The Ancient Americas

The Ancient Americas

A Brief History and Guide to Research

Hanns J. Prem

Translated by Kornelia Kurbjuhn

UNIVERSITY OF UTAH PRESS SALT LAKE CITY

Originally published as *Geschichte Altamerikas*, by Hanns J. Prem,

Updated for the English edition

Printed on acid-free paper

Library of Congress Cataloging-in-Publication Data

Prem, Hanns J., 1941–
[Geschichte Altamerikas. English]
The ancient Americas : a brief history and guide to research / Hanns J. Prem.
p. cm.
Includes bibliographical references and index.
ISBN 0-87480-536-8
1. Indians—History. 2. Indians—Antiquities. 3. America—Antiquities. I. Title.
D5.5.044 Bd. 23 1997
[E65]
970.01—dc21 97-3127

Contents

Preface

The original version of this volume was part of a series of similarly constructed books about different sections of the history of central Europe and the Mediterranean area; it was the first attempt to transpose this concept to areas outside of Europe. The basic idea of the series is the combination of an overview presentation of historical situations and sequences (Part I, Delineations) with an overview of important questions and approaches to research (Part II). While Part I describes knowledge thought to be secure in a conclusive and very summary fashion and so can dispense with scholarly documentation, the overview of research in Part II is meant not only to characterize briefly the significant contributions to the state of knowledge but also to make problems and unsolved questions clear and accessible by indicating and commenting on contributions thought to be seminal. It is obvious that the selection of literature, its evaluation, and the subjects discussed will be subjective. Still, one's own position cannot dominate. Finally, the extensive bibliography allows the reader access to scholarly discussions of presentation and commentary.

Despite the adoption of the described concept of a historical handbook, an overview of the history of ancient cultures and states on the American double continent before the contact with Europeans clearly has to be different from one of certain areas in Europe, the Mediterranean, or even South and East Asia. These differences, which are reflected in the structure and mode of presentation in this book, have several causes:

The spatial and temporal framework. Ancient American cultures existed in an area which combined had a length of nearly ten thousand km; however, the two major sectors were separated by almost a quarter of this distance. A sense of the differences of ancient American cultures is conveyed by the fact that at the time of the Spanish conquest in this area the languages spoken belonged to at least seven different language families, which have no discernible relationship with each other. The uniformity that can be suggested by the term "ancient America," therefore, was not at all present, although similarities, even if they are often only superficial, should not be ignored. In time the discussed cultures reach back more than two thousand years.

The lack of indigenous written records. Only very few cultures of ancient America developed written historical chronicles, and of these many have not been preserved or have been destroyed on purpose. For the remaining cultures only the conditions prevalent at the time of the Conquest can be used to project backward. Since the roots of these conditions can be assumed to be in earlier periods, backward projection has an invaluable significance. Finally, archaeological research supplements this, and indeed is the only tool for reaching time periods that are further removed.

The cultural environment foreign to people from the old world. A member of the western civilizations rightfully sees himself as an heir not only of the recent past but also of the antiquity of his culture area, and he therefore thinks (if rightfully so remains to be seen) he can understand the conditions prevalent in ancient times; when he is confronted with the indigenous culture of the Americas, he finds himself in a completely foreign world. What should be familiar seems to be reduced to a general humanness, the foreign nature is overpowering and makes access difficult, the often unavoidable impression of the exotic frustrates and obstructs the path to understanding.

The state of research in a comparatively young specialty. An adequate study of source materials has only just begun, and complete access to all data is by no means possible. Intense historical research into ancient American civilizations has been conducted for less than a hundred years, and for much of that time there were only a few specialists involved. Results are still limited to individual points and many of these are controversial, so they have hardly been entered so far in summary presentations.

Indian revivals and apologetics. In the areas of the old American civilizations the direct contact to the indigenous past has been disrupted through the cut caused by the Conquista and the half millennium of European dominance. While historical researchers are conscious of the limits of their possibilities of insight and statements, some modern heirs of the old cultures and their sympathizers claim that they have a direct access, but this cannot be checked scientifically. Their assertions do allow insights into the thought processes of contemporary societies, but often falsify the image of past ones.

This complex situation had to be taken into account in the present volume. The temporal and spatial extent and the difference of the cultures demand a concentration on the latest periods, especially the states of the Aztecs and the Incas, which were then the largest indigenous powers and as such commanded the center of attention of the conquerors, so that they were documented in the most extensive way and can be most clearly recognized. Even so an often extreme compression of contents could not be avoided. The imbalance between the Mesoamerican area and the Andes can be traced back to a lack of indigenous sources for the latter, making reconstruction difficult and uncertain. The other later cultures, whose examination is much more fragmentary, had to recede disproportionately. As indispensable as the early periods are for understanding later large states, they also could be treated only briefly and lastly in an inadequate way because of limitations of space in both the presentation and the discussion of archaeological evidence. They had to be limited to the large, supraregional cultural horizons and the decisive changes. For more information there is the cited archaeological literature. The uneven state of research is reflected in the overview presentation (Part I), which may appear erratic; this section could not be kept entirely free of tendencies or even fads. Some subjects, on which research is still in a state of flux, had to be transferred more than is common to the research part of the book.

The investigation of the history of ancient America is, as it has been for a long time, a domain of ethnology and archaeology (which under the roof of anthropology are much closer to each other in the United States than in central Europe). This modifies the approach and the terminology. In this volume I have tried to dispense with technical terms whenever possible. The use of old-world historical terms was avoided to prevent any suspicion of unjustified equations.

This volume could hardly have been created without the assistance of two colleagues, who collaborated on individual parts or assisted with the literature: Ursula Dyckerhoff (Aztecs) and Elisabeth Giesel (social and economic organization of the Andes). Henning Bischof and Albert Meyers have read an early version of the text pertaining to the archaeology of the Andes. My discussions with Barbara Göbel about her dissertation on the domestication of American plants have helped me in the appropriate section. Agustín Seguí pointed out mistakes and incongruities in the first (German) edition. To them all I owe a world of gratitude; responsibility for the final version is entirely mine. The translation by Kornelia Kurbjuhn provided the rare and good experience that a colleague not only transposed every one of my words into another language, but examined them and often discussed them with me in detail.

The time and freedom to write this book I owe to an academic grant from the Volkswagenstiftung. The manuscript of the first edition was finished toward the end of 1987. Literature published later was incorporated into the new edition as much as the framework allowed.

Names and terms of Indian languages are given in the traditional orthography, which stems primarily from sound values of sixteenth-century Spanish, and they are not at all uniform. The modern orthography, which often is quite different, was not adopted for a volume of this nature. The most important features of the employed representations are as follows:

Aztec (Nahuatl): *tl* stands for an alveolar "t" combined with a voiceless lateral "l." The sign sequence *uc* (after a vowel) equal to *cu* (before a vowel) designates an alveolar "k" combined with "w." Stress is always on the penultimate syllable. Glottal stops were not indicated.

Maya (Yucatec): contrary to Spanish usage, *c* before *i* and *e* also corresponds to "k."

Quechua: the double sign *ll* is to be pronounced as in the Spanish *calle.*

All terms from Indian languages were used in the singular and in forms roughly corresponding to languages inflecting nominals. The correct form of plurals was abandoned because there are often substantial changes as compared to the singular (therefore regularly for the Nahuatl *teteuctin* the singular *teuctli* [Lord] is given, for Quechua *runacuna* the singular *runa* [human being]). This rule was broken only for Nahuatl terms that are unusual in the singular, those designating groups of persons (*pochteca,* long-range merchants) and ethnic groups (*Mexica*).

Modern authors (contrary to Colonial authors) are referred to in the text without their first names. Exceptions are made only when otherwise there could be confusion.

PART I

DELINEATIONS

1

The Prehistoric Period

Relatively late, possibly during the last Ice Age, people who came from eastern Asia stepped onto the American continent. Some time between 70,000 and 8000 B.C. northern Asia and Alaska were connected by a broad, ice-free land bridge, because the sea level was substantially lower than it is today. First traces of human activities are dated to 50,000 and 35,000 B.C., possibly even much earlier. Through a narrow corridor in the continental ice shelf at the eastern edge of the Rocky Mountains, which was closed only during the height of icing, simple hunters and gatherers made their way south and reached the highlands of Mexico prior to 20,000 B.C., and a short while later the northern part of South America. Their purely acquisitive mode of economy necessitated a constant or periodically minor change of habitat according to the ripening periods of wild plants and the seasonally different stands of wild animals. The area extensively utilized by one band must have been large and contained a broad spectrum of small, ecologically differentiated zones whose exploitation could guarantee a continuous minimal food supply. This mode of economy kept the population density at a constant and low level.

AGRICULTURE ≡ In parts of the areas later developing into civilizations, the domestication of wild plants began around 7000 B.C. Several varieties of squash, gourds, beans, and maize were planted, which later formed the basis of the diet, and in the Andes root crops were added.

Contrary to widely held opinion, the introduction of agriculture is fraught with a series of disadvantages and risks. While those working the soil need to labor more than hunters and gatherers to gain their food, their diet is not well balanced overall, and failed crops are a greater danger due to a dependence on fewer sources of food. It has been suggested that human beings were forced into such disadvantage when their attempts to feed a constantly rising number of people could not be managed any other way. It is doubtful if early cultivation was consciously used to solve nutrition problems, or if it was even capable of doing so. Among the earliest cultivated plants were many that were not used for food; besides, the raising and harvesting of domesticated plants, which is a long-term process, could hardly have been foreseen. The problems generated by agriculture are offset by obvious advantages: yields on the same limited space are much higher and allow a larger population, which in turn creates the prerequisite for more complex forms of social organization and finally "civilization" (societies with state organization). Such developments took place almost simultaneously in two areas of the American continent: in Mesoamerica and in the Andes.

Of special interest is the almost total lack of domesticated animals in prehispanic America. In Mesoamerica the number of tamed animals—dog and turkey—was even more modest than in the Andes, where guinea pigs, ducks, and herd animals such as llamas and alpacas were added to dogs. A lack of wild lifeforms, especially of large mammals (whose extermination had been caused to a large extent by early man in America), has been cited as a reason for the lack of domesticated animals.

2

The Preclassic and Classic Cultures of Mesoamerica

THE AREA

CULTURAL SPACE ≡ The area occupied by the high cultures on the middle American land bridge is called Mesoamerica. The delineation of this area is determined by the existence of specific cultural traits that were not distributed evenly at all periods. Therefore, Mesoamerica at the beginning of the evolution of civilization was a small area; it grew consecutively due to the spread of characteristic civilization elements but fluctuated along its borders all the time, because groups from outside arrived and their culture adapted to that of Mesoamerica. In the period directly prior to the arrival of the Spaniards, Mesoamerica was comprised of the modern states of Mexico south of 21° latitude, Guatemala, Belize, Honduras, and El Salvador, roughly west of 88° longitude.

NATURAL SPACE ≡ The natural environment of Mesoamerica is marked by highlands to about two thousand meters, bordered by mountain ranges in the east and west, which run from the north to the Isthmus of Tehuantepec ever closer to each other and finally merge. About 19° latitude the highlands, which are comprised of different-sized valleys, are cut by a zone of volcanoes. At the Gulf of Mexico there is a partially hilly, partially flat coast. South of the isthmus the landscape is dominated by mountain ranges running east to west with deeply cut valleys and a coastal plain bordering the Pacific Ocean. To the north of that there is the peninsula of Yucatán, a low mesa with distinctive karst formations.

CLIMATE ≡ Climate and vegetation in Mesoamerica are determined by altitude and a position aweather or alee of the mountain ranges. The valleys between the north-south ranges are dry, often resembling steppes, and depending on the altitude they can be cool, moderate, or warm with a distinct rainy season in the summer. The coastal plains are tropical and humid; there is a zone of clouds along the rising mountains. The Yucatán peninsula is warm, due to its lack of altitude; it has a tropical rain forest in its southern part, but becomes gradually drier toward the north.

CULTURE AREAS ≡ The considerable ruggedness of the Mesoamerican area, with many valleys and basins of different size divided by mountain ranges hostile to traffic, promotes small-scale cultural phenomena. In the few large and more open basins of Central Mexico (corresponding to the Mexican federal states of Mexico, Hidalgo, Puebla, and Mexico City) and in Yucatán this tendency is less pronounced.

CULTURAL EPOCHS ≡ The course of cultural development has been classified as archaeological time spans called Preclassic, Classic, and Postclassic in the terminology most widely used. Today these terms denote only temporal spans and should not be understood as brief summaries of cultural situations. They allow a clear arrangement of cultural events, which will be adhered to in the following chapters as well (see Chronologies).

SETTLEMENT ≡ The most important requirement for an evolution toward civilization—and not only for Mesoamerica—is permanent settlements. These appeared gradually in the second half of the Archaic period, which is prior to the Preclassic. A condition for founding permanent settlements was that throughout the year food could be found close to the habitation. There were only very few specially favorable locations, mostly at seacoasts, where this was possible without growing nutrients; otherwise settlements and the domestication of plants occurred at the same time.

CERAMICS ≡ Closely connected to settlements are a number of other cultural innovations, such as the invention of ceramics, which occurred on the Mexican Pacific Coast around 2900 B.C. Starting at this time one can recognize settlements of various sizes and ranks, centers of political and religious importance, solid "public" buildings for various purposes, artwork, and parts of the population who specialized in something other than direct food production.

THE OLMECS

Around 1500 B.C., the earliest typically Mesoamerican culture appeared, without any recognizable local precursors and in an ecologically unfavorable area on the southern Gulf Coast near the Isthmus of Tehuantepec. This culture is called Olmec (a given name that unfortunately is identical to the name of a tribe). Knowledge about the Olmecs, as well as about all other Preclassic and most of the Classic cultures, is quite limited, because there are no written records or oral traditions reaching back that far.

STONE RELIEFS AND BUILDINGS ≡ A characteristic style of stone sculpture and reliefs and of the architecture of a few religious centers is all that allows access to Olmec culture. General analogies created the opinion that in the ceremonial centers (the most important ones are La Venta, San Lorenzo, and Tres Zapotes) only a small elite, comprised of rulers (chiefs) and priests, lived next to specialized artisans and architects. The rest of the population stayed in small hamlets around the centers, providing foodstuffs and other goods. They entered the centers only to work on public structures, here platforms of sand and clay, and to bring in gigantic stone sculptures transported over long distances.

RELIGION ≡ The subject matter of the masterfully crafted stone reliefs seems to be mainly a strange half-human creature with features of a jaguar, the mightiest beast of the Americas. Frequent depictions of a seated male with a small child in his lap are completely mysterious. Many of the monuments were carefully and intentionally damaged, then most or all of them were ceremonially buried.

EFFECT ≡ Olmec culture was not an isolated development on the coast of Tabasco and southern Veracruz. Characteristic cultural expressions, especially the artistic style of stone work, have another focal point in the southern slopes of the Mexican highlands in Chalcatzingo (relief sculpture on rock faces) and in Tlalcozotitlan (also called Teopantecuanititlan, monumental stone architecture), and reach from the Valley of Mexico to El Salvador. The background for this common style may have been a common ideology, for there are no signs of military expansions or an empire of this extent.

THE OLMEC PERIPHERY

OAXACA ≡ After Olmec culture subsided in the core area around 500 B.C., there were a few weak florescences in the former border areas but also some powerful new cultural developments. Despite the relative closeness of the Valley of Oaxaca to the core area, it was only slightly influenced, and around 400 B.C., on the isolated hill of Monte Albán, a center was formed that was characterized by intense architectural efforts and a substantial population. A reason for its formation may have been its sheltered and central position at the intersection of three valleys, which forms the basin of Oaxaca. Altercations with the rulers outside of the valleys possibly necessitated an alliance centered in Monte Albán, where the chieftains of the three valleys sent parts of their population. One interpretation of the many similar-looking relief tablets there suggests that they represent subjugated and eliminated enemy leaders. The short inscriptions in the earliest script in Mesoamerica cannot be read. Slightly later, lengthier inscriptions on the outer wall of one of the central buildings seem to publicly document victories. On the other hand, the fortifications built around that time indicate that the center was threatened.

At about 300 B.C. there is another cultural innovation in Oaxaca, the ritual ball game. Documented by the first ball court structures and relief sculptures of players, the game was to become a characteristic aspect of ceremonial life in Mesoamerica and beyond.

VALLEY OF MEXICO ≡ Even in the early Preclassic there had been a few hamlets and several larger settlements on the shores of the large lake, which had no drainage, in the area of today's Mexican capital, in the Valley of Mexico. Olmec influence can be shown in the ceramics. When this influence ceased in the middle of the Preclassic, Cuicuilco on the southern shore had become the dominant center of the region. On earthen platforms, which were later faced with stone, there were temples made of perishable materials. In the following centuries, in a procedure used later as well, important platforms were refaced several times, among them the large round pyramid consisting of several flat cones piled one upon the other. The eruption of the small volcano Xitle, which buried a large part of the fields around Cuicuilco, forced the population of the site to abandon it. Its significance passed on to Teotihuacán in the north of the basin.

TEOTIHUACÁN

No other period is defined as exclusively by the aura of one dominant center as the Classic is by Teotihuacán. The position of the site in an arid pocket off the Valley of Mexico was not at all propitious, hence it is hard to explain why Teotihuacán suddenly grew rapidly in the first century A.D., when it had not been very different from other small sites in the vicinity. The population numbers rose quickly and a part of the inhabitants specialized in making tools out of the volcanic glass, obsidian, that was found at the eastern edge of the valley.

RISE OF TEOTIHUACÁN ≡ In the second century the settlement already occupied twenty square kilometers, although building was sparse. In the disproportionately large ceremonial center the Pyramids of the Sun (the base of which measures fifty thousand square meters, the height about sixty-five meters) and the Moon, as they were later called, appeared almost simultaneously with the broad axial avenue and many of the characteristic building complexes, consisting of courtyards faced on three sides by temples. While the site's core grew to monumental proportions there were signs of far-reaching political power. Although the local obsidian mines were soon exhausted, the manufacture kept growing, for expeditions seem to have brought the material from other mines about seventy kilometers away. Around a new axis south of the old core the city achieved a new focal point in a court whose sides were four hundred meters long. Buildings were organized on a grid that ran parallel to the site's main axes. In compact living quarters the city could accommodate a constantly rising population, although the outer perimeters were hardly extended.

ZENITH ≡ Between A.D. 200 and 600 the city's population probably numbered one hundred thousand to two hundred thousand; new arrivals from the immediate surroundings added substantially to these figures. But even from remote areas like Oaxaca there were people who lived in their own quarters in Teotihuacán and followed their own customs there. More and more a shift of emphasis from religious-ceremonial to civil areas of life can be noted.

STRATIFICATION OF THE POPULATION ≡ Statements about the presence of social groups can be supported only by indirect evidence. At the head of society there were administration officials; possibly the same persons held the higher priestly offices (a theocratic system often is visualized). Their tasks were administration and organization of a large community that had to be supplied from the outside, planning of building concepts, and supervision of construction. Then there were artisans for shaping obsidian, manufacturing ceramics, building houses, painting murals, and making stone sculptures. Long-range traders saw to the flow of Teotihuacán merchandise to the borders of Mesoamerica. Finally, the city contained a large peasant population that assisted in construction and other tasks during the dry season. There must have been a large number of porters, who were the only available means of transportation for the mass of goods.

CITY PLANNING ≡ City planning in its strict grid order, which was dominated by a broad north-south street and an axis cutting it at right angles, sheds an indirect light on political structures. In the northern half the street is formed in part by sunken courtyards, surrounded by stepped dams, and contains a broad zone of administrative and representational buildings. There are numerous court-pyramid complexes and groups of buildings that are called palaces because of their structural opulence, which probably served as living quarters for the elite. This zone was separated from the rest of the city by walls. Beyond this zone living quarters predominated, walled-in rectangles measuring fifty to seventy meters a side with few entrances. These led through hallways to sunken courtyards surrounded on all four sides with often symmetrical structures that had porticos facing the yard, stood on low platforms, and possibly were intended for representation. In the corners of the courtyards there were doorways to the actual living rooms. Walls were often painted, in either simple repetitive designs or elaborate figures.

DECLINE ≡ By A.D. 650 Teotihuacán continued to build but started to shrink at an ever faster rate. The surrounding area also lost inhabitants. Reasons for this demographic development are unknown. By A.D. 750 there was a sudden collapse; many buildings in the center were burned down and presumably devastated on purpose. There were still people at Teotihuacán for a hundred years or more, but they were unable to maintain the former quality of craftsmanship or revive the destroyed core of the city.

FACTORS OF GROWTH ≡ Reasons for the founding and florescence of Teotihuacán cannot be separated from those of its decline and fall. Teotihuacán shared its location near an advantageous traffic lane between the Valley of Mexico and the central Gulf Coast with many other sites. Other advantages of place did not exist, so there had to have been irrational reasons—such as a cult in the cave over which the largest pyramid was built, and which became a pilgrimage center. Also the monumental pyramids were built very early in the city's history. The completion of these structures, and also the city planning, cannot have been achieved without a good-sized administrative organization, which later on was free for other tasks, and which allowed the subsequent change from a pilgrimage center to a political-economic power. The administrative capacity thus released was able to assure the supply of the city even from a distance and could organize a dependably functioning system. The turn to worldliness at Teotihuacán had consequences in all of Mesoamerica. The economic activities at Teotihuacán, especially the obsidian industry, became a decisive factor. Even in the latest period there was a new enterprise in the form of cinnabar mining in remote quarries.

FACTORS OF DECLINE ≡ The cessation of the far-flung Teotihuacán influence around A.D. 500 caused cultural crises in the affected areas, such as the "hiatus" in Maya culture from A.D. 540 to 600. The decline of Teotihuacán first touched the outer periphery. The economic role of the city was not at all as unique or irreplaceable as the original character of the religious (or ideological) center and could be taken over by regional competitors. When the weakened centralized power could no longer secure the supply and cohesion of its own city, it had to be given up by its inhabitants within a short time.

TEOTIHUACÁN'S NEIGHBORS

CHOLULA ≡ At about the same time as Teotihuacán another center rose ninety kilometers to the southeast, in Cholula in the Valley of Puebla. At first a religious function seems to have been the focus there as well, manifested in a mighty pyramid; unlike the larger one at Teotihuacán, this one was constantly enlarged and built up during the centuries, until it finally covered two and a half times the area of the Pyramid of the Sun. It was given up after A.D. 700, later than the one at Teotihuacán. In Cholula a site with an originally religious orientation had also become a trading center. The combination of both functions secured the life of the city beyond the conquest into the present time.

NORTHERN MEXICO ≡ During the Classic, Mesoamerica extended to the northernmost basin and valley regions, which were still suitable for agriculture, into today's Durango and Zacatecas. After the late Preclassic there was the culture of Chalchihuites, named after a ceremonial center now called Alta Vista, founded around A.D. 500. Its building concept had been borrowed from Teotihuacán. The attractiveness of Chalchihuites was enhanced by a precious stone that was mined there, but of great importance was also the protection of the route to Arizona and New Mexico, where the Hohokam culture showed increasing Mesoamerican influences. However, the decisive factor for the placement of the center was its closeness to the Tropic of Cancer. A unique observatory was built to allow astronomical observations, which are particularly clear in the region. Chalchihuites ended as had Teotihuacán around A.D. 700.

EL TAJÍN ≡ The ceremonial center El Tajín in the area of the northern Gulf Coast was influenced by Teotihuacán as well. However, only when that influence waned around A.D. 500 did El Tajín start to flourish. Despite a comparatively low number of inhabitants, just a few thousand, it became an important center of remarkable cultural singularity with a far-flung sphere of influence. The innovativeness of El Tajín's architects is of note. They experimented with many new construction solutions, such as interior rooms held up by pillars, mock staircases, and rooms that are arranged not around a courtyard but around a rectangular hallway. The dominant decor of temple facades, niches with inlaid meanders, also shows a willful stylistic concept.

BALL GAME ≡ A still dim insight into a characteristic and important aspect of Mesoamerican culture, which was a focus of attention at El Tajín, is provided by a cohesive group of stone implements called *palmas* (palm leaves), *yugos* (yokes), *hachas* (axes), and *candados* (locks), because of their shapes. They were used as grave goods, but seem to be stone versions of pieces made of other materials that were among the accoutrements of ball players, as shown by numerous depictions. The many ball courts at El Tajín and other contemporary sites such as Catona (Puebla) also emphasize the importance of the ball game.

OAXACA

MONTE ALBÁN ≡ Contemporaneously with Teotihuacán, the center of Monte Albán reached its maximum significance and influence between A.D. 250 and 450. Up to thirty thousand inhabitants, now securely identified as Zapotecs, lived on the slopes of the mountain, while the monumental buildings of the Great Plaza were constructed on the flattened summit of the central peak; separate complexes, supposedly the residences of rulers, and the most important shrine adjoined. The economic role of Monte Albán was probably always minor; only about 10 percent of the population are estimated to have been engaged in crafts, much less than at Teotihuacán. The nature of the relationship between Monte Albán and Teotihuacán is not well understood; Teotihuacán did not dominate over Monte Albán, but appears as an equal, if not equal-weighted, partner. Contacts had existed since A.D. 150 but broke off after A.D. 400, when Oaxaca entered a noticeable isolation. Possibly the Oaxacan quarter at Teotihuacán, mentioned above, was constituted just at this time and it continued to exist until the fall of the host city.

DECLINE OF MONTE ALBÁN ≡ Around A.D. 700 Monte Albán stopped being the power center of the valley and its large elite groups. The area of the Grand

Plaza with its ceremonial structures and ruler residences was given up, while the general population dwindled in numbers only gradually, and retreated behind a fortified wall on the side not facing the valley. It is still not clear why this development occurred at Monte Albán, despite its isolation at the very time Teotihuacán fell. Unlike Teotihuacán, Monte Albán kept its transcendental importance as the preferred place for elaborate burials.

ZAPOTEC CITY-STATES ≡ After A.D. 700 Monte Albán was only one of a dozen city-states in the valley, each consisting of a main site and several associated hamlets. A trend to move the settlements from the open valley floors to better sheltered heights, and the construction of associated fortifications, seem to indicate that the times were turbulent.

THE LATE CLASSIC

When the influence of Teotihuacán started to fade around A.D. 500, several local cultures rose, each focused on an important central place and based on the indigenous development of Teotihuacán concepts, enriched by new forms. It is noteworthy that an only partially apparent basic flow of shared forms and themes can be observed from the central Mexican basin to the Maya area.

XOCHICALCO ≡ In the southern reaches of the central Mexican mountain range, Xochicalco was situated on the tops of several connected hills, the slopes of which were fortified by concentric walls. The largest part of the interior area was occupied by buildings for representation and religious ceremonies, with ground plans resembling those of Monte Albán. Next to them was one of the largest ball courts in Mesoamerica, situated near the flank of a hill supported by a giant retention wall. There were only a few luxurious living quarters, so the number of inhabitants was probably small.

It is obvious at Xochicalco that there were far-reaching connections, as evidenced by borrowings from Maya culture and by sacrifices in the interior of religious buildings, where red seashells and snail shells brought in from large distances were important religious objects. The most significant difference from Xochicalco's central Mexican neighbors is the fact that there are numerous brief inscriptions. There is a vague resemblance to signs from eastern Mesoamerica and to Maya hieroglyphs. There is a second family of signs on other monuments, which were later utilized by the Aztecs and their neighbors. Possibly this is showing either a parallel or a change in ethnic-linguistic affiliation.

After a brief florescence Xochicalco saw a rapid decline around A.D. 800 and was abandoned in a hundred years. In this period there was a conscious "killing" and "burial" of monuments and other precious objects, probably because a fleeing population could not carry them along.

CACAXTLA ≡ Another aspect of the same cultural tie to eastern Mesoamerica can be recognized in the unique murals of Cacaxtla in the western part of the Valley of Puebla-Tlaxcallan. Dated A.D. 700 to 900, the murals deal with two subject matters. On the base of one structure there is an almost life-sized battle scene painted in breathtaking realism: a group clad in jaguar skins fights man to man against another with bird helmets, whose features seem to be Mayan. In a second series of paintings inside a temple, victors and losers of the battle are confronting each other, illuminated and now complementing each other. Their disagreement, incomprehensible in its details, has been resolved into myth and presents the opposing pairings jaguar–feather serpent, night–light, and earth–sky.

EASTERN MESOAMERICA

Around the peninsula of Yucatán man first conquered the coastal areas and later proceeded along the large rivers inland, mainly in the south. Since 1000 B.C. there had been settlements with ceramics and permanent buildings in central Yucatán and in the northern part of Belize. In the final part of the Preclassic, at about 300 B.C., the population numbers rose quickly, and suddenly small and large settlements emerged everywhere, with ever more numerous and elaborate ceremonial architecture. Monumental stucco heads flanking central staircases can be taken as a special marker for this time. The origin of these early settlers is unknown, but linguistic considerations place them in the western highlands of Guatemala. An additional cultural impetus from outside may have been created by a natural catastrophe in western El Salvador. The volcano Ilopango had buried the fertile region around the Olmec-influenced ceremonial center at Chalchuapa in A.D. 260 under a blanket of ashes and forced the population to emigrate. From this area or even from regions with an Olmec tradition farther west may stem the prototype of the Maya hieroglyphic writing system and the complex calendric calculations.

CITIES ≡ There was a varied monumental architecture in the ever-increasing number of cities: rectangular plazas sided by high pyramidal stepped platforms topped by temple buildings with extraordinarily small inner rooms. On the other sides of such plazas there were long buildings with many narrow rooms covered by corbelled vaults; these are considered to have been palaces, where the nobility either lived or executed numerous administrative and ceremonial tasks. The representative structures in the center of sites were built of stone and covered by corbelled vaults. The walls and also the floors of interior rooms and courtyards were faced with a hard stucco layer, carefully burnished. In courtyards stone monuments were erected with inscriptions, extolling the martial deeds of rulers, their ritual and civil activities, and their genealogical origins.

Murals also served the same purpose. On the outskirts of ceremonial centers and in hamlets all over the countryside were the living quarters of the common people, made of wood, daub, and wattle with palm-thatched roofs, always standing on small platforms grouped around a courtyard. Population density of sites was only a fraction of that of Teotihuacán, considering the airy placement of structures (Tikal had possibly a mere sixty thousand inhabitants on 120 square kilometers), but overall there was a remarkably high number of settlers.

INFLUENCE OF TEOTIHUACÁN ≡ In the middle Classic the influence of Teotihuacán also reached the Yucatán Peninsula, probably via Kaminaljuyú. In the lowlands it is most evident at Tikal and its southern periphery and is expressed primarily in architectural forms, ceramic types, and depictions of deities. In the highlands of Guatemala, where there were Maya as well, the similarities to Teotihuacán are so strong in Kaminaljuyú, whose cultural definition originally was built on a basis attributed to the Olmec periphery, that a direct political or military involvement seems possible. While the zone dominated by Kaminaljuyú was small, there was an indirect influence spreading to the Pacific Coast where an unusual mix of cultures was developed near Cotzumalhuapa.

POLITICAL HIERARCHIES ≡ Political organization in the lowlands of Yucatán consisted of a stratified network of small polities, similar to city-states, ruling over hamlets and small settlements within a circumscribed zone. Aside from possibly boastful inscriptions, it is still not clear how large was the area under the direct authority of quite important sites. Fortifications and the reach of the few, elaborately built roads also suggest fairly small zones of domination. Whether there existed four supraregional powers on the highest level, as has been asserted again recently, opposing each other and with spheres of influence that were subject to dramatic changes, has not yet been conclusively determined. Independent of site size and sphere of influence there were several areas where there was supraregional exchange on many nonpolitical levels: priest/astronomer discussions, marriage contracts among leading noble families sometimes spanning huge distances, and a widely spread trade network.

The population was divided into two classes of extremely uneven numbers. The nobility, numbering perhaps 10 percent of the population, headed by the rulers of city-states (*k'ul ahaw*) and their families, were followed in rank by the governors of dependent sites (*sahal*), and a broad noble group comprised of specialists like scribes, painters of luxury ceramics, and the carvers of stelae, and also those with various administrative tasks. An ostentatious court life and elaborate ceremonies were minutely portrayed on the outside of painted cylindrical vessels. In contrast to the nobility there were the common people, who lived in sparsely settled townships and scattered rural settlements, and who supported the entire population with their agricultural products. The peasant population probably also engaged in all crafts, except the ones that demanded specialists.

RELIGION AND RITUAL ≡ Rituals undertaken by the nobility and the rulers were depicted in paintings and stone relief. Intentionally painful castigation and bloodletting, intake of psychotropical substances, and other techniques were employed to receive visions. A central place is occupied by the ritual time span of 260 days, divided in ever new segments in pictorial manuscripts as well, which was tied to very specific augury-prognostic statements.

SCRIPT AND CALENDAR ≡ The writing system of the Maya, called hieroglyphic, appeared in the third century A.D. in fully developed form without recognizable precursors, as a combination of syllables and ideographs, and remained largely unchanged through more than a millennium. In this system a high level of abstraction is combined with very complexly designed, partially descriptive signs, precisely organized and at the same time unusually flexible. The large distances between the different regions, where in part there were different languages spoken, did not disturb its uniformity. The same is true for the calendar, where cycles used in all of Mesoamerica (the ritual calendar of 260 days and the normal year of constant 365 days) were combined with others, especially a continuous day count from a point zero far in the past. Calculations of the moon's phases were connected to these cycles as well as prediction tables for eclipses and the visibility phases of the planet Venus.

ECONOMY ≡ The basis of food provisions at first had been slash-and-burn agriculture, which demanded large areas. Only a small portion of the land was cultivated in rotation; maize, beans, and squash were planted simultaneously. Most likely the array of useful plants was considerably larger and encompassed also root crops. As the population numbers rose, this system was more and more supplemented by house gardens, which were intensively utilized, and by several improvements of the fields, such as terracing on slopes, raised fields in swampy areas, and guards against erosion, which allowed a constant use of fields. The extent and hence the effect of these measures is still a matter of debate. Trade of goods for daily consumption took place over considerable distances, because hard stones and obsidian had to be imported in the lowlands, which were poor in raw materials. This was true even more so for luxury items. Whether there was a specific group of people who specialized in such trading (this was attributed to the group *putun*) or not is uncertain.

TECHNICAL KNOWLEDGE ≡ The technical knowledge of the Mayans was comparable to that elsewhere in Mesoamerica. However, as a special invention of their own, bottle-shaped hollows were sunk several meters deep into the limestone and served as storerooms in the southern lowlands and as cisterns in the northern lowlands.

LOCAL HISTORY ≡ Despite a large number of partially legible stone inscriptions with a historical content, it may still take a long time to write a descriptive history of these people and places. Even at a place like Yaxchilán on the Usumacinta river, the inscriptions of which have been analyzed the longest and the most intensively, the results (here summarized as an example) remain rather vague and bloodless. Although the sequence of fifteen rulers in the Classic has been deciphered, their names are merely fictitious surrogates for the most part based on paraphrases of glyphs. Their recorded deeds seem to consist of successful raids against powerful, often far removed, other rulers, raids which, however, did not lead to conquests.

The thirteenth ruler of Yaxchilán, Itzam Balam (formerly called "Shield Jaguar"), came to power in A.D. 681. It is known that he achieved seven victories over adversaries; he boasted about them all his life. It was also deciphered that his two wives had an unusually important role in public. One of them, Lady Xoc, has been portrayed in a temple she had built, as she engaged in bloody castigation rites, supported by her husband, to achieve contact with a mythical dynasty founder. Her importance is also documented by the fact that after the death of her husband in A.D. 742 she ruled in his stead for a decade. However, not she but Lady Ik' Kimi was the mother of his son and successor Yaxun Balam IV (also "Bird Jaguar"), who could not begin his rule immediately after the death of his father. The reason may have been weighty difficulties in the recognition of his succession claims despite or because of this alliance. Therefore he tried intensively and finally with success to legitimize his position and that of his mother through a multitude of inscribed monuments. Only after ten years, at the age of forty-three, after successful wars that were celebrated in reliefs, and after the birth of a successor, could he assume power. In subsequent years he developed an intense building activity and recorded what amount to paraphrases of the same themes on monuments in inscriptions and pictures. His reputation was expressed through visits in neighboring sites, where he assisted in stabilizing the claims of the local dynasty. Under his son, Itzam Balam II ("Shield Jaguar"), there were numerous wars, which seem to have shaken the stability of the site. His son, "Mahkina Tab Kimi," is the last known ruler; after him the inscriptions fall silent in A.D. 808.

At the site of Palenque one can see how the ruling families portrayed themselves over a similarly lengthy time span. The mythical history begins in B.C. 3121, a short time before the beginning of the present calendrical cycle, with the birth of a deity couple. They in turn produced three gods who were venerated in historical times in three adjoining temples in Palenque, as well as others. The genealogy begins with a strangely early ancestor in the tenth century B.C. and jumps to the first historical ruler, K'uk' Balam, in A.D. 397 (see genealogy of Palenque). Until the end of the sixth century little more than the names are known of the successive rulers. Then wars are reported, albeit without details, between sites like Pia (modern: Pomoná) and Toniná and Palenque, where the political stability may have suffered because of difficulties in the succession of rulers. In any event, twice within a few decades women became rulers, which each time caused the lineage of rulers to shift to their marriage partners. Possibly encouraged by this situation, the enemies from Pia reached the center of the site on November 24, 610. At this time the deity images were desecrated and the rulership was lost; elsewhere cities boasted of their captives from Palenque. Under the very able ruler Hanab Pacal II, Palenque once again achieved its independence. On August 7, 659, the ruler of Pia was captured and either was held with others for a long time or was sacrified upon the inauguration of a specific building of the Palace. The site substantially enlarged its territory and remained unchallenged for quite a long time. His son and successor created some of the esthetically most impressive buildings at Palenque, consisting of three temples devoted to similar subjects, where he venerated his mythical ancestors (see above). The next successor but one of Pacal, K'an Hok' Chitam II, who became ruler when he was almost sixty years old, was defeated and captured by Toniná on August 30, 711. After several years of an interregnum a rightful ruler once again acceded to the throne at Palenque, but the site never again reached its former standing, and soon the decline of Maya culture became apparent.

WAR AND EXPANSION ≡ Contrary to earlier opinion, advances in decipherment and other discoveries have elucidated the role of martial activities in Maya culture. War, which took place earlier, presumably on a small scale and concerned mostly the gain of high-ranking captives and tribute payments, later changed and became a means to subjugate neighboring sites or those even farther away. Especially in the core area of the lowlands military confrontation occupied an important place, while most of the periphery provides a more serene picture. However, marriage alliances across large distances and peaceful contacts among the high nobility of various sites have also been documented.

COLLAPSE OF SOUTHERN MAYA CULTURE ≡ In the Terminal Classic the fate of two branches of Maya culture separated. The classical version ended in the eighth and ninth centuries in the southern part of the Yucatán Peninsula and the adjoining highlands. The temporal sequence of the collapse can be recognized on dated monuments, which were erected at regular intervals. The largest number of simultaneously erected monuments occurred as late as A.D. 721. But within a few decades the number of sites that adopted this custom had become lower than the number of sites no longer able to continue. The sites in the east and west, including the very large ones, ceased to function before A.D.

790. After A.D. 830, aside from a few highland centers, only sites in the small region between the upper reaches of the Río de la Pasión and the Río Hondo still erected monuments—strangely enough this is also the region where the first ones appeared. It can be said then that the collapse spread inward from the eastern and western peripheries.

REASONS ≡ At the end of the Classic there was a destruction of central power in the city-states. The collapse occurred everywhere, not at the same time, but so fast that frequently half-finished buildings were not completed. Population numbers and complexity were drastically reduced. The nobility, experienced in rituals and specialized techniques, seemed to have vanished. Reasons for the decline are still obscure. The simple hypotheses based on one main reason, which have so far been suggested in large numbers, usually are not satisfactory explanations. As far as can be recognized now there had to have been multi-leveled effect contexts, chief among them a drastically worsening ecological situation due to overuse of arable land.

RESCUE ATTEMPTS ≡ A conspicuous omen of the collapse was something like the overheating of culture. It seems as if the Maya elite were aware of dangerous problems, but according to their contemporary world view saw causes that by modern standards were incorrect. Measures taken were therefore without effect. They seem to have consisted of constructing ever more buildings and erecting more and more stone monuments in more places; the impression is that by appealing to supernatural forces and by constant demonstrations of power and fame they could avert the threat of disaster. These efforts must have tied up more and more of the work force, which consequently were missing in more productive areas that were geared to secure the continuation of the population more effectively by intensifying agriculture. At the same time, the constantly growing nobility and the rise of specialized artisans meant that the part of the population working the land shrank, while the part that had to be supported rose steeply in numbers. Growing social disproportion seems to have contributed a great deal to the collapse.

RÍO BEC REGION ≡ A somewhat different picture is presented by the region north of the core area, the center and north of the Yucatán Pensinsula. In the Río Bec region, the southernmost of the provinces, there was a substantial increase in population in the Late Classic. At the same time the slopes of the lime hills were terraced to accommodate fields that should have secured the food supply for some time. Numerous, mostly small centers with ostentatious architecture went up, characterized by a building style that occurred only in this region; there were mock facades in the shape of steep towers, which held on their apex small temples with pseudo-entrances. With a minimum of effort the optical impression of temple pyramids of the Maya core area was meant to be suggested. However, unlike these, the mock pyramids were accessories of relatively small palaces, a clear indicator of the lack of recognition of their power from outside, and the agglomeration of numerous small polities.

CHENES REGION ≡ Due to a lack of excavations the knowledge of cultural developments north of the Río Bec region is based almost exclusively on a stylistic analysis of architecture. Many of the characteristic elements of the Río Bec style were transposed into the architecture of the Chenes region, adjoining to the northwest and hardly researched, where the style made its appearance early in the seventh century. While mock pyramids appear only in derived forms, the Río Bec stylistic element of shaping a central building entrance into a dragon mouth was willingly adopted.

PUUC REGION ≡ North of the Chenes region, in the Puuc area, there was an incredible density of settlements of all sizes starting at least in the middle of the eighth century. They impress by a masterly building technique and mosaic facades of stone. Stylistic elements from the Chenes region melded with a long indigenous tradition, to which traits from the Gulf Coast probably were added. Such influences from areas outside of what comprised classical Maya culture became more and more apparent in the Late Classic and through all of the Postclassic. The originators were peoples living on the western edge of Maya culture, probably in coastal Tabasco, who had close contacts with the Maya, but were oriented toward central Mexico. How long the development of these three stylistic provinces took has not yet been determined. The scattered ceremonial buildings and the few larger structures in the Río Bec region were given up around A.D. 825, but the Chenes region flourished far into the tenth century, the Puuc region possibly even longer. By now there are indications that here the end of the classical cultures was not as abrupt, and there definitely was no end to the settlements. Rather, there probably were social changes that affected the power of local elites and led to a general cultural decline, which manifested itself by the sudden end of constructing representative buildings.

3

The Early Postclassic in Mesoamerica

The early Postclassic is the time between ca. A.D. 800 and 1250. Investigations are marked by the competition of two kinds of sources: archaeology and historical reports. Our knowledge reflects their frequent incompatibility.

TULA

After the decline of Teotihuacán there was a vacuum in central Mexico, where city-states dominated small regions. Two centuries were to pass before there was a new large city in central Mexico around A.D. 1000, Tula.

THE CITY OF TULA ≡ The city of Tula and its ceremonial center were situated about sixty-five kilometers northwest of Teotihuacán in an open plain at the edge of an area that was at that time fertile, close to major obsidian mines, and on an important traffic route. It cannot have been agriculture alone that allowed Tula to become the largest city of Mesoamerica. Rather, Tula inherited the significance of Teotihuacán as a central manufacturer of obsidian as well as miner of the volcanic glass at Pachuca, which Teotihuacán had begun to do. This craft apparently occupied half of the inhabitants. They also worked travertine into transparent vessels and made ceramics. In addition to a pompous ceremonial center Tula contained widely spread living quarters for its approximately thirty thousand inhabitants.

SOCIAL STRUCTURE ≡ The main ceremonial area was full of architectural innovations that indicate decisive sociocultural changes. In the center there was a huge plaza with enough space for a hundred thousand people. On three of its sides were elongated meeting halls, with ceilings supported by several rows of wooden columns, open to the plaza. In them several thousand people could stay at the same time; the length of stone benches along the walls of these halls measures more than one thousand meters. Users of these halls and benches had themselves and their social functions depicted in numerous stone reliefs: warriors galore, stiffly arranged in processions. The ever-present theme of war repeats in a telling metaphor, when eagles and jaguars form processions like the warriors and swallow bloody human hearts, or when symbols like bones and skulls are repeated.

In Tula, the change manifested itself from an esoteric cult of the Classic, celebrated by a small group of prominent people in the narrow interiors of temples, to ceremonies demanding the participation of a large number of equally ranked officials, and hence interiors with enough space for them. As in later times, warriors dominated these ceremonies. There may have been various societies and ranks.

FAR-REACHING CONTACTS ≡ Tula must have had long-range contacts of various kinds, as ceramics imported from eastern Mesoamerica show. There was grey-green plumbate from southern Guatemala, but also polychrome wares from Costa Rica. In exchange Tula, just as Teotihuacán had earlier, may have sent obsidian tools in large quantities. Toward the north the situation was quite different, since the borders of civilization were not too far away. There were connections to Río Gila, where Mesoamerican influence grew even after the fall of Teotihuacán, but neighboring hunter and gatherer groups must have appeared as a threat; just one hundred kilometers north of Tula defensive mountain forts, such as Las Ranas and Toluquilla, were manned.

THE END OF TULA ≡ According to the archaeological record, the florescence of the large city of Tula didn't last long. The living quarters examined so far may have been abandoned by A.D. 1050; it is unknown when the ceremonial center fell. Fire consumed the halls; later the pyramids were destroyed in a gigantic effort, and columns and caryatids were toppled. A sketchy description of these dramatic times is given in an Aztec report written half a millennium after the events.

THE TOLTECS OF THE REPORTS

With the end of the last ramifications of the Classic the first reports appeared, laid down as picture manuscripts or written after the Conquista based on oral traditions. However, the statements are largely fragmentary and it is hardly possible to separate mythical parts from reality. In particular there is one early subject dominating the reports that seems to have fascinated people until the Conquista: the fate of the marvelous city of Tollan, its inhabitants, the Toltecs, and their famous ruler, Ce Acatl Quetzalcoatl. Tollan with the epithet Xicocotitlan is identical with the excavated city of Tula on only one of several levels of understanding. Tollan had become a kind of honor title and was important in religious terms, so other cities were called by that name as well. In fact, many cities in Postclassic Mesoamerica tried to create or cement their status by showing their roots to be in such a Tollan.

THE TERM "TOLTEC" ≡ In pre-European times it was not only the inhabitants of Tollan Xicocotitlan who were called the Toltecs (the Aztec *tolteca* means "citizen of a place called Tollan"), but also other groups who were or who claimed to be associated with this Tollan or another town of that name. Finally, "Toltec" was used for people or groups who were as good as the inhabitants of Tollan Xicocotitlan in crafts, knowledge, and wisdom (as the sources idealize it). Much confusion and misunderstanding stem from these numerous meanings, which often cross each other.

TOLLAN ≡ The descriptions of Tollan as written down after the Conquista can be divided into two groups. On one hand Tollan is described as a paradise, a marvelous place, whose inhabitants owned all earthly goods in abundance, and due to their piety had learned incomparable wisdom and mastery of all crafts and sciences from their god. Opposed to this are sections of reports that, although also showing mythical elaborations, give a very earthly picture of interior strife in a city headed for its downfall. Only these last may portray the Tula excavated by archaeologists. There can be no question that the mythical, idealized Tollan can not be found.

ETHNIC COMPONENTS ≡ Tollan Xicocotitlan, like many Mesoamerican cities, was settled by people of various ethnic backgrounds. The dominant group were the Nonoalca, who had probably come from the southern Gulf Coast. In contact with the Maya they had experienced a civilized refinement that was unknown at this time in central Mexico. The other leading group were the Tolteca-Chichimeca. They had come to Tollan from the northern border of Mesoamerica, but they had previously lived already in a more central location. There they had adopted a sedentary way of life based on agriculture, which differentiated them from the nomadic Chichimecs.

QUETZALCOATL ≡ In the reports (possibly influenced by Christianity), the inhabitants of Tollan are said to have venerated only one deity, Quetzalcoatl ("feathered serpent"). Instead of the multiple human sacrifices that later became so common, the god is said to have enjoyed a gentle cult and demanded only serpents, flowers, and butterflies as sacrificial offerings. But Quetzalcoatl was also a name for the highest priest of the god.

TOPILTZIN CE ACATL QUETZALCOATL ≡ The most important ruler of Tollan, Topiltzin ("our revered prince"), who also was called by his birthday's day name Ce Acatl ("One Reed"), is often referred to only by his title Quetzalcoatl. Details of his origins and life are not clear. He must have reigned in the final period of Tollan, a time fraught with catastrophes brought on by the leaching of soil and a climatic change of around A.D. 1000 that made a large region north of Tollan barren. At the same time nomadic groups of Chichimecs pushed south from the ever-expanding steppes in the north. Internal strife between the two most important groups of people at Tollan, the Nonoalca and the Tolteca-Chichimeca, finally resulted in the collapse. The conflict between the two populations is reflected in the Quetzalcoatl myth in the reports: although he was a picture of modesty, Quetzalcoatl succumbed to diabolical temptation by demons (who had the names of major Aztec deities), was a prey to debauchery, and thus brought ill fate to his city. Plagued by afflictions, he had to flee the city with his adherents. Rulership in Tollan was seized by Huemac, who then was also subjected to visitation by demons, sought refuge in a cave, and vanished there or killed himself. Which of the two antagonists belonged to which population group has not been conclusively determined.

Topiltzin, at this stage more often called Quetzalcoatl in the descriptions, went from place to place for a while, performed numerous miracles, and ended up at the coast of the Gulf of Mexico. There he is said to have immolated himself, turned into the morning star, or gone away over the sea.

DISPERSEMENT OF THE TOLTECS ≡ Those who had fled from Tollan assembled near the city of Colhuacan in the Valley of Mexico, the second place Topiltzin ruled, where according to other reports he finally arrived and where he remained until his death. Others settled in several different places, stretching from the southern side of the Valley of Mexico into the Mixtec area and beyond.

NEIGHBORS AND HEIRS OF THE TOLTECS

MIXTECS ≡ The picture manuscripts of the Mixtecs in the modern state of Oaxaca reach back to the Late Classic; some are preserved as originals, others are Colonial adaptations. Although decipherment of hieroglyphic names of people and places has been achieved in only a few cases, pictorial descriptions of activities of rulers of many city-states and their dynastic connections in the valley regions in the north of modern Oaxaca show that they were often involved in petty disputes. The most important of these—here with their better known Aztec names as well—are Yancuitlan (today Yanhuitlan), Tepozcolollan (Teposcolula), Coaxtlahuacan (Coixtlahuacan) and Tlillantonco (Tilantongo). The rulers of Tototepec (Tututepec) on the Pacific Coast were engaged in military expansion toward the end of the Postclassic.

EIGHT DEER ≡ In the pictorial manuscripts the probably most successful conqueror of the Mixtecs is especially highlighted. He was named "Eight Deer" according to his birthday in the year A.D. 1011; the hero from the dynasty of Tilantongo also had the apt epithet "Tiger Claw." His unusually extensive biography is typical of the political situation in his time, but also of what his contemporaries and descendants considered to be important (and therefore worth telling): Eight Deer was the son of Lord Five Alligator and his second wife, Lady Eleven Water Precious Bird. After the death of his father, his older half-brother inherited the throne, and Eight Deer at nineteen years of age turned to Tututepec; from there he undertook a large number of successful raids. After he had acquired the fame of a great warrior, he had a jewel placed in his nose in an elaborate ritual, a mark of distinction. According to a report in one source this happened at Tollan—whether this was Tollan Xicocotitlan is doubtful. When he was forty years old he married Lady Thirteen Serpent Flower Serpent. In all Eight Deer was married to five women and had at least eleven children. One of his greatest successes was that eventually he managed to gain rulership of his hometown, Tilantongo. After a failed conquering raid against the home of his second wife, Eight Deer was captured in A.D. 1063 and sacrificed. The family of his wife apparently had a decisive role in this.

VALLEY OF OAXACA ≡ When Monte Albán ceased to be the political center, the Valley of Oaxaca had been divided into a large number of Zapotec city-states. They shared a religious center, Mitla, where the deities of the underworld were venerated. In the palaces of Mitla, the facades of which were decorated with rich stone mosaics, the highest ranking Zapotec priest was in residence, and he was also buried there. Possibly around A.D. 1280 the Zapotec ruler of Zaachila had formed a marriage alliance with Mixtecs from Yanhuitlan, who brought along a large number of relatives and retinue. Their claim that in the following time they managed to subjugate almost the entire Valley of Oaxaca and throw the Zapotec rulers back to the area around Tehuantepec probably does not correspond to reality.

YUCATÁN

CHICHÉN ITZÁ ≡ Intruders from the southern coast of the Gulf of Mexico impressed themselves on the Postclassic city of Chichén Itzá, situated on the flat karst in the northernmost part of the Yucatán Pensinsula, next to a deep, water-filled cenote, which was venerated as a sacred well. The traditions of the Maya, written down very late, form a contrast to the results of archaeological work, which has led to contradictory explanations. According to traditional views the architecture of Chichén Itzá is the manifestation of two cultural phases: one is Terminal Classic Maya (the same who created the Puuc style), the other the Mexican-influenced Itzá. Both finally formed a cultural amalgamation with each other. The historical sources seem to support this in part when they describe the rulers of Chichén Itzá, the Itzá, as foreigners who could speak only broken Maya. Scholars liked to see in their leader Kukulkan the Toltec Quetzalcoatl (translated, this is the same name), driven from Tollan, who had ventured, according to some reports, to the land of Tlillan Tlapallan, which they interpret as the Maya area. This scenario is questioned more and more, because it is incompatible with historical chronology and archaeological dating, but a satisfying alternative has not yet been offered. More modern opinion has it that instead of a massive intrusion there was a slow, and most likely peaceful, trickle of people and cultural ideas, which contributed to a short-term regional florescence of the dying Maya culture. Around A.D. 850 they were followed by less peaceful "Toltec" warriors from the coastal regions of the Gulf, who may represent the small militant group of the Itzá.

These conquerors made Chichén Itzá their capital and settled also in other cities. Chichén Itzá was a very important pilgrimage center because of its sacred cenote, where countless offerings were thrown, and where human beings were sacrificed as well. Izamal functioned as a shrine of the sun god Kinich Kakmo and the island of Cozumel as one where the moon goddess Ixchel was venerated. The duration of Chichén Itzá's dominance was two hundred years.

DECLINE ≡ The fall of Chichén Itzá is clothed in the later sources as a personal dispute between the ruler Chac Xib Chac and the ruler Hunac Ceel of Mayapan. Hunac Ceel presumably came from a modest background. He had become ruler of Mayapan by an uncommon act. Regularly people were thrown into the sacred cenote at Chichén Itzá to ask the deities supposedly residing there for a fertile year. If none of the victims survived to be pulled out after a few hours and be questioned as to the answers of the deities, it was a sign that they were angry. When this happened at one time Hunac Ceel jumped into the cenote of his own free will and brought back a seemingly good answer.

The background for the rivalry between Chichén Itzá and Mayapan is not clear. The cause for the dispute was created by Hunac Ceel, who employed sorcery to make Chac Xib Chac desire the bride of Ah Ulil, ruler of Izamal, of all times at their wedding feast. Ah Ulil's answer was war; he went against Chichén Itzá. His absence was used by Hapay Can, who obviously stood on the side of the Itzá, to raid Izamal and make it a tributary. Now Hunac Ceel himself attacked Chichén Itzá, probably in A.D. 1194. He was aided by seven generals, whose names tell us that they belonged to a Nahuat-speaking group. Together with their troops they had been hired as mercenaries from the Gulf Coast (Tabasco), to which there were obviously close ties. Chichén Itzá was conquered, its inhabitants left, and some of them went to Lake Petén more than four hundred kilometers away. In this secluded spot they could maintain their independence from the Spaniards until A.D. 1697.

4

The Late Postclassic

The Late Postclassic, lasting from the middle of the thirteenth century to the Spanish conquest, is known in many regions mainly through written sources. Its beginning almost everywhere is characterized by migrations in which small bands of warriors often tried to conquer a local population and enforce their own rule. These conquerors liked to claim connection with "Tollan," but it cannot have been the same historical site in all cases.

YUCATÁN AND GUATEMALA

MAYAPAN ≡ The previously described victory over Chichén Itzá and the elimination of Izamal at the same time allowed Hunac Ceel to make his city Mayapan the political center of northern Yucatán. In Mayapan the descendants of Hunac Ceel ruled under the name Cocom together with the Tutul Xiu. The rulers of various provinces also resided there, hardly of their own free will, but rather to guarantee the good behavior of their home sites. Overall Mayapan was prey to anxiety: the entire city with its religious and ceremonial buildings, which were built in quite a slipshod way, and thousands of small compounds were surrounded by a wall—in this form a real innovation.

DECLINE OF MAYAPAN ≡ The joint rulership in Mayapan probably presented some conflicts. Again, the Cocom brought in warriors from Tabasco, who tyrannized the population. Finally, around A.D. 1445, there was a conspiracy under the leadership of Ah Xupan, a member of the Tutul Xiu family, and all members of the ruling family of the Cocoms were killed. Parts of Mayapan were burned and the city was abandoned. Only one Cocom escaped, because he was in Ulua (Honduras) on a trading mission. He called his people together and settled them in the province of Sotuta. The Tutul Xiu made Maní their capital, while the auxiliary troops from Tabasco, who must have reached a large number in time, lived in the province Ah Canul ("body guard"), in the particularly barren and dry far northwest of Yucatán. The sixteen regional chieftains of northern Yucatán were engaged in constant strife. Despite this inner instability the Spaniards managed the conquest of Yucatán only after several failed attempts (1527–34) in A.D. 1540–46.

"TOLTEC" CONQUERORS IN GUATEMALA ≡ In the Postclassic small groups of warlike intruders repeatedly invaded the highlands of Guatemala and Chiapas, populated by the Maya. Within a short time they often usurped rulership and became dominant powers in small regions. A good example for this procedure is given by the Quiché, Cakchiquel, and Tzutujil in the highlands of today's Guatemala. These Maya groups were settled in a wide area around Lake Atitlán. In the beginning of the thirteenth century warriors invaded the region who came from the area south of the Laguna de Términos on the Gulf Coast, where they were exposed to massive central Mexican influence. These new elites claimed to originate from "Tollan" to legitimize their rank and rulership claims; however, this was definitely not identical to Tollan Xicocotitlan. The few invaders melted into the original population's language and culture, but established central Mexican culture elements. The Quiché, Cakchiquel, and Tzutujil formed a military alliance, which was strengthened by marriage ties.

QUICHÉ ≡ In the early fourteenth century the Quiché became the most important expansive power. A first step to subjugate the previous population was the mythically embellished battle on the fortified mountain Jacavitz. The military might of the Quiché was supplemented by the allied Cakchiquel, who overcame the local Pokomam. After the first generation of rulers had died the Quiché tried to strengthen their "Toltec" legitimization with office titles and insignia brought back by ambassadors to the great ruler Nacxit, about whom nothing else is known. In the following period the Quiché moved their capital several times, finally to Utatlán. The rulers Cotuja and Kucumatz enlarged their territory substantially; under Quikab, the next ruler, it reached its largest extension and was secured by numerous fortified mountain strongholds. Nevertheless, in the second half of the fifteenth century there were serious uprisings. Shortly afterwards there was a break with the Cakchiquel, with whom the Quiché had a series of skirmishes. There was also a war with the Tzutujil, which cost the Quiché dearly.

The attempted expansion of the Aztec Triple Alliance beyond Xoconochco (Soconusco) also resulted in contact with the Quiché. In the reign of Ahuitzotl *pochteca* came as far as Utatlán, and in A.D. 1510 the Quiché may have started to pay tribute. The vicinity of the Aztec Empire ended the constant squabbles of the Quiché. Moteuczoma is said to have warned the Quiché of the Spaniards. When the military might of the Quiché was weakened by an epidemic preceding the Spaniards, and the Tzutujil and Cakchiquel refused assistance because of dissension with the Quiché, the tactical military superiority of the Spaniards made the A.D. 1524 conquest by Pedro de Alvarado inevitable.

CENTRAL MEXICO

With the fall of the barrier created by Tollan and forced by climatic changes, numerous small and larger ethnic groups pressed down from the northwest into the central Mexican valleys. They preserved descriptions of their emigration that formed an integral part of their ethnic identity despite the somewhat stereotypical contents. Usually the point of departure was a place with seven caves (Chicomoztoc), from which the tribes proceeded in easy stages, led by a "sacred bundle" (*tlaquimilolli*), the imaginary resting place of their god. They finally passed through Tollan, which was already deserted and ruined, and then migrated quite directly to their later homeland, where they had to make a place for themselves among the local population.

VALLEY OF PUEBLA-TLAXCALLAN ≡ Even before the fall of Tollan the two ethnic groups settled there had left to move farther into Mesoamerica. In the area of Puebla they met with the Olmeca-Xicalanca, with whom (or with their allies) all immigrant groups leaving the Valley of Mexico toward the south had to contend. The capital of the Olmeca-Xicalanca and the seat of their two jointly appointed rulers was Cholollan (Cholula).

NONOALCA ≡ As the sources attest, groups of the Nonoalca under their leader Xelhua settled in a large region extending almost to Veracruz, south and southeast of the sphere of the Olmeca-Xicalanca. Their political centers, among them Teotitlan del Camino and Tehuacan, preserved until the Conquest a cultural tradition that had clearly more ancient traits than that of their neighbors.

TOLTECA-CHICHIMECA ≡ The Tolteca-Chichimeca and other groups coming after them settled in the area of Cholollan, where they suffered from the tyranny of the Olmeca-Xicalanca. According to their tradition, they were able to topple them in an uprising, which was skillfully started during a banquet. As a consequence of these events an alliance was formed to allow the Olmeca-Xicalanca to regain possession of Cholollan.

CHICHIMECS ≡ Other groups coming into the Valley of Puebla and Tlaxcallan called themselves Chichimecs—a term that indicates a nomadic lifestyle and not a name of a defined ethnic or linguistic group. According to their traditions they had been called in as auxiliary troops by the Tolteca-Chichimeca. Just as the Chichimecs of the Valley of Mexico had done, they also claimed origin from the mythical Chicomoztoc, where Mixcoatl was one of their numerous leaders. Unlike their predecessors in Puebla, the Chichimecs did not follow a civilized mode of life. With their assistance the Olmeca-Xicalanca could be vanquished and forced out to the east; most likely this meant their elite only. They settled in the area of the Sierra de Puebla. In consequence, a new regional supremacy had been firmly established in Cholollan toward the end of the thirteenth century, deriving legitimization from one of the population groups of Tollan-Tula, who later on were themselves called Toltecs.

CHICHIMEC RULE ≡ After they had conquered other areas and made the inhabitants tributaries, four Chichimec tribes founded what became the leading political units in the area until the Conquest: Tlaxcallan (Tlaxcala), Huexotzinco (Huejotzingo), Cuauhtinchan, and Totomihuacan (Totimehuacan). The Chichimec leaders had married women from Cholollan. The shrine of Quetzalcoatl at Cholollan remained the focus of religious-political reference, where the investiture of local chieftains was performed by inserting the Toltec nose ornaments. The consolidation of the states had been achieved by the middle of the fourteenth century. Other, possibly small, groups that had immigrated from the north or the south did not form new powers but were integrated into states already established.

HEGEMONY OF HUEXOTZINCO ≡ Following the consolidation of Chichimec supremacy there was a period of military altercations for regional power, where Tlaxcallan and Huexotzinco stood in opposition. Huexotzinco was supported by their ethnic relatives, the Acolhua of the Valley of Mexico, but Tlaxcallan was able to avoid a resounding defeat thanks to help from Cholollan, Cuauhtinchan, and Totomihuacan. In the early second half of the fourteenth century Huexotzinco defeated Cholollan in another war, resulting in a lessening of its political and territorial significance. It did keep its significance as a religious center and as the city of merchants. The overall result of the fighting was a political-military balance in the region, which formed the basis of joint actions under Huexotzinco's leadership.

TARASCANS ≡ In the Postclassic the western part of central Mexico was dominated by the Tarascans, whose nobility also belonged to a semi-nomadic Chichimec group, who had immigrated late. Their military prowess allowed them to assume power over the previous population, peasants and fishermen of various language groups. Men from the immigrated group married important women of the local population. The founder of the empire was Tariácuri, who came from one of those marriages, and who had his capital in Pátzcuaro. It was probably in his time that the Tarascan language was generally accepted. In the course of a history full of changes the empire became an alliance of three powers under a son and two great-nephews of Tariácuri. Starting from the three capitals around Lake Pátzcuaro, Pátzcuaro, Tzintzuntzan, and Ihuatzío, more territory was conquered. Tangaxoan of Tzintzuntzan, one of the great-nephews of Tariácuri, was the founder of the Tarascan dynasty, which provided the *cazonci* (ruler) of Tzintzuntzan at the time of the Spanish conquest.

VALLEY OF MEXICO ≡ The archaeological findings show that after the fall of Tula the population numbers and the number of settlements dwindled rapidly in the area north of the Valley of Mexico and in its northern half. In that period the bulk of the population could be found at the fertile southern end of the Lake of Mexico, where the creation of *chinampas* guaranteed sufficient provisions. *Chinampas*, a method of land gain employed in Mesoamerica in several variations, consist of long, narrow, parallel-running, raised beds that were situated at the shores of sweet-water lakes or on swampy valley floors. That nomadic groups from the sparse north were attracted to them is quite understandable.

CHICHIMECS ≡ After the fall of Tollan several groups of diverse ethnic backgrounds also progressed into the Valley of Mexico. The leader of one of these groups, possibly of several, who called themselves frequently Chichimecs, had the name of Xolotl; in other sources somebody called Mixcoatl was in his place. Supposedly he entered a ruined and deserted land, where he was able to acquire a huge territory without resistance; however, his interest was limited to the Valley of Mexico. He had hardly anything in common with the few Toltecs he encountered. Xolotl started Chichimec settlements apart from them, founded his capital in Tenayocan, and conquered the Toltec capital of Colhuacan a short time later in the southern part of the Valley of Mexico.

Only a few decades after the Chichimecs of Xolotl, three other groups of people under their leader Acolhua arrived in the Valley of Mexico: the Tepanecs, the Acolhua, and a group of Otomí. They settled in Xolotl's territory—in the west, east, and north of the valley. In a complicated dense net of marriage alliances they affiliated themselves to each other and to the most important ruling families of the previous population, especially the Toltec dynasty of Colhuacan.

TEPANECS ≡ The ethnic and linguistic makeup of the Tepanecs is contradictory in its details. The Mexica counted them among those groups who had come from Chicomoztoc, but their language is related to Otomí. In the opinion of the dynasty of Tetzcoco they migrated with their leader Acolhua (according to other sources, Matlacoatl) into the valley later than Xolotl's Chichimecs and founded their capital Azcapotzalco not far from Tenayocan. Their early history is obscure. The leader of the migration was followed by his son and two grandsons as rulers. Rise to the dominant power of the Valley of Mexico was achieved by the fifth ruler of the Tepanecs, Tezozomoc (ca. 1365–1426). Although they were allied to the Chichimecs through marriages, the Tepanecs and the Mexica—whose island settlement in the Lake of Mexico fell under Tepanec rule—were successful in a war against the Chichimec center Tenacoyan and thus gained the important title Chichimecateuctli for their dynasty.

OTOMÍ ≡ The second group of immigrants was called Otomí, but they consisted only of a small part of a larger population in central Mexico, who all shared the Otomí language. The immigrants under their leader Chiconcuauh settled in Xaltocan, in the arid north of the valley. They were the group that least conformed to the cultural standards of Mesoamerica.

ACOLHUA ≡ The Acolhua under their leader Tzontecomatl settled on the eastern shore of the Lake of Mexico and made Coatlichan their capital. Possibly to balance the power politics, Xolotl's oldest son Nopaltzin established his son Tlotzin Pochotl in the Toltec city of Tlatzallan south of Acolhuacan. Like others of the Chichimec elite, the Acolhua married into the Toltec population that had settled there earlier.

CHICHIMEC-TOLTEC DYNASTY ≡ Nopaltzin's son and successor, Tlotzin Pochotl, who had Toltec roots through his mother from Colhuacan, furthered Chichimec cultural adaptation to their Toltec neighbors. At the same time, the capital was moved from Chichimec Tenayocan to Tetzcoco, founded by Nopaltzin. From Tetzcoco, which took over the role of Tlatzallan, the distance to the centers of the Acolhua could be lessened. This change was also expressed in the adoption of the Toltec investiture ceremony by Quinatzin. At this time the actual authority of Xolotl's descendants receded and comprised hardly more than the area around Tetzcoco under Quinatzin (?–1377), the successor of Tlotzin. Quinatzin continued the political and cultural consolidation of the still minor city-state. The decisive factor was the expulsion of Chichimec groups, who had refused for a long time to adopt agriculture, into border zones of the highlands and to Tlaxcallan. Together with his more important allies in Huexotla and Coatlichan, or by himself, Quinatzin achieved numerous conquests, which reached into present-day Morelos. Under Quinatzin Tetzcoco gained political weight among the confederates.

OTHER IMMIGRANTS ≡ Quinatzin's position was strengthened further by the immigration of Toltec-influenced Tlailotlaques and Chimalpanecas from the Mixteca (today the border region between Puebla and Oaxaca). In order to neutralize the ethnic plurality caused by the different immigrations, Quinatzin's successor Techotlalatzin (1377–1409) introduced Nahuatl as the state's language. The Tepanec conquest of Colhuacan had caused large population groups to leave the southwestern valley. Members of four ethnic groups had arrived in Tetzcoco, perhaps already in Quinatzin's times, and the Otomí from Xaltocan followed after the victory of the Mexica there. Techotlalatzin settled the immigrants in various hamlets in his realm, and he created four ethnically different quarters in his capital Tetzcoco. It is doubtful, though, if it was he who gave the state a firm inner structure by integrating the subordinate *tlatoani* (rulers) into the administration. In the final years of Techotlalatzin the realm of the eastern valley chiefs was curtailed by the advances of the Tepanecs and their Mexican auxiliary troops.

CHALCO ≡ A comparatively detailed example for the origin and composition of an ethnically complex community is Chalco in the southeastern pocket of the Valley of Mexico. The population of Chalco was supposedly the result of five major immigration waves, which reached this area in the thirteenth and fourteenth centuries. At least eight groups with up to five subgroups each came into the area and continued in settlements and thirteen local political units until the Spaniards arrived.

COLHUACAN ≡ Colhuacan, in the southern center of the Valley of Mexico, was the true Toltec center, and is said to have formed an alliance with Otompan at the time of Tollan. The dynastic sequence, which reaches far beyond the invasion of Chichimec groups, provides a bridge to Tollan, which has been placed into an unusually distant past by the appropriate sources. After Tollan's fall Colhuacan continued, less as a factual power than as a grand name.

MEXICA ≡ The Mexica, who were called Aztecs only in modern times and that not appropriately so, claimed origin from a mythical place called Aztlan, situated on an island in a lake far to the northwest of their later home. Possibly emerged from a cave, they migrated from there, led by their tribal god Huitzilopochtli, at first with the main ethnic groups of the highlands and founders of later states (the different sources do not enumerate the same tribes), but soon separated from them. The first identifiable station for them was also Tollan, where they stayed for several years. Then the Mexica went by the shortest route to the Valley of Mexico, with mostly four-year stops during which they farmed. Finally, around A.D. 1250, they reached the hill Chapultepec on the western shore of the lake (where the life of Huemac of Tollan had ended in a mythical cave). The local population went against the intruders. After a victory they divided the Mexica up among each other, and a remnant was allowed to settle in the region of Colhuacan. After some skirmishes they were forced out there as well; finally in the first half of the fourteenth century they found themselves on a remote reed island, where a prophecy of their god came true. Archaeological research has not been able to resolve whether the future capital Tenochtitlán was founded with this, or if it existed already. Tlatelolco, the sister city, situated on a neighboring island, became independent a few years later.

SOCIOPOLITICAL ORGANIZATION IN CENTRAL MEXICO

In the second half of the fourteenth century everywhere in central Mexico there were similar sociopolitical conditions, which changed in later times only in quantity, not in quality.

CITY-STATES ≡ The basic political units—in the Valley of Mexico alone there were forty to sixty of them—can be best characterized as city-states. Each of them consisted of a more or less urban center with a palace and temple, living quarters for the elite, and the institutions integrating the whole community, accompanied by an agricultural hinterland with villages and hamlets. In this densely populated area, each territorial expansion of one of the states had to be at the cost of a neighbor. Often the states entered into changing confederations, which had the tendency to expand. Such confederations were initiated or confirmed by dynastic marriages of the rulers. The same is true for areas adjoining the Valley of Mexico, whose populations also spoke Nahuatl. The religious customs were also largely homogenous, marked by the meaning accorded to the sacred human sacrifice, which was intended to secure the continuation of the world. Local color appeared only in the veneration of different patron deities, which in the final analysis were just aspects of the same main gods. A code of behavior recognized everywhere provided free access to sacred sites and to the markets, in general protected ambassadors, and regulated formal declarations of war.

SOCIAL HIERARCHY ≡ The inhabitants of the states formed two social levels. The nobility was in its majority noble by birth (*pilli*) and constituted about 10 percent of the population. Commoners differed by their obligation to pay or work for the states, the states' representatives, or specific nobles.

SOCIAL ASCENT ≡ Nobles and others were able to climb the social ladder by performing war acts. Their ascent was expressed in visually apparent status and formed the prerequisite for achieving public offices. For commoners social advances could lead to freedom from tribute and acquisition of land (use of it was somewhat restricted); thereby a noble rank of worth and service was formed that could not be inherited. Similar procedures applied for the priesthood.

BIRTH NOBILITY ≡ Nobles by birth formed numerous dynasties and families, differentiated by ethnic extraction, descent, possessions, and power, whose heads often had specific historical titles that included the word *teuctli* (Lord), which also denoted generally a member of the high nobility. A successor for the head of a noble family was usually selected by observing agnatic principles; however, he had to prove himself first through valor in war and skill in certain high administrative offices. In some cases women could rise to this position. Final selection needed the consent of equals or of the head of state. The center for a family and living quarters for their head was a "palace" (*tecpan* or *teccalli*, "mansion"). Often there was substantial land associated with it, which either was directly farmed for the family head or had been given to relatives or a sideline of the family. Land of the nobles (*pillalli*) was bequeathed to heirs, often also to females, and was treated as a private possession. A specific form of land ownership (*teuctlalli*) was tied to the title *teuctli*. As members of the propertied class, nobles generally were able to afford to marry several women and run a large house. On the other hand, lower ranking nobles often could not be distinguished from the peasant population.

NOBLE HOUSES ≡ The lands of a noble family were not in one piece, but were distributed over the entire area of influence of the family, or even throughout the territory of the state. They were farmed by dependent peasants, who gave part of the production to the landowners, as did the artisans belonging to a noble house; they and their families were obliged to perform numerous services in the households. Every larger noble house thus formed a corporate economic unit, whose clan head also held political and judicial powers over land and dependents. The power of a noble hinged on the number of his dependents.

RULERS ≡ Every city-state was governed by one or more rulers from the local leading noble dynasties; a ruler had the title *tlatoani* ("speaker"); his territory was called *tlatocayotl.* The historical legitimization of the *tlatoani* was derived from the status and merit of his ancestors at the time of immigration and land gain, and supported by marriage with women of Toltec ancestry. Succession was much like that in noble families. The rulers had religious, judicial, and administrative functions; their palaces were economic and political centers of the state; they represented the state as the highest authority, and also had the last word on questions of land.

FUNCTIONARIES ≡ Nobles by birth provided for the most part the judges and other high- and middle-level administrative officials of the central state organization, and also the military leaders. In the priestly hierarchy nobles dominated as well. They could shift between religious and secular offices according to their personal predilections. The *tlatoani* and the other office holders were entitled to the yields of land connected with the office.

COMMONERS ≡ Commoners provided the majority of the population; they lived mostly as peasants or craftsmen, often in addition to farming. In general sons followed in the professions of their fathers. The smallest economic unit was the family of more than one generation with lateral extensions, where monogamous marriages predominated. There could be others in the household not belonging to the family. Following several early sources, the term *macehualli* is used today as a generic term for all commoners.

DEPENDENTS ≡ Some commoners lived as dependents of noble families. As peasants they mostly lived on the land they worked or in a neighboring hamlet, and for generations they cultivated the same fields. Like the artisans they delivered a part of the produce, objects, and services to the owner of the land or to the head of a noble family. Theoretically these people could move away and settle elsewhere, in order to work land under more or less the same conditions. The category of dependents appears under different names in the sources. As a general term the Spanish *terrazguero* of Colonial administrative documents is commonly used.

RURAL COMMUNES ≡ Other commoners lived in corporate groups, which socially were only slightly stratified, as collective owners of a piece of land, whose size depended on its location. Part of it was farmed for community institutions (temple, young men's houses, place of education for the military); part went to support the "Elder," whose status was like that of a low-ranking noble, and who headed and represented the community. The largest portion of this land was individually farmed by members, and could be bequeathed to heirs, but not sold. Each household contributed a part of the community's tribute to the *tlatoani*, according to the size of land parcels they worked. Moreover, the community as a whole was responsible for farming the land that belonged to the ruler, for delivering the yields, and for providing other regular services for the ruler or the state. Sometimes special groups of members provided only certain valued services. These corporate groups of commoners are often called *calpulli* (literally "great house"), a term also used for other circumscribed groups of people. The impression created by Colonial authors that this was a basic form of organization for the common population cannot be upheld. In fact, this structure was probably not preserved in Central Mexico until the Conquista, except in a few areas.

MERCHANTS ≡ The merchants (*pochteca*) saw to movement of goods, especially into remote areas, to specialized markets, and to international ports of trade, and formed a supraregional infrastructure. They were probably of Toltec origin, and lived in special quarters in the cities, venerated their own god, and had a much-differentiated internal structure. In particular, long-range traders, who imported luxury goods and tropical raw materials, could amass substantial riches. At least some could attain a status in society by wealth that was comparable to that of nobles, by organizing expensive ceremonies and providing slaves for sacrifices. Their obligations toward the ruler and the state were paid by delivery of objects and services.

The corporate association of merchants (*calpulli*) subjected its members to strict rules, and to a certain extent had its own judiciary system. At the time of the Aztec Triple Alliance the living quarters of the *pochteca* were concentrated in twelve cities in the Valley of Mexico, whose merchant corporations were organized in one common, strictly hierarchical order. The highest status belonged to the merchants of Tenochtitlán, Tlatelolco, and Huitzilopochco (Churubusco). Probably there was a similar regional organization around the old trading city of Cholollan (today Cholula).

ARTISANS ≡ Highly specialized artisans (gold- and silversmiths, precious stone cutters, and feather workers) had also formed corporate professional groups, similar to the merchants, and venerated their own deities. It is not clear if these special professional corporations existed outside of the large cities.

"SLAVES" ≡ The persons called *tlacotli*, for whom the Spanish translation "slave" in the sense of human "merchandise" is erroneous, appeared only seemingly outside the firmly structured social groups. *Tlacotli* had "pledged" their services to another person for a time, either of their own free will against payment (because of gambling debts, waste, bad harvests, and such), or because they had been sentenced to this condition as a penalty and reparation after a crime they had committed. After the determined period was over or the debt was paid, the person once again was his own master. Children born in the meantime were always free. Only repeatedly relapsing criminals stayed *tlacotli* all their lives; they could be sentenced to be sold in the marketplace. Such slaves could be sacrificed.

It is thought that there may have been a form of slavery, corresponding better to the term, that applied to persons captured in a war. Such slaves could be traded over long distances, but there is hardly anything known about their living conditions and their status.

PORTERS ≡ Beasts of burden and wagons did not exist, so porters (*tamemes*, derived from the Nahuatl *tlameme'* or *tlamama'*, "porter") had to perform all transports other than the ones on water. The number of porters must have been high; their work was hard and not much respected. The sources do not mention explicitly if porter services were performed as part of the current duties of the professionally otherwise occupied commoners. Much can be said for a separate professional caste of porters.

WOMEN ≡ The scope of action for women was limited mostly to home and children, as is common in societies with clearly defined levels. The social standing was determined by many factors—it was emphasized that one of the wives of Nezahualpilli was at least his equal in education and wisdom. Within commoner families women contributed to services and tribute payments by grinding maize, preparing tortillas, spinning, and weaving. Personal participation of women in long-range trade and status in the hierarchy of the *pochteca* seem to surpass other possibilities of female activity directed toward the outside. As mothers of future soldiers women among the Aztecs received a special religious valuation. Women played an active and central role in the temple cult of several female deities.

YOUTH ≡ The basically different roles of both social strata were expressed among others in public education. There were two kinds of schools to prepare especially the male youths for adult life: *calmecac* were part of the important temples and reserved for nobles with few exceptions. Military training there was supplemented by teaching knowledge in religion, administration, and the fine arts. In the young men's houses (*telpochcalli*), run by experienced warriors, the military education was dominant, but there was also instruction in the execution of general community services.

MULTI-ETHNIC STRUCTURE ≡ Differentiation between nobles and commoners and between the different professional groups and their organizational forms within the population was mainly ethnically determined and the result of multiple migration movements and conquests. Many of the city-states, as late as the time of the Conquista, were determined by their ethnic pluralism, expressed in some of them by the fact that the *tlatoani* originally belonged to different peoples. Ruling dynasties everywhere were identified with a specific ethnic group and derived part of their legitimization from this membership. Immigration and conquests were also at the root of the regionally very differentiated population of dependent or land-owning peasants.

EARLY HISTORY OF THE AZTEC TRIPLE ALLIANCE

THE FIRST RULERS ≡ In the second half of the fourteenth century the Mexica's position in their island settlement was so far consolidated that they founded their own ruling dynasties in their two capitals, Tenochtitlán and Tlatelolco. The rulers were selected from the dynasties of other sites that had long been prestigious: Cuacuauhpitzahuac (1372–1407) of Tlatelolco was a son of Tezozomoc of Azcapotzalco, who descended from an ancestor not well documented. By choosing Acamapichtli (1371–1391) for Tenochtitlán a Toltec line of ancestors was utilized. The minor social differentiation of both groups may explain why two men from "outside" were elected, since none of the local families lent themselves automatically for the position; a ruler from elsewhere supposedly stood above the probably rival groups. Certainly the influence of the Tepanecs can be supposed, because there were no basic changes in the dependent relationship of the Mexica. Acamapichtli's marriages to daughters of the leading men of various subgroups of the Tenochca created a dense net of relationships that later became the basis of the Mexican elite.

CONSOLIDATION OF THE MEXICA ≡ The reigns of both Acamapichtli in Tenochtitlán and Cuacuauhpitzahuac in Tlatelolco can be regarded as a period of consolidation. Safe from outer dangers, the island settlements could be developed. As auxiliary troops of the Tepanecs, or in their name, the Mexica undertook important conquests, but also made raids on their own behalf. In this way the warriors gained experience, loot, and above all self-esteem.

HUITZILIHUITL ≡ When Acamapichtli died and his son Huitzilihuitl (1391–1417) became his successor, his marriage to a woman from the Tepanec dynasty showed the ongoing integration of the insular population into the political community in the Valley of Mexico. Around this time the historical reports of the Mexica lose their legendary, anecdotal style and become descriptions closer to reality.

CONQUESTS OF HUITZILIHUITL ≡ The official lists of Acamapichtli's conquests contain only few settlements, but the list of Huitzilihuitl's is roughly double in size. This reflects not only the aggressive politics and expansion of the Tepanec Empire, but also the impact of Mexican auxiliary troops. In the southern lake district tribute from the first of three conquered cities, Cuitlahuacan, Mizquic, and Xochimilco, had benefited the Mexica of Tlatelolco and Tenochtitlán. Further conquests had been achieved south of the Valley of Mexico. An important success was the victory of the Mexica over the Otomí dynasty at Xaltocan in the northwestern valley in the year 1395, which secured this area for the Tepanecs.

WAR AGAINST ACOLHUACAN ≡ The four-year-long war of the Tepanecs against Acolhuacan, in which the Mexica military had the decisive role, was started during the reign of Huitzilihuitl. The Tepanec area and Acolhuacan shared a long common border, and the troops of Tezozomoc had already entered into the sphere of Acolhuacan's influence and had undermined its position. Under Techotlalatzin's son and successor Ixtlilxochitl Ometochtli (1409–1417) there was the decisive conflict with Azcapotzalco. The reason for it was that Ixtlilxochitl, by proclaiming himself the Chichimecateuctli, had provoked Tezozomoc, who claimed the same title, so laden with symbols, for himself.

The clashes started in 1414. Ixtlilxochitl had at first answered the attack of the enemy in a clever strategy by hitting their core area, but could not withstand his enemy's superiority, especially as several *tlatoani* of the Acolhua had left his cause because they were influenced by Tezozomoc. Huitzilihuitl of Tenochtitlán and Tlacateotl of Tlatelolco were reported to be conquerors of the important Acolhuacan towns Acolman, Otompan, Tetzcoco, and Tollantzinco. Ixtlilxochitl's empire disintegrated; he himself was finally murdered in 1418. His young son Nezahualcoyotl fled to Huexotzinco and then to Tlaxcallan. Tezozomoc took the largest part of the Acolhua area for himself, but left Tetzcoco to the Tenochca and Huexotlato to the Tlatelolca, who were thus made allies, even if they were not yet independent. Other Acolhua areas (Coatlichan, Acolman) were released into a half-autonomous status, still depending on Tezozomoc's mercy. After this victory there were no more rivals for Tezozomoc and he had himself proclaimed highest ruler and Chichimecateuctli.

THE TEPANEC EMPIRE ≡ Under Tezozomoc of Azcapotzalco, who had come to rule shortly before Acamapichtli, the Tepanec Empire had reached its largest extent, thanks to the effective troops of the Mexica. It consisted of the core area northwest of the lakes, the entire Valley of Mexico, and other territories, which may have reached almost from the northern borders of Mesoamerica to today's Morelos and northeastern Guerrero (Tlachco, today Taxco), and also lands in the Valley of Toluca. Sons and sons-in-law of Tezozomoc were rulers in numerous dependent city-states. Other important states (Coatlichan, Huexotzinco) were loosely allied with Tezozomoc.

CHIMALPOPOCA ≡ The third ruler of Tenochtitlán, Chimalpopoca (1417–1426), was a son of Huitzilihuitl, and as a grandson of Tezozomoc he had a good relationship with the Tepanec ruler. Not only did he and Tlacateotl, the ruler of Tlatelolco, receive tribute from conquered areas, the Mexica's own tribute obligations were reduced and they were allowed to build the first stone structures. In these years Tlatelolco started trading previously unavailable products from warmer climates. Many Tepanecs felt, though, that the Mexica were too self-confident and demanding, as they had already perpetrated small infringements on the Tepanec mainland, and had traded there as well.

CONFLICTS WITH THE MEXICA ≡ When Tezozomoc died in 1426 at a very old age in Azcapotzalco, a Tepanec faction hostile to the Mexica won the upper hand. His son Quetzalayatl, chosen by Tezozomoc as his successor, was ousted by his older half-brother Maxtla, who had ruled Tepanec Coyoacan since 1410. Maxtla immediately raised the tribute payments of the Mexica again. His subsequent politics led to a series of murders in various cities; among the victims were Chimalpopoca of Tenochtitlán (probably 1426), in circumstances never fully explained, and Tlacateotl of Tlatelolco (1427), who both had wanted to remain loyal to the legitimate successor.

ITZCOATL ≡ Subsequently, in Tenochtitlán the energetic and experienced warrior Itzcoatl (1427–1440) was elected as ruler. He was about forty years old and a son of Acamapichtli and uncle of Chimalpopoca. With his election, for the first time at Tenochtitlán a son did not follow his father; the succession began to go by special (uniquely Mexica) rules observed from then on. In Tlatelolco, Cuauhtlatoa became ruler. The political constellation was changed irrevocably when Nezahualcoyotl, already recalled from exile to Tetzcoco in the lifetime of Tezozomoc, had to flee from Maxtla to Tenochtitlán; his mother, a daughter of Huitzilihuitl, came from there, and he and Itzcoatl found themselves allied as opponents of the Tepanecs. This move may seem surprising, after the Mexica had been instrumental in the victory over Nezahualcoyotl's father, but it is typical for the often changing alliances determined by events of the moment.

WAR AGAINST THE TEPANECS ≡ For an open war the available forces were not sufficient, because Nezahualcoyotl did not command a home base. But he managed to win as allies the states of Huexotzinco and Tlaxcallan, now wooed from all sides, where he had previously been allowed to stay as a refugee. Tlatelolco and Cuauhtitlan also joined against the Tepanecs, whereas Chalco stood aside, despite great efforts by all involved parties. Thanks to the allies (there were large troop contingents especially from Huexotzinco), parts of the area of Tetzcoco could be taken back, and an attack could be mounted on the most important Tepanec town, Azcapotzalco, which had been fortified in the meantime. After a siege of almost four months Azcapotzalco could be taken late in 1428, not least because the *tlatoani* of the Tepanec Tlacopan (today Tacuba, a quarter of Mexico City) refused to assist Maxtla. After the fall of Azcapotzalco more Tepanec places could be conquered, while Maxtla had retreated to Coyohuacan, still representing a power. Finally, additional campaigns forced Maxtla to flee in 1431; supposedly he died soon afterwards. The high ruler of the Tepanecs had fallen for good. Nezahualcoyotl was installed as ruler of Acolhuacan; this had to take place in Tenochtitlán, because there were still single *tlatoani* in parts of his realm who refused to follow him out of loyalty to the Tepanecs.

RESULTS OF THE WAR ≡ After the end of the war large tracts of land in the Tepanec area, especially at Coyohuacan, were taken over by Tenochtitlán and given to successful generals of past campaigns, most of them descendants of Acamapichtli. After the nobles only a few of the commoner warriors received land, as did city quarters (*calpulli*) to support the religious institutions. Thus the stratification of the Mexica, based earlier primarily on status distinctions, was further accentuated by land ownership. This social change was explained by an anecdote in the sources (group of "Crónica X") that reflected the view of the Mexica elite: before the outbreak of the Tepanec war there was a pact between the fearful people and the courageous warriors and their generals to relinquish the help of the hesitant *macehualli*; they in turn promised that they would be of service for all time in the event of a victory. That is why the common people, who had not participated in the fighting, did not share in the distribution of the land.

BESTOWING OF TITLES ≡ Furthermore, on the most successful of the warriors Itzcoatl bestowed a series of titles, which until then had been held by Tepanec officials, and which became from then on the titles of high functionaries of the Mexican administration.

DEPENDENT MAINLAND ≡ The Mexica campaign to subjugate Xochimilco, Cuitlahuac, and other parts of the valley's southern lobe, begun in the final phase of the Tepanec war, as well as the conquest of the area around Cuauhnahuac (Cuernavaca), which was achieved by allied troops, had brought important places, which had been taken earlier by the Tepanec, into Mexica hands. With the exception of Chalco they now dominated the entire densely inhabited, fertile southern valley, which formerly had belonged to Colhuacan, and they could avail themselves of the services of the local population. The development of urban infrastructure, especially the construction of a drinking water aqueduct and a dam road from the mainland, was achieved with substantial services and materials from the conquered cities. The Mexica gained a foothold beyond the Valley of Mexico in several small but important zones of what today is Morelos.

ACOLHUACAN ≡ It was 1433 when the last resistance in Acolhuacan was overcome and Nezahualcoyotl was able to reign unopposed from his capital of Tetzcoco. Taking ethnically determined settlement structures into account, he organized the Empire of Acolhuacan into fourteen new local governments. He attempted to integrate also those *tlatoani* whose loyalty in the past war had left much to be desired. The organization of the Acolhuacan Empire created by Nezahualcoatl remained intact until the Conquista.

FOUNDING THE TRIPLE ALLIANCE ≡ The joint victory over the Tepanecs provided the basis for an enduring coalition, now called the Aztec Triple Alliance, which was aimed at subjugating other states for tribute. It consisted of the two victors over the Tepanecs, Tenochtitlán and Tetzcoco, and the capital of the new Tepanec realm, Tlacopan. A new dynasty from the house of Tezozomoc had begun to rule there in the person of Totoquihuaztli. The three great rulers (*huey tlatoani*) indisputably used the traditional titles of Colhuateuctli (Tenochtitlán), Chichimecateuctli (Tetzcoco), and Tepanecateuctli (Tlacopan). The forceful acquisition politics of the Triple Alliance dominated the almost ninety-year period of western Mesoamerican history until the Spanish conquest.

MOTEUCZOMA I ≡ After the death of Itzcoatl, his nephew Moteuczoma I Ilhuicamina (1440–1468) became ruler in Tenochtitlán. His half-brother Tlacaelel took over the second most important office in the state; as Cihuacoatl he was mostly concerned with interior political functions. Both Moteuczoma and Tlacaelel had earned exceptional merits as generals in the Tepanec war. Today they are regarded as the determining personalities in the state created by the Mexica.

POLITICAL REFORMS ≡ In the reign of Itzcoatl and even more in the reign of Moteuczoma I the state of the Mexica received its definitive form. The highest ruling entity was a council of four, under which at a lower level there were a number of other high officials with elevated titles. The basic qualification for offices was success in war. Title holders and numerous other officials were given the right to use conquered areas, which were farmed for them, in exchange for their services. Successful warriors were rewarded by the ruler for their achievements with titles and insignia; if they came from the common people they could rise on the basis of specific accomplishments to a form of merit nobility. "Luxury laws" gave them and the nobles additional privileges, and after the victory over the Tepanecs the stronger social stratification between the two large population strata was made publicly visible by differences in costume and house construction.

WARRIOR IDEOLOGY ≡ Around this time in religion the so-called warrior-religious complex became quite apparent: Huitzilopochtli, originally the local tribal deity of the Mexica, had become the god of war in the central Mexican pantheon, where he was understood as an aspect of the sun. To guarantee the path of the stars and the existence of the cosmos, the willfully acting deities had to be supported by numerous sacrificial acts. The most valuable sacrifice of all was that of the human being. Warriors had the task of bringing in these victims as captives.

WAR AGAINST CHALCO ≡ Shortly after his election Moteuczoma had resumed the campaigns against Chalco, which controlled one of the important passes to climatically more favored areas. For these and other campaigns an incident was regularly fashioned that was supposed to justify the subsequent formal declaration of war: ambassadors of the Mexica demanded some service, whose acceptance would have publicly signaled subjugation. In the case of Chalco they demanded construction materials for the new temple for Huitzilopochtli. The expected refusal was followed generally by years of fighting, involving losses for both sides, but in this case the war was interrupted by natural catastrophes.

CATASTROPHES ≡ The series of catastrophes began in 1449 with a heavy flood, which devastated Mexico City (Tenochtitlán and Tlatelolco). To protect the city, construction of a dam diagonally through the lake was necessary; this was built under the personal supervision of Nezahualcoyotl. Following this there was a famine, the result of several years of failed crops. The stores in palaces were insufficient; malnutrition furthered several plagues, and many people died or fled to climatically more favored areas, especially to the Gulf Coast. The first normal harvest occurred in 1455.

EXPANSION TO THE SOUTHEAST ≡ Despite the fact that after overcoming the famine the war against Chalco was resumed, the years after 1455 saw large-scale conquests mainly outside of the Valley of Mexico. Conquest of the northern part of what is Guerrero today, begun under Itzcoatl, was resumed, but the main thrust of expansion was aimed at the tropical and subtropical areas in the east and southeast, where maize was grown all year and promised to fend off future famines. There were the main ports of trade and the sources of luxury goods, which served as status symbols. Moteuczoma no longer participated in these campaigns, but the creation of a tropical garden in his summer residence Huaxtepec (in northern Morelos) showed the longing of highlanders for more abundant regions.

The first objective in the southeast was Coaixtlahuacan (in Oaxaca), capital of a larger Mixtec chiefdom and an important port of trade on the road to the southern Gulf Coast, and it fell into the hands of the Triple Alliance in 1458. Then the armies of the Triple Alliance went against Ahuilazapan (Orizaba) and Cuetlaxtlan in today's Veracruz, where there was a strong defense mounted due to the participation of chiefdoms from the Valley of Puebla and Tlaxcallan. Moquihuix from Tlatelolco became the hero of the finally successful campaign. A subsequent raid secured the area around Tepeyacac (Tepeaca), where the Triple Alliance had been called to assist in a quarrel between local noble groups. After a large section of the middle Gulf Coast with the larger part of adjoining inland areas and parts of today's states of Guerrero and Hidalgo had been won, the Triple Alliance controlled a territory that was at least as large as that of the preceding Tepanec Empire, when Moteuczoma I died in 1469.

FLOWERY WARS ≡ The beginning of the so-called flowery wars between the Aztec Triple Alliance and their linguistic and cultural neighbors Cholollan, Huexotzinco, and Tlaxcallan, occurred in the second half of Moteuczoma's reign. Tradition has it that the flowery wars were not conducted for conquest, but provided realistic war training opportunities for the warriors of both sides; in addition, sacrificial captives could be gained with a minimum of effort. This "sports" war gave the two social classes a chance to gain prestige and climb to the next social level through military success. But this describes only one aspect of the flowery wars. The pugnacious but territorially weaker former allies and now "family foes" lived in an area of similar ecology to the Valley of Mexico, which therefore was not attractive economically, and at first did not justify a conquest. On the other hand they controlled the trading routes to the Gulf Coast, and were subjected to constant erosion in the flowery wars, where they could cause big losses to the armies of the Triple Alliance; but in the long run they held the shorter end of the stick. Although most of the sources place the beginning of the flowery wars a short while after the famine, they probably did not begin before the final subjugation of Chalco in 1465.

HEIR OF MOTEUCZOMA I ≡ The principle of avoiding a direct succession of father to son seems to have been in question once again when a successor to Moteuczoma I was needed. In the sources there is reference to the reign of Moteuczoma's daughter Atotoztli; on the other hand his son Iquehuacatzin is mentioned as an elected successor.

AXAYACATL ≡ However, most often Axayacatl (1469–1481) is called the immediate successor of Moteuczoma. Through his father he was a grandson of Itzcoatl and through his mother a grandson of Moteuczoma I; moreover, his father was a son of the dynasty founder Acamapichtli, and his mother a granddaughter of the same important ruler. This meant that Axayacatl was in a genealogically advantageous position. Although at barely twenty years of age he was a relatively inexperienced young man, he was preferred over his two older brothers, who indeed also got to rule at Tenochtitlán later. One possible explanation is that Axayacatl is supposed to have been the first candidate of Tlacaelel. It may have spoken for him that in his military campaigns he never shied away from personal involvement (as attested by a duel in the Valley of Toluca, the unhappy ending of which caused him to limp for the rest of his life).

The beginning of Axayacatl's reign marked the end of the epoch of great warriors, who had occupied important offices since the victory over Azcapotzalco. These were not only Moteuczoma I, Tlacaelel, whose year of death is unknown, and Nezahualcoyotl, but also other men, whose names were not recorded and who had high positions in the state due to their merits in Tenochtitlán.

NEZAHUALPILLI ≡ Nezahualcoyotl was succeded in 1472 by his still fairly young son Nezahualpilli. During his reign the political weight in the Triple Alliance shifted more and more to favor Tenochtitlán, while Tetzcoco became famous as a city of fine arts and sciences.

SUBJUGATION OF TLATELOLCO ≡ The most important political event of the reign of Axayacatl was the military altercation with the sister city Tlatelolco, where Moquihuix had started to reign in 1467. Dynastic quarrels presented an inducement to let long-term rivalry break out, possibly caused by the position of Tlatelolco as a trade center and market. Moquihuix had tried in vain to win allies in the Valley of Toluca, also in Huexotzinco and Tlaxcallan. War was inevitable, and in it Axayacatl participated in the fighting; Moquihuix was killed in 1473. After this Tlatelolco was placed under the reign of Mexican military governors. With the subjugation of the trading center Tlatelolco, the important military-political activities of the *pochteca* enabled them to play a part in the acquisition politics of the Triple Alliance.

CAMPAIGNS IN THE WEST ≡ Axayacatl could consolidate the conquests of Moteuczoma in the area of the Gulf Coast and trade routes leading there. His great military campaigns, however, were in the west, where he subjugated first the Matlatzinca and Mazahua polities in the adjacent Valley of Toluca. The next thrust farther west was halted in 1478 by the Tarascans under Tzitzipandácuare, who not only annihilated the Mexican troops at Taximaroa (today Ciudad Hidalgo, Michoacán), but carried the war back into the Valley of Toluca; however, they were beaten there. The military stalemate caused a tense silence between the two rival states, and a thinly populated no-man's-land was created along the border area.

TARASCANS ≡ During the last century before the Spanish conquest the Tarascan state in west Mexico formed the counterweight to the Aztec Triple Alliance. As in central Mexico the political center of the empire was situated on a high plateau around Lake Pátzcuaro, where there were beneficial conditions for a dense population. Under the ruler (*cazonci*) Tzitzipandácuare (ca. 1454–1479) Tzintzuntzan had become the central government seat of a state more and more tightly organized. The Tarascan expansion, begun in his reign, finally created a long border line with the equally expansive Aztecs under his successors. Under Tzitzipandácuare numerous groups of non-Tarascan-speaking peoples, who had fled mainly from western areas conquered by Axayacatl, were integrated into the Tarascan state. Some of them were settled on purpose in border regions to the Triple Alliance, where they had to provide military service. Consolidation and centralization of the Tarascan Empire was probably hastened by the threat posed by the Mexicans.

TIZOC ≡ At the time of his election, Tizoc (1481–1486), older brother and successor of Axayacatl, had a successful career as one of the highest-ranking military leaders and was a member of the high council. His name is especially linked to the beginning of a new construction phase of the main temple of Tenochtitlán, which had been enlarged by his predecessors and fitted with new monuments. The sacrificial stone (*cuauhxicalli*) attributed to him is an excellent example of the style and artistic mastery that characterized the official art of Tenochtitlán and set it off from that of previous times and neighboring regions. In his conquest politics Tizoc was a less successful ruler than his predecessors. Because he could not fulfill expectations in this area, the rumor mentioned in the sources, that his death prior to finishing the temple construction was not natural, gains credibility.

AHUITZOTL ≡ The construction of the main temple was finished under Ahuitzotl (1486–1502), the middle one of the three brothers; it now had the same appearance as at the time of the Conquest. The consecration took place in 1486 and was accompanied by sumptuous religious ceremonies of previously unknown proportions. At the height of the four days of sacrificial acts an unheard-of number of war captives were sacrificed.

DEMONSTRATION OF POWER ≡ For the temple consecration, as for other public religious events, such as coronations of rulers, or the yearly Tlacaxipehualizitli festival, rulers from the neighboring areas were invited to watch. Even rulers of independent states or of states hostile to the Mexica attended the ceremonies, hidden of course from the people. All guests returned home after the exchange of precious gifts. These occasions were used by the Mexica to demonstrate openly their wealth, their power, and the abilities of their armies, in order to assure some of their friendship, others of the inevitability of a past or future subjugation.

REVOLTS ≡ When he assumed rulership Ahuitzotl had found a well-rounded area to rule; however, in its further reaches local rebellions had to be dealt with, especially after a change of rulers in Tenochtitlán, in his case the Chontal rebellion. Ahuitzotl was a popular military leader who was known for his cruel conduct of war. Even as *tlatoani* he personally led the Aztec armies and answered the defection of the Chontal (Alahuiztlan, Teloloapan in Guerrero) with a merciless carnage among the population. Other cities in the region escaped this fate by surrendering on their own. Other military campaigns of Ahuitzotl south of the Tarascan territory brought into Aztec hands settlements in the Valley of the Río Balsas and in the area of today's Guerrero.

POLITICAL ACTIVITIES ≡ Ahuitzotl's conquest politics are marked by the increased use of long-range merchants, active in the service of the empire. They served as ambassadors to foreign rulers and commission traders of their *tlatoani.* Furthermore, special groups of merchants had the official order to act as spies and *agents provocateurs* and thus acted as the advance for Aztec conquests. This second role resulted in the fact that they were generally exposed to attacks or chicanery by local rulers, leading sometimes even to murder, which was seen as a welcome reason for Mexican retaliatory expeditions.

FURTHER EXPANSION ≡ Mostly after 1495, there were other military campaigns and conquests in the Valley of Oaxaca, a thrust to the Isthmus of Tehuantepec and beyond to the region of Xoconochco (Soconusco) in today's border region with Guatemala. The Aztec troops had been preceded in the isthmus by warlike expeditions of the long-range merchants, and in the following period Aztec trading contacts with the remote southern areas still outweighed true political dependencies.

The northernmost conquest of the Aztecs was Huexotla (Huejutla in Hidalgo), subjugated by Ahuitzotl, and situated a little north of the 21° latitude. The traditional interests of Tetzcoco in the Gulf region were emphasized by the conquests of Nezahualpilli, who extended the conquered areas on the coast toward the south. Ahuitzotl's conquests did not lead to the incorporation of whole areas, but consisted only of tribute-paying enclaves, whose distance from the center of power could not be managed realistically by the available means of transport.

SECURING CONQUERED AREAS ≡ In order to secure the newly conquered areas despite the long distances, garrisons were installed under Ahuitzotl; at the same time colonists from central Mexico were settled in areas depopulated by the hostilities. This way, after a punitive expedition by Ahuitzotl, a line of fortresses was created near Oztoman (in Guerrero) at the southern border of the Tarascan-controlled Michoacán; following a proposal by Nezahualpilli, central Mexican families were settled in their vicinity; they were responsible for the defense of the fortresses and were asked to grow cacao as tribute. In Oaxaca a garrison with an Aztec colony was created as well. But such colonies seem to have been singular phenomena and were not part of an overall political concept.

DEFEAT OF ATLIXCO ≡ The Aztec troops were less successful in the ever more frequent battles against their "best enemy," Tlaxcallan, Huexotzinco, and Chlolollan, who had become allies. In 1499 their armies provided the Aztec warriors with the second heavy loss in their history in the Valley of Atlixco, claiming several members of Tenochtitlán's ruling dynasty, among them Tlacahuepan, a son of Axayacatl.

FLOOD ≡ Toward the end of the century (1498) a catastrophic flood was visited upon the island city Mexico and the villages on the lakeshore. Its reason is said to have been a misguided effort to collect sweet water from wells at the lake's southern shore and bring it into the city by aqueduct. By the time the out-of-control well water was stopped it had caused substantial destruction. The extensive restorations gave the city the look the Spaniards were to find when they arrived. Ahuitzotl did not see the end of the city's repairs. He died in 1502, apparently from a head injury he is said to have sustained during the flooding.

MOTEUCZOMA II ≡ A son of Axayacatl, Moteuczoma II Xocoyotzin ("the younger"), who had achieved important victories as a general under Ahuitzotl in Oaxaca, was elected as Ahuitzotl's successor. The goal of Moteuczoma II's expansion policy was the protection, supplementation, and creation of a territorial link to the areas Ahuitzotl had conquered. Therefore the list of conquests achieved in his reign under the leadership of his brother Cuitlahuac shows a concentration on Oaxaca and the routes leading there. A military expedition against the still-independent Mixtecs of Tototepec on the Pacific Coast, led by Moteuczoma himself for a change, was not successful: neither Tototepec, nor the warlike Yopi in Guerrero, could be subjugated, although both areas were almost completely surrounded by Mexican-dominated zones. In the east the Mexicans were successful in pushing a broad wedge of conquered towns to the middle Gulf Coast; in this way the rulers of the Valley of Puebla and Tlaxcallan were finally cut off from the coast.

EXPANSION OF THE EMPIRE ≡ The Aztec Empire reached its largest expanse under Moteuczoma II and achieved the form found by the Spaniards in 1519. The areas the Triple Alliance controlled, populated by peoples diverse in language and ethnicity, reached from the Gulf Coast to the Pacific, to the borders of Mesoamerica in the northeast and far beyond the Isthmus of Tehuantepec in the south to the borders of today's Guatemala. However, this was not a territory with a uniform structure or one that allowed a spatially even rulership. Rather the empire consisted of a patchwork of areas paying tribute and others with an unclear status. Up until the last moments prior to the Spanish conquest there were substantial changes here. Not all Aztec conquests, as reported in the sources, necessarily meant a dependency documented by tribute duty. Especially in the border zones large areas could maintain their independence despite military conflicts, such as the powerful empire of the Tarascans in the west, largely in today's Michoacán. In the eastern Sierra Madre, Metztitlan Tototepec stayed independent, as did Yopitzinco, and the Mixtec Tototepec on the Pacific Coast. Teotitlan del Camino on the border between Puebla and Oaxaca, which often is labeled as merely allied to the empire, clearly was paying tribute for a long time.

TLAXCALLAN AND HUEXOTZINCO ≡ The most important of the independent enclaves, because of their closeness to the capital, were the "best enemies" Chollolan, Tlaxcallan, and Huexotzinco with other small states; they had been weakened in Moteuczoma's time, and they no longer formed a closed block confronting the Triple Alliance. An old rivalry between Tlaxcallan and Huexotzinco blazed into open war. Tlaxcallan conquered large areas belonging to Huexotzinco and devastated the capital. Tecayehuatl, ruler of Huexotzinco, and several nobles fled to Tenochtitlán and persuaded Moteuczoma to station troops of the Triple Alliance in Huexotzinco; there they engaged in battles with the Tlaxcalteca, suffering many casualties. However, the armies of the Triple Alliance could not transport the Holy of Holies of the god Camaxtli (Mixcoatl) to Mexico. About two years prior to the landing of the Spaniards, the Huexotzinca returned from exile and once again joined the anti-Aztec alliance.

POLITICAL MEASURES ≡ Just as his predecessor Ahuitzotl had done, Moteuczoma raised the tribute of subjugated peoples in numerous cases. A series of measures were meant to aim especially at the centralization and consolidation of power in the empire by forging stronger ties to the areas close to the center, whose political-military leadership was now undisputed. Subjugated rulers had to reside in Tenochtitlán, both to be under supervision and to further integration; they could also send a prominent member of their dynasty there or have their sons educated in the city. The same goal was served by having more and more members of the ruling family of Tenochtitlán assume the throne in outlying towns from which their mothers hailed. Internal peace was also furthered by allowing conquered Tlatelolco to be free of tribute after it participated in successful military actions, and by letting Ahuitzotl's son Cuauhtemoc assume rulership there in 1519, instead of a military governor.

TEMPLE BUILDING ≡ Religious integration was the intention underlying the construction of the temple *Coateocalli* in the central temple complex; it was supposed to house the gods of the conquered peoples. By furnishing a rock temple at Malinalco outside of the valley, intended for ceremonies of warriors,

Moteuczoma allowed a conquered province to participate in official cults; however, in the view of this province it might have been just another instance of Moteuczoma's or Mexica despotism and lust for power that motivated this measure.

REFORMS ≡ The internal political reform begun by Moteuczoma was aimed at a clearer division of the classes. The opportunities of commoners to rise in rank were curtailed, and the *macehualli* and members of the merit nobility were removed from the immediate surroundings of the ruler and dismissed from palace service. A new, strict court etiquette surrounded the ruler with an aura of intangible remoteness. He now stood at a godlike distance from other people. The religious aspect of the legitimacy of rulership, which had always been there, was now emphasized visually. Like his predecessor, Moteuczoma II had his portrait carved in relief on the rocks of the tradition-laden hill of Chapultepec, wearing the costume of the god Xipe Totec.

NEZAHUALPILLI ≡ Nezahualpilli of Tetzcoco died in 1515 at a great age after a reign of more than forty years. He had the reputation of a wise statesman and poet and was credited with important innovations such as a revision of several laws at Texcoco and abolishing one of the forms of slavery, which had supplied one household or family through generations with a paid slave from another. Being an extremely moral-minded and just, but firm, ruler, Nezahualpilli even proceeded without regard against members of his immediate family. Thus once his son and heir apparent was sentenced to death and executed; at another time one of his wives, a daughter of Axayacatl, met with the same fate, which placed a burden on his relationship with the ruling family of Tenochtitlán. The worsening relationship between the two main partners of the Triple Alliance was also expressed by the suspicion of Tetzcoco that treason by Tenochtitlán was the cause of losing a war against Tlaxcallan in which heavy casualties were sustained. In the last decades of Nezahualpilli's reign, Tetzcoco had not participated in conquests with its earlier intensity, but had allowed leadership to pass more and more to Tenochtitlán, to a point where they even had to give up rights in areas they had conquered earlier.

NEZAHUALPILLI'S SUCCESSION ≡ After Nezahualpilli's death, rivalries about his succession broke out in Tetzcoco between his sons; Moteuczoma successfully supported his own nephew Cacama (1515–1520) against Ixtlilxochitl, designated by Nezahualpilli, which led to a complete dependency of Tetzcoco on Tenochtitlán. Ixtlilxochitl's fight for his rights was somewhat successful; he could salvage at least a part of Acolhuacan. Subsequently he and his brothers Cacama and Coanacoch—the latter used the situation to his advantage—entered into a treaty that divided Acolhuacan into three political units. Tenochtitlán's puppet Cacama kept the area with the capital Tetzcoco.

CONQUISTA ≡ The incredibly fast and forceful rise of the Mexica to the largest political power, which slowed down only slightly just prior to the conquest by the Spaniards in 1521, just as much as the fast collapse after the Spanish conquest, has always generated surprise and questions, which have either not yet been answered or whose answer is controversial.

Led by Hernán Cortés, the Spaniards arrived at the central Gulf Coast in the spring of 1519. In the beginning they formed an alliance with the Totonacs of the Gulf Coast, who had only recently been conquered by the Mexica, and later one with Tlaxcallan, which at first resisted, but then provided substantial services as porters and auxiliary troops—as did others in times to come. In Chalollan Cortés demonstrated through a supposedly unprovoked massacre that he was determined and capable of eradicating any resistance without pardon. On November 8, 1519, the Spaniards entered México-Tenochtitlán and were received by Moteuczoma II with full ceremony. Moteuczoma had probably received news of the appearance of Europeans on the southern coasts years ago, and his failed attempts to halt the march to the capital by diplomatic or magic means instead of military force therefore might have been the result of lengthy, and in his view well-founded, thoughts.

END OF MOTEUCZOMA ≡ Moteuczoma appeared as a generous host, but he was restricted in his movements by the Spaniards more and more during events not elaborated on here, so that he finally lived like a prisoner. These events caused Cacama of Tetzcoco to rise up, but he was brought to Tenochtitlán by order of Moteuczoma and handed over to the Spaniards. In similar fashion the ruler of Tlacopan, Moteuczoma's brother Cuitlahuac, who was the ruler of Iztapalapan, and others fell into the hands of the Spaniards and were put in chains.

During the absence of Cortés and a Spanish contingent, for no apparent reason his deputy Pedro de Alvarado attacked and killed the elite of the Mexican warriors, who had gathered in the temple district in the middle of May, 1520, to celebrate the Toxcatl feast; this caused Indian resistance to form in Tenochtitlán and upon his return Cortés and the Spaniards were locked in. Cuitlahuac was released from captivity to pass on Cortés' order to end the siege, but instead he organized the actions of the warriors as their commander in chief. The Spaniards were besieged and the followers of the captured ruler were eliminated. When Moteuczoma tried to persuade the Indians to keep peace, under orders from Cortés, he came to death in a fashion never clarified.

CUITLAHUAC ≡ Conscious of his desperate situation, Cortés attempted a technically well-prepared sortie from the city in the night of June 30, 1520, which was prematurely discovered and became a serious defeat for the Spaniards; despite being pursued they miraculously reached Tlaxcallan, which served them as a safe base.

In Tenochtitlán, Cuitlahuac was elected to be the successor of Moteuczoma and Coanacoch became the ruler in Tetzcoco. But in October 1520, after a period of only eighty days on the throne, Cuitlahuac died of smallpox, which had been introduced by the Spaniards, and for which the natives had no immunity. The epidemic, which preceded the Spaniards everywhere, demanded countless victims even in remote areas.

CUAUHTEMOC ≡ Young Cuauhtemoc, a son of Ahuitzotl, became Cuitlahuac's successor; he had recently been made *tlatoani* of Tlatelolco and had distinguished himself in the fight against the Spaniards. Tenochtitlán was now isolated, after the Tarascans had rejected a request for assistance and Ixtlilxochitl of Tetzcoco had joined Cortés. In the spring of 1521 the Spaniards, who constantly received reinforcements from their country, started a siege of the city, which was cut off from the waterside with the help of brigantines built in Tlaxcallan and Tetzcoco. After ninety days of furious fighting, the last Indian resistance ceased August 13, 1521, in the temple district of Tlatelolco. Cuauhtemoc and other rulers became Spanish captives. They were tortured a short while later in an effort to discover the whereabouts of the state's treasury, and hanged afterwards for a negligible reason.

Only a few years after the fall of the Aztec Empire, Michoacán, Guatemala, western Mexico, and the remaining Mesoamerica outside of Yucatán were conquered by the Spaniards and their Nahuatl-speaking auxiliary troops.

THE STRUCTURE OF THE AZTEC EMPIRE

TRIPLE ALLIANCE ≡ The Aztec Triple Alliance, formed by the states of Tenochtitlán, Acolhuacan with its capital Tetzcoco, and Tlacopan, did not have a common political head. Political action was determined by informal decisions made by the three rulers. During conquests they proceeded jointly, although each of the partners could also act independently, and there were rivalries. Depending on the geographical location of the three capitals, each ruler had precedence in political enterprises in a specific sector of the region. In internal politics the three states were independent of each other and each had its own institutions and administrative structures.

RULES OF SUCCESSION ≡ Basically the election of a successor for a dead ruler was each state's own prerogative. Originally, the ceremonial acceptance by the other two rulers did not provide the opportunity to object. However, under Moteuczoma Tenochtitlán assumed a decisive role.

RULES OF SUCCESSION IN ACOLHUACAN ≡ In Acolhuacan and its member states it was customary that a son follow his father as a ruler. Since the rulers of Tetzcoco married daughters of the ruler of Tenochtitlán, their sons were heirs apparent in Acolhuacan, and at the same time grandsons of the ruler of

Tenochtitlán, who was interested in their succession, because he thus gained influence as well. In the same fashion, the rulers of Tetzcoco made sure of their rising influence on the dynastic sequence in other areas later on, by giving one of their daughters in marriage to a dependent ruler, thus gaining the family loyalty of his successor.

RULES OF SUCCESSION IN TENOCHTITLÁN ≡ While originally also a son followed his father as *tlatoani* in Tenochtitlán, the later characteristic succession rule was begun with the election of Itzcoatl: the new ruler was chosen from a group of candidates among the descendants of Acamapichtli by a larger, not closely defined, panel, avoiding a direct father-to-son succession. Among the virtues demanded were intelligence, flawless conduct, modest behavior, and oratory skills. A candidate for the throne had to have one of the highest military ranks based on previous military success. Thus the number of candidates was narrowed to very few in the final analysis. A ruler could predetermine his successor to a large degree by placing him in offices seen as prerequisite. After Axayacatl it became common that first a brother of the deceased ruler was considered, and only if necessary would a son of one of his predecessors be elected. Within this rule there remained a certain amount of flexibility.

STATE STRUCTURE OF ACOLHUACAN ≡ Reorganization of the political internal structure of the Triple Alliance members after the victory over the Tepanecs had created state territories of substantial size. Nezahualcoyotl had anchored the supreme rulership in Tetzcoco and had divided power among fourteen local *tlatoani* in regions determined by ecologically diverse altitudes; among them were the rulers of the previous capital of Acolhuacan, Coatlichan, and the once-powerful Huexotla. These rulers acted independently in their territories, which were interlocking. They had judicial power over their *macehualli*, while nobles were judged in Tetzcoco.

On a central level the fourteen rulers occupied high offices of state. They had no other obligations toward the supreme ruler than following him in war; their appreciation of him was expressed by sumptuous gifts on the occasion of the great ceremonies. Their subjects did not have to pay tribute to the central state or to the ruler in Tetzcoco. Eight other areas not governed by *tlatoani* were ruled by tribute administrators (*calpixqui*) and had to provide objects and services for the state and the ruler in Tetzcoco. A rotation system for all parts of the land regulated services for the palace and public buildings.

STATE STRUCTURE OF TLACOPAN ≡ Tlacopan (today Tacuba) was the successor state of the former Tepanec Empire (Tepanohuayan) and the weakest partner in the alliance. Its territory was much smaller than the erstwhile Tepanec Empire, because many of the formerly Tepanec areas had to be conquered after the Triple Alliance's victory over Maxtla by additional military actions, in part by later rulers, and often they did not end up as part of Tlacopan. The former capital Azcapotzalco became one of several *tlatocayotl* organized under Tlacopan. The population, partly Tepanec, partly Mexican, was ruled each by its own *tlatoani.* Other than in Tetzcoco, there were several levels of dependent *tlatoani* in Tlacopan.

TERRITORY OF TENOCHTITLÁN ≡ As expressed in the ruler's title *colhuateuctli,* Tenochtitlán had inherited Colhuacan. The towns at the lakeshore in the southern lobe of the Valley of Mexico, which had at first belonged to Colhuacan and had been conquered under Tepanec leadership and later by the Mexica alone, formed the hinterland of the island city. They corresponded to the much-earlier-conquered territories of the other states. The administrative incorporation of dependent *tlatocayotl* in the vicinity, comparable to that of both partner states, can be made out only in traces at Tenochtitlán. The lake towns formed the central administrative unit of the tribute organization of Tenochtitlán, directly answering to the head tribute administrator (*petlacalcatl*), who worked out of the palace. Government participation of the *tlatoani,* as in Tetzcoco, certainly was not present earlier, but for later times there is some evidence of consultations with dependent rulers, who became ever more attached to the ruling house of Tenochtitlán by family ties.

GOVERNMENT OF TENOCHTITLÁN ≡ In Tenochtitlán the highest governmental power next to the *tlatoani* was vested in a council of four officials. Two were nobles and two commoners. Two of them had the highest military command. In addition, there was the Cihuacoatl and other high title-holders active on the highest level in functions not clearly delineated. A series of other titles were given to persons of middle and lower ranks of the executive. The inner-city administration was based on a separation into four quarters and a large number of smaller units.

JUDICIAL ORGANIZATION ≡ One of the criteria of the state is the presence of a constitutional legislative system and a judicial arm to enforce it. The judicial organization of the Triple Alliance can be shown best for Tetzcoco, where beneath the ruler and the state council there were four council and judicial boards, who operated out of the Tetzcoco palace, at the head of the territorially organized legal and administrative hierarchy. They were the supreme court, war council, council for music, arts, and sciences (also responsible for priests), and the council for treasury and tribute. Their judges were responsible for nobles of the respective ranks and professions. The supreme court with twelve judges (at least half of them nobles) had to deal with all cases not covered by any of the other three courts, or with cases in which one of the members of the other courts had been sued. Furthermore, it also functioned as the appellate court for sentences against commoners imposed by local judges in the fourteen *tlatocayotl.* Nobles could appeal sentences by the supreme court through two other supreme judges, whose sentences demanded the concurrence of the ruler.

The judges were functionaries whose honesty was subjected to particularly high demands. In Tetzcoco's higher courts there were several cases in which the office of a judge coincided with that of a *tlatoani.*

The judicial system of Tenochtitlán was organized in a similar fashion. The hierarchically structured justice organization reflected the state's monopoly on power. There were two high courts, one for nobles and one for commoners, as well as the opportunity to appeal. The legal systems in the states of the Triple Alliance were in force within each territory, but their validity did not extend to conquered areas.

AGGRESSIVE EXPANSION ≡ The Aztecs did not have a permanent army. Their aggressive expansion politics made them feared adversaries, for they used every pretext (or even created one) to attack all areas not willing to submit to them. As a reason for a war expedition into a remote area it often sufficed that a merchant had been robbed there or prevented from free passage. At the end of such war expeditions the Aztec troops raged among the population until the victims begged for mercy and declared themselves willing to pay tribute, which was determined on the spot.

TRIBUTE EMPIRE ≡ The Aztec Empire is often called a tribute empire because its structure depended on the delivery of tribute. The subjugated areas were organized in tribute provinces (thirty-eight for Tenochtitlán), which had to deliver at regularly determined times specific tribute, consisting of food, raw materials, luxury items, and consumer goods. Such tribute shipments consisted of goods specific for each region, or were determined by the region's closeness to the Valley of Mexico, because corn and other foodstuffs could be brought in only from a limited distance. In part the tributaries had to manufacture articles (such as clothing or precious warrior decorations) according to a given design from materials they had to purchase. The total of all goods delivered as tribute was so large that it played a decisive economic role in the time of Moteuczoma II.

In the centrally located conquered regions the subjugated population was utilized to work on buildings for the state and service in the army. Moreover, in such areas the use of large tracts of land had been taken from the rightful owners and tribute goods were grown there, or it was given to Aztec nobles in recognition of services in wars or offices. More remote provinces had to feed and otherwise support the army when it marched through.

DISTRIBUTION OF TRIBUTE ≡ Tribute deliveries were distributed among the members of the Triple Alliance according to strict rules. The manner of distribution clearly reflected early power structures, because Tenochtitlán and Tetzcoco each received two fifths, Tlacopan one fifth, of all incoming goods. There were also areas whose tribute was distributed according to other criteria, or was reserved exclusively for one or another member of the Triple Alliance. Political power shifts within the Triple Alliance in the course of time were acknowledged by shifts in the distribution of tribute as well.

INDIRECT RULE ≡ In the provinces an Aztec tribute administrator (*calpixqui*) and several local assistants took care of the fulfillment of tribute duties. At the same time the administrator functioned as the local representative of the Aztec state. Aztec military governors were rarely installed instead of a local ruler; in general the Aztecs ruled indirectly and dependent regions were given extensive autonomy. According to the circumstances of the conquest, the previous rulers were either left in office or exchanged for others who were more suitable or friendly to the Aztecs.

MILITARY PRESENCE ≡ There never was a network of troops covering the entire empire. Beginning with Ahuitzotl there were at least two permanent garrisons, one on the southern Tarascan border, the other in Oaxaca. Several other garrisons were situated in the vicinity of some borders as well, all in seats of a *calpixqui*, but there are no reports concerning their installment. Their function seems to have been internal and external security.

SPREAD OF NAHUATL ≡ The Aztecs did not introduce measures that would have unified or changed the ethnic differences prevailing in the provinces, although they knew about such settlement policies from the Triple Alliance member Tetzcoco in the fourteenth century. There seems to have been no official effort to spread Nahuatl; however, when the Spaniards arrived this language was the *lingua franca* in a large area.

SHARED CULTURAL TRAITS ≡ A feeling of common identity among the nobles in the Valley of Mexico and beyond seems to have surpassed ethnic diversity, which stayed quite relevant on the lower social levels. Differences were of a power-political, but not ethnic, nature, although groups were often formed along ethnic lines of demarcation. The feeling of a shared culture even embraced hostile states in Puebla and Tlaxcala, called "cousins" or "brothers," whose elite met with the Aztecs on the occasion of religious ceremonies and poets' meetings, despite constant wars.

REBELLIONS ≡ The loose organization of the Aztec Empire favored local rebellions against the Aztecs or their *calpixqui* that were suppressed by renewed military intervention. Sometimes such rebellions were caused by local factions competing for rulership, but mostly the reason was a refusal to deliver tribute. Despite the fact that the producing population had a double load to carry, because tribute for the Triple Alliance had to be generated in addition to duties to their own nobles, there is no record of any large uprising.

ASSOCIATED AREAS ≡ Besides areas fully integrated into the tribute system, there were others only loosely connected with the Aztec Empire that merely provided military assistance, allowed troops to march through and supported them, or simply expressed their friendly attitude by occasionally sending gifts to the rulers of the Triple Alliance.

ECONOMY ≡ The economy of the Aztec Empire was determined by two different but closely intertwined systems for the distribution of goods and services: tribute and trade.

TRIBUTE ≡ In an economic sense tribute served to skim off the surplus of agricultural and manufactured production and accumulate it in the hand of the ruler—as the center of the state—who supported the palace with it and fulfilled his obligations toward all subjects of all ranks. A part of the tribute goods was passed on as rewards to successful warriors or officials at important ceremonies, with all signs of ostentatious consumption, or was given out as food to the people on the occasion of religious feasts. Its use as wages for artisans, food for servants engaged in official works, or laying-in of provisions for hard times was less spectacular. Similar distributive mechanisms existed on the level of local *tlatoani* and noble houses as well. The *macehualli*'s tribute was exchanged for returns such as protection against attacks, right to use land, assistance in hard times, and the performance of rituals.

TRADE ≡ Trade was conducted in public markets, where those who produced something sold it themselves; also there were professional traders, who operated on a local or regional level. In the Valley of Mexico, where there was a regionally organized market system, the largest was the daily market of Tlatelolco. Other markets specialized in specific products. The trading of goods beyond the region was in the hands of professional long-distance merchants. Besides exchange trade some standardized value indicators were used that took the role of money. These items were also consumer goods.

Tribute and trade were intermingled on several organizational levels. Economic transactions in local or regional market places were conducted by producers, middlemen, or consumers, and there was also trading in goods that came from tribute or that were necessary for the manufacture and delivery of future tribute. Finally, the rulers contributed goods to an exchange of merchandise in international ports of trade through long-range merchants, where the many artisans gained raw materials for the manufacture of luxury goods as well.

CITY STRUCTURES ≡ In the time of Moteuczoma II the City of Mexico had reached a size previously unknown on the continent; its 150,000 inhabitants were double the number of the next populous city, Tetzcoco. Mexico City was urbane in character, true to its size. Among the heavily stratified population, members of the elite, warriors, and artisans were over-represented. A multitude of people were engaged in various other professions, important among them public service. Only very few lived off the land or fished. Thus metropolitan Mexico formed not only the political center of the empire, but also its demographic and economic core, whose support had generated a tightly integrated, differentiated economic system throughout the Valley of Mexico.

5

The Andes: Landscape and Climate

MOUNTAIN STRUCTURE ≡ The Andes are a tertiary mountain range running from north to south, which has been compressed by the western drift of the South American continent and consists of several parallel ranges. In the north the width of the Andes is a mere two hundred kilometers, while in the south it reaches eight hundred kilometers near Lake Titicaca. The height of the mountain ranges is between three and four thousand meters, cut by valleys one thousand meters deep. The coastal plain in the west of the central Andes is narrow and consists of alluvial deposits brought by short, torrential rivers, which break out of the mountains and run to the west.

CLIMATE ≡ The area that later developed civilizations is situated roughly between the equator and 20° latitude near the Tropic of Capricorn. The climate is determined by the winds that dominate in these latitudes: near the equator there is a tropical circulation, a south- to southwesterly wind, which regularly causes greatly abundant precipitation. Farther south the southeastern trade wind dominates. While crossing the Andes the air masses lose moisture, so that the coastal zones west of the mountains are extremely dry and desertlike. A cold current (the Humboldt) running near the coast to the north makes the winds directed toward the land shed rain over the ocean and thus furthers the creation of desert zones. The temporary overlay of a warm northern counter current, which occurs every few years and has become known as El Niño, has dramatic consequences for the abundance of fish and the climate of the coastal plains.

DIFFERENT ALTITUDES AND FLORA ≡ As in other parts of Latin America the climate is determined by the altitude as well as by exposure to atmospheric currents. It was Humboldt who proposed a division into the hot lowland zone *tierra caliente,* the temperate zone *tierra templada,* and the cool highland zone *tierra fría* followed by the highest region, *tierra helada.* The high valleys situated on the leeward side of the mountain ranges are cold and dry. The highly dissected mountain mass causes a small-scale alteration of very differentiated local climates, where typical wild and cultivated plants grow accordingly.

IMMIGRATION ≡ Mankind entered South America from the Central American land bridge about fourteen thousand years ago and reached Tierra del Fuego about two thousand years later. Living conditions were those of the ending ice age; all mountains down to three thousand meters height had formed glaciers. In the extensive grasslands created by a moister climate, human beings found an amazing diversity of game. Hunting these animals and, of course, collecting wild plants provided a living for a modestly sized human population, who also occupied the highlands after the end of the ice age.

PRE-CERAMIC TIMES ≡ On the coast, where the sea provided continuous nourishment (and where archaeological preservation is better), the first permanent settlements can be shown to have existed by 4000 B.C. The beginning of agriculture seems to be concentrated at first on inedible plants. Both in the highlands and on the coast the first temple buildings appear at the end of the pre-ceramic phase (among others Kotosh near Huánuco, La Galgada on the upper Río Santa, Aspero at the mouth of the Río Supe, and El Paraíso on the Río Chillón). The effort invested in these buildings (in El Paraíso alone more than a hundred thousand tons of stone were utilized) allows us to recognize a central authority of an as yet undetermined nature. Differences in burials allow us to recognize a social differentiation. Possibly the beginning of the constructions at Cerro Sechín in the Valley of the Río Casma can be placed at this time as well. This was an impressive religious center with a large ceremonial building but no living quarters, whose dominant ideas can be interpreted only through pictorial representations: processions of officials, intermingled with mutilated bodies and body parts, which probably were human sacrifices, while outsized fish in similar contexts may refer to sacrificial rituals connected with the sea.

6

Early and Middle Horizons in the Andes

INITIAL PERIOD ≡ The manufacture of ceramics (this introduction characterizes the Initial period) occurred in the central Andes around 2100–2500/2800 B.C., but it seems to have been taken over from northern South America, where the place of origin is still unknown. At the site of Valdivia in Ecuador the pottery has an age of 3500–3200 B.C. At about the same time there is true weaving of cloth in the Andes as opposed to the earlier braiding techniques. The earliest signs of gold work in the Andes and of copper work in the area of Titicaca also stem from this period.

Movement of settlements from the coast into river valleys indicates that the main nutritional basis now is agriculture; maize, peanuts, and manioc were added to existing plants and the arable land was enlarged by artificial irrigation. In this period, starting at ca. 2000 B.C., advanced ceremonial architecture of many sites in central and northern Peru generally followed a basic design (terraces, circular sunken courtyards, outer walls at right angles, pyramid bases of adobe, low relief depictions made of unfired clay) that often was embedded in extensive, structured settlements. These centers (e.g., Huaca La Florida, Garagay, Cerro Sechín, Sechín Alto) could have been supported only by a large population, one which was somewhat structured and which had a production capacity directed both to the production of food surplus and to elaborate building construction. The amount of material and work invested in the erection of ceremonial structures needs a motif, which must have been religious.

CHAVÍN

Starting at 1200/1100 B.C. an iconographic style was spreading that determined the Early Horizon and indicated a religious complex and a culture characterized by it. Its most important focal point, which also gave it the name, was Chavín de Huántar, situated in a high side valley of the Río Marañón in northern Peru. The paraphernalia of this cult are tendentially connected with the local elite, for whom it possibly meant a strengthening of their own legitimation. All implications for political domination by Chavín are missing.

The central temple building of Chavín is unique because several massive, rectangular parts, connected to each other, are pierced by labyrinthine, narrow corridors. The facades were designed of stone inset with grotesque heads sculpted in the round, characteristic low reliefs, and a portal with contrastingly colored stones. The function of this complex cannot yet be determined. Of numerous large ceremonial complexes only these have been examined: Cerro Blanco (Nepeña Valley), Garagay (Rimac Valley), and Huaca de los Reyes (Moche Valley); they share brick walls with painted reliefs. The main pictorial subjects, mostly executed in low relief, include frightening feline deities in a characteristic, flowing, curvilinear style; the apparently absurd confluence of several beings into one probably has to be understood as a metaphor.

CITY-STATES ≡ The end of the Early Horizon was indicated by the fact that the long-lived, dominant Chavín style broke up into ever more strongly differing local variants. At the same time small city-states appeared, in whose centers lived not only the elite but also numerous craft specialists. They were supported by a peasant population living in the surrounding areas.

THE EARLY INTERMEDIATE PERIOD

The Early Intermediate period, which started around 400–200 B.C., brought an increase in population especially to the valleys of the Peruvian north coast and Ecuador. Settlements were moved to the less fertile valley rims, agricultural activity was increased through irrigation. Increased construction of fortresses seems to show resource conflicts, possibly caused by population pressure.

MOCHE ≡ Everywhere on the coast of north and central Peru giant pyramids made of adobe were constructed, visible signs of political-religious power. The largest of these (340 by 160 meters base measure, 40 meters high), together with administrative structures and living quarters, was erected in the Moche Valley, where there may have been the capital of a far-flung state.

The discovery of the first untouched noble tomb in a monumental platform complex of adobe at Sipán (Lambayeque) yielded a very complex tomb architecture and furnishings, the incredibly rich endowment with valuable costume parts and paraphernalia expressing the power and position of the rulers.

CERAMICS ≡ The expressive, finely painted or sculpted vessels of the Moche, decorated with line drawings in one or two colors, offer a unique glimpse at life in those times, although one has to take into account that the function of most preserved ceramic objects was to serve as grave goods and this may be reflected in depicted subjects. Often there are fighting scenes with warriors and captives, which probably do not depict actual events but rather vary a conventional theme: the victor grabs the loser by the hair and pulls him off by a cord around his neck, after he has taken his clothes away. Finally the captive, destined for sacrifice, stands before the seated ruler in front of the pyramid. These are excerpts from the imagination of a military-aggressive society with a central power. The more peaceful daily life of hunting and fishing was depicted as well on vessels; however, agricultural activity was neglected almost entirely, certainly not by chance. Another facet is elucidated by the three-dimensional depictions containing scenes of mythology or of the pantheon, or the minute registry of body changes caused by either age or disfiguring diseases. Often there are sexual subjects depicted on ceramics, sometimes as caricatures (e.g., oversized sexual organs), or as scenes from everyday life. The careful portraiture of faces on the front of vessels allows only a vague interpretation; perhaps they depict local rulers or army leaders.

NAZCA ≡ The development of the remaining coastal region progressed in a similar fashion; however, lack of such informational ceramics as they occur in the Moche valley prevents further insights. This does not devalue the artistic merits of the ceramics of Nazca on the southern coast with its multicolored, flat, stereotyped figures and faces and their metaphoric associations. The significance of spectacular, giant, incised pictures of animals, also of lines and areas in the desert floor around Nazca, is still unknown; often astronomical references are suspected.

METALLURGY AND WEAVING ≡ Among the technical innovations of the Moche period are the perfection of metallurgy by the lost wax method, welding, and gilding by the *mise en couleur* technique. Elaborate weavings (gauze, tapestry, later decoration by embroidery), partly known since the Early Horizon, appear now in much refined form.

PUCARA ≡ The region north of Lake Titicaca was dominated by the center of Pucara, which was characterized by highly developed stone reliefs, the motifs of which were repeated in a refined pottery, and architectural accomplishments. The style of Pucara and Tiahuanaco seems to have a joint ancestor in the Titicaca area.

THE MIDDLE HORIZON

Around A.D. 600 a long-range influence became apparent, emanating from two sites: Huari in the highlands of central Peru and Tiahuanaco in the southeast of Lake Titicaca. Some sites have been interpreted as showing signs of political dominance, such as secondary administrative seats around Huari, or secondary ceremonial centers connected to Tiahuanaco. However, the Middle Horizon is primarily identified through the supraregional distribution of some ceramic and art styles, whose significance is a matter of debate. According to stylistic-iconographic findings, a third center of supraregional importance could have been Pachacamac on the central Peruvian coast; the northern coast may have preserved its independence from Huari as well.

TIAHUANACO ≡ The ruins of Tiahuanaco are situated in a high but still fertile basin. The basic food crops were tubers and grains of the genus Chenopodium. In zones with a very high groundwater level plants were grown in ridged fields. Large herds of domesticated Andean camelids (llama, alpaca) supplied wool, meat, and dung and also served as pack animals. In the vicinity of the lake fish enlarged the food selection. Provisions were secured by freeze-drying the tubers, also by the plain drying of meat and fish.

The ceremonial center of Tiahuanaco has two types of building complexes: large buildings shaped like pyramid stumps faced with stone blocks, and sunken courtyards surrounded by stone walls. The entrance to these complexes consisted of monolithic gates. Between them there were palaces and living quarters. These building components can also be found at ceremonial centers dependent on Tiahuanaco. Their function remains completely unexplained.

The beginnings of Tiahuanaco as a center chiefly of local importance are in the Early Intermediate period. The site hardly headed a far-reaching empire—most of the administrative provincial centers are in the immediate vicinity—but its long-range influence, particularly toward the south, may have been due to its role as a pilgrim center and religious focal point. The decline of the site around A.D. 1000 was signaled by the collapse of its intensive agriculture.

HUARI ≡ The first state with a large territory probably appeared around A.D. 650 in the area of modern Ayacucho, and was centered at Huari. The little-explored site had at least two phases of building activity, the first reminiscent of the stone work of Tiahuanaco. Two-story chambers made of big stone blocks are quite peculiar; possibly they served as mausoleums for ruling families. Elevated platforms with sunken courtyards are similar to those of Tiahuanaco as well. The site was heavily fortified with walls.

Starting at Huari a probably military expansion to the north took place, with the ceramic style suddenly shifting from indigenous to Huari-derived forms without any transitional stages. This expansion lasted about a century and encompassed a large part of the Peruvian mountain zone. The area was made accessible by elaborately built roads and was governed, as was shown for Ayacucho, by administrative centers (such as Piquillacta near Cuzco, and Viracocha Pampa in the northern highlands) arranged in three hierarchic levels, according to their scale, where large granaries were created. The local population was made to live in cities controlled by garrisons. The coastal area may have been dependent on Huari only indirectly. Huari lasted merely two hundred years; by A.D. 850 the capital was deserted for unknown reasons and the empire disintegrated into small units that made war on each other. It should be pointed out that evidence interpreted here as traces of an expansive state may instead reflect religious concepts.

PACHACAMAC ≡ The influence emanating from Pachacamac, which was without doubt the longest-lived religious center of the Andean region, remained limited to a part of the coast. As the significance of this place shows in later times, its influence was not political, but religious. Although it was at times under the supremacy of Huari, Pachacamac seems to have remained relatively independent.

THE LATE INTERMEDIATE PERIOD

By definition the stylistic-cultural unity expected of the Middle Horizon did in fact exist only for the beginning of this period. The regional break-up that marked the Late Intermediate period (A.D. 1000 until the Inca conquest of the Chimú Empire ca. A.D. 1476) began much earlier. After what was only a short intermission, with regionalization the conditions of the Early Intermediate period returned.

Outside of the Chimú Empire there were several small political entities in the area of Lake Titicaca; these were later conquered by the Incas. Most important among them are those of the Lupaqa and the Colla (with the sites Chucuito and Hatuncolla south and north of Puno). The restless character of this period can also be recognized by the existence of numerous fortified settlements in northwestern Argentina and northern Chile. Irrigated terraced fields of these sites, ceramics, and metal objects found there show their ties to the central Andes cultures.

CHIMÚ EMPIRE ≡ The Chimú culture on the northern coast derived from remnants of Moche. According to archaeological evidence its beginnings can be dated to A.D. 1200. The Chimú Empire, which is mentioned in written sources, was probably formed much later. Its capital was Chan Chan, situated in the Moche Valley, where supposedly its mythical founder Taycanamo lived. His son and grandson extended the territory to encompass the whole valley and the closest neighboring valleys. The continuation of its history almost until the conquest by the Incas remains in the dark; even the rulers' names are not known.

Chan Chan was one of the largest urban agglomerates in the coastal area of Peru. This well-organized city was laid out according to a plan consisting of at least ten characteristic, identical sectors with buildings of adobe surrounded by high walls, each constructed by one of the successive rulers as a palace, administrative seat, and storage house of precious goods. It is speculated that after the death of a ruler the palace complex was changed to a burial area kept up by his family, where the deceased was surrounded by his treasures. The majority of the city population lived outside of the palaces in sprawling living quarters. The population of outlying districts was brought in for the massive construction.

In order to feed the obviously dense population of the Chimú Empire, the arable areas were extended by a complicated system of water distribution, which included aqueducts from one valley to the next. In dependent areas there were administrative centers with the added economic task of collecting goods and services as tribute.

Beyond what can be gleaned through archaeology, knowledge of the culture of the Chimú Empire is very limited. In religion, deities representing the moon and the sea were at the center of veneration, while the sun was accorded little importance.

Around 1465 the Inca ruler Tupac Yupanqui conquered the Peruvian north coast and also subjugated the Chimú Empire, which was allied with Cajamarca and other small political entities at that time. On one hand he deported the ruler Minchançaman to Cuzco and married him to one of his daughters, on the other hand he made Chumun-Caur, a son of Minchançaman, ruler in Chan Chan. The dynastic sequence of Chimú remained unbroken until the seventeenth century.

At the time of its maximum extension, shortly before the Inca conquest, the empire probably reached a length of one thousand kilometers, but was only fifty to 150 kilometers wide along the coast (although there the arable land was restricted to valley oases between broad strips of desert).

7

The Inca Empire

The imperial expansion of the Incas occurred in a very short span of time about one hundred years before the Spanish conquest. Details of origin and growth of the Inca Empire may never be completely recognized; Colonial sources are simply too vague and contradictory in details (concerning even the attribution of specific events to the different rulers). They stem on one hand from Indian traditions, whose task was more the support of state ideology than the transmission of historical facts, and on the other hand from the influence of the political situation of the Colonial period, identifying the Incas as late usurpers. When early Inca history is studied, both tendencies have to be taken into account. Archaeology of the Late Horizon, which is defined by ceramic and architectural styles emanating from Cuzco, basically cannot explain historical questions. Therefore every description of early Inca history remains on extremely shaky ground.

PREHISTORY

MANCO CAPAC ≡ The origin of the Incas is unknown. Several creation myths, which usually take place in the area of Lake Titicaca, rival each other. The half-mythical founder of the Inca dynasty, Manco Capac, is surrounded by a multitude of different and contradictory legends. Together with three brothers and four sisters, among them his wife Mama Ocllo, he led the Inca *ayllu*, here probably an ethnic segment, from a place of miraculous origin, through several places where extraordinary events took place, to Cuzco, their future capital. His *ayllu,* called Chima Panaca, was first situated in lower or Hurin Cuzco. At the time of their immigration, which probably took place in the early thirteenth century, the Incas met a local population with whom they engaged in small-scale disputes; some of these very small groups are said to have been eradicated completely. For quite some time the Incas were unable to assume the upper hand.

SINCHI ROCA ≡ Sinchi Roca, the son and successor of Manco Capac, was born in Tamborquiro before the Incas had reached Cuzco. Even in descriptions of him nothing characteristic can be learned. He also did not make important conquests, because in his time the Incas were one small group among many. Although their sphere of influence probably did not extend beyond Cuzco, there may have been small-scale alliances with neighboring *curaca*, local rulers, possibly even recognition of a leading role. Sinchi Roca founded the *ayllu* Masca. His successor was not his oldest son, Manco Sapaca, but a younger one by the name of Lloque Yupanqui.

LLOQUE YUPANQUI ≡ During the period of the ruler Lloque Yupanqui, alliances with other rulers in the neighborhood were formed, either of free will, or after military coercion led by his son Cusi Huaman Chire, who also stamped out "revolts" of the indigenous population, such as the Hualla. Presumably the Inca rulers of that time could manage little more than small raids performed by a few dozen warriors, which were upgraded and glorified only in view of the later empire.

MAYTA CAPAC ≡ The fourth ruler, Mayta Capac, was born when his father was already quite old. It is said that he performed miraculous deeds when he was a mere child, and as a young ruler he withstood attacks of people who had lived in Cuzco before the Incas, thereby stabilizing alliances with neighboring sites. Remarks about his offspring are contradictory.

CAPAC YUPANQUI ≡ Most likely Capac Yupanqui was not the oldest son of his father. In any event he was forced to prevent succession disputes by drastic measures. The first conquests outside the Valley of Cuzco are attributed to him. Nevertheless, hostile groups kept bringing armed conflict right into the vicinity of Cuzco. On the other hand the obvious strength of the ruler of Cuzco made the inhabitants of other sites acknowledge his supremacy of their own free will and thus secure his military protection for themselves. At first Capac Yupanqui was married to Chimbo Mama, who "fell ill," and later possibly with Curihilpay from Ayarmaca, or Cusi Chimbo, who presumably poisoned him. During the confusion surrounding the death of Capac Yupanqui, Hurin Cuzco suffered a defeat and the dynasty there came to an end.

THE DYNASTY OF HANAN CUZCO ≡ Like many other sites and regions in the Andes, Cuzco was divided into two halves even before the advent of the Incas, one called "upper" (Hanan Cuzco) and the other "lower" (Hurin Cuzco). The rulers, including Capac Yupanqui, belonged to the latter. Organization by halves allows a parallel existence such as a dichotomous rule as an alternative to a sequence of dynasties.

INCA ROCA ≡ The new dynasty from Hanan Cuzco started out with Inca Roca, who was the first with the title "Inca." The beginning of his ruling period was marked by revolts in the subjugated sites of the area, as well as of the *ayllu* in Hurin Cuzco, who probably wanted to take advantage of the insecurity generated by the violent change of rulers; suppression of these must have been one of Inca Roca's priorities. In his time there may have been the start of the long-lasting altercations with the Chanca, who settled along the Río Pampa (mythical tradition has it that they originated from its well), and with the region of Ayacucho, when they began to expand toward the east and Cuzco.

Inca Roca was no great conqueror. Instead, his period was marked by internal changes. Rather than using the old ruler's seat in the Temple of the Sun Inticancha in Hurin Cuzco, he built his own residence in the upper part of the city. The construction of the first water main through Cuzco is also attributed to him.

Inca Roca was married to Mama Micay, daughter of the chief of Huallaca. Because of this marriage there was a dispute between the Huallaca and Ayarmaca that culminated in the kidnapping of the oldest son of Inca Roca, Titu Cusi Hualpa, to Ayarmaca. He was able to return to Cuzco only after several years and then became co-regent with his father. The solution of this conflict was reached by an exchange of marriage partners between the ruling houses of Cuzco and Ayarmaca.

YAHUAR HUACAC ≡ Titu Cusi Hualpa followed his father as a ruler under the name of Yahuar Huacac. Like his predecessors, he had to prove his supremacy against the same neighboring sites, which shows how little they were consolidated. By threatening an attack he was able to have the Colla and their allies recognize his rulership. Conquest or self-subjugation apparently were not followed by a lasting political or military control. After a comparatively brief reign, which made him seem quite bland, Yahuar Huacac became the victim of a murderous attack in Cuzco by members of subjugated groups from the south, which did not lead to the proper consequences. He had designated the middle one of his three sons, Cualpa Maita, as his heir, but the young man was ambushed by the Huallaca and murdered with his entourage. After the violent death of Yahuar Huacac, this led to succession problems.

VIRACOCHA INCA ≡ It is not completely clear if Viracocha Inca was Yahuar Huacac's son Hatun Topa; another opinion has it that he founded a new dynasty. He had to crush immediate rebellions as well, even in the vicinity of Cuzco, and fight countless small skirmishes with neighboring chiefs who felt independent. The number of conquests in his reign is low and doesn't reach far beyond Cuzco. The exception was a raid to the southeast in the region of Collao on Lake Titicaca, where two rival rulers had asked the Incas for assistance. As the dispute had already been decided when the Inca army arrived, there was only a festive sealing of the friendly union with the successful group.

Viracocha Inca had to overcome resistance in his own camp as well. The attempted riot of a brother of Yahuar, who had been incited by people from Hurin Cuzco, broke down due to lack of general support, and the leader poisoned himself. Even the priests from Hurin Cuzco, feeling rejected since the sovereign power had been passed to a dynasty from Hanan Cuzco, conspired with the Chanca, who threatened Cuzco from nearby. Despite the fact that Viracocha Inca had four children with his wife Mama Runtu from Anta, of whom the oldest was Inca Roca and the third oldest Cusi Inca Yupanqui, he made his son Urco, child of the secondary wife Curi Chulpa from the *ayllu* Ayauilla, his co-regent and therefore future ruler.

INCA URCO ≡ The reign of Inca Urco was so brief that many chroniclers don't even mention it. The others describe him after his assumption of power in the worst possible way: he had not constructed a single building, had not liked weapons, and had just followed his pleasures, which were exorbitant drinking and an insatiable appetite for women. Among those who planned his downfall were Apo Mayta, a grandson of Capac Yupanqui, and Vicaquirao, a brother of Yahuar Huacac, who both had served as army leaders under the two previous rulers, Yahuar Huacac and Viracocha.

The situation came to a head during an attack on Cuzco by the Chanca, who came from Andahuaylas and had been stationed nearby for some time. At this critical moment Viracocha, who was still alive and the ruler, and his son Urco preferred to flee from the city and offer their submission to the Chanca, while Cusi Inca Yupanqui organized resistance with the two aforementioned generals. The defenders of the city could overcome the Chanca only with supernatural assistance (so the records say). They put them to flight and also got hold of the deity image they had brought along. After this victory over the Chanca and another, final one a little later, young Cusi Yupanqui—now with the honorable epithet Pachacutec—was designated somewhat unwillingly by his father as his successor, while Urco lost his life, an event in which Pachacutec was apparently involved. This way Pachacutec's accession to power was indisputable.

THE EXPANSIVE EPOCH

PACHACUTEC INCA YUPANQUI ≡ Pachacutec is unanimously seen as the able creator of the Inca Empire. His enthronement probably took place in the early fifteenth century. His father died about ten years later, in his old-age residence outside of Cuzco. At the beginning of Pachacutec's reign numerous polities, even close to Cuzco, once again tried to avoid recognition of the new Inca ruler and regain their independence. Their suppression was a prerequisite for a further consolidation as well as for future expansions of the Inca Empire. A first task was finishing the subjugation of the Chanca and bringing in still independent sites and areas. In the west there were Sora and Vilca, and other groups around Ayacucho. Later military expansion was directed to all sides. Farther to the west, at the Pacific Coast, the Chincha acknowledged the Incas' sovereignty of their own free will, when faced with superior power, and could thus keep considerable autonomy. From there the political entities of the numerous coastal valleys toward the northwest were subjugated up to the Yunga on the eastern slope of the Andes, which included the important pilgrimage center Pachacamac. Toward the southeast the Incas pushed forward to Lake Titicaca and brought the Colla and others into their fold.

However, not all military expeditions were equally successful. On a march into the region east and north of today's Lima, rivalry with the Chanca troops incorporated into the Inca army broke out openly because of their success; to escape the planned murder of their leaders, the Chanca separated from the army and retreated into the jungle of the eastern Andean slopes, where their pursuers could not reach them. During this pursuit the Inca army, led by a brother of the Inca, Capac Yupanqui, went farther into the north than the ruler had allowed. Despite the fact that this disobedience had led to the incorporation of the large and wealthy province of Cajamarca, requital was the death of the general. It is possible that the ruler feared that his successful brother, supported by the army, could push him from the throne, or that he would—equally fraught with danger—favor the Chanca mutineers and was not seriously pursuing them.

A failed military raid to the eastern slope of the Andes northeast of Cuzco also does not fit the picture of the constantly victorious Inca. The second attempt, led by Pachacutec himself, remained unsuccessful as well, since it had to be abandoned due to a revolt in the area of Lake Titicaca. Pachacutec used the suppression of the revolt immediately to enlarge his empire toward the southeast to the Chicha and Charca, although his son and co-regent, Amaru Yupanqui, proved his military ineptitude on this occasion. Also during this campaign it was shown that the Inca warriors could not handle tropical jungles, while they seemed to be invincible in the highlands and coastal regions.

REFORMS ≡ Next to the military exploits the outstanding accomplishment of Pachacutec was the creation of the Inca state's organizational base. The visible expression of this political transformation was the conversion of Cuzco into the representative, symbolic center of the empire. The Temple of the Sun, Inticancha, was furnished splendidly and subsequently called Coricancha ("Golden Court"). In it the deceased Inca rulers were venerated in the form of golden statues. Besides spreading the Inca sun creed also in the conquered areas, Pachacutec inaugurated an esoteric cult, reserved for the elite, for the creator god Ticsi Viracocha.

Aside from furnishing the representational buildings, the rest of the capital was completely reconstructed; in order to gain space for new buildings a part of the population was settled elsewhere. The arable land around the city was made even more productive by terracing and irrigation. In order to feed the workers brought in from far afield, specially constructed warehouses served to store food and other necessary goods. Extensive construction was going on at the same time all over the empire. This not only enlarged the arable land, but made the building and improvement of roads one of the most important prerequisites of the expansion of the empire.

Pachacutec was credited with the long-drawn-out process of consolidating the empire's administration. By incorporating local institutions originally meant for small polities but now adapted to the needs of a supraregional state, a mostly homogenous administration for the entire empire had become possible that was also equipped with sophisticated instruments of central direction and control. The (re-)distribution of goods and spoils of war in the form of gifts to neighboring rulers, who accepted a certain subordination when they took them, was another means of expansion. Among the measures of unification was the introduction of the Inca language (Quechua, or *runa simi*) as the general communication and trade language, even in areas with originally different tongues.

Pachacutec increased the Inca nobility by incorporating a large Quechua-speaking population living in the vicinity, who were distributed among ten additional *ayllu*.

TUPAC YUPANQUI ≡ During his lifetime Pachacutec named his oldest legitimate son, Amaru, as his co-regent. When Amaru did not live up to expectations he resigned from the succession, possibly urged by his father, in favor of his much younger brother Tupac Yupanqui.

For quite some time Tupac Yupanqui ruled next to his father, who immediately charged him with new conquests. The first goal was to stabilize the area up to Cajamarca and to extend the realm to the north; the most important event was the subjugation of the Chimú Empire on the Pacific Coast and coastal valleys dependent on it. At that time this was the Incas' only rival going by the size of controlled land; from Chimú the Incas may have taken over organizational elements, city plans utilizing the right angle, and craft techniques employed on the coast.

Another thrust led to Chachapoyas northeast of Cajamarca. Extension of the empire beyond Huancabama to the north probably happened only after several years of rest in the form of a second long military campaign, which started at the coast near Piura. Later the Inca army had to contend with an unusually violent resistance in the area of the Cañari, but were able to subjugate cities in today's Ecuador, among them Tomebamba (now Cuenca), which was very generously rebuilt by the Inca. Now the road to Quito lay open. In these conquests the generals were brothers and older half-brothers of the ruler by the names of Tilca Yupanqui, Auqui Yupanqui, and Tupac Capac. It has been said that Tupac started an expedition of more than one year's duration in order to check out reports of islands in the Pacific Ocean, sailing off with a huge flotilla of balsa rafts. It is not clear which coasts or islands he actually reached.

After Tupac Yupanqui had substantially enlarged and secured the empire, his father Pachacutec died at an old age. Tupac Yupanqui was the first ruler (aside from the dynasty founder, Manco Capac) to marry his sister, Mama Ocllo; she gave birth to several sons. Possibly still influenced by his father's experience, Tupac Yupanqui named his youngest son Titu Cusi Hualpa his successor, but failed to make him co-regent. It is not clear if he altered this decision a short time before his death around 1493—he may have been assassinated—to favor Capac Huari, son of his secondary wife Chiqui Ocllo, whose partisans tried without success to make Capac Huari the ruler. Chiqui Ocllo was sentenced to death.

HUAYNA CAPAC ≡ Tupac Yupanqui's son Titu's coronation as ruler was undisputed after his rival was removed, and he chose the name Huayna Capac. Because of his youth a brother of his father, Hualpaya, was made regent. Later Huayna Capac undertook several military expeditions aimed at independent groups on the eastern slopes of the Andes and in the area of the Bay of Guayaquil, and he moved the northern border of the empire to the Río Ancasmayo in southern Colombia after fierce battles. Neither this border nor the one on the Río Maule (Chile) in the south, established by his predecessor, was ever crossed again by the Inca army. All actions aimed at the Indians in the jungle on the eastern slopes of the Andes seemed to hit a void and remained without success. The empire had reached its maximum expansion; by now it could no longer be meaningfully governed with available means of communication and tools of administration, which meant that the realm's integrity could not be lastingly secured.

It turned out that succession was a problem for Huayna Capac. He was the second Inca ruler to have married his sister, but they had no children. However, some children by secondary wives became important: Ninan Cuyochi, Atahualpa (mother: Tocto Coca), and Huascar (mother: Mama Rahua Ocllo). Several chroniclers report that Huayna Capac, who spent his last years in Tomebamba, the city of his birth, had designated Ninan Cuyochi as his successor. However, when father and son died at almost the same time around 1525—presumably victims of a devastating smallpox epidemic with severe demographic effects preceding the Europeans—several parties were trying to achieve a solution in their own interests, as had happened before.

SUCCESSION DISPUTE ≡ When they began to be factors in the succession, the position of the two sons, Atahualpa and Huascar, was contradictory. The first, supposedly the favorite son of Huayna Capac, had failed to show his leadership qualities on the occasion of a military expedition, but had some backing in the army. The latter, who was governor of Cuzco during his father's absence, could count on the support of nobles at the court. In consequence the empire was split into two areas of dominance. In the south Huascar was made ruler in Cuzco, and in the north Atahualpa ruled from today's Ecuador. After several altercations at a distance there were several heavy battles, won at first by Huascar and then by Atahualpa. During a final confrontation near Cuzco, Huascar's army was routed and he was captured. His closest relatives were later killed by order of Atahualpa.

THE SPANISH CONQUEST

The fraternal wars had just ended when Francisco Pizarro landed in 1532 near Túmbez with 180 Spaniards. Pizarro and Atahualpa met in Cajamarca, where the Spaniard took the Inca ruler captive in a surprise attack. In order to avoid Huascar's accession to rule, Atahualpa had his half-brother killed while he was on the way to Cajamarca as a captive. Despite a famous last-ditch effort by the empire to fill a room up to the ceiling with gold as ransom, Atahualpa did not gain his freedom, but was sentenced to death in a trial based on fictitious accusations. After he had been baptized the sentence was commuted from burning to strangulation and was carried out on August 29, 1533.

In order to use the authority of an Inca for his own ends, Pizarro enthroned a brother of Huascar, Tupac Hualpa, but he died a short time later. After several maneuvers aimed at setting the still-existing hostile factions at each other's throats, Pizarro made a son of Huayna Capac, Manco Inca, the new ruler. The Spaniards held him in Cuzco under humiliating conditions, either confined to his house, or as a captive. Finally he escaped, started a rebellion, and laid siege to Cuzco from April 1536 to August 1537.

After this first phase had failed, Manco Inca retreated first to Ollantaytambo and finally to Vilcabamba (about two hundred kilometers from Cuzco on the eastern slope of the Andes), where he established an independent state that posed a constant threat to Spanish towns and roads. The continuation of factions in the Indian elite, which had become apparent in the disputes between Atahualpa and Huascar, and the memories of many Indian ethnic groups of their negative experiences in the Inca Empire, which had caused them to join the Spaniards during the Conquest, did not allow an uprising of the whole land. Manco was killed in 1545 by a Spaniard who had found asylum with him. Despite occasional contacts with the Spaniards and adoption especially of military techniques, the life of the Inca in Vilcabamba remained mostly traditional.

Manco's son Sayri Tupac became his successor, and a regent was named for him. After complicated negotiations Sayri Tupac, overall a colorless person, came to Cuzco in 1558 and was given the title Adelantado, an income, and some property. His brother Titu Cusi usurped his power in Vilcabamba, and wanted to bring the Spaniards to recognize his sovereignty. Starting in 1568 a Franciscan was allowed to missionize in Vilcabamba. In 1571 Titu Cusi died; his successor was Tupac Amaru, who was captured in 1572 in a military action by the Spaniards and beheaded, which meant the end for the neo-Inca state. Its fate had always been influenced by the long-drawn-out disputes between two dominant factions of the Spanish conquerors, the Almagros and the Pizarros, as well as by different Spanish rebellions, but it had no chance under the accomplished viceroy Toledo.

SOCIAL AND ECONOMIC ORGANIZATION BEFORE THE DEVELOPMENT OF THE INCA EMPIRE

AYLLU ≡ The basic social unit beyond the family was the *ayllu*, a related, localized group, which laid claim to common ancestors and a common place of origin, designated by a common name. Marriage partners were usually found within one's own group. An *ayllu* had common land in the form of fields and grazing grounds and therefore formed also an economic unit. Some *ayllu*, especially on the coast, were specialized in a specific craft. An ayllu had its own head (*curaca)* and took care of its own affairs. Several *ayllu* formed a larger political unit with a local head.

A differentiation both of *ayllu* and of larger units into moieties was widespread. They were localized and in part separated by landscape features, such as streams. The preferred designation was an "upper" and "lower" half of settlements or regions, such as Hurin and Hanan Cuzco, which has only classification character. These units were exogamous; marriage partners were found in the complementary "half" of each.

ECONOMIC METHOD ≡ Dispersed settlements containing one or several *ayllu* provided themselves with the goods of daily use. All necessary resources were available. Depending on size, member families were given a part of the arable land for their use; however, new distributions or redistributions happened regularly. Families also produced clothes, tools, and the sparse furnishings of houses themselves.

A local head of a larger unit was freed of work; the other members saw to his needs by collectively working special parcels of land. In a similar fashion the community took care of members who could no longer or could only partially take care of themselves, because of either age or disease.

COMMON WORK ≡ Tasks meant to benefit the community were undertaken by all; these included the construction of agricultural terraces, irrigation channels, work on the *curaca's* fields, and all work that one family could not handle alone, like building a house. In this case a duty to reciprocate was imposed.

ECOLOGICAL COMPLEMENTARITY ≡ The ecology of the Andean area is characterized by numerous horizontal zones that have different agricultural potential depending on the altitude. The potential of their own agricultural zone was used by families. Other more attractive zones of different altitude, which could be far away, were utilized by the entire ethnic group, who started small settlement enclaves there.

ORGANIZATION IN THE DEVELOPED INCA EMPIRE

RULERSHIP ≡ The Inca was the head of state and was venerated as an offspring of the sun (*Inti*). He represented the state and under all circumstances his was the decisive voice. He was surrounded by a strict formality, which granted contact with him only to a few as an extraordinary privilege. His chosen successor was basically that son of the main wife (*coya*) who seemed to be most able. The successor often had to prove his qualification as a co-regent, but also could be relieved of these duties. Intrigues and disputes about power and the succession occurred frequently. Even if the power of the Inca seemed to be fathomless in theory, he was nevertheless clearly dependent on the interests of the high nobility, who formed factions again and again. Military leaders especially had an important role in this.

The actual power structure is hardly transparent. Lately it has been suggested (against the evidence of the majority of sources) that just as settlements and ethnic groups were dualistically classified, there were in Cuzco and in other areas two parallel rulers, each with an assistant. Other offices had the same principles of sharing power.

As counselors of the ruler there was a council of twelve or of four high officials, according to different sources, also the governors of the four empire quadrants, members of the high nobility who in turn supervised provincial governors, whose exact functions are hard to determine. They were stratified by rank according to the number (a multiple of ten) of subordinates (tribute payers). The provinces were examined regularly by emissaries of the ruler; commoners could perform only lower administrative tasks. A large number of symbols made visible the status of the highest ruler and the nobility. Among them were special rights of behavior and of dress.

The leaders (*curaca*) of subjugated political entities, who recognized the supremacy of the Inca, usually kept their functions and were still provided for by their subjects who worked their land for them, and ruled, albeit clearly in a limited way, indirectly as representatives of the central state. However, they had to send their children to the capital for education, and as guarantee for the good behavior of their parents. The succession of a local ruler apparently was regulated by the Inca central administration.

THE CENTER OF CUZCO ≡ The center of the empire, Cuzco, which was built as such by Pachacutec, is described by the conquerors as alien but impressive. There were around seventy-five thousand inhabitants. Surrounding an almost square central plaza around the *unshu*, a stone pillar with the throne of the ruler, the palaces of previous rulers were located. The Spaniards noticed that neither on this square, nor elsewhere in the city, was there a market. Close by there was the monastery-like complex Acclahuasi, a little farther on, the sun temple Coricancha. Only the high nobility lived in the core of the city. Four streets divided the city into quadrants. The houses were built of stone, but had roofs of straw. Between them there were narrow streets. The fortress Sacsahuaman with its cyclopean walls was situated on an elevation west of the city.

ORGANIZATION OF THE EMPIRE ≡ Expansion of the empire had necessitated the introduction of higher levels of organization. Therefore the realm was divided into four parts (*suyu*), which met in Cuzco as the symbolic central point: Chinchasuyu (northwestern Peru up to Ecuador), Antisuyu (northeastern Peru, mainly eastern slopes of the Andes and adjoining lowlands), Collasuyu (southeastern highlands, Lake Titicaca, Bolivia, northwestern highlands of Argentina, northern Chile), and Cuntisuyu (southern Peru).

STATISTICS ≡ In order to govern their huge empire the Incas had specially trained persons (*quipu-camayoc*) prepare statistical material mainly about population numbers, tribute payments, and resources of the state. As their only means of recording they had knotted strings (*quipu*), which worked in this way: to a main line numerous counting strings were attached, with different knots expressing numbers in a decimal system. Categories of counted objects could be indicated to a limited extent by different colors. The *quipu* could not be used to record texts, so all further information had to be memorized and passed on verbally. This must have made administrative tasks such as the efficient planning of construction (buildings, water mains, roads) incredibly difficult.

DECIMAL ORGANIZATION ≡ With the rise of organizational structures the population, but especially the army, were subjected to an administrative technique meant to facilitate bookkeeping by forming units of multiples of ten. However, a rigorous execution with exact numbers would not have been practical or very meaningful.

EXPANSION OF THE EMPIRE ≡ One of the most remarkable achievements of the Inca Empire was its fast expansion over a huge area. The strategy of this expansion did not rest alone on military action, but included "peaceful" means. In some cases the threat of incorporating independent small political entities was announced by the formal presentation of gifts, such as were exchanged among neighboring equally ranked chiefdoms. Presents that were reciprocated on this basis were interpreted by the Incas—in terms of their imperial politics—as an acknowledgment of their supremacy and gave rise to administrative intervention in the area. This difference in interpretation provided a constant germ for disputes that the Incas had to understand as rebellions and end by military means. Even if the Incas tried to secure border regions by sometimes dense rows of fortifications, and further integrate them by political and administrative measures, the outlying areas often were only formal rather than real parts of the empire.

ARMY ≡ It is doubtful if the Inca Empire commanded a substantial permanent army. After their subjugation ethnic groups like the Cañari were utilized for permanent military service, and settled near Cuzco. Other than this service they had no others to perform. Members of the different ethnic groups fought in their own units within the army, where they could be recognized by their indigenous costumes, traditional weapons, and their own leaders. Close relatives of the Inca ruler served as commanders in chief of the army, which sometimes marched in two or three divisions. There were two parallel command positions, each ordered according to the dualistic principle. Women were also placed in the army, where they supplied food. Common weapons were slings to hurl stones, metal-studded clubs, and lances. The same weapons were also used by the neighbors and opponents of the Inca Empire, and therefore a technical advantage as a reason for military success can be ruled out.

AYLLU ≡ When the population of the Inca Empire was organized in the fifteenth and early sixteenth centuries, other levels of social organization were superimposed on the *ayllu*, which remained the basic unit. The *ayllu* of a specific region were combined in groups that formed provinces of the Inca Empire (often following previously independent political or ethnic units). The separation of the commoner majority of the population from the nobles became more pronounced; a vertical mobility no longer existed.

PANACA ≡ At the center of the Inca Empire the *ayllu* had lost its decisive meaning. The *panaca* in Cuzco have to be understood as a development of the *ayllu*. They consisted of descendants of each of the Inca rulers. Therefore they contained exclusively nobles, who furnished the empire with officials and administrators. The original functions of the *ayllu* regarding land ownership and economy had been changed accordingly. The mummy of a deceased ruler stayed in the hands of his *panaca* and was venerated as if it were the living man.

AGRICULTURAL LAW ≡ In the Inca Empire land was valuable only with a corresponding access to a work force, which was accessible either from belonging to a network of social reciprocity determined by relationships or from the prevailing power configurations. The centralized state took the right of unlimited seizure of any land. This became particularly prevalent at a time when a new region was added to the empire. However, the largest part of the land remained in the hands of the *ayllu*, which allowed its families or households to use an area according to the number of persons involved. The remaining land, whose size is described differently in the sources, was worked collectively and with priority. The yield of the land and the proportionate part of herds of Andean camelids were destined for the needs of the state; they were collected, stored, and redistributed by state functionaries. In areas conquered by the Incas, this meant an additional burden on the population: they had to supply the local nobility and also provide extensive service on fields taken over by the centralized state for its use. Although there were measures to increase the agriculturally usable areas and enhance productivity, still the demands of the centralized state caused a reduction of the yields available to the local population.

Yields reserved for the centralized state benefited primarily the nobility and numerous functionaries of religious institutions. Another matter was the not only central but still local supplying of specialized artisans (*camayoc*), who did not work on fields themselves, and those who could not take care of themselves because of either age or disease.

In this system the nobility had a hereditary right to yields not only of specific parts of the state land, just as did other non-agrarian parts of the population, but also of individually acquired land. Each Inca ruler owned several large tracts of land, primarily in the vicinity of Cuzco, which were worked by thousands of dependents (*yana*). When the ruler died this land and those who worked it belonged to the *panaca* he founded. Therefore, his successor had to acquire new lands, which according to some scholars became one of the motors of expansion. The Inca ruler also could give land to persons who had proved deserving in the state.

ECONOMIC SYSTEM ≡ In the Inca Empire as in other typologically comparable societies, the exchange of goods and services was marked by a reciprocal relationship. Members of the lower population strata were obliged to deliver a part of their yields to the state (and the nobility representing it) and provide services. In return they received the state's political and administrative efforts, security within and without, ritual communication with the supernatural, and also goods as a reward, as compensation for services, and as provisions in times of need. Whether these relationships were felt to be equal-sided can no longer be determined. The system was at the same time both centralized and decentralized, depending on the category of goods and services. In this system there was no room for a market exchange, except for regional deviations, and there was no need for one.

PROVISIONS ≡ All produce collected by the state from the population was either used up immediately or preserved by different methods such as freeze-drying, then kept in storage houses of the state, which were situated all over the country, particularly near the main roads. The mass of these provisions was so enormous that they could feed more or less the entire population in times of need. Primarily and under normal circumstances the stored goods (which functioned as the state's finances) were used for the upkeep of persons in the service of the state. In this system there was hardly any need, nor any possibility, for trade. An exchange of a few goods took place among individuals, and the value of one commodity was expressed in relation to others. There were standardized weights and dry measures, but no money equivalent.

TRIBUTE IN FORM OF SERVICE ≡ Following annexation to the Inca Empire, tasks formerly undertaken by all were enlarged. As a rule commoners were obliged to work on state fields and participate in tending the state's llama herds, weaving, and gathering fruits and plants. Furthermore, there were other services (*mit'a*) required: construction and maintenance of roads, bridges, fortresses, settlements, and storage houses, work on remote state-owned fields, service as a courier, and work in mines. For these tasks all able-bodied, married adults were requisitioned in a rotation system. Accordingly, the service in the army was regulated. During the duration of service the state provided for all needs from its storage houses. If those in such service were required at a remote location for a length of time their *ayllu* took over their current agricultural duties.

Mit'a has to be understood as tribute in the form of human work. Therefore the state demanded defined service, not a specific mass of goods, even when what was finally delivered was harvested produce or craft items. Demands of service or products were always oriented toward local conditions. Especially precious products were sent to Cuzco, while foodstuffs and consumer goods were collected in local storage houses, whose impressive dimensions have been shown by excavations. The local *curaca* were not expected to deliver tribute, but they made precious gifts to the central ruler and also received comparable ones from him.

SOCIAL CATEGORIES ≡ While the state did not touch traditional rights and duties of individuals for their own group, when it demanded tribute service from agrarian *ayllu* members (*hatun runa*), it made additional use of traditional social categories in the form of *yana* and *mitmac,* whose members—

probably since Pachacutec—were divorced from their original group in differing rates and who directly depended on the Inca state.

YANA ≡ The term *yana* encompasses a very heterogenous category of dependents (sometimes imprecisely called "slaves" in Colonial sources), whose common denominator was the fact that they had been extricated from their *ayllu* of origin, although it is possible that not all connections had been severed. They provided services (from simply working fields and tending herds all the way to higher administrative tasks) exclusively for institutions of the state or for members of the Inca family or local upper crust. In turn they were spared from *mit'a* service. It was the *yana* who worked on the fields of the *panaca* in the environs of Cuzco. There is little known about the recruiting of *yana.* Their personal freedom was hardly curtailed, except for the choice of residence. They could be given to other persons as gifts. Membership was inherited up to a point. In some regions it went from a father to one son, while the rest of the children presumably returned to their *ayllu.*

ACLLA ≡ A category comparable to *yana* was *aclla,* which was restricted to women. They were selected for their grace from the populations of the *ayllu,* and also from the nobility, and educated in their own boarding houses especially in ritual-religious activities. The majority of *aclla* living in cloistered seclusion performed crafts for the needs of the central state. Others could become concubines of the rulers, while still others served in eternal chastity in the Temple of the Sun. Finally, *aclla* could become human sacrifices on special occasions.

MITMAC ≡ *Mitmac* (hispanicized: *mitimaes*) was a category of persons who were ordered away forever from their original place of origin due to a specific task, and settled in a new place, but who could remain members of their ethnic group, keep the original characteristics such as costume and customs, and often keep a connection with their place of origin. In the Inca Empire *mitmac* were formed by state order and often settled far from their homes in enormous numbers, partially in opposite regions of the empire. Sometimes a regular exchange of the population took place. A welcome side effect of such resettlements was the spread of the official language of the state and cultural unification. There were numerous tasks for *mitmac*: political and military control in insecure regions or border areas, and also mobilization for productive labor in agriculture or mines. Many *mitmac* brought to Cuzco were artisans.

NOBILITY ≡ The Inca high nobility, which presumably consisted only of the descendants of past rulers, was too limited in number to fill all administrative offices and high military ranks of the rapidly growing empire. Members of other ethnic groups around Cuzco therefore were made members of the Inca nobility and educated to fill positions reserved for nobles. A third category of nobles was the elite of subjugated areas, who could be given substantial privileges by the Incas.

JUDICIAL SYSTEM ≡ The legal organization was not constitutional in the strict sense of the word, but was based on rights; specific legal institutions did not exist. Execution of laws depended on the gravity of the crime and was in the hands of lower or higher administrators. Penalties ranged from public admonition to physical punishment to death, but for the same crime there could be a different punishment depending on whether a noble or commoner was the offender. This meant by no means that nobles could hope for a lighter penalty, because punishment was determined by the offender's circumstances, and rose with his means.

RELIGION ≡ It is necessary to differentiate between the faith of the majority of the population of the Andes and official religion; the latter, of course, was intimately entwined with the state. The legitimization of the ruler was derived from the conviction that he was the son of the sun (as his wife was the daughter of the moon). The ancestors of the Inca families were revered as deities, and their *malqui* (mummies or their replicas) were kept in the Temple of the Sun.

The most important personified deities of the official religion were the sun (Inti), visualized as male and closely connected to the ruling dynasty, complemented by the moon (Quilla) as the female side, also viewed as earth mother (Pachamama). Also important was the personified lightning (Illapa, probably at home in the southern highlands), who gave fertility to the earth in the form of rain. Viracocha combines the traits of a culture hero with those of a shaper of the world, creator of humans and animals.

The Incas demanded the veneration of their deities in conquered areas, especially of the sun, but as a rule they recognized also religious traditions that existed there already. By bringing the foreign gods in the form of their images or representations to Cuzco, they used religion as a means of political integration. Parts of the population in revolt were punished by the destruction of their gods or deity representations. The decisive feature of the faith of the agrarian population was securing nourishment through fertility bestowed by supernatural forces. Without doubt the deities of their own region and their *ayllu* were the most important for them.

Religious concepts indigenous to the Andes, which were found in both state and popular religion, are the *huacas*, a local manifestation of the sacred in the form of stones or rocks, and *camaquen*, corresponding in the widest sense to the old-world concept of the soul.

HUMAN SACRIFICE ≡ In specific periods of the yearly cycle, but also on the occasion of special political events, children were regularly sacrificed. The killing of companions for high-ranking deceased persons cannot be regarded as human sacrifice, because it was thought that they would continue their services in the beyond.

CALENDAR ≡ Knowledge about the calendrical systems of Andean peoples is very limited, again due to the lack of an efficient and permanent recording device. Common opinion has it that the solar year was divided into lunar months. It is unknown how the difference of 10.88 days between twelve lunar months and one solar year was evened out. Inca Pachacutec is credited with the construction of observation towers that allowed the determination of the position of the sun from a specific place in Cuzco for calendrical purposes.

The *ceques* also are thought to have had religious-calendric functions. They were forty-one imagined lines, which started in the center of Cuzco and led to 328 sacred places (*huacas*) in a diameter of less than fifteen kilometers, where sacrifices were made on specific days.

COMMUNICATION ≡ The entire realm of the Incas was covered by a relatively tight net of roads. The most vital artery ran through the Andean highlands from Ecuador and Cuzco to today's Santiago, Chile. A parallel, but less important, road ran along the coastal plain. A lack of vehicles meant that the roads were used only by walkers, and therefore could be adapted more easily to the landscape, but the construction efforts needed to build and preserve them, especially in the mountains (dams, cuts, steps, pavements, water holes, and bridges), were substantial. These efforts were made by inhabitants of each area as part of their service duties. A special technical achievement were the many hanging bridges with often substantial spans, which had to be renewed almost every year. At intervals of maximally a one-day journey hostels (*tampu*) had been built, where transients could rest. Their management was part of the service duties of the local population. Different from these were small huts, each for two runners (*chaski*), who were part of a courier system for passing on messages. Since a writing system was lacking, messages had to be transmitted verbally—practical disadvantages in view of the quality of transmissions are evident.

The fact that this serious shortcoming in old-world eyes did not make the administration of this huge empire impossible shows (as do numerous other examples as well!) that human societies can choose quite different solutions to the same problems, and that to judge one culture by experiences from another has to lead almost necessarily to faulty evaluations.

As remarkable as the technical, administrative, and political achievements are that mark the Inca state and that allowed it to exist in the first place, they should not induce an uncritical admiration or apologetics. The Inca Empire was not, as can be read repeatedly, a mainly well-meaning rule with the goal of welfare for all and the providing of a state for its members. Equally, and possibly even characteristically, the empire was marked by force, oppression, and massive, merciless interference in the lives of its people. This should not be ignored, when the no less brutal act of the Spanish Conquista is evoked.

PART II

Basic Questions and Approaches to Research

8

Ancient American Studies as Science

THE SUBJECT

Complex societies, which are commonly called civilizations, were developed in two areas of the American continent long before the conquest by Europeans in the sixteenth century. There has never been an independent discipline for the research of these ancient American civilizations. In the United States this area of research (frequently called "Precolumbian Studies") is incorporated into (cultural) anthropology, in Europe into ethnology. The Anglo-Saxon concept of the contents and methodical breadth of anthropology corresponds to the manifold research points of departure within this specialty, which interact without subject divisions in intense cooperation: archaeology, ethnohistory, linguistics, history of art, epigraphy, philology, and ethnology of the Indians in this area.

Because of this situation, tendencies of research were strongly influenced by directions, emphases, and theoretical discussions in anthropology (mainly in the United States), which, in turn, put a decisive stamp on the archaeology of the Latin American area. Therefore, a predominance of formal anthropological literature has to be stated here.

In the United States several art historians (such as George Kubler, Donald Robertson, and Elizabeth Boone) and historians (such as Charles Gibson, Woodrow Borah, and Howard Cline) have been quite successful in making ancient American cultures their specialty, as opposed to developments in Europe. Thus they helped to break up Eurocentric fixations in their area of research. Moreover, the historians have substantially contributed to the formation of a very independent ancient American ethnohistory, which according to its subjects and theories is basically ethnology, but uses as sources historical documents, and utilizes methods of both disciplines.

The trends of ethnohistorical research are more and more determined by a dichotomy caused by the sources. The reports of Colonial authors of the sixteenth and early seventeenth centuries have been known for more than a hundred years. The amount of information from this catalog of sources has not been raised since then, so modern historical analyses and interpretations based on them (like the sources themselves, these claim to be valid in general) can differ from each other only by theoretical-conceptual basic assumptions (paradigms in the definition proposed by Kuhn), which are often substantiated by the preference of sources showing suitable tendencies. The goal of regionally limited research, which uses Colonial documents, is often diametrically opposed to these studies, and shows through local diversity that global statements are inadmissible and produce senseless leveling. The rising use of these administrative sources in such studies is also coupled with an overemphasis on specific subjects.

TEMPORAL-SPATIAL PLACEMENT

Mesoamerica is the part of present-day Mexico, Guatemala, Belize, Honduras, and El Salvador where there existed complex societies and economies before the Conquest at least for some time (see the listing of traits by Kirchhoff [1952]). Dividing the area into a half west of the Isthmus of Tehuantepec and an eastern half seems to make sense. In a similar definition the civilizations of the Andes comprise the territory of modern Ecuador, Peru, Bolivia, and Chile, or the mountains of the central Andes and the coastal strip to the west. This area corresponds to the territory governed by the Incas at the time of the Conquest.

TEMPORAL LIMITS ≡ The section of history to be observed here is placed between the formation of early states and the effective end of self-determined Indian lifestyles. The beginning in time cannot be placed exactly: all transitions toward the political structure of the state always have happened surely by degrees; all attempts to be precise have to be artificial and depend on the criteria chosen for the definition of "state." Moreover, the transition in the different areas in ancient America happened repeatedly each time; at the decline of the individual states the pendulum swung back again and again to political systems of lesser complexity and centralization. These "secondary" smaller political entities, which lacked the structures of states, have to be treated here as well.

TEMPORAL CLASSIFICATION ≡ Archaeological research has applied a classification of three periods to the two civilized areas of the Americas. The evolutionary classification of culture epochs employed in the Andes is independent of temporal placement and its terminology changes depending on criteria of evaluation. The criterium of political organization yields this sequence: folk communities, theocratic states, regional states, cyclical conquests, Inca Empire (Steward and Faron 1959:67); the criterium of economic-political constitution yields this sequence: formative, cultist, experimental, florescent, expansionist, urbanist, imperialist (Mason 1957 [revised in 1964]). For Mesoamerica a temporal classification is used almost exclusively: Preclassic (starting there about

1500 B.C.), Classic (starting at A.D. 300), and Postclassic (starting at A.D. 900) (Willey, Ekholm, and Millon 1964). A classification deliberately free of connotations by temporal sections, characterized by cultural concurrence beyond a single region ("horizons") and by regional differentiations, has been adopted especially for the Andes: Initial period (starting at 1700/1600 B.C.), Early Horizon (starting at 900 B.C.), Early Intermediate (starting at 200 B.C.), Middle Horizon (starting at A.D. 600), Late Intermediate (starting at A.D. 1000), and Inca Horizon (starting at A.D. 1450) (Rowe 1962a), but it is also proposed for central Mexico (identically designated horizons begin there in 3000, 1700, 1150 B.C., A.D. 200, 700, 1400 (Tolstoy et al. 1977:96; Parsons 1974:90). A more precise subdivision of the final periods before the Spanish conquest, which is documented by historical sources, could not prevail.

CONQUISTA ≡ The conquest of Mesoamerica and the Andes by the Spaniards, the Conquista, has to be seen as an approximate final point of the temporal span discussed here, the moment when indigenous central-state authority collapsed under the military pressure of the Spanish conquerors. For central Mexico and the areas depending on the Mexica this happened in the middle of 1521 (conquest of Tenochtitlán); since a central power was not present in Yucatán at that time, an artificially fixed point in time has to be chosen (1542: Mérida was founded in the Maya city of Tihoo); for the Andes the murder of Atahualpa (middle of 1533) will serve.

AFTER THE CONQUISTA ≡ Several considerations cast a doubt on the significance of these temporal segments. Although the Conquista represents a clear cut-off point on the highest political level, since the conquerors were able to achieve a position of power quickly thanks to their military, the government of the lower levels soon adapted to their ideas, because functioning indigenous structures were kept in place at first. On the other hand, the Conquista took effect in the cultural areas very gradually and selectively, despite the fact that missionizing began very soon. As their own written remarks suggest, parts of the Indian population remembered Precolumbian times very consciously, often with immediate objectives in mind, and tried to relate their memories to both their European and Indian contemporaries.

Furthermore, the execution of political power by the Spaniards was limited in remote areas for a long time, either because inhabitants could maintain a formal independence (the remnant state of the Inca in Vilcabamba, engaged in constant disputes with the Spaniards until 1572; Maya Indians at Tayasal in Lake Petén almost without European contacts until 1697) or engaged in rebellions, flaring up repeatedly, and shedding European government at times (the longest lasting that of the Cruzob Maya in today's Quintana Roo during the so-called Caste Wars from 1840 to 1901).

PRECOLUMBIAN/INDIGENOUS ≡ Faced with this situation it is practical to adopt a terminology differentiation. Cultural events are called "Precolumbian" when they happened before a contact and hence influence by Europeans, while "indigenous" describes contents of Indian traditions, independent of the time when they manifested themselves.

9

Sources

The sources on the cultures and history of ancient America can be classified in three large categories: archaeological evidence, Indian traditions from a period prior to the Conquista, and the cultural situation of the period after the Conquista, when Precolumbian culture gradually became intermingled with European and turned into a mestizo culture.

THE ARCHAEOLOGICAL EVIDENCE

Except for the last centuries before the Conquista, which were described by written sources of quite differentiated quality and density, especially in areas of politically centralized government, and with great reservations as to Classic Maya culture, results from archaeological excavations offer the sole entry to cultures of ancient America.

ARCHAEOLOGICAL SOURCES ≡ Archaeological sources are all material objects that have been manufactured, treated, or used by people prior to a specific time, the objects' spatial-temporal configurations, and all material remnants of these people, regardless of their physical presence, if their one-time existence has been proven indirectly. It is important for the evaluation of archaeological sources that the persons who generated these remains by doing so did not intend to inform anyone of their own cultural status. In this they differ from the authors of written or orally transmitted texts, who always pursued some goals with their remarks.

POSSIBILITIES OF INTERPRETATION ≡ In archaeological evidence common stylistic features and changes of style can be recognized best in objects of daily use or luxury items, other artifacts, and architecture. Traditionally, archaeological research has concentrated on them and sought to describe them as formally defined, temporal-spatially limited archaeological "cultures," a term that has little more than the name in common with what ethnologists call culture. Even the identification of human carriers with known ethnic groups is possible with some assurance only, if at all, for late periods. Political units and their changes seem to be hardly ever clear. It has long been recognized that stylistic change in general cannot be attributed to shifts in population ("migrations").

Cultural relations are frequently expressed by bloodless terms such as "exchange" and "contact," which are meant to explain stylistic congruencies.

LIMITS OF INTERPRETATION ≡ If the mentioned limitations should be overcome, the material heritage, which is all archaeological research deals with directly, has to be recognized basically as the result of function and interaction of all culture areas. Assuming the existence of efficient analytical tools, statements about other, if not all, culture areas should therefore be allowed to be made. In fact, not all culture areas are represented in archaeological evidence in the same way, so that statements based on observation remain limited to very few areas in reality. The observation and documentation of the archaeological contexts and human activities above or in the ground is still in its infancy.

NEW ARCHAEOLOGY ≡ "New Archaeology" in the United States tries to extend interpretation possibilities beyond the areas immediately connected with the origin of archaeological evidence, such as craft techniques and architecture (Binford 1962; 1986; overview: Trigger 1978:2–18). "New Archaeology" attempts to adapt anthropological thought processes, in order to recognize and explain regularities in different situations through generalizations, and therefore arrive at general laws of human behavior. At first social, economic, and political organizational forms were the focus of attention (in the lead: Willey 1953). Led by Kent Flannery, possibly the most productive theoretical thinker of ancient American archaeology, research was extended to processes of cultural change (Flannery 1967; *1972a) as well as to interactions between human populations and ecosystems, which only seemingly do not affect cultural areas not addressed directly (Flannery 1972c), and which are accredited with a significance that generally determines culture. In order to address the system character of "culture" the incorporation of systems theory, albeit only partially possible, was attempted (Flannery 1968; *1972b). Influenced by anthropologists like Marshall Sahlins and Elman R. Service, the interpretational frame for cultural situations was an evolutionary sequence of sociocultural types, which were not understood as unilinear.

Starting ca. 1985 "New Archaeology" is faced increasingly with criticism; "Postprocessual Archaeology" has emerged as the main opposition, which is oriented toward an "understanding," hermeneutic view of history (Renfrew [1994] prefers to speak of a cognitive archaeology). In this new or broader direction areas such as ideology and the use of symbols are given the attention missing so far, to come closer to the thinking and the concepts of the peoples of the past. Moreover, the dependency of the reconstructed past on the actual position of the researcher is recognized. A suitable method for the transformation is still missing. Possibly this is why cognitive archaeology has not been applied to Mesoamerica or the Andes (as is shown in Cowgill 1993, especially pp. 564–69). The majority of field archaeologists keep a distance to the theoretical discussion outlined here.

HISTORICAL PROCESSES ≡ Progressively, the incompatibility of a nomothetic viewpoint, established by the "New Archaeology," with an ideographic historical science is seen as a meaningless dichotomy (Trigger 1970; *1978:19–36), because both disciplines undertake the examination of historical processes, albeit on the basis of different data (critical: Hole 1983). In consequence, the archaeological supplementation and examination of statements in written sources has been demanded and is now undertaken (Murra and Morris 1976).

In terms of history of science we must note the rapid change of archaeological explanatory statements, whose trends actually correspond to contemporary ideological drifts or political events (Wilk 1985).

INEVITABLE AND CALCULATED INCOMPLETENESS OF DATA ≡ Another problem of interpretation is the inevitably substantial incompleteness of data: there are cultural activities of which no permanent trace can be expected, or traces have been completely or partially destroyed by natural events or conscious as well as unconscious intervention of man, or were ripped from their context by illegal excavations. On the other hand, the large number of existing remains allows only a representative collection by methods with calculated incompleteness. The most often employed method for this is the surface survey, which deals with large areas by assessing only a small section, selected at random. This method has been rightfully criticized as fraught with mistakes (Sanders, Parsons, and Santley 1979:491–532). More specific problems of the interpretation of archaeological evidence will be dealt with in later sections.

DATING PROBLEMS ≡ An absolute chronology of archaeological data is sought by employing scientific dating methods, which are constantly refined. Such methods, however, have narrowly limited uses and contain methodological problems that can be only touched on here in passing to explain their impact on archaeological temporal sequences.

The most important method, radiocarbon dating of vegetal remains, determines the time when life functions ended. The age thus determined is only an approximatimation; its exactness can also be affected by other circumstances. In the United States an increase of precision can be achieved by utilizing a calibration curve developed for the year rings of the setaceous pine (Stuiver and Reimer 1993). Dates referred to in this volume have been corrected ("calibrated") by this method. Tree-ring dating, which is basically very precise, has not yet been employed successfully for the area of ancient American civilizations and probably will not be viable at all.

Thermoluminescence dates the time span between the firing of a ceramic product and the examination. It and other scientific dating methods have not yet led to the desired precision of dating cultures represented only by archaeological remains, due to their still relatively small numbers and inherent errors. Comprehensive discussions of the state of knowledge on chronology have been presented for only a few regions: early western Mesoamerica (Tolstoy 1978), eastern Mesoamerica (Lowe 1978), and northern Chile (Nuñez A. 1978).

INDIGENOUS TRADITIONS

In most cultures of ancient America there was no recording device for texts. Therefore, historically relevant reports existed only in the form of oral traditions, which have been preserved only if they were recorded after the Conquista in European script. This is true for the entire Andes region and for large parts of Mesoamerica. In only a few areas of Mesoamerica was historical information recorded before the Conquista in the form of pictorial manuscripts (central Mexico, Oaxaca), or inscribed monuments, and sometimes in other media (Maya). Their authors are always anonymous; only in Maya culture have scribes and sculptors or painters sometimes signed their work with their names.

MESOAMERICA ≡ A comprehensive listing of the written sources of Mesoamerica has been compiled only for writings on paper or similar media (*Handbook of Middle American Indians*, vols. 14 and 15: *Guide to Ethnohistorical Sources* 1975, individual chapters cited below). The following overview is based to a large extent on this listing. Limitation of space precludes a complete citation of all sources as well as their publications. Therefore, if there are several editions of one source, only the one with the best quality will be quoted; if necessary, deficiencies of editions or translations will be pointed out. A complete evaluation of sources, their tendencies, contradictions, and dependencies is still missing (partial statements among others: Duverger 1983; 1987, part 1).

MESOAMERICAN PICTORIAL MANUSCRIPTS ≡ In western Mesoamerica only eleven pictorial manuscripts from Precolumbian times (traditionally called "Codices") have survived. They come from only three regions, namely, the Valley of Mexico, a region not yet precisely identified, but supposedly situated in the south of the modern Mexican state of Puebla, called "Mixteca-Puebla" (Nicholson 1960), and the western part of the modern state of Oaxaca. Whether or not there have been pictorial manuscripts in other or earlier cultures (especially Teotihuacán) remains speculation, lacking discoveries.

FORM ≡ Pictorial manuscripts consist of long strips of leather or paperlike prepared plant materials, which were screen-folded and protected by wooden covers. In them depictions of episodes that needed to be relayed are combined with isolated written signs. The depictions follow a diversely stringent code of pictorial conventions; the goal is a transmission of information in as clear a manner as possible. The composition of historical pictorial manuscripts is chronological.

PRECOLUMBIAN PICTORIAL MANUSCRIPTS WITH HISTORICAL CONTENTS ≡ Of all preserved Precolumbian pictorial manuscripts from western Mesoamerica only five deal with historical subjects: Codex Becker I (*Codices Becker I/II*, Nowotny 1961; later discovered additional fragment: *El Fragmento de Nochistlan*, Nowotny 1975), *Codex Bodley* (Caso 1960), *Codex Colombino* (Caso and Smith 1966), Codex Nuttall (*Codex Zouche-Nuttall*, Anders and Troike 1987) and Codex Vindobonensis (*Codex Vindobonensis Mexicanus 1*, Adelhofer 1963) deal with the genealogies of Mixtec rulers in western Oaxaca (especially from Teozacoalco and Tilantongo), their origin in mythical times, their deeds, and their fate.

EASTERN MESOAMERICA ≡ Since inscriptions carved in stone found in Classic Maya culture contain mostly genealogical-dynastic information with a few historical side remarks and Colonial records contain such references as well, it can be assumed that other than the exclusively ritual subjects of the preserved pictorial manuscripts, some existed that also had historical contents.

NONHISTORICAL PICTORIAL MANUSCRIPTS ≡ The other preserved Precolumbian pictorial manuscripts from western Mesoamerica and the area of the Classic Maya culture have exclusively calendric-augury and ritual contents; they inform us only about these areas of Precolumbian culture. Among them are the five Mixteca-Puebla manuscripts: Borgia, Cospi, Fejérváry-Mayer, Laud, and Vaticanus B. They are accessible in partially commented editions (*Codex Borgia*: Nowotny 1976; *Codex Fejérváry-Mayer*: Burland 1971; *Codex Cospi*: Nowotny [introduction and summary] 1968; *Codex Laud*: Burland [introduction] 1966; *Codex Vaticanus 3773*: Anders [introduction, summary] 1972). An extensive synoptic commentary by Nowotny (1961) highlights structural mechanisms; the facsimile editions with commentaries by Seler (*Codex Borgia*: 1904–9, 3 vols.; *Codex Fejérváry-Mayer*: 1901; *Codex Vaticanus 3773*: 1902, 2 vols.), who strongly preferred stellar myth interpretations, are now for the most part obsolete.

MAYA PICTORIAL MANUSCRIPTS ≡ The four preserved Precolumbian pictorial manuscripts of the Maya deal with astronomical-augural subjects in table form, supplemented by pictures and texts. The time of their origin is given inconsistently: Codex Dresden (*Codex Dresdensis*: Anders and Deckert 1975) is dated to the early thirteenth century (Thompson 1972:16). For Codex Paris (improved reproduction of an edition of 1887: *Codex Peresianus*: Anders 1968; a new black and white reproduction of pp. 2–11 in Treiber 1987) and Codex Madrid (*Codex Tro-Cortesianus*, Anders 1967) Thompson (1950:25–26) suggested an origin in the fourteenth and fifteenth century, while Edmonson and

Bricker (1985:44) see these two and the recently discovered controversial *Codex Grolier* (first reduced reproduction in Coe 1973:150–54; preferred Lee, Jr., 1985, with reproductions of all four Maya pictorial manuscripts) as early Colonial period copies of older manuscripts; undoubtedly the Codex Madrid is such a copy.

MONUMENT INSCRIPTIONS ≡ Only in Classic Maya culture (between ca. A.D. 300 and 900) were stone inscriptions with historical references carved in large numbers in the area of the Yucatán Peninsula. The inscriptions appear on free-standing high monoliths in the shape of rectangular columns or plates ("stelae"), on low circular stones or boulders ("altars"), or on specific parts of the architecture, mostly of stone, such as lintels, or on monumental staircases. The inscribed texts refer in part to the parallel depictions. There are hieroglyphic texts on mural paintings as well, and also on painted or incised ceremonial ceramics (here almost exclusively as standardized ritual texts, as ownership reference or purpose indication). The length of the texts is quite variable.

It is very hard to gain an overview of these inscriptions. A complete documentation is only in its beginnings (Graham, *Corpus of Maya hieroglyphic inscriptions*, 1975–present [so far sixteen volumes have been published]). An older compilation concentrated on the calendrical parts of the inscriptions, which then appeared to be the only comprehensible sections (Morley 1937–38). There are also complete documentations of single ruined sites (among them the most important, Copán: Morley 1920, since then numerous new evidences; Chichén Itzá, not published in the form of complete inscriptions: Beyer 1937; Tikal: Jones and Satterthwaite 1982; Palenque: Greene Robertson 1983, 1985a, 1985b, 1991 [and continuing]).

In other regions of Mesoamerica there were no lengthy inscriptions in stone because there was no appropriate writing system available. In central Mexico inscriptions contain isolated dates or personal or place names without any context, or else they have unspecified depictions. In Oaxaca there are a number of monuments from the Terminal Preclassic with slightly longer text passages, but so far they cannot be read (short analysis by Marcus 1976b; Whittaker 1992:5–19). The same applies to contemporary texts from the central Gulf Coast (see below: Epi-Olmec inscriptions). The Late Classic inscriptions with genealogical-dynastic contents from the region around Oaxaca contain hardly any texts besides very standardized depictions (Marcus 1983c) and thus probably lead to Mixtec pictorial manuscripts in style and structure. Listings or analyses of the few scattered inscriptions have not yet been published.

COLONIAL PICTORIAL MANUSCRIPTS ≡ Besides manuscripts physically stemming from Precolumbian times, there are a large number that were written after the Conquista but refer to sources lost since then, which deal with the period before the Conquista. In their depictions the measure of influence by European examples fluctuates between imperceptible and dominant. Many of these sources also have comments written in Latin letters. *Codex Boturini* is historically important because, first of all, it deals with the early history and immigration of the Mexica (hardly available edition: Corona Núñez 1964). Its authentic commentary by anonymous Indians in the Aztec language, called *Codex Aubin*, has to be positioned at the transition to text sources described below (Lehmann, Kutscher, and Vollmer 1981).

The schematic construction of central Mexican historical manuscripts is also preserved in the *Anales de Tula* (Zantwijk [commentary] 1979) and the *Codex Mexicanus* (Mengin 1952; with separate facsimile; for the most part the commentary is restricted to listing parallel passages from written sources). Manuscripts of only partially historical contents, such as *Codex Vaticanus A* (1979) and *Telleriano-Remensis* (Quiñones Keber 1995) are in the format of European books, with extensive explanations by Europeans.

Two very different manuscripts in the indigenous tradition have no authentic commentary in the form of included texts: the *Códice en Cruz*, so called because its year columns from 1402 to 1557 are arranged in the form of a cross with the events indicated by personal and place hieroglyphs (Dibble 1981), and the *Codex Xolotl*, a series of cartography-like depictions of the Valley of Mexico, interspersed with pictures of the migration and events surrounding the Chichimec leader Xolotl as well as later incidents (Dibble 1980).

Codex Mendoza, mainly devoted to listing Aztec tribute provinces and their regular delivery of goods (Berdan and Anawalt 1992), also contains a part describing culture and a listing of conquests attributed to the individual rulers. Pictorial and hieroglyphic notations are copiously commented on in Spanish. Only the tribute lists and small fragments of a historical part are preserved of the uncommented manuscript *Matrícula de Tributos (Códice de Moctezuma)* intimately related to the former (Berdan and Durand-Forest [commentary] 1980).

INDIAN AUTHORS ≡ After the Conquista, Indian manuscripts became victims of missionary zeal, which saw in them delusions of the devil without exception. On the other hand, soon after the Conquista a large number of sources were created with an emphasis on history and technicalities of tribute; these can be positioned in quite different degrees of closeness to preserved written sources and oral traditions. Their Indian authors transposed the indigenous historical texts, which existed mainly in oral form or as pictorial annals, into European script, often preserving their own language. The amount of their editorial input can hardly be determined.

CENTRAL MEXICO ≡ In Mesoamerica the largest number of these sources comes from the Valley of Mexico and the Valley of Puebla. The texts were composed in the sixteenth and early seventeenth centuries by often unknown Indians and conform to an indigenous structure, which is that of annals interrupted by lengthy discourses. Among the most important sources are the following: the earliest source, the *Anales de Tlatelolco,* some of its sections allegedly already written in 1528, mainly confined to this sister city of Tenochtitlán (edition, deficient translation, and commentary: Mengin 1939 and 1940). The *Anales de Cuauhtitlan,* written in the middle of the same century and dealing with the northern Valley of Mexico, may be the historically most fertile source of this type. The compilers brought together traditions from several areas, and marked them as partially contradictory (edition and translation: Lehmann 1938; Bierhorst 1992a, 1992b). The *Historia Tolteca-Chichimeca* (facsimile edition with Spanish translation and commentary: Kirchhoff, Odena Güemes, and Reyes García 1976) comes from Cuauhtinchan in the southern Valley of Puebla. The *Crónica Mexicayotl,* the early history of the Mexica, was written mostly by Chimalpahin, but there are parts by Alvarado Tezozomoc and Alonso Franco (edition and translation inferior: León 1949).

Among the sources in the Aztec language the literary production of Domingo Francisco de San Antón Muñón Chimalpahin Quauhtlehuanitzin is remarkable. He was a noble from the region of Chalco, who wrote in the beginning of the seventeenth century. Most important for the Precolumbian history of central Mexico—but also the first hundred years of the Colonial period—are his very detailed *Diferentes historias originales de los reynos de Culhuacan y Mexico y de otras provincias* (about the lost sources: Romero Galván 1977). So far, only the Aztec text has been edited completely and coherently (Zimmermann 1963). The published translations are not always trustworthy (Rendón 1965; Lehmann and Kutscher 1958; Mengin 1950; Durand-Forest 1987).

INDIAN AUTHORS IN SPANISH ≡ Indian authors also wrote extensive historical presentations in Spanish, which in part show a lack of mastery of this language and the influence of European literature (bio-bibliographical overview: Carrera Stampa 1971). At the center of the amply narrative, incredibly detailed, and without doubt enhanced *Historia Mexicana* by Hernando Alvarado Tezozomoc (Orozco y Berra 1878), is the establishment and expansion of Aztec rule, which seems to be quite close to a lost Nahuatl work. Extensive similarities of contents with other sources (see below) have led to the postulation of a *"Crónica X,"* an original source not preserved (Barlow 1945a). Fernando de Alva Ixtlilxochitl, a member of the royal house of Tetzcoco, composed five historical treatises, which overlap one another, about the Acolhua in the eastern part of the Valley of Mexico, who were the last to become Mexica allies (O'Gorman 1975–77). Among others he used the *Codex Xolotl,* mentioned above, as a source. In order to comply with an order of the Viceroy to deliver *Relaciones Geográficas* (see below), the half-caste Diego Muñoz Camargo (1984) wrote in his *Descripción de la ciudad y provincia de Tlaxcala* . . . an overview of his own region, which far exceeds the format both in size and nature, and which represents the most extensive historical work on Tlaxcala. The *Relación de Tetzcoco* by Juan Pomar (1891; *1941; Garibay K. 1964) was created under similar conditions.

SOURCES BY SPANISH AUTHORS OR COMPILERS ≡ A large number of the reports on Precolumbian central America are linked directly or by conjecture to the names of persons of Spanish extraction. They either appear as the actual authors or remain anonymous as compilers of Indian communications.

SOURCES OF INDIAN TRADITIONS COMPILED BY SPANIARDS ≡ The degree of collaboration or influence by Spaniards on these sources varies and in each case it can rarely be determined with precision. A typical example for this group is the creation of the most voluminous of these sources, which was composed for areas outside of the Aztec Empire, and which has been preserved. Known as *Relación de Michoacán*, the work was written in 1541 and describes the culture and history of the Tarascans, the most important military and political opponents of the Aztecs. The compilation is attributed to the Franciscan Jeronimo de Alcala, who followed a wish of the Viceroy and expressly felt himself not the author but the trusty translator of statements made by Indian elders he had assembled (Tudela 1977). The explanations provided by Indian informants about pictorial manuscripts now lost were collected in the *Historia de los mexicanos por sus pinturas* (Garibay K. 1973:23–79), possibly written by the Franciscan Andrés de Olmos (see below). Two parallel, though in part contradictory, texts contain information about the family of Moteuczoma II. They were written by two anonymous Franciscans in order to support claims by his daughter Isabel (García Icazbalceta 1941a; 1941b).

SOURCES WRITTEN BY SPANIARDS WITH DATA FROM INDIAN TRADITIONS ≡ After the Conquista authors of Spanish extraction wrote numerous books about the history and culture of the conquered areas. Almost all of these authors spoke one or more Indian languages, so they had direct access both to verbal reports of indigenous informants and to the writings of Indian authors. It is common to differentiate religious and secular authors.

RELIGIOUS AUTHORS ≡ In simplified terms, the main interest of religious authors, who were often members of a mendicant order (mostly Franciscans), and later Jesuits, were subjects that had a bearing on their missions. However, the range of such subjects was quite extensive.

FRANCISCANS ≡ Among the first Franciscans, who arrived in New Spain as early as 1524, was Toribio de Benavente, called Motolinía, who wrote an eyewitness report *De moribus indorum* in 1540, which has vanished. An incomplete copy has been preserved, also a short version of the work written by an unknown editor (joint, reconstructive edition: Benavente 1971).

The monumental work *Historia general de las cosas de Nueva España* by the Franciscan Bernardino de Sahagún (Aztec text with translation: Anderson and Dibble 1950–1982; Spanish text: Garibay K. 1956; the chapter divisions are valid for both editions) is of unique importance. His goal was to set down a comprehensive, philological description of Aztec culture in the language and in the words of its members, and to support missionary work, so the religious subjects clearly dominate. His very systematical working method was to assemble competent Indians, discuss individual subjects with them (López Austin 1974a), and have students of the Indian college at Tlatelolco write everything down. Sahagún's influence consisted of posing the subjects, organizing the statements and editing them, and providing an exact translation (in part with philological comments). The complicated history of the complete work and the relationship of the different parts (Aztec and Spanish) is extensively discussed by Nicolau d'Olwer, Cline, and Nicholson (1973).

DOMINICANS ≡ The Dominican Diego Durán, who came to Mexico as a child and mastered the Aztec language at an early age, wrote the earliest comprehensive report about the history and culture of the Aztec Empire in the second half of the sixteenth century. The historical part of his work *Historia de las Indias de Nueva España y Islas de Tierra Firme* (1967; the historical part is in vol. 2) uses the hypothetical, aforementioned *"Crónica X."* In turn, it served as a source for parts of the anonymous *Codex Ramírez* (Couch 1991), which also contains independent information, underlining the complex nature of these sources.

LOST SOURCES ≡ A series of sources is no longer available. Their existence is known from direct references or quotes by other authors. Among the possibly most important are the writings of the following religious authors. Andrés de Olmos, a competent philologist, wrote in 1533 the *Libro de las antigüedades de México, Tezcuco y Tlaxcala,* on orders from his superior. After it was lost in Spain, he prepared a summary (*Recopilación de las Antigüedades*), which was also lost. The following anonymous works are presumed to be by him: *Historia de los mexicanos por sus pinturas* (see above), *Histoyre du Mechique,* which is preserved only in a French translation (Garibay K. 1973:23–79), and *Codex Tudela,* which deals with calendars and rituals (Códice Tudela 1980; discussion: Wilkerson 1974). The position of the *Codex Tudela* within the group around the *Codex Magliabechiano* is also discussed by Boone (1983) and Riese (1986c).

JESUITS ≡ According to the wishes of the viceroy, the Jesuit Juan de Tovar (1972) had written a historical description around 1578 that used indigenous informants and, after it was lost, he prepared a revision for Acosta (see below) that substantially refers to Durán.

EARLY RE-WORKED PRESENTATIONS ≡ A substantial number of sources stem less from indigenous tradition or eyewitness accounts of their authors, but incorporate other works by Spaniards (often summaries as well) that seem to have been widely circulated in manuscript form in those times. The importance of these works comes from the fact that information is presented that is no longer available in its original form. Of these only a few will be mentioned. Bartolomé de las Casas, later bishop of Chiapas (1967), is known as an ardent advocate of Indian rights; the evaluation of his source has to take this into account. The Franciscan Geronimo de Mendieta deals with aspects of indigenous culture in the second book of his *Historia ecclesiástica Indiana*, written after 1596, and mainly discusses the history of missions (1860; *1945). The work of the Jesuit José de Acosta (1940) depends on Tovar for a large part.

One of the most important summarized historical sources of New Spain was written in the beginning of the seventeenth century, *Los veinte y un libros rituales y monarquía Indiana* . . . by the Franciscan Juan de Torquemada, first printed in 1615 in Seville and then, in corrected form, in 1723 in Madrid (critical edition with a substantial bibliography: 1983). Torquemada's work, which intended to justify the victimization of Indian culture by missions, was evaluated by Alcina Franch (1975); his indigenous sources were examined by Cline (1968).

A fierce dispute at first about the right to conquer and subjugate the Indians, which had raged since the Conquest, had an effect on considerations of the indigenous cultures. They appear in two political-literary extremes: the *leyenda blanca*, which justifies the Spanish conquest because it brought higher culture to the Indians, and which emphasizes or exaggerates reprehensible traits of Indian culture, and the *leyenda negra*, which stigmatizes the conquerors as destructive (in the sense of Las Casas), and for whose invasion and subsequent actions Indian culture provided no excuse.

INDIAN SOURCES FROM OTHER REGIONS OF WESTERN MESOAMERICA ≡ Historically relevant Indian sources in languages other than Nahuatl, which was the predominant language of the Aztec Empire, practically do not exist. An exception is the *Codex Huichapan*, which contains in one part annals of Precolumbian times in picture writing and corresponding texts in Otomí; the historical part is available only in an inaccurate edition and translation (Alvarado Guinchard 1976).

EASTERN MESOAMERICA ≡ East of the Isthmus of Tehuantepec the source situation is clearly different from the western areas. At least for the lowland area of Maya culture it can be supposed that hieroglyphic texts with historical contents, preserved mostly on stone, supported and strengthened oral traditions beyond the Conquest.

THE MAYA OF YUCATÁN ≡ Sources that were written after the Conquista in European script have been preserved from two areas populated by Mayan peoples: the northern part of the Yucatán Peninsula and the highlands of Guatemala. From the first area come a large number of so-called Books of Chilam Balam, which are differentiated by their places of origin. They are manuscripts of the eighteenth and nineteenth centuries, whose texts reach far back and in part might even contain transcriptions of hieroglyphic texts. Here Indian traditions and texts of obvious European origin about history, calendars, astrology, and medicine are intermingled. Historical remarks, which are incorporated into an analytical framework of *katun* segments (ca. twenty years) and prophecies mixed with history for cycles of thirteen *katun* each, are often difficult to understand. The historically most important Chilam Balam book is from Chumayel (Roys 1967; Edmonson 1986), from Tizimín (Edmonson 1982), and the collection *Codex Pérez* from Maní (Solís Alcalá 1949; Craine and Reindorp 1979). A translation of a reconstructed text from common historical sections has been prepared by Barrera Vásquez and Rendón (1948). Present-day knowledge about the historical sources of this area has been brought together by Edmonson and Bricker (1985).

MAYA OF THE HIGHLANDS ≡ The three most voluminous historical sources from the Guatemalan highlands are of a totally different character. Beginning in mythical times, they recount the immigration of the Quiché and Cakchiquel and their conquests until the fifteenth or sixteenth century. The most important source is the *Popol Vuh*, which has been translated many times (among others Schultze-Jena 1944 with a Quiché dictionary; Edmonson 1971; Tedlock 1985). The *Título de Totonicapán* was also written in the Quiché language (Carmack and Mondloch 1983). A similar structure is observed in the *Anales de los Cakchiqueles* (Recinos 1950; *1953). The most comprehensive overview of all sources in this area is by Edmonson (1985).

INDIGENOUS TRADITIONS REFLECTED BY SPANISH AUTHORS ≡ The best early source for Indian culture and history in the northern part of the Yucatán Peninsula (containing an attempt to record a misunderstood alphabet in the Maya script, which nevertheless became the key to its decipherment) is the *Relación de las cosas de Yucatán* by the Franciscan Diego de Landa, who later became bishop of Yucatán (1959; English translation with an extensive and very valuable commentary: Tozzer 1941).

THE ANDES ≡ The sources from the Andes have been influenced decisively by the lack of a functioning indigenous system for writing texts. In Precolumbian times historically important descriptions could be transmitted only verbally (a differentiation of traditions was postulated by Wedin [1966:34–39], who sees an official tradition with various degrees of access by the public, and another one consisting of personal memories). In addition, the indigenous interest in writing down historical events apparently was not well developed. This is probably the main reason why the character of traditions became more and more anecdotal, legendary, and mythical after a short time. It also lacked a trustworthy chronological framework.

Corresponding to the nature of tradition in the Andes, there was no extensive recording of indigenous traditions in European script after the Conquista, as there was in Mesoamerica. The number of Indian and mestizo authors is very small. Also the period of their writing is comparatively late. Rather, the descriptions by Spaniards are predominant. These Spaniards had different goals in mind and their competence varied greatly, especially when it comes to the history of Inca rulers, the expansion of their rule, and, to a lesser degree, to the situation before the Incas were established. A comparable density of facts does not reach beyond the middle of the fifteenth century. To works composed later than ca. 1570, even if the authors refer to Indian informants, little originality beyond folklore and the continuation of folk religion is attributed by recent research (Wedin 1966:96).

A detailed, strongly biographical overview of the most important authors of the sixteenth century is provided by Means (1928). However, there are hardly any references to interdependent sources and to tradition lines, and both the evaluation of the quality of sources and the bibliographical notes are often old-fashioned. An evaluation of the sources is also given by Wedin (1966:41), who discusses in a mostly positive stance the comprehensive overview by Porras Barrenechea (1986, with in-depth characterization of authors, extensive bibliography, and text samples; latest summary: Pease G. Y. 1988a).

INDIGENOUS TRADITION PUT IN WRITING ≡ The so-called *Huarochirí Manuscript* of ca. 1598, anonymous and without a title, is the only source about the Precolumbian culture of the Andes completely written in an Indian language. It appears to be the summary of depositions of several informants. The role and the person of the editor, his temporal placement, his position, and perhaps his identity as Francisco de Avila (see below) is seen controversially (discussion in the following editions: Trimborn 1939; *enlarged and with additional material: Trimborn and Kelm 1967; Arguedas and Duviols 1966; Taylor 1980; *1987; about this in detail: Hartmann 1981; answer with a detailed discussion of paleography and translation variants: Taylor 1982; latest edition: Urioste 1983).

INDIAN AUTHORS IN SPANISH ≡ Three historical sources by Indian authors from the Andes have come down to us. It is remarkable that they all wrote in Spanish, contrary to Mesoamerica, although two of them injected Quechua inserts of varying length as well (Salomon 1982; Chang-Rodríguez 1982).

Felipe Guamán Poma de Ayala, supposedly a grandson of the Inca Tupac Yupanqui through his mother (Padilla Bendezú 1979), composed his rather voluminous work *Primer nueva corónica y buen gobierno* for the Spanish king in the beginning of the seventeenth century (Murra, Urioste, and Adorno 1980). The text (in a Spanish influenced by Quechua) is riddled with shorter or longer passages in Quechua and contains four hundred full-page illustrations. Historical remarks retreat behind others. Guamán Poma obviously had access to contemporary sources (critical treatment of recent examinations: Adorno 1981; 1986).

Joan de Santa Cruz Pachacuti (1968), a member of a provincial noble family of the Colla, who spoke Aymara, composed a report in the beginning of the seventeenth century that is strongly influenced by Indian-Christian legends and fantasies and has little historical value.

The report by Titu Cusi Yupanqui (Urteaga and Romero 1916), also written for the Spanish king in the year 1570, and meant to prove his descent from an Inca family, does not deal with Precolumbian history but with the time of the remnant Inca state in Vilcabamba (critique of the source's value: Regalado de Hurtado 1981).

MESTIZO AUTHORS WRITING IN SPANISH ≡ The following two mestizo authors tried to make the Inca Empire appear in a positive light in European eyes (Murra 1958:35). The author Inca Garcilaso de la Vega (actually García Lasso de la Vega) deserves special attention; he was the son of a Spanish noble and of the granddaughter of an Inca ruler. The value of this source is diminished by the fact that in 1560, at age twenty, he left Peru forever for Spain to try to get compensation for his father's services and restitution for the lands of his mother—however, in vain. After a military career and other literary activities he wrote his famous *Comentarios Reales* around the turn of the seventeenth century (1960). Their core is the history of the Inca as it was seen by his family, who were in opposition to Atahualpa; he also quotes the work of earlier authors under their names. Garcilaso is the most important in the group of sources that glorify the Inca past. The *Comentarios Reales* have been criticized as a source and examined as literary history numerous times (showing many single examples: Durand 1976; his trustworthiness is doubted by Rostworowski de Diez Canseco 1953:55–70). A reason for his deviant statements can be his intention to make the history of his own people appear positive in the eyes of the conquerors. It is not clear how much of his book is really based on his memories of statements made by his family members, and how much is literary embellishment or adoption from contemporary Spanish authors, also in the sense of literary opposition (Rostworowski de Diez Canseco 1953: 60–68).

The Jesuit Blas Valera is also of Indian extraction on his mother's side. His *History of Peru*, written in Latin around 1590, is known only through numerous quotations by Garcilaso de la Vega; several other authors (Means 1928:503–6) attribute to him a *Relación de las costumbres antiguas de los naturales del Perú* published anonymously (1968), which has little historical value.

INDIAN TRADITIONS RELATED BY SPANIARDS ≡ The most important Spanish author for the Precolumbian history of the Andes is Pedro Cieza de León, who collected his data soon after the Conquista, when he was a soldier in Peru, especially in Cuzco. The second part of his work, written about 1550, is of historical interest for Precolumbian times (1985), while the third part is mainly concerned with the events of the Conquest (Pease G. Y. 1984). The value of the source is increased because most of the time Cieza de León gives the origin of his information.

The historical work of Juan Diez de Betanzos (Martín Rubio 1987), who commanded splendid access to information due to his marriage to a member of the Indian nobility of Cuzco and his mastery of Quechua, was written in 1551. The description starts with the mythical history of pre-Inca times; however, it deals mainly with Inca Pachacutec. The complete text of the work, which was previously known merely in sections, was rediscovered in 1986 (Pease G. Y. 1988a).

As a lawyer, Juan Polo de Ondegardo occupied the office of Oidor in the Audiencia of Lima starting in 1545, as well as other positions in the military and administration. His short *Relación* is important for the history of the Incas (Urteaga and Romero 1916b), as well as two works about continuing elements of Precolumbian religion (Urteaga and Romero 1916a; 1917). The priest Miguel Cabello de Balboa incorporated an important description of history in his main work (1951), written in 1586, which is especially valuable for the coastal area.

The historical work by the priest Antonio de la Calancha (1981), produced at the beginning of the seventeenth century, contains one of the most extensive descriptions not only of late Inca history, but also of the history of earlier periods and of the Chimú Empire. Means (1928) presumed that this work is based on interviews with Indian informants, preserved in an anonymous version he attributed to Calancha (Urteaga 1920).

Another priest, Francisco de Avila, collected texts toward the end of the sixteenth century in the province of Huarochirí, mainly of religious contents, but also legends going back to pre-Inca times. Most authors see him in connection with the origin of the so-called *Huarochirí Manuscript* (see above). He wrote an incomplete summary of the text called *Tratado y relación de los errores, falsos dioses y otras supersticiones y ritos diabólicos* . . . (published in Arguedas and Duviols 1966:199–217).

A part of the often peculiar and confused historical description by the Italian Jesuit Juan Anello Olvia (Pazos Varela and Varela y Orbegoso 1895), who wrote in the early seventeenth century, supposedly comes from an Indian *Quipu* expert, whose name is preserved. The Augustinian Alonso Ramos Gavilán (Muñoz Reyes 1976), whose book was printed in Lima in 1621, reports from and about the region of Lake Titicaca, where he was a missionary for quite some time.

The work of the following two authors is quite obviously coined by political goals of the Colonial period, especially the justification of Spanish government: Pedro Sarmiento de Gamboa, whose *Historia General llamada incaica* (edition with translation 1906) attests to the same deeply rooted enmity toward the Inca ruling family as the contemporary *Información y probanza . . . del orígen y descendencia de la tiranía de los Ingas* . . . , which was compiled in connection with it by order of the viceroy Francisco de Toledo (Levillier 1924; partial publication in Levillier 1940; see also *visitas*), and which contains no authentic statements, despite the formal questionnaire. The actual information, the origin of which is obscure, is really contained in the questions. The obvious dependence of Colonial authors on each other has not yet been studied thoroughly. Only Davies (1995:89–100) deals with this question, albeit in a cursory fashion, and tries to reconstruct the information basis of early and later authors as well.

EARLY DESCRIPTIONS, BASED ON OTHER WORKS ≡ The earliest compiler, who preserved the contents of numerous lost reports, is Gonzalo Fernández de Oviedo y Valdés (Pérez de Tudela Bueso 1959), who in 1532 became royal chronicler for Spanish holdings in the Americas and hence was in a uniquely advantageous position regarding information. It has been remarked that in his work he used an uncritical method. He had never visited Peru in person.

The Jesuit Bernabé Cobo (1956), who knew large areas of the Spanish holdings from personal experience, wrote a description of natural science and history in the first half of the seventeenth century in which he incorporated, besides verbal information, mainly statements by earlier authors. Secondary authors are the already mentioned Las Casas (O'Gorman 1967) and Acosta (O'Gorman 1940). The latter mainly used works by Polo de Ondegardo for Peru.

CONDITIONS OF EARLY COLONIAL TIMES

It has to be understood that the Conquista by no means completely extinguished traditional ways of life, despite the enormous changes it brought to all areas of Indian culture. Therefore the conditions prevailing in Colonial times among the Indian population basically can be used—with limitations even in such sensitive areas as religion—for a critical backward projection to pre-European times, and as such are also historical sources.

REPORTS ≡ Even during the Conquista, single conquerors began to compose reports about their activities of the moment, mostly for the superficial reason of justification; their reports also contain statements about the Indian cultures they encountered. For Mesoamerica the letters of Hernán Cortés to the king belong in this category (1963), as do the letters of Pedro de Alvarado (1954) about the conquest of Guatemala, the description by Gómara (1954), published in 1552 and based on verbal communications by Cortés among other known sources, and the reports by various conquerors written later, among them the most voluminous by Bernal Díaz del Castillo (1960). In this group are other authors such as Francisco de Aguilar (Gurría Lacroix 1977), who entered the Dominican order soon afterwards, and others (Andrés de Tapia 1866) as well as the unknown author—maybe not an eyewitness—whose work has been preserved only in an Italian translation, *Relatione di alcune cose della Nuovo Spagna* . . . (Ramusio 1556). The latter form a transition to the numerous *"relaciones de méritos,"* written retrospectively and partly in greater temporal distance to the moment of contact, in which their authors tried to prove their personal merits during the Conquest and give other information as well. Many of these have been put together by Icaza (1923); others were published by themselves, because they were more extensive (Vázquez de Tapia 1972). Authors writing as eyewitnesses and participants in the Conquest, whose reports are historically and in view of the cultural situation they encountered of little value, were soon replaced by scientifically educated and interested administrators and missionaries. If they reported on indigenous historical traditions they have been named above. Of interest here are works about the contemporary situation. Two reports by the long-term Oidor of New Spain, the Indian-loving jurist Alonso de Zorita, are exemplary, because they contain the most in-depth general information about the social life of the indigenous population. So far only the shorter of his works has been published (1891).

In the Andes a comparable report is the one composed prior to 1570 by the Oidor of the Audiencia of Lima, Fernando de Santillán (1879), after he returned to Spain; he places special emphasis on social stratification. A separate category of sources deals with the continuation of indigenous religious forms, among them Cristobal de Albornoz (1967). Reports written later than the middle of the seventeenth century have not been included here because attention to the Indian world of the colony and especially Precolumbian history has lessened substantially compared to the earlier period. By definition, ethnographic reports of recent times, which allow the continuation of Indian cultural elements to be recognized, also belong in this group of sources. Their relevance for pre-European times is a corroboration at best.

ADMINISTRATIVE AND JUDICIAL DOCUMENTS ≡ The evaluation of an enormous number of documents prepared by the Spanish administration during the Colonial period promises valuable insights, which shed light on pre-European times, but such work was started seriously only around 1950 (Murra 1970; *1975e). These documents show less of a slant than reports written to inform and probably influence a reader (often the king). Administrative documents have been composed for an immediate goal. Also statements contained in them by parties involved or not involved are biased without a doubt, but the goal of the examinations and actual thrust of an administration is usually obvious and can be taken into account when evaluated. The voluminous documents of courts of law may be stifled by formal details, but usually they contain the statements of both sides, the evaluation of each other's assertions, and the assertion of the court—invaluable assistance in modern research.

For backward projection to the times before the Conquest it must be remembered that changes that appeared in the meantime may not be recognizable as such, especially if they took place in the framework of pre-Colonial institutions, such as quantitative areas of social or economic structures.

EXAMINATIONS OF LARGE AREAS IN COLONIAL TIMES ≡ The administration of Spanish holdings in the Americas created data through a series of ambitious examinations that need to be much differentiated in singular instances, but are often of excellent quality and cover large areas in a remarkable degree of completeness. Soon after the Conquest the *visitas* were created. By 1580 they were replaced by *Relaciones Geográficas*, which covered large areas thoroughly and were structured systematically.

VISITAS IN PERU ≡ In the vice-monarchy of Peru regional examinations (*visitas*) were undertaken beginning in 1540. Some of them are accessible (Cajamarca: Barrientos 1967; Conchucos: Espinoza Soriano, ed., 1974; Jayanca: Espinoza Soriano 1975:260–72).

The first comprehensive series of seventy-two *visitas* was compiled in 1549, in the second decade after the Conquest (Murra 1970; *1975e). In it there were statements not only about the present situation, but also about the past before the Conquest, which were given by Indian local rulers and their *quipucamayoc*. So far only a few of these *visitas* have been found, evaluated and published (Helmer 1955 [*visita* Chupachos]; Galdos Rodríguez 1977 [*visita* Atico and

Caraveli]; Rostworowski de Diez Canseco 1975a [*visita* Chinchaycocha]; Espinoza Soriano 1975b [*visita* Ochoc-Huánuco]; Murra 1991 [*visita* Sonqo]; Rostworowski de Diez Canseco 1978a [*visitas* to Canta, Huaura, and Maranga]).

In the next decade there were no comparable large-area examinations, but instead there was some local gathering of data (Bandera 1965, of 1557; Castro and Ortega Morejón 1974, of 1558; Ortiz de Zúñiga 1967–1972). Starting in 1565 there were regular yearly *visitas*, which were meant to remedy local grievances between the Indian population, the Colonial administration, and single Spaniards. These goals resulted in the fact that *visitas* had a special value for sectors of Precolumbian history that concern tribute technicalities in Colonial times (Murra 1964; on evaluating *visitas* as sources: Salomon 1980; English original 1986:38–47; commented publication of a *visita*: Zevallos Quiñones 1975).

Another series of *visitas*, whose importance is mainly statistical, were ordered by the viceroy Toledo in 1571 (publication: Colonial-period condensation of two-thirds of the *visita*: Cook, Málaga Medina, and Boyssee-Cassangne 1975; a complete, but even more abbreviated version: Levillier 1925; of individual reports only 10 percent are known, for instance: Ramírez Horton 1978; Espinoza Soriano 1963).

VISITAS IN MEXICO ≡ After single collections of data had been undertaken very early in the vice-monarchy of New Spain, which contained at first all of Mesoamerica (1524 in Michoacán, summary fragments preserved: Warren 1985:73–80, 248–59), there were early examinations in the form of *visitas* between 1547 and 1550, which, however, have not been preserved in full form or have not yet surfaced at all. A summary containing mostly statistical data is called *Suma de visitas de pueblos por orden alfabético* (Paso y Troncoso 1905; evaluation and discussion: Cook and Borah 1960). Local census documents with further remarks are obviously quite rare from the early times in New Spain. Exceptions are the ca. 1540 examination in Nahuatl from the area of Cuernavaca-Tepoztlan (Hinz, Hartau, and Heimann-Koenen 1983; Díaz Cadena 1978; Carrasco P. 1964a), the census of 1553 in Coyoacan (Santillán 1976), and the voluminous 1560 census from the area of Huexotzinco, partly written in hieroglyphs (Prem 1974).

RELACIONES GEOGRÁFICAS ≡ In an attempt by the Spanish Crown to gain more detailed information about numerous features in the newly won areas, questionnaires were developed between 1569 and 1573 and sent to local administrators. They were used also in Spain in 1574 and, starting in 1577, in the American dominions. There were fifty questions posed about geography, climate, fauna, flora, minerals, economy, and history (background and questionnaire are thoroughly discussed by Cline 1972b; 1972c). A large part of the administrative units answered by sending reports of different volume and precision; many are now the only historical statements for their area. A detailed listing of preserved *Relaciones* from Mesoamerica was published by Cline (1972a). The majority of *Relaciones Geográficas* of this area was published by Francisco del Paso y Troncoso (1905). The bibliographical notations of *Relaciones*, which Vargas Rea had imperfectly published, and which Paso y Troncoso had planned to use for volumes 7 and 8 of his series, were put together by Cline (1972c:392). A new publication series has appeared recently (Acuña 1981–88 [the volumes are 1: Guatemala, 2–3: Antequera, 4–5: Tlaxcala, 6–8: México, 9: Michoacan, 10: Nueva Galicia]). The *Relaciones* from Yucatán are published together (Garza et al. 1983). The preserved *Relaciones* from the Andes have been published by Jiménez de la Espada (1881–97). Series of *Relaciones geográficas* from the seventeenth century are not really significant for Precolumbian history.

UNPUBLISHED ADMINISTRATIVE DOCUMENTS ≡ In all Spanish-held areas in the Americas the Colonial administration produced huge numbers of documents, which often allow a quantitative analysis of Colonial conditions. Ethnohistorical inference methods can then contribute to elucidate the pre-European period.

Two classes of data have to be differentiated here: orders of various kinds coming from the king or the viceroy and going to Colonial officials have indirect information contents, insofar as they confirm, modify, or dissolve continuing Indian institutions. They are indirect proof for indigenous, continuing situations, insofar as they turn expressly or implicitly against them (not complete, but the most comprehensive published collection: *Recopilación de Leyes de los Reynos de las Indias* . . . , 4 vols., 1681; facsimile edition: 1973; also, all relevant archives own large numbers of "*Reales Cédulas*"). The fact that many of these orders were rarely or never enforced is not relevant to the suggested examination.

The second class of data is formed by documents that were written in the course of official or semi-official business. Despite the fact that they appear within Colonial judicial forms, they allow the recognition of facts existing since Precolumbian times, or document these facts extensively. Among them are last wills and testaments, where Indian titles, rights, and possessions are passed on, civil trials with single Spaniards or Colonial institutions with the goal to gain back or defend traditional rights or inherited goods, official examinations at the time of land investiture to Spaniards (and Indians!), when conflicts with older rights were researched, applications to be free of tribute duties, where Indian nobles prove their origins, and other categories of documents. They are hardly published at all. Substantial numbers of such documents from former Spanish holdings can also be found in European libraries (Bibliothèque Nationale Paris, Fonds Mexicain) and in the United States.

COLONIAL PICTORIAL MANUSCRIPTS ≡ Documents that were compiled by Indians as a reaction to Colonial conditions and that contain descriptions of Precolumbian circumstances belong in this context as well; they reproduce more or less indigenous pictorial conventions, which are supplemented most of the time by explanatory written texts (examples: *Códice Osuna,* Chávez Orozco 1947; *Codex Mariano Jiménez*: the first part published as *Códice de Otlazpan,* Leander 1967), or form proof as parts of larger document collections. Many of these documents, often cartographic in nature, are published only partially or not at all.

ARCHIVE MATERIAL ≡ Large, often hardly touched numbers of applicable documents are located in numerous local archives in Latin America (especially in notary's archives, the archives of towns, villages, and churches). As a rule the holdings of central archives are more accessible; they are located at the seats of former *Audiencias* (e.g., Mexico: today Archivo General de la Nación; Guatemala: today Archivo General de Centroamérica; Lima: Archivo General de la Nación) and the Indian Archives in Sevilla (Archivo General de Indias), as well as several other archives in Spain. Overviews for the Andes were written by Murra (1981b) and by Fisher (1981).

Of little interest are the church books and papers of Colonial criminal courts, which were begun only toward the end of the sixteenth century. An exception are documents of the relatively rare trials when somebody was accused of Precolumbian religious practices.

EVALUATION OF INDIGENOUS WRITTEN SOURCES

In four areas of Mesoamerica there was a writing system, albeit of different levels of competence, that helped to preserve material of historical significance in amounts worth mentioning. The epigraphic analysis (reading) and interpretation of contents have progressed depending on the preserved corpus and the complexity of the material.

CENTRAL MEXICAN PICTORIAL WRITING ≡ From the Valley of Mexico and neighboring regions no Precolumbian pictorial manuscripts with historical contents have been preserved. Colonial versions show that events were depicted in a form with relatively few conventions, while personal names and dates were recorded by standardized glyphs. Their reading can be viewed as accomplished within a system that cannot guarantee unequivocal limits (Prem 1974, with extensive glossary; 1979b; 1992; Dibble 1971).

MIXTEC PICTORIAL WRITING ≡ Interpretation of the contents of the five preserved Precolumbian Mixtec pictorial manuscripts with historical subjects, and the reading of place and personal names expressed in hieroglyphic writing, are extraordinarily difficult because corresponding information from other sources seems for the most part to be missing. However, Caso (1949) has shown that early Colonial documents do provide assistance in the interpretation of events in past epochs. He has analyzed and presented the contents of these codices in a monumental index (1977–79). Mary E. Smith (1973) also identified and read names of places by mainly using Colonial information. An overview is provided by Jansen (1992).

EPI-OLMEC INSCRIPTIONS ≡ The few known and often short inscriptions found along the southern coast of the Gulf of Mexico and along the Pacific Coast from the Isthmus of Tehuantepec to western El Salvador allow the recognition of a relatively complete writing system, which probably has to be classified as an ancestor to Maya writing. It seems to date to the time around the birth of Christ, if the preserved dates are calculated according to the conventions of the Maya calendar. The recent discovery (under dubious circumstances) of a long inscription (La Mojarra Stela: Winfield Capitaine 1988) and renewed study of the longer-known, small, duck-billed and winged "Tuxtla Statuette" (Méluzin 1987), inscribed on all sides, allowed a still hypothetical reading in an ancient Proto-Zoquean language, which yielded historical information much like the subjects of Maya inscriptions (Justeson and Kaufman 1993; another position is taken by Anderson 1993 in a catalog-type overview).

MAYA INSCRIPTIONS ≡ The reading of Maya hieroglyphic writing, which is very complicated as a system and as graphic designs, started with calendrical parts of the preserved pictorial manuscripts and stone monuments. Reading noncalendrical sections started only with the work of Tatiana Proskouriakoff (1960; less technical summary: 1961) and Berlin (1958; history of decipherment overview: Stuart 1992). Both could prove the historical, genealogical, and local political contents of a series of such inscriptions. They disproved the predominant opinion of the day that contents were mainly chronological, astronomical, and speculative ("I do not believe that historical events are recorded on the monuments," Thompson 1950:64).

Since this breakthrough, research of Maya writing has taken an impressive and ever accelerated turn (history of research up to about 1990: Coe 1992). The decisive factor was that the approach of scholars such as Knorozov (1967) and Kelley (1976), who were regarded as outsiders up to that time, that Maya writing was a combination of syllables and ideograms was accepted and became the basis of analysis (Lounsbury 1973, a treatise far surpassing the subject of the title, and 1984). On this basis it was possible to recognize structures of texts preserved in hieroglyphic writing (Schele 1982, Bricker 1992). The alternate scribal variations by substitution often encountered in the texts allow testing and additions to the corpus of readings. There are now so many decipherments that they can be presented in dictionary form (Kurbjuhn 1989).

The actual state of epigraphic research is subject to constant and fast changes and cannot be discussed here. In particular, the discovery of the genealogical history of a growing number of sites is of historical interest (of a multitude of studies here only some examples: Kelley 1968; Houston and Mathews 1985; Grube 1986; Closs 1984; 1985; 1989). The political structure of the Maya area can be recognized in part (Marcus 1976a, in part out of date; revised: Marcus 1993; Mathews 1985; Johnston 1985). More and more single political or military events can be found in the inscriptions (Riese 1982), as well as other relations between political entities (Schele and Mathews 1991). However, it remains unclear if these statements always reflect real history or represent an "official" declaration intended to raise status (Mathews 1985:52). The evolution of the Maya script can be seen only in fragments (Grube 1990). Its origin is without doubt in the environs of Olmec culture, something that can be supported by linguistic evidence (Justeson et al. 1985).

METHODS OF RECORDING IN THE ANDES ≡ If one disregards the ever repeating attempts to find an undiscovered writing system in graphic designs on textiles or other media, only the knotted strings, *quipu*, represent an actual recording system. They served to record numbers in a decimal system. The numbers were expressed by the number of turns in a knot; the value "0" was an empty space (Locke 1923). Special ties of knotted strings to the main rope designated the strings that expressed (sub)totals. The subject areas could be differentiated only by colors (extensive, mainly descriptive literature, e.g., Radicati di Primeglio, n.d.; mathematical in orientation and constructed as a workbook: Ascher and Ascher 1981). The statement by Colonial authors (Bernabé Cobo 1956) that historical information could be recorded on *quipu* or by *quipu* specialists (Yeakel 1983), regularly finds modern champions, but cannot be supported.

10

General Tendencies of Archaeological Research

Up to the recent past special tendencies in the examination of ancient American cultures cannot be determined. Only the above-mentioned "New Archaeology" has brought a substantial change and caused a turn to model-oriented analyses. The results thus achieved, however, frequently are on a highly abstract level, which hardly offers a point of departure for a simple synthesis.

SUMMARY PRESENTATIONS ≡ This became evident in summary presentations. For the period shortly before the Conquista authors of overviews were satisfied with repeating descriptions of Colonial authors; for the times before that, which provided only archaeological evidence, they extrapolated backwards and otherwise described and grouped the archaeological data. Even in this the majority of books written for a large audience do not reflect the actual state of research; they will not be mentioned here or appear in the bibliography. There are only very few works about all of ancient America where the theoretical discussion and the state of knowledge up to the publication date are aptly covered (Katz 1972; with a strong art-history slant: Willey 1974a; even more outdated: Disselhoff and Linné 1960; far exceeding the restrictions mentioned in the title: Kubler 1984). Recently, several notable summaries were published that deal with Aztec culture in modern monographic form (Townsend 1992; Carrasco P. 1976a [the first edition has many production mistakes; later editions are preferable]; Berdan 1982; León-Portilla 1992; an eclectic view of the Aztecs: Clendinnen 1991; Prem 1996).

THE ANDEAN AREA ≡ The first modern description of the Inca Empire was written by John Rowe (1946). Mason (1957 [revised 1964]) writes in depth, but is somewhat outdated in the unusually voluminous historical area of economic and social organization. An uncritical summary based exclusively on sources without attention to analytical literature is provided by Brundage (1963; book review by R. T. Zuidema 1965; response by Brundage and answer by Zuidema 1966). The most recent overview is by Davies (1995). The other presentations emphasize the account of archaeological insights. The most thorough and constantly revised presentation with huge amounts of detail is by Kauffmann Doig (1983). More concise overviews, which complement each other spatially, are given by Bushnell (1956) and Meggers (1966). Lanning reflects archaeological data of the pre-Inca period (1967).

MESOAMERICA ≡ Marked by the theoretical concept of cultural ecology is Sanders and Price (1968). The overview by Adams (1977) prefers archaeological areas. An up-to-date overview with fifteen richly illustrated single descriptions is provided by Prem and Dyckerhoff (1987). The voluminous, partly outdated, but still often-cited summary by Krickeberg deals only with western Mesoamerica (1956). Summary presentations about eastern Mesoamerica deal mostly with Maya culture and will be quoted in the appropriate place. The same applies to Aztec civilization.

ORIGIN OF INDIANS

IMMIGRATION FROM ASIA ≡ It is uncontested that the inhabitants of the American continents originated from northern Asia, but the dating of their migration across the Bering Strait is controversial. The majority of authors assume that the first groups of people came to Alaska after the beginning of the Wisconsin icing, 70,000 B.C. (Müller-Beck 1966). The very latest findings in the Old Crow basin on the northern Yukon may even indicate that an immigration could have been possible around or after 150,000 B.C. (summary: Irving 1985). People reached more southern parts of North America only considerably later and entered South America well before 10,000 B.C.

TRANSPACIFIC CULTURE CONTACTS ≡ The majority of authors assume a basically independent development of cultures on the American continent. They do not reject the possibility of sporadic contact such as by ships from East Asia wrecked on the American west coast, but think for numerous reasons that these would have no effect on local culture, as evidenced by the irrefutable presence of Vikings on the Atlantic shores of North America (Ingstad 1969).

Contrary to this stance a substantial group of archaeologists believe that many cultural elements and complexes come from Asia. The hypotheses differ much as to time, duration, regional point of origin, and influenced area of supposed contact (Olmecs: Meggers 1975; Ecuador: Estrada and Meggers 1961; single subjects: Marschall 1972; overview presentation: Heine-Geldern 1966; Bosch-Gimpera 1970; Jett 1983; critical overview presentation: Phillips 1966; Davies 1979b; *1986; history of science, especially fantastic-speculative works, treated paradigmatically: Wauchope 1962).

Methodologically, proponents of transpacific culture contact use two main directions in their arguments: conformity is too great to be satisfactorily explained by independent invention, and contacts were technically-logistically possible. Most of the works do not evaluate all solutions to problems ever found in the world (as an indicator of proof of similarity). Faced with the real possibility of ship travel from East Asia to America, one has to ask how often such trips took place and if they were planned, and finally state the complete lack of a single true East Asian import (Caso 1962; *1964; Tolstoy 1974, with commented bibliography; Mundkur 1978; 1979; Prem 1979a).

The idea that all civilizations, including the ones from the New World, originated in Egypt or Babylon has been around since the nineteenth century, but is now only rarely brought up (Heyerdahl 1971).

DEVELOPMENT OF AGRICULTURE

SIGNIFICANCE ≡ In general agriculture is seen as one of the most important prerequisites for the development of hierarchic societies and as the basic economic condition for the formation of the state. Only the growing of food by planting allowed the feeding of a dense, settled population and also made possible the accumulation of surplus.

EARLIEST EVIDENCE ≡ Evidence for the invention of agriculture is difficult to find archaeologically, because the beginnings of the domestication process, artificial propagation of plants by man, cannot be recognized by archaeologically visible morphological changes of plants, especially since the wild forms of the most important American hybrids have not been clearly determined. Also, indirect evidence in the form of special tools is either found for relatively late times, or is not verifiable.

The rise of agriculture in the mountain regions of Mesoamerica and the Andes has been examined by several large projects: in the Tehuacan Valley of central Mexico (summarized with bibliography: MacNeish 1973; 1981), in the Valley of Oaxaca (Flannery 1986; 1968; *1972b), in Ayacucho in the Peruvian highlands (MacNeish 1977), and in the Callejón de Huaylas in northern Peru (Lynch 1980), where it can be recognized in lengthy sequences of evidence that early agriculture was joined to an economy based on hunting and gathering. Some excavation results (Fritz 1994) and the dating of the beginning of agriculture and cultivations (for maize in Mesoamerica: Fritz 1994) are still controversial.

On the desertlike Peruvian coast early agriculture has been present in preceramic levels since at least 3000 B.C. (best known site Huaca Prieta: Bird and Hyslop 1985). For northern Chile and northwestern Argentina very early dates are quoted for the rise of agriculture as well.

MOTIVES FOR AGRICULTURE ≡ At the core of the discussion about the historical reconstruction of the rise of agriculture is the question "why." Hunters and gatherers are optimally adapted to their living conditions. As an explanation for the shift to a more work-intensive and more risky economic system only an enforced situation such as a rise of population numbers or nutrition problems seems to serve. As a trigger two variants have been proposed: local disturbances of a population normally regulated below the capacity of a given area (Bray 1976; Flannery 1968; *1972b), or a continuous global growth of population, which triggered the step toward cultivation simultaneously in many parts of the world (Cohen 1977). The hypothesis of an inherent population growth has been challenged (Hassan 1981). Populations seem rather to grow after cultivation has started (Roosevelt 1984). It seems that domestication started with valued, rare, but not life-supporting plants (Bronson 1977). The ability of early cultivation to alleviate nutritional problems has been doubted, while it is not debated that intensifying existing cultivation will do this. The rejection of global models led to an emphasis on models with regional importance (Flannery 1986). Rindos (1984) developed the new thought that the domestication of plants is a symbiotic interaction between man and plants, not consciously directed by man, which precedes agriculture. Especially the prevailing insight that hunters and gatherers have the technical prerequisites for an agricultural economy, by developing and practicing methods for the care of plant life, should lead in the future to another viewpoint about the rise of agriculture.

TECHNOLOGY

CERAMICS ≡ The development and origin of ceramic manufacture in Mesoamerica and the Andes is not clear; the possibility that it was taken over from another area is discussed in a controversial way. For the Valdivia ceramics from Ecuador a take-over from the Japanese Yomon culture was suggested because of formal similarities (Meggers and Evans 1966). This thesis was shaken by the evidence of older, local ceramics (Bischof 1979; also Lumbreras 1981:133–68; Feldman and Moseley 1983:149–55). Despite the fact that ceramics occur distinctly later in Mesoamerica, archaeological evidence is not sufficient to demonstrate an inner-American spread of ceramic technology (see especially the discussion published with the following article: Paulsen 1977).

METALLURGY ≡ Metals had been prepared and worked in the Andes since the first pre-Christian millennium to make decorative objects, first by hammering and later by casting techniques (Bergsøe 1937; 1938; Lothrop 1951; about smelting techniques based on a three-dimensional depiction in a ceramic bowl: Donnan 1973). In Mesoamerica metalwork appeared only by the end of the Classic, at first in western Mexico. Later, metallurgy remained limited to the manufacture of ornaments in large areas and was never utilized for significant technical purposes. A connection to Andean metal techniques is so far unproven conjecture. The sometimes suggested origin of metallurgy from Asia has to be rejected (Heine-Geldern 1954).

DEVELOPMENT OF EARLY STATES

The impressionistic but yet correct designation of large political units by Spanish conquerors in the central Mexican highlands and the Andes as "states" or "empires" leads to the question: Which time depth can be assumed for this form of political organization in the pertinent areas of the Americas? It is obvious that in this discussion development theories are given special importance. The suggestion by Fried (1967; 1974) to differentiate so-called ranked societies by cultural evolutionary terms such as chiefdoms and stratified pristine states caused a renewed intensity of the discussion about time and reasons for the development of early states (Service 1975; Carneiro 1970): Not only do the natural limits (Carneiro: "circumscription") of living space further the elaboration of political structures as a counter measure, but also restrictions by human neighbors. New data show that the development takes place much faster than assumed by Service and Carneiro, when following times of cyclical conflicts and restricted growth (Wright 1986:358). An overview with a thorough discussion of proposed assertions is given by Haas (1982) and more briefly by Burger (1992:220–27).

The unilinear neo-evolutionistic explanation models for the emergence of complex societies mentioned above are criticized by, among others, Blanton et al. (1996); these authors emphasize the role of individuals and of groups of people who influenced political institutions in a shaping and preserving fashion by their craving for wealth, status, and power. They see two different power strategies at work, one that attempts on one hand to centralize and monopolize power in a small leadership group, and the other that wants to prevent this and settle power in large corporate groups. A visible expression of the latter would be the horizon styles of large parts of Mesoamerica (Olmecs, Teotihuacán, Puebla-Tlaxcala; the change possibly needed for cultural development from local to large-scale integrative phases is emphasized already by Willey [1991]). Apparently the authors realize that they cannot yet prove these contexts.

CHIEFDOMS ≡ The evolutionary level of social order preceding chiefdoms ranked society on the basis of individual achievement; this was replaced in chiefdoms by an inherited division of the whole society into a lower and an upper class. One of the archaeological markers for this are child burials with a noticeable high status, since children could have attained this elevated position only by birth (as long as they were not sacrificed) (Flannery 1972c:403).

The classification of sites in the Andes and in Mesoamerica, from which the Early Horizon emanated, into this category of political systems has been accepted by most modern authors (Olmecs: Sanders and Price 1968:126–28; Chavín: Price 1974:75; Sanders and Webster 1978:288–91; summary: Wright 1977:389–92; Haas 1982:184–208) without expectation of conclusive proof.

EARLY STATES ≡ In a state there is a much diversified and ranked society under a mostly centralized government and with an effective economic structure, which does not necessarily encompass markets. Archaeological evidence for the presence of a state organization are work-intensive "public" constructions (Haas 1982:214–15), especially if they serve obviously to further the personal fame of high-ranking individuals or to demonstrate the power of the state or the state religion, the rise of specialists working only on their own projects (artisans, administrative officials, priests, soldiers, and dependents), which satisfy the needs of the elite and the state's apparatus, as well as human sacrifices in large numbers (Trigger 1971; *1978). Early states recognized in Mesoamerica are the political units of the Maya (without political or economic integration) and Teotihuacán, while in the highlands of Guatemala a secondary development of a state supposedly occurred through the influence of Teotihuacán (Sanders and Webster 1978:284–97). In the Andes the level of state organization is first assumed for Tiahuanaco and Huari according to prevailing opinion. The classification is naturally dependent on applied criteria for "state," as well as on the interpretation of archaeological data; therefore it is by no means of one accord.

REASONS ≡ The search for mechanisms that effected the transition from chiefdom to state (prime mover) has a long tradition (overview with discussion: Flannery 1972c:405–21). Which main factors are seen as decisive depends to a large extent on the point in time during a per se continuous evolutionary process of change when one is willing to call a political unit a state (pointedly: "what you look for is what you get," Webb 1987:162). If one disregards the fact that the state has also been called (at least in the beginning) a side issue of a general evolution pressure in the direction of centralization (Cohen 1981:122), the criteria listed below are seen as especially significant for the cultures of ancient America (a critically considered evaluation of proposed models by special consideration of the Maya is provided by Demarest 1992).

POPULATION PRESSURE ≡ If a population subjected to area limitations (caused by the environment or other people) grows beyond a certain threshold, the inescapable dispute about diminishing resources necessitates an ordering state organization. However, archaeology cannot regularly demonstrate the parallel between a rise in population and a resulting complex political-administrative structure demanded in theory.

WAR ≡ On the basis of the classic thesis by Spencer (1880–96) that war has a decisive evolutionary significance, Carneiro (1970) developed a modern version, influenced by the situation prevailing in Peruvian coastal valleys. Extensive examinations of settlements have modified this precept to include the thought that disputes with neighbors from farther distances (other valleys) constituted an essential trigger (Wilson 1983). A necessary restructuring of agricultural use due to military preparations against invasion attempts caused a concentration of power in the hands of a few (Lerche 1986). However, according to Carneiro (1981:63), military disputes had the decisive role not only in the formation of states, but also in the formation of chiefdoms. Impressed by the discovery of early defensive constructions, this thesis was applied to Maya culture, which no longer can be viewed as extremely peaceful (Webster 1977). The thesis also is supposed to be valid for the expansion of Huari, provided that trade is included (Webb 1975).

TRADE ≡ The necessity of acquiring lacking but indispensable raw materials through supraregional trade is also thought to have led to the rise of state institutions to organize such trade and distribute the goods (core-periphery model for the rise of classic Maya culture: Rathje 1972). However, this thesis cannot explain the formation of states in areas with sufficient raw materials.

SMALL-SCALE DIVERSITY ≡ Sanders (1956) departs from the central significance of small-scale diversity of the environment in close, neighboring (vertically staggered) zones of natural resources. Given these conditions, a network of regional exchange relationships was developed, while in the lowlands the uniformity of natural conditions acted as an obstruction (Sanders and Price 1968). Sanders (1977a) counters a possible argument that states can be found early also in the lowlands with the evidence that the lowlands in the interior of the Yucatán Pensinsula contain unexpectedly severe ecological differences, which probably influenced cultural changes.

HYDRAULIC MEASURES ≡ The assumption that the need for regional hydraulic measures for a more intense usage of land or as protection against floods generated a centralized political power was advocated for ancient American cultures in a very dogmatic fashion by Wittfogel (1972, instead of his main work, which refers to ancient America only in passing). The decisive significance of agriculture with irrigation is stressed by Sanders (1968) for Teotihuacán. Contrary to this theoretical viewpoint the archaeologically discovered and dated irrigation systems in Mesoamerica are limited to a small area between the Valley of Mexico and the Valley of Oaxaca (Woodbury and Neely 1972; O'Brien et al. 1980; Nichols 1982; Fowler 1968). Especially at Teotihuacán, where the explanatory model of hydraulic activity has been used many times, no early irrigation has been discovered. Other archaeologists turned against this simplified model with local discoveries and other models thought to provide a better explanation (Peru, Lurin valley in the Early Intermediate period: Earle 1972; Teotihuacán: Kurtz 1987).

RELIGION ≡ The undoubtedly strong religious component of early states (and chiefdoms) in Mesoamerica and in the Andes led more and more to a rejection of the assumption of the strictly material bases for the development of states and the adoption of ideological factors in the broadest sense (Keatinge 1981; Coe 1981a). As is really not remarkable, the incredible achievements of early cities were due not to force but to a successfully implanted conviction (Kurtz and Nunley 1993; the hermeneutic interpretation of archaeological evidence as texts seems to be exaggerated).

Overall, the weakness of the cited explanatory attempts is that they are concentrated on one decisive trigger. Instead, more complex causal contexts should be considered, where ideological (ethnic and religious) elements as well as material ones have their place (excellent theoretical discussion: Flannery 1972c; see also Hole 1983:13).

MULTILINEARITY ≡ A basic difference of opinion about the evolutionary process of the origin of the state exists between the assumption that a development exists where by necessity all stages are passed even if not at the same speed (unilinearity), and the assumption of different sequential patterns (multilinearity). Which of the competing patterns occurs is supposed to be determined by external factors such as climatic risks and degrees of difference in soil composition, which affect plant cultivation (Sanders and Webster 1978: 277–83).

LATER STATES ≡ While the attention of scholars was focused so intensely on the origin of a state in one cultural space, the secondary formation of state organization received little attention. It is obvious that societies below the integration-level "state" react to the political-military pressure of neighboring states by adopting the successful organizational forms. It is more difficult to explain the repeated formation of states without such an external stimulus. Brumfiel (1983) designed a differentiated step model for the Aztec Triple Alliance. A first phase of stepped-up military disputes between small political units, which led to the formation of the Triple Alliance, was followed by political restructurings that strengthened the central political and economic position of Tenochtitlán; the increase of power by access to and use of work forces for public construction was followed by the formation of a complex and specialized bureaucracy only a relatively short time before the Conquista. This sequence is at least partially supported by the written sources.

When authors such as Rounds (1979) see the development of the Aztec state as an example of the development of political organization on the state level, this can be proven true only with reservations. It is not considered properly that this is just the last in a series of state formations in Mesoamerica, which took place in a politically and historically prepared environment. The states surrounding the Mexica on the mainland all had a ranked society at that time, and at the latest since Teotihuacán the Mexican highlands knew complex, centralized states, summarized in the sources by the name of Tollan. The question of whether the Aztecs could have escaped this development in the first place has never been posed.

DEVELOPMENT OF CITIES

The development of settlements into cities is seen as dependent on the development of the state and as happening simultaneously. For the Andes it is not yet decided if there were cities in the Early Intermediate period (Nazca) or if they can be securely confirmed only later with the expansion of Huari and Tiahuanaco (Schaedel 1978c:39–42). The discussion concerning the city in Latin America up to the present has been conducted at a series of voluminous symposia, starting with the International Americanist Congress 1966 in Mar del Plata (a selection of the most important contributions is contained in Schaedel 1978c). Older overviews, mostly descriptive in character, are therefore outdated (for instance: Hardoy 1973 [revised translation of 1964]).

11

Central Problems of Historical Research

CHRONOLOGY AND CALENDARS

In ancient America contemporary historical chronicles were not prepared; at least none have been preserved. The available indigenous descriptions are all retrospective and often lack a dependable chronological framework, so that the events that are related "swim" in a hardly structured temporal depth. The establishment of a relative, and hopefully of an absolute, chronology therefore is a prerequisite of a dependable historical reconstruction. It needs an analysis of indigenous time-counting systems.

INDIGENOUS CHRONOLOGY ≡ The investigation of indigenous calendars in ancient America is confronted by two problems. The statements of Colonial authors have to be treated with skepticism, because their understanding of the complex matter of both the European and the divers indigenous calendars is often inadequate. Moreover, Colonial descriptions of indigenous calendars are often mingled with attempts of reform and adaptation if not amalgamation of Indian and European calendars. This is particularly obvious when it comes to the complex calendars of Mesoamerica (Prem 1983).

Several misjudgments about indigenous calendars exist in modern scholarly literature as well. So as a reason for the assumption that it was essential for determining planting times it has been said that a society based on an agricultural economy urgently needed an exact solar calendar (compare: Valcárcel 1946:471). In reality, numerous climatic and botanical indicators are observed in such societies, allowing a much better adaptation to the conditions, which change slightly from year to year, rather than adherence to a fixed calendar.

CENTRAL MEXICO ≡ The complete structural unity of the calendar in central Mexico and the meaning of the glyphs for the ritual calendar have been established (detailed summary: Tena 1992); however, for historical chronology the important question is discussed, whether regional calendar styles, while calling years by the same name, have shifted against each other (Caso 1967), which would explain contradictory date notations of the indigenous historical tradition (Jiménez Moreno 1958; Kirchhoff 1954; skeptical: Prem 1983). Based on ambivalent statements and nonauthentic calendar tables by Colonial authors, the often-voiced assertion that the Indian year had a leap similar to that of the Julian year cannot be maintained (the latest: Castillo Farreras 1971).

MAYA ≡ The basic principles of the calendar used by the Classic Maya and the hieroglyphs employed to fix it in writing have been understood since the end of the nineteenth century and have been described repeatedly (Morley 1915). The correlation with the European calendar has been controversial for a long time. Following the conversion by Spinden (1924), favored at first, the Classic would have ended around A.D. 650, which means that the time span up to the advent of the Europeans would be too long. An end of the Classic around A.D. 900 would coincide better with the Colonial sources and archaeological evidence and is supplied by Thompson's (1950, among others) equation, the one most recognized today, even if his deductions are not considered above reproach. This equation is also supported by an astronomical control of planetary dates in a Maya pictorial manuscript (Lounsbury 1992). The latest demands by archaeologists for an even later correlation (which would place the end of the Classic at A.D. 1150) have not yet led to an exact alternative, acceptable in terms of the sources (Chase 1985).

MIXTECS ≡ The few Precolumbian pictorial manuscripts from the Mixtec area contain both historical and nonhistorical matters. The chronological scale is predetermined by the endlessly revolving calendar cycles, which can be distinguished from each other only by the relative sequence in the manuscript. The nonhistorical descriptions, taking place in mythical times, elucidate the metaphorical function of some highlighted dates, which may exist as well in the historical sections (Furst 1978b), and could put into perspective some common interpretations that assume that these sections contain references exclusively oriented toward reality.

ANDES ≡ The superficial statements of Colonial authors, who hardly wrote down more than the names of Indian months and their approximate correspondence to Christian ones, and who had no tolerance for the mechanics of the indigenous calendar, are the reason for contradictory modern statements about the calendar of the Inca Empire. It is particularly nebulous how many lunar elements had been built into the solar calendar (Zuidema 1987:17; see Rostworowski de Diez Canseco 1953:220–28; the following summary contains mistakes: Valcárcel 1946). Contrary to the most often voiced opinion, Zuidema (1966) speaks of solar months. Bauer and Dearborn (1995:59–66) assume that a solar calendar was developed only in later times (and only in Cuzco), in addition to the generally used simple lunar calendar.

Archaeoastronomical measurements seem to confirm sources (Juan Polo de Ondegardo 1916b) that place the beginning of the year on the last new moon before the summer solstice (June 21). With the help of *ceque* lines Zuidema (1966; 1977b; *1980) was the first to examine, he attempted to elucidate this, but his results are not convincing. The categories of months with different lengths he postulated remain speculation. Despite different opinions about the yearly calendar, the existence of a counting of many years or another chronological system beyond the course of one year has not been stated anywhere.

INTERPRETATION OF INDIGENOUS TRADITIONS

SOURCES OF MISTAKES ≡ The 52-year cycle (Nahuatl *xiuhmolpilli*) is the ordering principle of source reports of indigenous traditions in central Mexico and Oaxaca. Individual years were differentiated from each other by a corresponding number of successive year names. Since the sequence of year names could be easily derived from the mechanics of the calendar, a basically functioning dating method existed for shorter time spans; however, it cannot be determined to which of the ever repeating cycles a specific date has to be assigned.

Despite the impression of a chronicle caused by date statements in which an author writes down directly the events of his present time, the preserved form of sources is the result of later compilations of statement units, whose closeness to reported events remains as undefined as the number, size, and background of the compilations and revisions. Since year names returned in identical form after a cycle was completed, Indian chroniclers and advisors were unable to assign isolated dates and associated events clearly to a specific cycle and therefore to an absolute date. Without additional ordering information unintentional distortions, even reversal of a temporal sequence, could hardly be prevented (Prem 1984b); however, this could be shown up so far only for a few events, for instance the earliest parts of the dynastic sequence of Tollan and Colhuacan (Davies 1977, especially pp. 441–51; Prem 1984a).

COMPETING CALENDAR STYLES ≡ An additional reason for distortions of calendric structures could be similar year name sequences that are shifted against each other, since in the sources the same events are often recorded as taking place in different years. Finally, it has been assumed that a reason for inconsistent dates can be the reduction of a lengthy procedure to a specific time slot in the sources (contrary to a technical-calendric explanation of the same process: Kirchhoff 1950). An extreme position has been taken by Edmonson (1988), who proceeds from a much larger number of calendars shifted against each other; some of his data are based on questionable evidence. He reconstructs hypothetical calendars back to Olmec times.

CHRONOLOGICAL CONCORDANCE ≡ In the meantime, the concordance of the year designation used by the Aztecs at the time of the Spanish conquest with the European year count is established securely: the Indian year *1 Acatl* corresponds to the European year 1519 (except for a shift of several weeks caused by the different beginnings of each of the years). A day concordance is accepted generally as well (thorough discussion: Caso 1967; Prem 1983:147–59).

MIXTEC YEAR COUNT ≡ Jiménez Moreno (1940) has proposed a formula for the Mixtec year count that equates a year *1 Acatl* with 1507. So far, this has not been thoroughly tested. There is another reason why the correlation of early dates of Mixtec pictorial manuscripts with the European calendar has not been securely established. While Caso (1977–79:181) sees the earliest discernible date (the birth of a noble lady) as corresponding to A.D. 692, other authors feel that the points of departure should be moved as many as three calendar cycles (156 years) forward (E. Rabin, Some problems of Chronology in the Mixtec historical manuscripts. Unpublished lecture, México 1974). Furst (1978a:69) has pointed out the problems associated with the often attempted date correlation of mythical sections in the reports.

INDIGENOUS VIEW OF HISTORY ≡ It is generally assumed that ancient American cultures saw time in cycles. This is clearly the case in the Colonial Chilam Balam books from Yucatán, where events, whether political or natural, "lose much of their specificity and become types of human experience" (Farriss 1987:577). Something that happened once at a specific moment of the repeating time scale will happen again when the same cycle date returns. In other cultures of ancient America the inevitability of these repetitions is less clearly expressed or recognizable. Things are made more difficult by the fact that indigenous history concepts were all passed through the filter of the European Christian world view, since almost all texts were written under that influence (Salomon 1982; Eschmann 1976:39–49). Past events, when they return, offer assistance for orientation, understanding, and behavior. However, this does not mean that contradictory source statements can be disregarded, and that descriptions can be labeled generally as mythical, and therefore a historical chronology lacks relevance (Pease G. Y. 1978). Simplifications of the time scale in Aztec sources seem to be historical-interpretative and not prognostic: specific types of important events seem to be assigned to special dates—whether by manipulation of the events themselves, or by mechanical adaptation of the reports cannot be decided (Gillespie 1989). A linear concept of time was developed by the Classic Maya and expressed both by events placed far beyond the longest cycles in the past (the origin of ruling dynasties) and by a purely linear time recording system (long count) (Farriss 1987).

POPULATION FIGURES

Eyewitness reports of the Conquista offer only very rough estimates of the density of the population that was encountered; large areas were not even considered. The population numbers at that time can only be estimated. As a point of departure the earliest dependable figures from Colonial times are used. The population numbers at the time of the Conquista rise as research progresses. In examinations around 1940 low figures were assumed (central Andes: 6 million [Rowe 1946:184]; central Mexico from the Gulf to the Pacific Coast: more than 2.5 million [Cook 1947:49]), while later examinations arrive at much higher numbers (central Andes: 30–37 million [Dobyns 1966:415]; central Mexico: 25–27 million [Borah and Cook 1963:88; Cook and Borah 1971:115; critical and in turn controversial discussion: Sanders 1976]). Later estimates view these figures with skepticism, but are quite different from each other (central Andes: 12 million [Smith 1970:459–60]; 9 million [Cook 1981:108–14]) or incredibly low (2–3 million [Shea 1976:174]; central Mexico: 5–10 million [Zambardino 1980:25]). The methodological problems allow the recognition of a controversy about the value of estimates from the contact period in Mexico (Henige 1992, while Dobyns [1993] is opposed; continuously critical: Smith 1994). Population numbers for the old culture areas of the Americas are an important argument in the discussion of food supply, of pressures in overpopulated areas leading to expansion, of inner stability—all factors that are regarded as instigating or furthering numerous historical processes.

12

Mesoamerican Cultures in Archaeology

THE PRECLASSIC

OLMECS ≡ Only two—probably the largest and most important—Preclassic centers of the Olmec core area at the Gulf Coast in southeastern Veracruz have been excavated, and that with different intensity: La Venta by Drucker, Heizer, and Squier (1959) and San Lorenzo Tenochtitlán by Coe and Diehl (1980; short summary: Coe 1981b).

CHRONOLOGY ≡ The chronological position of Olmec culture, controversial for a long time, has been determined by radiocarbon dating first at La Venta and then at San Lorenzo Tenochtitlán (Coe 1981b:122; Rust III 1992). The sensational recovery of the second fragment of Tres Zapotes Stela C ended the dispute about the reading of the date, at first hypothetically completed (by using Maya mathematics: 31 B.C.), and attributed the stela to a later offshoot of Olmec culture.

Knowledge of Olmec culture so far has been gained mainly by analyzing the style of monuments, which established chronological sequences, areas of contents (Clewlow, Jr., et al. 1967; Clewlow, Jr., 1974; Milbrath 1979), and iconographic interpretations of the depictions. How the ethnohistorical method of "upstreaming," which extrapolates from known periods to earlier ones, is able to result in dependable work, is an open question (Nicholson 1987a, vol.7:21–22).

RELIGIOUS CONCEPTS ≡ Especially the dominant role of the jaguar, the largest feline of the Americas, has triggered thoughts that depictions of jaguar-man composites refer to shamans (based on ethnographic analogies: Furst 1968). Attempts to find deities known from the Postclassic in Olmec depictions have to appear doubtful (Joralemon 1971; jaguar as Tezcatlipoca: Coe 1972) as well as the analogous interpretation based on modern ethnographic evidence (Köhler 1985). Despite several suggestions, the intentional and partially quite elaborate mutilation of sculptures has remained without explanation (Grove 1981).

TECHNOLOGY ≡ Proven technical achievements of the Olmecs are not confined to exquisite stone sculpting and the transport of tons of monolithic basalt blocks by land and by sea over substantial distances, but also encompass difficult production methods such as concave mirrors made of hematite (Heizer and Gullberg 1981; Carlson 1981), which were worn by officials around the neck (as one can see in depictions). Their optical properties allow the starting of a fire, but also have other effects. The interpretation of an object as a compass has been attempted (Carlson 1975).

OLMECS IN GUERRERO ≡ In the area of the southern slope of the central Mexican highlands (modern state of Guerrero), monuments were found of such a close stylistic resemblance to the ones on the Gulf Coast that one can speak of a second Olmec culture area (prescient: Covarrubias 1961:123). While the rock carvings at Chalcatzingo and the cave paintings of Oxtotitlán have been known for some time (Gay 1971; Grove 1970), stone buildings were uncovered in 1983 in Tlacozotitlan on the Río Balsas that in many details are reminiscent of San Lorenzo (Martínez Donjuán 1986). Lately several similar sites have been discovered.

The results of recent examinations seem to make the available summaries about the Olmecs somewhat redundant (Piña Chan, Covarrubias, and Covarrubias 1964; Coe 1965, mainly describing Olmec influence in the valleys of Mexico and Puebla; Bernal 1968; *1969, establishing the circumference of Olmec culture indefensibly wide; also in a similar vein, Soustelle 1979, who apparently requires another calculation mode for inscriptions with dates).

OLMEC PERIPHERY ≡ The Olmec periphery does not yet present a complete picture. Along the Pacific Coast from Tehuantepec to northern El Salvador there are sites that belong to the Olmec periphery according to the style of their monuments (Parsons 1981). A few readable inscriptions in stone with dates of 35 B.C. (Chiapa de Corzo, Stela 5) and A.D. 103 (Abaj Takalik, Stela 5) (Graham, Heizer, and Shook 1978) assign this complex to the late Preclassic and the transition period to the Classic. For the Olmecs there is a monument index available (Fuente 1973) as well as a voluminous bibliography up to 1978 (Gutiérrez Solana and Schávelzon 1980).

MAYA ≡ Modern research into the Preclassic and Protoclassic on the Yucatán Peninsula takes place almost exclusively in Belize for reasons of research policy. The existence of a ceramic-producing population before 2000 B.C., which had been assumed at first, had to be revised (Hammond 1977; Hammond and Miksicek 1981; Hammond 1980). The earliest cultural period defined by ceramics in Belize is of the same time as others farther inland (Andrews V 1990; Andrews V and Hammond 1990). However, the settlements spread from the coasts and neighboring lowlands along rivers and lakes to the interior (Puleston and Puleston 1974, in part redundant because of new excavations; Rice 1976). In the Late Preclassic important centers arose both near the coast and in the interior with complex systems to intensify plant yields (Scarborough 1983), and with a sumptuous ceremonial architecture on a grand scale. One of the most remarkable features of Late Preclassic and Early Classic architecture are monumental stucco relief masks on pyramids, until recently known only from Uaxactun. They are discussed at length by Freidel (1981:205–23), on the basis of his excavations at Cerros. The existence of fortifications is proof of a time of substantial strife (Becan: Webster 1976; Muralla de León: Rice and Rice 1981; and a growing number of other sites).

THE CLASSIC IN WESTERN MESOAMERICA

The majority of modern authors recognize the supraregional, dominant cultures of the Classic in Mesoamerica and of the Middle Horizon in the Andes as states in the sense described above.

TEOTIHUACÁN ≡ The huge pyramids of Teotihuacán near the Valley of Mexico commanded attention even in Precolumbian times; they were excavated and consolidated as early as 1906 by Leopoldo Batres. Since then excavations have been conducted off and on at Teotihuacán, although there is a strong emphasis on exposure and restoration for tourists. Focus of examinations was the north-south axis (*miccaotli*) and adjoining building complexes, the ciudadela, and a few outlying living quarters. Reports have been published on only a few of these excavations (Acosta 1964). The most important information comes from the Teotihuacán Mapping Project, a very detailed surface survey encompassing more than thirty square kilometers (Millon 1973), which formed the basis for most of the analyses and interpretations accepted today. The state of research until ca. 1979 was summarized by Millon (1981, with an extensive bibliography; somewhat more current and incorporating the area of influence of Teotihuacán: Millon 1988). Later excavations (Report Volume: Cabrera Castro, Rodríguez G., and Morelos G. 1982) have shown the general correctness of the surface survey interpretations, but naturally numerous points of imprecision and mistakes have been revealed (Cabrera Castro 1986:127–46), which suggest that survey results should be evaluated with care.

DATING ≡ A precise temporal positioning of the phases of Teotihuacán is still a problem. A good dozen radiocarbon dates from the area of the north-south axis yield unrealistically early values (around A.D. 200) for stylistically late buildings; it has been suggested that beams of older structures sometimes were reused. Samples from other parts of the site are dated between A.D. 290 and 700 (Millon 1973:60–61). The earlier interpretation that the ceremonial center was in ruins long before the rest of the site is no longer upheld. The continuation of Teotihuacán to the sixth century at least is also derived from ties to Maya culture, which has absolute dates. The contradiction inherent in the radiocarbon dates of the ceremonial center has not yet been resolved.

Chronological discrepancies are also apparent in connection with the living quarters of people from Oaxaca. Monte Albán ceramics found there (transition of Monte Albán II to IIIa) date from A.D. 150 to 250 (Paddock 1983a), but according to the strata they belong to a Teotihuacán sequence beginning at A.D. 400 (Millon 1973:41). Spence (1992:79) explains the temporal discrepancy by suggesting that an anachronistic home culture was "frozen" for a lengthy time due to an enclave situation.

CITY PLAN ≡ More and more an ideological reason is assumed for the founding of Teotihuacán. The cave under the Pyramid of the Sun, used for ritual activities, is accorded special importance (Heyden 1975; Millon 1992:382–90 with daring conclusions). The grid underlying all city structures deviates by 15 ½ degrees to the right of the world directions. This orientation is often seen as astronomically determined (Chiu and Morrison 1980, sunset on August 12, also on April 29, distance 260 days equals 1 *tonalpohualli*), which cannot be proved; the orientation of the city can be explained as well by a sightline from the Pyramid of the Sun to the summit of Cerro Gordo, a mountain dominating the valley. Numerous circles incised in the stucco floors of buildings and plazas may have been used for measuring, but they were also found outside of Teotihuacán (Aveni 1978).

ARCHITECTURE ≡ The characteristic feature of Teotihuacán's architecture is facades designed with the so-called *tablero-talud*, a boxlike protuberant upright area with a sunken, often painted inner square above a slant going up and inward. The *tablero-talud* is quite widespread in the Mesoamerican Classic and should not be regarded as an indicator of domination by Teotihuacán outright. In fact, it is possible that it has its origin elsewhere (García Cook 1981:254) and has become a general stylistic tool. The murals of Teotihuacán, dominated by extremely conventionalized depictions of officials and jaguars with obviously symbolic functions (Miller 1973), show how the ruling class wanted to be perceived. The lack of clear indicators of individuality, status differences, or subordination was taken as evidence for a hardly developed centralization of the rulership (Cowgill 1992). Reconstruction of a religious system based on depictions in the murals cannot be supported (summary: Heyden 1987).

POPULATION NUMBERS ≡ Millon (1973:45) estimated the population to have numbered at least 75,000 and more likely 125,000, based on the presumed number of sleeping quarters within the constructed space, and then raised his figure freely to 200,000. A more realistic figure is probably between the two high numbers (Prem 1977). Scattered around the valley there may have been an additional population numbering about 10 percent of the inhabitants of the city.

PROVISIONS ≡ Even if area yields of today are assumed, the valley of Teotihuacán was not able to support a city of this size. For an estimated 30 to 50 percent of the inhabitants food had to be brought in from neighboring valleys (Valley of Mexico, southern valley of Pachuca). Year-round artificial irrigation in a part of the valley could not substantially raise the yields. Climatic conditions always presented the danger of frosts or droughts, which further diminished the securing of provisions (Prem 1977).

ECONOMIC BASE ≡ For a long time the dominant estimation of Teotihuacán was that it must have been a mainly theocratically governed center with religious functions. That had to be revised after its economic importance was discovered. The mining of obsidian in the valley, and after that was exhausted in the Pachuca area, had to be organized by the state, as well as its manufacture on a large scale (Spence 1984; 1981); however, the part of the population involved in obsidian manufacture is controversial. To supply Teotihuacán with obsidian products ten artisans would have sufficed. The problem here is the interpretation of surface finds. The largest part of obsidian found in areas called "workshops" does not consist of manufacture debris, but of used objects (Clark 1986). Luxury items needed in substantial amounts were cinnabar for the paint used on walls of ceremonial structures, as well as turquoise and turquoise-like materials for the decoration of ceremonial objects. Since the beginning of the Classic this material had been brought from the area of today's New Mexico, at least part of it in the form of expeditions. Chalchihuites (Zacatecas) was the most important base on this road and by itself a mining site (Weigand, Harbottle, and Sayre 1977). The fortress La Quemada, situated closer to central Mexico, may date from the same period (Nelson 1990; Trombold 1990), which contradicts the common assignment, based on architectural elements, to the early Postclassic and thus precludes a suggested connection with Tula on one hand and with the Chaco Canyon in New Mexico on the other.

Kurtz (1987) recognizes the ability of Teotihuacán to generate work in production and distribution of goods as the decisive factor in population density and the formation of the state at Teotihuacán, contrary to ecologically determined models.

WRITING ≡ The amazing lack of writing in the archaeological evidence of Teotihuacán has furthered the search for so far unrecognized forms of a notation system in the rich iconography (voluminous documentation: Winning 1987). Caso (1967:143–63) thought he saw a system limited to calendric information based on very few and often dubious examples. Other approaches as well (readable texts: Barthel 1982) have not been accepted generally so far, or limit themselves by speaking of rudimentary forms of graphic notations (Langley 1986). It is important to recognize that, contrary to old-world examples, the existence of a developed writing system is by no means necessary for the functioning of an administration in an urban state system.

DECLINE OF TEOTIHUACÁN ≡ Archaeological evidence allows the recognition of large-scale destruction mainly by fires in the center of Teotihuacán. Although Millon (1988) assumes that the city's inhabitants caused the fires in a tremendous rebellion, there has been no indubitable proof for that. After a brief break (less than fifty years) there was a resettlement of marginal parts of the city, but no continuation of the cultural tradition. The induced decline lasted for quite some time (Diehl 1989). Multiple reasons are given for the ruination of the city. The suggested dependency of the city on the function of the wide-flung trade network controlled by the state is supposed to have been its weakness. Teotihuacán could not survive the formation of competing trade centers during the middle of the Classic (Santley 1984:80–85).

MONTE ALBÁN ≡ Monte Albán, situated southwest of the capital of the modern state of Oaxaca, is one of the few Precolumbian sites that not only was excavated at the core but also was surveyed all around. The results, therefore, are relatively dependable (Blanton 1978). The cultural phase Monte Albán II (ca. 100 B.C. to A.D. 200), which cannot be identified with an ethnically known population, is called an early state (Flannery and Marcus 1983a:80). The reasons for creating the center in that place (at the intersection of three hypothetical confederate political units) seem to have been purely political, since the hill, rising four hundred meters above the valley floor, shows substantial disadvantages of location.

ECONOMIC BASE ≡ Only a minute part of the provisions for the population of Monte Albán could be grown on the slopes of the hill, even with partial irrigation (O'Brien et al. 1980). Irrigation by various methods was and is employed on the floor of the Valley of Oaxaca, and it is examined intensively in the light of its importance for the development of political systems according to the above-mentioned thesis of Wittfogel (Hopkins III 1984; Kirkby 1973).

EXPANSION ≡ Signs of the expansive character of the confederation of Monte Albán may be contained in the stone slabs of structure J at Monte Albán, which are covered with often brief hieroglyphic inscriptions, most of the time interpreted as victory announcements (Marcus 1983a; Whittaker 1982). The importance of war at the creation of early states in Carneiro's (1970) thesis, and that of others, lends central significance to these inscriptions. Redmond (1983) and Spencer (1982) assume a military expansion beyond the Valley of Oaxaca into the southern Tehuacan Valley. The Zapotec militarism that can be recognized in the sources of the sixteenth century (including institutional details of the Postclassic from other regions) is here transposed to a period one and a half millennia earlier and used for interpretations (persons in jaguar clothes are supposedly Zapotec warriors belonging to a jaguar order). The expansion of the agricultural potential in the conquered Cuicatlán Valley beyond the needs of the local population is thought to indicate a tribute duty, which cannot be proven by the presence of imported goods at Monte Albán. However, a construction of fortifications in a border zone is directly recognizable in an examined region of the valley facing away from Monte Albán.

CONTACTS WITH TEOTIHUACÁN ≡ The contacts between the center of Monte Albán and the metropolis Teotihuacán, which determined the Classic, can be recognized in both places. In Teotihuacán there was a colony from Oaxaca (see above), while on monuments at Monte Albán possibly a delegation from Teotihuacán is depicted (Marcus 1983). Contrary to earlier research, which deduced a dominance of Teotihuacán through a variant of the *tablero-talud* design on the facades of Monte Albán, today the differences between the two sites are emphasized (Flannery and Marcus 1983b, and other contributions in the anthology).

REMOTE ZONES OF TEOTIHUACÁN INFLUENCE ≡ The influence of Teotihuacán in the form of stylistic elements and customs, as can be determined in many regions with varying intensity, has been examined as to its nature in only a few cases. In Kaminaljuyú in the highlands of Guatemala there was an obviously small group, at the outskirts of the site, that could not prevail in all of their own cultural practices (such as burial customs). Sanders (1977b) is of the opinion that there were men from Teotihuacán who married into the local upper class and slowly adopted Maya customs. The lack of evidence for an intrusion by force allows the conclusion that a peacefully introduced colony in the port of trade Kaminaljuyú was present; its influence could be successfully curbed by political measures (Michels 1977).

A particularly strong and direct presence of Teotihuacán, probably even in the form of an enclave, has been shown to have existed at Matacapan in the volcanic region of Santiago Tuxtla (Veracruz). The close relationship is expressed not only by the characteristic facade design of *tablero-talud*, known for some time now, but also by numerous ceramic types of ritual significance, by burials under living quarters, and finally by the identical craft specialization in obsidian working and ceramics. As a motif for the existence of this outpost it has been suggested that raw materials (volcanic stones, kaolin) needed to be protected (Santley, Ortiz Ceballos, and Pool 1987).

PERIPHERY OF TEOTIHUACÁN ≡ The florescence of several sites in the periphery has been dated to the late period of Teotihuacán and to the first two centuries after its decline. The most important of these are Xochicalco, situated on the southern incline of the central Mexican highlands, a place with extensive ceremonial architecture and large palace-like living compounds, fortified by walls and citadels (Litvak King 1974), and Cacaxtla, also fortified, in the northwestern part of the Valley of Puebla. In both places there are growing indications of a cultural tie to the Classic Maya culture, at least to the western border areas. They were suggested for the relief depictions at Xochicalco long ago, but can no longer be rejected since the discovery of large murals at Cacaxtla (Kubler 1980). The temporal placement of these indicators (Cacaxtla A.D. 700–850 [López de Molina 1981:173]) is still a problem.

THE CLASSIC MAYA CULTURE

The fascinating culture of the Classic Maya has challenged numerous authors since it became known through the reports by the North American traveler John L. Stephens (1841; 1843). Due to the rapid developments in decipherment and large archaeological projects, the older standard works reflect not at all, or only in revised form, the current status of knowledge. Topical summaries are often coined by the oppositions of research, which is still in flux (Schele and Freidel 1990). The most current summaries can be found best in anthologies with contributions by numerous authors on one broadly treated subject.

FACTORS OF THE RISE ≡ The question of the reason for the rise of Maya culture in the Classic in the ecologically far from advantageous center of the Yucatán Peninsula crosses with the theoretical discussion about the rise of early states (see above). The explanations proposed for the Maya have to be seen against this background.

IMMIGRATION OR STIMULUS ≡ Ceramic evidence is cited as evidence of a population influx from the Gulf Coast or the highlands of El Salvador and Guatemala, possibly in connection with the eruption of the volcano Ilopango (Sheets 1976; Gifford 1976), an influx that induced development and acted as a cultural stimulus. Opposed to this is the notion that there was an independent development based on the Yucatecan Preclassic (Hammond 1977; Willey 1977).

MODELS ≡ Singular factors or several connected ones have been made responsible for the cultural development in the Classic. Based on his examinations of the fortification at Becan, Webster (1977) saw a decisive reason in the wars about land, caused by a rise in population numbers; the victorious group then was obliged to build up its military and political organizations. Frequency and importance of war in the early Classic has been doubted, since there are few fortified areas and depictions of warlike subjects, compared to the Late Classic (Dillon 1982; Demarest 1978). Contrary to the war thesis, which is derived from Carneiro (see above), Rathje (1971; 1972) saw a driving force in the attempts by the core area around Tikal to obtain missing materials, such as volcanic stone for *metates*, obsidian for knives, and salt, by long-range trading systems, whose organization furthered the formation of state institutions. Exchange trade goods should be independent of natural prerequisites: luxury ceramics and whole complexes of religious paraphernalia for elaborate rituals. The surrounding zone, which was closer to the raw materials ("buffer zone"), would not have needed the expenditure, and therefore did not experience this developmental thrust. This thesis was criticized by pointing out that suitable materials were indeed present in the core area and were used there, and that long before a complex organization developed, obsidian and other raw materials could be obtained by long-range trade (Hammond 1982:131).

TEOTIHUACÁN INFLUENCE ≡ The influence of Teotihuacán in Maya culture can be best observed in the core area around Tikal and its immediate environment in the form of building styles, sculpture, and ceramics, but it can also be recognized in sites closer to the borders. Rathje (1977) explains this by enlarging his model, described above, to point out that the core area, with its access to many areas producing raw material, was an ideal trading partner for Teotihuacán. Influence by Teotihuacán is also made responsible for the development of Maya state structures (Tourtellot and Sabloff 1972).

"HIATUS" ≡ Between A.D. 534 and 593 the erection of stone monuments with inscriptions and dates ceased almost completely. This can be best observed around the centrally located Tikal. But during the "hiatus," building activity also was interrupted and styles of sculpture and ceramics changed noticeably. The question of the reasons for this period of weakness leads naturally to a comparison with the final decline of Maya culture. According to Willey (1974b) the main difference was that after the "hiatus" there was a fast recovery, and Maya culture emerged more resplendent than it had been before.

POLITICAL ORGANIZATION ≡ The political structure could be interpreted only through archaeological evidence until recently, except for inferences from the Late Postclassic conditions in the north of Yucatán. Indications for a central political power are missing. Often political dependencies have been inferred through the spatial arrangement of centers of different rank; resulting rulerships were different from each other, but never very large. An interesting interpretation model has been proposed by Renfrew (not specifically for the Maya Classic: 1986) in the form of equally ranked political units. In this model a special role is given to the demonstration of communal splendor, both to impress neighbors and competitors, and also to confirm one's own value. Progress in the decipherment of Maya writing has led to a modification and a somewhat refined precision of concepts. The ordering of the southern part of the Yucatán Peninsula into four large state units, based on a single, somewhat obscure, inscription, proposed by Marcus (1976a) is no longer upheld. She herself (1933) emphasizes the fluctuation of political units on several hierarchic levels in a "dynamic" model (the state of research is similarly summarized by Demarest 1992:139–41).

WARS ≡ The progressively more apparent, all-encompassing presence of warlike disputes in inscription texts and pictorial representations among the Maya, who had been labeled as strictly peaceful by previous examinations, is interpreted as a form of elite action that obeys strict cultural rules and is almost ritual. Except for the final period, the goal was not territorial gains but the achievement of personal prestige (Freidel 1986; Webster 1993).

ECONOMY ≡ The basis of nutrition was corn, which was grown with other plants in fields cleared by slash-and-burn, a method that needed long recovery periods and therefore large areas, thus limiting the possible density of the population. Supplemental use of tree fruit (nuts of *Brosimum alicastrum*) (Puleston 1982) and tubers is hypothetical. Measures to intensify yields in areas with a high groundwater level ("raised fields") or terracing have been shown for some regions (anthology: Harrison and Turner 1978, provides a summary of present-day knowledge, but should be read with the review by Sanders [1979]). Rivera Dorado (1982) reconstructs the economic system on the basis of "Asiatic production methods" beyond the knowledge provided by the data.

TRADE ≡ Reports of the Colonial period confirm the existence of far-reaching maritime trade routes used by the Maya, which fell into the hands of the ethnic group called Putun toward the end of the Classic and later (Thompson 1964; slightly more extensive, *1970). In the interior the water routes, where they existed, were preferred for traffic as well, instead of porters. The amount of luxury goods and mass articles from the highlands (jade and other decorative stones, obsidian, lava, ceramics, Pacific shells, precious Quetzal feathers) far superceded what was exported from the lowlands.

ARCHITECTURE ≡ In many regions of the Yucatán Peninsula knowledge about the cultural situation is determined very much by stylistic examinations of architecture (Gendrop 1983) and the study of city planning concepts (Andrews 1975; Hartung 1971). Still, very few buildings have been adequately examined by archaeology and the resulting evidence published (Ruz Lhuillier 1973; Bolles 1977).

ART ≡ A summary examination of the many scattered murals is still missing (with emphasis on Postclassic paintings on the east coast: Miller 1982; anthology: Lombardo de Ruiz 1987). Proskouriakoff (1950) developed a basic temporal sequence of stelae based on dates contained in the inscriptions and stylistic criteria. Paintings on the walls of polychrome cylinder vases, which are often accompanied by stereotypical texts in hieroglyphic writing, were examined and published (Coe 1973; 1978).

RELIGION ≡ The approach to Maya religion is possible only by interpreting pictorial depictions and incorporating reports by Spanish missionaries about what they found. The best overview is given by Thompson (1970:159–354; see also this summary: Anders 1963). The image of the classical cultures of Mesoamerica as peaceful has been changed dramatically in recent years. Accordingly, the role of human sacrifice in Maya culture has been clarified (Schele 1984; Helfrich 1973, with a complete presentation of data).

SCIENTIFIC KNOWLEDGE AND WRITING ≡ For centuries the Maya employed a unified hieroglyphic script with a few small regional variations since the Early Classic, which allows us to deduce that the priests, probably responsible for the script, were tightly connected and exchanged their knowledge constantly. This connection becomes especially obvious when date notations of stone inscriptions are given that also contain complex calendrical calculations and astronomical references. Thus a method of calculating moon phases developed in Copán, spread within a short time through the entire Maya area, and was used during fifty years in a homogenous and synchronous manner (Teeple 1927). The sum of scientific knowledge is unknown because only four pictorial manuscripts have been preserved and among them only one contains complicated mathematical and astronomical tables about phases of the planet Venus and predictions of solar eclipses (Thompson 1950:208–62; 1972). This knowledge, as well as the ability to create the complex glyphs, was probably limited to members of the nobility. A slightly larger number of people may have been able to read the script, but surely not more than a very small percentage of the population (Houston and Stuart 1992, as method-critical commentary on Brown 1991).

In the complicated matter of decipherment of the Maya script the recent years have seen more progress than expected, which is the result of extensive collaboration with linguists. The progress is so speedy that it cannot even be followed through publications of details (summaries are soon out of date: Kelley 1976, representing the status of 1965; more recent: Schele 1982; Bricker 1992; see also above under Maya inscriptions). Text statements are becoming readable in their actual language. The reconstruction of genealogies of important centers proved to be particularly fertile ground (Schele 1992; Riese 1992; Houston 1992), because their friendly or hostile relations have been discovered and political structures, alliances, and dependencies have been recognized. The reconstruction of statements about individual events is commonly presented in a highly technical manner (for instance: Riese 1986b). The dynasty of Yaxchilán, mentioned in the Delineation part, has been taken from Mathews (1988), Josserand and Hopkins (1991), and Schele and Freidel (1990); very thoroughly Riese (1986a; date material from Proskouriakoff 1963; 1964; details on Yaxun Balam IV: Bardsley 1994; and Grube 1996).

END OF CLASSIC CULTURE ≡ After a maximum of dated monuments were erected on the period-ending date of October 13, 790, more and more centers stopped setting these monuments at regular intervals. At first sites in the far west and east were affected: the area from Palenque to Bonampak in A.D. 800, the region of Copán in the east in A.D. 830. At this time in most centers a lessening of building and sculpting activities has to be noted. Finally around A.D. 900 the decline reached the core area around Tikal and several sites along the edge of the Guatemalan highlands. About fifty years later most of the centers were abandoned and large areas of the lowlands except the eastern coasts, the area around the lakes in the middle, and the flatlands in the northern half of the Yucatán Peninsula, seem to be almost deserted. However, it is out of the question that a massive population shift took place, as had been assumed earlier ("Old" and "New" Empire).

DIFFERENCES FROM THE END OF TEOTIHUACÁN ≡ Despite obvious parallels in the rise and fall of Teotihuacán and the Maya, they are outweighed by the differences. In Teotihuacán (where the lack of inscriptions limits the precision of statements) the population number and building activity reached a plateau quickly and started to sink only a short time before the fall; in the Maya area population and building activity saw a gradual rise, interrupted by times of stagnation and regression ("hiatus"), a short peak period, and a fast fall. The difference in progression also may have been caused by the higher political stability of Teotihuacán as the undisputedly largest and most powerful city of central Mexico, whereas the Maya lacked a large political unit and lived in numerous centers of different size levels (Cowgill 1979).

REASONS FOR THE FALL ≡ In his discussion of the "hiatus," Willey (1974b: 427) had seen as a reason for the fall of Classic Maya culture that a ring of small political units formed around the borders and strangled the important economic interaction with areas farther away. Culbert (1988) is of the opinion that a constant worsening of the nutritional situation caused by the more productive, but also more risky, intensive agricultural methods damaged the entire ecological balance. Other reasons proposed are a series of failed harvests, diminution of animal protein through intensifying agriculture at the cost of forests, diseases that could spread through a dense population, stress of the work force by disproportional ceremonial building construction intended to outdo the neighbors, and finally a rebellion of the simple people, who were overworked and badly fed (Willey and Shimkin 1971; *1974; 1973).

COMPLEX REASONS ≡ Contrary to monocausal reasons, systems-theory approaches try to reconstruct the combination of multiple factors in a model, which gains importance by the need to formulate precisely the causal contexts. In a simulation of the factor bundle mentioned by Willey and Shimkin, it was shown (Hosler, Sabloff, and Runge 1977) that a recovery occurred, as after the "hiatus," which means that internal factors alone could not have caused the final collapse. A model concentrating only on food production and work output seems to be able to accurately describe the cessation of monument erection (Lowe 1985:183–99).

ECOLOGICAL CHANGES ≡ Apparently profound natural changes affect the basic life of a population less than changes caused by man himself, even if they were not intended. The intensive use of erosion-endangered areas in slash-and-burn agriculture caused soil to be deposited in shallow lakes and turn them into swamps. Afterwards, the high beds in these lakes ("raised fields") (Puleston 1977; Siemens and Puleston 1972) could not be used any more for growing food (Harrison 1977).

CORE-PERIPHERY INTERACTION ≡ The model proposed by Rathje (1972) for the rise of Maya culture in the core area also contains an explanation for the fall: while in the beginning the core area alone produced luxury items, for which it could exchange the needed raw materials, the periphery areas slowly took over this manufacture themselves and thus took away from the core all ability to exchange goods (Rathje 1973).

REBELLIONS ≡ Almost all explanations assume a rising pressure, which may have exploded among the lower strata of the population, who suffered the most from deficiencies, especially in cities. Thompson (1954; 2nd revised edition 1967) sees indications in the intentional damage of stone monuments depicting members of the upper classes, as well as in the continued ceremonial use of the centers for some time after the fall, by people who had neither the knowledge nor the means to continue the rituals properly. A mathematical test of the temporal and spatial progression of failure to erect monuments seems to confirm this thesis (Hamblin and Pitcher 1980; rebuttal: Lowe 1981).

INVASION BY WAR ≡ In the area of the Río Pasión the intrusion of a militant group from outside the Classic Maya culture was deduced from archaeological evidence (Sabloff 1973; Adams 1973). The time of this suggested, in any event only small-scale, successful invasion is in the middle of the collapse. The intruders therefore used a situation favorable for themselves, which they could not have caused in the first place because of their numbers. They did cause, for a brief time, a stylistically foreign continuation of Maya culture limited to Seibal and Altar de Sacrificios. Epigraphic evidence was used to put the importance of this intrusion into perspective (Stuart 1993).

PUTUN MAYA ≡ The intruders appearing at the end of the Classic were identified by Thompson (1970:3–47) as the Putun, a group in the area south of the Laguna de Términos, known from early Colonial sources, who clearly adopted central Mexican traits. The Putun are said to have devoted themselves to trade by sea around the peninsula. The decisive role in the Late Classic and Postclassic history of Yucatán, attributed to the Putun by Thompson, is doubted more and more.

RÍO BEC ≡ In central Yucatán there is a region around the site of Río Bec that differs in style from the core area. Excavations in Becan and Chicanna have resulted in dates between A.D. 650 and 830, contrary to earlier datings (Eaton 1972:55–56). In this area terracing on a grand scale was discovered (Turner 1979); however, its use in intensifying agriculture is a matter of debate (Carrasco, Boucher, and Peña 1986).

PUUC AND CHENES ≡ The temporal and genetic position of the closely related style groups Puuc and Chenes is not cleared up satisfactorily, as is the more and more questionable traditional delineation, because the material data base is insufficient (the monumental architecture survey by Pollock [1980] so far is singular) and dated objects are missing. Andrews (1986; 1985) developed the presently accepted chronological sequence. The attempt by Potter (1977) to define Río Bec and Chenes as one stylistic region does not lead anywhere.

"MEXICAN" INFLUENCE ≡ It cannot be denied that similar foreign elements appear toward the end of the Classic (around A.D. 800) in the Río Pasión area, and also in the region of Puuc. Their ethnic and cultural classification is still speculative, even if the carriers have been called Putun (Thompson 1970). They may have created the Puuc style and spread it close to the northern coast (Chichén Itzá and Culubá: Shuman 1977:10). It has been proven that the island of Cozumel occupied an important position as a trade center (of the Putun?) on the northern tip of the Peninsula until the Spanish conquest (Sabloff 1977). The problem of Chichén Itzá's temporal and cultural position and its alleged special development due to "Toltec" immigrants is discussed below.

13

The Postclassic

Most often the year A.D. 900 is taken for the beginning of the Postclassic. This temporal delineation is useful in the southern lowlands of Yucatán, because it was there that the characteristic classic form of Maya culture with its dated monuments had ended a century earlier. For the northern part of the peninsula it is at least a century too early, since Late Classic features continued there for a while longer, while in the highlands of western Mesoamerica the typical Classic culture had ended one or two centuries earlier with the fall of Teotihuacán.

The connecting feature of the Postclassic is the slow, regionally different appearance of reports on indigenous traditions that have been preserved in sources written after the Conquista. For the early Postclassic they are so mythical-legendary that the historical facts (provided they exist in every case) can rarely be reconstructed with any confidence. From the middle of the Postclassic (thirteenth century) the reference points become more and more trustworthy, but it is only for the last one or two centuries before the Spanish conquest that a true picture can be gleaned.

The Toltecs are the dominant subject of early Postclassic history. With the term "Toltec" Mesoamerican peoples referred to many different concepts. The same is true for modern research. One possibility for differentiating the terms, which is not always observed, may be derived from the associated place names: Tula (called after the immediately adjoining modern city Tula de Allende in the Mexican state Hidalgo) refers to the archaeological site. In the meaning of indigenous central Mexican traditions it was identical with the Tollan Xicocotitlan of the sources, although its description includes many mythical or legendary features that cannot be reconciled with the evidence at Tula. The generic term "Tollan" (without the additional Xicocotitlan) has to be separated from this. It was used to refer also to places like Cholollan and other, not identified, sites in the southern Gulf Coast region, which were claimed as a place of origin by Maya groups. In places called Tollan persons were in residence who had one or several of the following names (or titles): Quetzalcoatl (also in Maya versions Kukulkan or Cucumatz), Nacxitl, or Tepeuh.

THE EARLY POSTCLASSIC IN WESTERN MESOAMERICA

TULA ≡ Archaeological excavations at Tula were almost exclusively restricted to uncovering and restoring the ceremonial center; to an unconscionable degree results from Chichén Itzá were used and thus the strong resemblance that existed anyway was further enhanced (Molina Montes 1982). The temporal position is usually based on the end of Tollan, the dates of which have either been taken from the sources or calculated backwards (Acosta 1976:158; different position for living quarters: Diehl 1981:281). After the end of excavations of the ceremonial center there were two surface surveys at Tula (Diehl 1974; Yadeún Angulo 1975). Most recently the role of Tula as a manufacturing center for obsidian has been proven by excavations (Healan, Kerley, and Bey III 1983). Mastache F. and Cobean (1985) provide a summary of present knowledge.

VEHICLES ≡ The example of Tula lends itself to demonstrating the lack of one of the most important technical advances in old-world eyes, the vehicle with wheels. Wheels were found exclusively on ceramic animal figurines (and only in the early Postclassic Mesoamerica) (Diehl and Mandeville 1987:244), but since there were no draught animals, they were not utilized for vehicles. Accordingly, the streets (in Mesoamerica mostly within settlements) served only pedestrians.

PERIPHERY OF TULA ≡ The situation in the Valley of Mexico during the early and florescent periods of Tula is well known through large area settlement surveys. A reconstruction of political conditions (Alden 1974) supports the assumed "balkanization" of the valley after the fall of Teotihuacán and the subsequent dominance of Tula.

TOLLAN ≡ The marvelous city Tollan Xicocotitlan, as described in the sources, was equated for a long time with the largest Mesoamerican metropolis, Teotihuacán (the last proponent: Séjourné 1954). In 1941 Jiménez Moreno could show that the Indian sources refer with that term to the city of Tula, which still exists today. Subsequently, Tula was excavated intensively (see above). The partially very idealized reports may also contain vague memories of Teotihuacán, whose fall may have contributed to this amalgamation (Wagner 1971b:171; 1971a).

ETHNIC GROUPS IN TOLLAN XICOCOTITLAN ≡ In Tollan Xicocotitlan two ethnically different groups lived side by side: the Nonoalca and the Tolteca-Chichimeca. Their origin is not very clear. The name Nonoalca may be derived from an abode on the southern Gulf Coast in the region of Nonoalco, something that cannot be placed in time. It remains speculation that they acquired there, in the vicinity of Maya culture, the refinement that was characteristic of Tollan (Florescano 1963:225). A complicated origin is proposed by Jiménez Moreno (1966b:55, 65). The Nonoalca could be remnants of a population that left Teotihuacán after its fall, stayed in the southeastern part of the highlands (Teotitlan del Camino, Coatzacoalcos), and later moved to Tollan. Scholars commonly accept that the Toltecs spoke Nahuatl, as Sahagún reported (Canger 1988:63). On the other hand, the archaeologist Paddock (1966:380) asks if the culturally dominant part of the population of Tollan Xicocotitlan (he probably means the Nonoalca) could not have been Mixtecs who returned to their home after the fall of Tollan.

The constituent population segments did not leave the city at the same time it collapsed. The sequence that can be reconstructed depends on the ethnic attribution of the most important persons, Quetzalcoatl and Huemac. Only if Quetzalcoatl is seen as a member of the Tolteca-Chichimeca can the diverging assertions be integrated into the following picture (Davies 1977:356): part of the Tolteca-Chichimeca left Tollan Xicocotitlan some time before the fall and went to Chalollan. From there they called on a supposedly non-Nahuatl-speaking group from the north, the Teochichimeca, one of whose leaders was one Mixcoatl, to assist them. The migration path of the Chichimecs led in a large curve through the Valley of Mexico and through Colhuacan (Kirchhoff 1958). The sources tell in a legendary, imprecise story that a person by the name of Mixcoatl ruled in the first half of the twelfth century in Colhuacan. His son and successor was Topiltzin, who soon took over the government of Tollan. Against this reconstruction many objections can be raised. By trying to combine contradictory source assertions, Zantwijk (1986) put out the hypothesis that Topiltzin Quetzalcoatl and Huemac were half brothers, sons of Totepeuh-Mixcoatl, and had ruled together.

TOLTEC EMPIRE ≡ The sources of the indigenous traditions do not make any trustworthy statement about the existence, spread, and inner structure of a "Toltec Empire." The reconstruction of such an empire, separated into four provinces, by Kirchhoff (1962; *1985; accepted by Zantwijk 1973:15; 1985) rests on the biased interpretation of a single passage in the source *Historia Tolteca-Chichimeca* and is not at all conclusive. According to Kirchhoff the configuration and inner order of the provinces had conformed with a cosmological structure widely spread in Mesoamerica (four world directions and a center). Another prerequisite of this reconstruction is the identification of Culiacan (state Guanajuato) in the west with Colhuacan of the migration reports, which is situated near Aztlan, where the Aztecs originated; this is not generally accepted. The assertion in the *Historia Tolteca-Chichimeca* can be interpreted rather as the real (or claimed) area of influence around their place of origin Cuauhtinchan (Prem 1991). Kirchhoff blames the end of the presumed Toltec Empire on a vaguely identified group from west Mexico, who governed Tollan for a while, but then could not persevere there due to internal strife, and later occupied the Valleys of Mexico and Puebla.

QUETZALCOATL AND HUEMAC ≡ The source reports about Tollan, thoroughly compiled by Wagner (1971b), highlight the two opponents, Quetzalcoatl and Huemac. Even their position in either the early period or the time of the fall of Tollan is seen controversially: according to Jiménez Moreno (the results of his examinations have never been published in detail: in Jiménez Moreno, Miranda, and Fernández 1965:100–102) Quetzalcoatl was the rightful heir of the Tolteca-Chichimeca dynasty of Colhuacan in the Valley of Mexico; he moved the seat of his government to Tollan. Probably in A.D. 987 he had to leave Tollan, because he had not been able to successfully oppose the introduction of human sacrifices. One of the later successors in the rule of Tollan, Huemac (ca. 1095–1156), was forced out by a rebellion of the Tolteca-Chichimeca and the Nonoalca, which initiated the collapse of Tollan. Contrary to this, Kirchhoff (1955) was of the opinion that both persons were contemporaries and had lived in the final period of Tollan. Huemac was a priest of the god Quetzalcoatl, but had been forced to give up the office due to a violation against the rule of chastity provoked by an opposing religious faction, and had then taken over the government. His immediate successor as high priest was soon followed by Topiltzin, who became known by the name, or rather title, Quetzalcoatl. Both left Tollan in the same historical situation, but chose different routes. Davies (1977:360–77) does not negate the existence of a Topiltzin-Quetzalcoatl in the early period of Tollan, although he leans toward the latter version, and claims that his amalgamation in the sources with the later Quetzalcoatl is the reason for the confusion. He also feels that Kirchhoff's separation of a secular and a religious ruling power in Tollan is unrealistic. Instead, Huemac, who was descended from an old ruling family, probably of Nonoalca roots, had driven the usurper Topiltzin from the city, but was himself forced out by the resulting riots. It remains unclear which role was played by attacks of intruders from the northern Gulf Coast. It depends on the time of the fall of Tollan Xicocotitlan and the position of Topiltzin in it, if one wants to see the refugee Topiltzin in Kukulkan, when he arrived in Yucatán (as do Morley and Brainerd 1956:81), a supposition strictly denied by Davies (1977:224).

The relationship between a historical figure with the title or additional name Quetzalcoatl and a mythical being apparently cannot be clarified (myth analysis incorporating iconography, see Florescano 1993; abbreviated *1992).

MIXTECS ≡ History of the Mixtecs in the western part of the modern Mexican state Oaxaca, as relayed in indigenous written sources, reaches back the furthermost, to far into the Classic. However, the information concerns almost exclusively small-scale dynastic matters. The temporal priority of preserved historical reports does not mean that they are models of contents for other, later ones. This was suggested in the unanimously rejected thesis by Chadwick

(1971), who proposed that reports on the later Toltec history were an adaptation of Mixtec reports about the first and second dynasties of Tilantongo.

The political and the social organization of the Postclassic Mixtec cannot be reconstructed on the basis of their pictorial manuscripts. It may not have been much different from the better known organizations in the Valley of Mexico, according to backward projections from Colonial period conditions. A stratification of society into rulers, nobles, landowners, and workers without any land, who planted the fields of rulers and nobles, probably was present here as well (Spores 1984:64–96). Support is expected from archaeological work; its status is summarized by Spores (1967:30–50; later additions: 1984:10–63).

The expansive force of the Mixtecs is illustrated by their presence in the Valley of Oaxaca, which can be proven beginning about A.D. 1280 (Whitecotton 1977:94). The extent of Mixtec presence is discussed partly in a heated manner. Opinions go from a complete conquest of the valley by the Mixtecs on one side to a regionally limited enclave on the other, which had no effect on the rest of the valley (Paddock 1983). Colonial-period *Relaciones Geográficas* mention a marriage tie between Mixtecs from the region around Yanhuitlan and the Zapotec ruling house of Cuilapan; there is no reason given for this alliance, nor can it be fathomed if this was the only such union. Moreover, pictorial sources of the indigenous tradition seem to indicate that Macuilxochitl in the eastern part of the Valley of Oaxaca was governed by a Mixtec ruler from Tilantongo and Teozacoalco (Paddock 1982). The dwellings often seem to have been settled by members of both ethnic groups (Whitecotton 1977:97). Available archaeological evidence does not allow an ethnic interpretation of Postclassic ceramics and building styles.

THE EARLY POSTCLASSIC IN EASTERN MESOAMERICA

TULA AND CHICHÉN ITZÁ ≡ The somewhat striking similarity in the structures and numerous details of buildings in the center of Tula with the ones especially in the northern part of Chichén Itzá in the modern state of Yucatán cannot be denied. For a long time the opinion was that immigrants from Tula were the creators of those buildings at Chichén Itzá. Even identical artists were postulated. After the beginning of excavations at the archaeological site of Tula it was thought that a direct influx of a possibly small group of people from Tula to Yucatán had taken place, influenced by the reconstruction of the history of Tollan that was presented at that time. Kubler (1961; reply: Ruz Lhuillier 1962) proposed an influence in the opposite direction based on another time frame that he favored. The discussion resulted in a more balanced approach to the original assertion.

Today an indirect "Toltec" influence on Chichén Itzá by intruding Mexican-influenced middlemen from the area of Champoton on the Gulf Coast near Tabasco is accepted most of the time. Only rarely it is assumed that there was a direct control by Tula over Chichén Itzá (Shuman 1977:10–12).

CHICHÉN ITZÁ AND PUUC ≡ Until recently it was believed generally that the architectural phase at Chichén Itzá, which was influenced by the "Toltecs," had followed the period of Puuc style after A.D. 950 without noticeable overlapping. Today, two different opinions have been voiced. In some cases a complete contemporaneity of the Puuc style and "Toltec" Chichén Itzá is assumed (Lincoln 1986), which makes a shorter time span for the Postclassic almost inevitable. The majority of archaeologists tend to assume a time span, albeit of diverse duration, where both styles overlapped (Ball 1979; Andrews V and Sabloff 1985). There was no agreement on a completely contrary variant that placed "Toltec" Chichén Itzá far into the Classic, and instead of a contact with Tula one with Teotihuacán was proposed (Parsons 1969:172–84; Cohodas 1978).

PROBLEMS OF INTERPRETATION ≡ The descriptions contained in the texts about Postclassic northern Yucatán history can hardly be unraveled, because apparently identical events are connected with persons of different names. This is particularly obvious in the case of Hunac Ceel. The victor over the Itzá in some passages is called among other names (Cauich, Ah Tapay Nok Cauich) by the name or title Kukulkan (Maya translation of Quetzalcoatl) or Ah Nac Xiu (corresponding to the epithet of Quetzalcoatl, Nacxitl). He also has a connection to somebody definitely called "Quetzalcoat" (Tozzer 1957:48, 258; Seler 1898; *1902). A similar source of confusion is suspected on the subject of place names in the sources, where ritual epithets and actual names need not correspond (a correlation of archeological evidence and indigenous sources has been proposed by Ball [1985] on this basis, which leads to the inescapable conclusion that everything can be identified as anything).

KUKULKAN ≡ In the source reports there appear by the name or title Kukulkan so many clearly different persons at different times involved in such different action sequences that they cannot have been one and the same. One Kukulkan came around A.D. 987 to Chichén Itzá from the west, as has been related above. Another Kukulkan was the founder of Mayapan (maybe 1283) together with Tutul Xiu (a Nahuat name, a variant of Nahuatl), and finally he (or another?) went peacefully through Champoton to "Mexico" (data presentation with different conclusions: Tozzer 1957:39, 51).

ITZÁ ≡ The exact determination of the place of origin of the ethnic groups who immigrated in the Postclassic from an area outside of Classic Maya culture into Yucatán has not been achieved to everyone's satisfaction. The most prominent group for whom a foreign origin is claimed are the Itzá. The Maya regarded them as strangers with a foreign language and characterized them often in a derogatory way. Especially their purported shamelessness was criticized. They claimed to have come from Chakanputun ("province of Putun"), from whence they migrated to Chichén Itzá. Thompson's (1970:14–17) arguments are not totally convincing that they were members of the Putun, who lived on the Laguna de Términos near the Gulf Coast. In that area the Maya languages Chol and Nahuatl coexisted and supplied most place names and many personal names (Scholes and Roys 1948:1–67). The same types of names are very common among groups who migrated into Yucatán, among them the Tutul Xiu, who claim to have come from Tulapan (corresponds to a Tollan), from the "House of Nonoal" (corresponds to Nonoalco), and the Canul, who descended from settled warriors called into the country from Tabasco. The opposite position, that the Itzá were Maya, is presented by Kelley (1968).

ROUTE OF THE ITZÁ ≡ According to Thompson (1970:11–14), the Itzá may have come to Chichén Itzá around A.D. 918. Before that their last station was on the island of Cozumel on the Caribbean coast of Yucatán. They entered the mainland through the harbor of Polé and subsequently wandered around in northern Yucatán until they settled in Chichén Itzá. Later, in 980, another group led by Kukulkan followed them; they reached Chichén Itzá from the west coast.

CHICHÉN ITZÁ ≡ The descriptions of the fall of Chichén Itzá can be found mainly in the Chilam Balam books of Maní and Tizimín (Craine and Reindorp 1979; Edmonson 1982). The temporal placement and the sequence of events are doubtful because they are expressed in repeated *katun* cycles. A thorough reconstruction attempt, still accepted except for the temporal placement, was prepared by Tozzer (1957). The Hunac Ceel episode can also be found in Roys (1967:177–81).

CHRONOLOGICAL QUESTIONS ≡ The exact temporal ordering of events in the Maya Postclassic is met with two difficulties. The first is the expression of year dates, which was unique in northern Yucatán in the Postclassic. Unlike the Classic system, instead of an exact counting of the days since a zero date, only the name of the pertaining twenty-year period (*katun*) was given in abbreviated form, which would repeat after thirteen periods (256 years). Dated statements in the sources, especially in the Chilam Balam books, where this system continued to be used, can therefore be correlated with different dates in the European calendar that are the length of such a period apart. The sequence of the statements is not secure either, because *katun* names revolve. The second, related difficulty is the day equation between the Maya (as used in the Classic) and the European calendars, where only variants that differ by 256 years are acceptable as sources. The argument leading to the correlation accepted now is open to criticism (its core is an argumentation by Spinden [1924] adopted by Thompson [1935] that the calendar related by Landa [1959] with dates from both systems corresponds to the year 1553). Nevertheless, the equation itself seems to be correct. Archaeologists on one hand have demanded correlations that prolong the time span between the end of the Classic and the Spanish conquest (Andrews IV 1965), and on the other hand an abbreviation of the time span (Chase 1985), but they could not prevail.

CONCEPTION OF HISTORY ≡ The Maya concept of the run of history becomes clear in the Chilam Balam books. According to a cyclical concept of time, past events were seen as predictions for future events, which would occur again and again in the same calendar periods. However, one cannot be certain if this one-sided view is not specific to this one group of sources only, which by chance were the only ones to survive. Another question is whether events were truly directed according to calendric-cyclical concepts, or whether they were only represented according to these conceptions; there is no answer. Therefore Edmonson (1979:163) pondered whether the often-reported abandonment or destruction of cities was not a symbolic act, only described as happening in the texts, which had to occur at the end of cycles of 256 years.

QUICHÉ AND CAKCHIQUEL ≡ The martial groups who made themselves the elite of diverse Maya peoples in the highlands of Guatemala in the early thirteenth century have left their historical traditions to us in three important sources (*Annals of the Cakchiquels* and *Título de Totonicapan*: Recinos 1950; Recinos and D. Goetz *1953; *Popol Vuh*: among others Edmonson 1971), and several small documents (Recinos 1957). As a place of origin or starting points of their migrations they often give names whose composition contains Tulan (probably Tollan) (Carmack 1968:55); however, this cannot be Tollan Xicocotitlan in the highlands of Mexico. Other statements and names (Nonoalcat, Coatzacam) help to determine as the place of origin the lowlands of the Gulf Coast between Laguna de Términos and the mouth of the Río Grijalva (Coatzacoalcos), which was called Nonoalco by the Aztecs. It remains unclear if there had been a place called or titled Tollan, or if the statements contain a reference to a local legend about a connection with the central Mexican Tollan. The name Vucub Pec points in this direction ("Seven Caves," the same as Chicomoztoc, a variant of the often-quoted central Mexican place of origin). "Toltec" influence can also be recognized in the archaeological evidence, especially in settlement patterns, and refers to Chichén Itzá and Mayapan (Fox 1980).

The history of the Maya peoples of the highlands has been presented in recent decades in monographs based on archaeological and historical data. The examination of the Quiché has been particularly thorough (Carmack, Fox, and Stewart 1975; Fox 1978; Carmack 1977; 1981), while other ethnic groups, such as the Tzutujil (Orellana 1984), are clearly neglected. Other regions, such as the Chuchumatanes mountain ranges, are hardly known, because there are no detailed sources (Lovell 1985:37–57).

POST-TOLTEC HISTORY OF CENTRAL MEXICO

COLHUACAN ≡ The Toltec origin of the ruling family of Colhuacan at least is extensively documented in the sources. The dynastic sequence indeed does lead back to a time before the fall of Tollan Xicocotitlan (Prem 1984a; Kirchhoff 1959). The shorter version from the sources from Tetzcoco is incompatible with this and has caused Davies (1980:23–41) to drastically shorten the longer list, an attempt that has to be rejected. Colhuacan presented an easy chance for many of the groups that immigrated later to establish a connection with the prestigious Toltecs.

VALLEY OF PUEBLA-TLAXCALA ≡ Although the Valley of Puebla-Tlaxcala is rich in historical documents, their inherent ethnocentrism and the lack of correlation possibilities with the Valley of Mexico impede a comprehensive reconstruction of the historical sequence of the region. The main source for Precolumbian history is the *Historia Tolteca-Chichimeca*, which concentrates on the southerly situated Cuauhtinchan (Kirchhoff 1947). Davies (1980:90–95 a.o.; 1977:363–68) tries to uncover the correspondences in the migration story, for in both areas the same Chichimec groups were involved. The origin of the dynasty of Cuauhtinchan and its multi-ethnic population, whose rivalries decidedly determined the history of southern Puebla until the fifteenth century, was conclusively examined by Reyes García (1977).

OLMECA-XICALLANCA ≡ The Olmeca-Xicallanca, whose name suggests a connection to the Gulf Coast, are also called "historical Olmecs," to avoid any confusion with the prehistoric Olmecs of the La Venta culture. As one of the civilized peoples of Mesoamerica they formed presumably a major counterweight to Tollan-Xicocotitlan, but there is hardly anything known about their political history (Kirchhoff 1960:96–101). The same is true for the Xochiteca and Quiyahuizteca, who were related to them and lived farther west in the border region to Chalco. The role attributed to the historical Olmecs in pre-Toltec times by Jiménez Moreno (1966b) cannot be tested. The date he (1954–55:220) deduced for the conquest of Chalollan by the Olmeca-Xicallanca around A.D. 800 is contested by Nicholson (1978:315; Davies 1977:113–20). Based on a statement by the Tlaxcallan historian Muñoz Camargo at the end of the sixteenth century, the Olmeca-Xicallanca are attributed with the construction of the fortress-like ruins of Cacaxtla (Tlaxcala), which cannot be verified by archaeology.

CHICHIMEC RULERS IN PUEBLA AND TLAXCALA ≡ The early Colonial sources of the area describe in detail the sociopolitical organization of the Chichimec rulerships, who show a lesser degree of political integration compared with the later Triple Alliance states in the Valley of Mexico, despite their considerable extent and expansive politics. The history of events outside of Cuauhtinchan, even for the late period of the confrontation with the Aztec Triple Alliance, can be fathomed only in fragments, lacking suitable sources (overview of development and discussion of chronology: Dyckerhoff 1978).

XOLOTL ≡ In a number of sources a Chichimec group that invaded the Valley of Mexico from the north in the twelfth century has commanded special attention. Their leader Xolotl is described as the founder of an empire that encompassed the Valley of Mexico, Toluca and Puebla, and the areas north of them; however, this may be rather a retrospective expression of legitimation aspirations of the ruling dynasty he founded.

ORIGIN OF THE MEXICA ≡ In their traditions the Mexica trace their origin to a place called Aztlan. The meaning of this Nahuatl name is obscure, contrary to others that can be easily understood. Despite the somewhat imprecise direction "in the northwest" of the Valley of Mexico, even the Mexica were unable to clarify the exact location. They described the place as being on an island in a lake, so scholars were afforded many interpretation and localization variants. Here only the most important ones will be mentioned: an area (no island) west of the Río Lerma and north of the Laguna de Yuriria (Kirchhoff 1961), if the modern mountain Culiacan can be identified with Colhuacan; the island in the Laguna de Mexcaltitlan on the coast of Nayarit (Jiménez Moreno, et al. 1965:115), if the province Aztatlan can be equated to the place Aztlan. Maybe the description given for Aztlan is nothing more than the situation in the Valley of Mexico, where the historical Colhuacan was situated, projected to ancient times (Seler 1894; *1904), which had to serve as a later-developed, ideological legitimization for the pathetic goal of Aztec migrations (Duverger 1983; *1987).

According to their own traditions, the Mexica left Aztlan together with up to eight other tribes (called *calpulli*), who later settled in their vicinity, but who are not the same in all sources. The stations of the migration roughly correspond in the sources as well, but by no means in details (Acosta Saignes 1946; Duverger 1983; *1987:170–71). Moreover, there are parallels to the migration of Xolotl and his Chichimecs. Michael Smith (1984) deduced that migrations from Aztlan belong to a larger complex of Chichimec migrations, where a wave of speakers of other languages at the end of the twelfth century was followed by three waves of Nahuatl speakers in the thirteenth century. Of those three the first wave settled in the Valley of Mexico, the second in the surrounding highlands, and the third consisted of the Mexica. Opponents deny the historicity of the reported migrations outright (in a decidedly materialistic historical view: Price 1980).

MEXICA: CULTURE OF THE MIGRATION PERIOD ≡ The Mexica were part of an originally sedentary and corn-growing population from the borders of areas under Toltec influence. Starting with applicable thoughts of Kirchhoff, Martínez Marín (1964; *1971) has compiled the cultural elements present among the Mexica during their migration.

Recent examinations of non-Aztec areas (but with a Nahuatl-speaking population) have shown everywhere a similar basic model of economic, social, and political structures, from which the special development of the Mexica can be differentiated. It has not yet been discovered if these were the Mexica's own innovations or if they were adopted from other political units of the area.

14

The Aztecs

NAMES AND TERMINOLOGY ≡ The name "Aztec" is by no means clear. In the early sources it appears only in single instances in connection with "Aztlan," the mythical place of origin of the Mexica. Only at the end of the eighteenth century did the Jesuit Clavijero (1964:65) establish its use, employed until today. The sources of the highlands call the migration group in question Mexitin or Mexica (Spanish: *mexicanos*) (background of this terminological question: Barlow 1945b; Kirchhoff 1962; *1985:262). To be exact, the inhabitants of the two sister cities Tenochtitlán and Tlatelolco are called Tenochca and Tlatelolca. As is common in the modern literature, in the following "Aztec" will be used to designate the ethnically and partly linguistically heterogenous population of the valley, their mostly similar cultural traits, and their political organization within the Triple Alliance formed of Tenochtitlán, Tetzcoco, and Tlacopan. Members will be called by the more precise name Mexica for the dominating ethnic group, or Tenochca, Tlatelolca, Tetzcoca, etc. For the most widespread language of the inhabitants of the Valley of Mexico one often finds "Aztec," which is not quite correct. As this language was spoken also outside the area dominated by the Triple Alliance, the indigenous word for it, "Nahuatl," is preferred.

OVERVIEW PRESENTATIONS ≡ Recently several overview presentations were published that treat the culture of the Aztecs in the form of topical monographs (Townsend 1992; Carrasco P. 1976a [later editions are preferred; the first one has many production mistakes]; Berdan 1982; an eclectic view of the Aztecs: Clendinnen 1991). Although many details are no longer up to date, the monograph by Soustelle is still recommended (Soustelle 1955; similar in subject but of lesser quality and full of mistakes in Aztec terms: Soisson and Soisson 1977).

The history of the Mexica and their immediate neighbors has not yet been presented as a summary. Exceptions are the monographs by Davies (1973b; early period of the Mexica: 1973a; parts of this book were incorporated in 1980, where also the history of neighboring peoples is included. Single analysis of states independent of the Aztecs: 1968; a political history that is not quite convincing: Brundage 1972).

EARLY HISTORY OF THE AZTEC TRIPLE ALLIANCE

TLATELOLCO AND TENOCHTITLÁN ≡ The settling of the Mexica on reed islands in the Lake of Mexico is described by the sources as an event directed by the gods, but it is not dated uniformly. The most often quoted calculation of the year 1325 (overview: Duverger 1983:158–66; *1987) was moved by Jiménez Moreno (1954–55:233) and Davies (1980:191) to 1345 by calendrical manipulation. In any case, when the Mexica arrived, there was an older population settled there, at least in Tlatelolco, about whom the sources say nothing. However, these people most likely participated in the development of Tlatelolco, which possibly was meant to be different from Tenochtitlán. Nevertheless, the early situation of Tenochtitlán and Tlatelolco overall is difficult to judge. According to the sources following the Mexica traditions, the so-called first ruler of Tlatelolco, Cuacuauhpitzahuac (1372–1407) was preceded presumably by Teuhtlehuac, who was also responsible for the Tenochca (Barlow 1944).

ACAMAPICHTLI ≡ The year when the first ruler of the Tenochca, Acamapichtli, who may have had at first only the office of Cihuacoatl, started his rule (*Codex Mendoza*, Berdan and Anawalt 1992, folio 2r), cannot be determined exactly, but it is commonly taken to be 1370. Equally unclear is his exact descent and that of his wife Ilancueitl (Davies 1973a; Zantwijk 1982:25). Davies (1973a:55–65) emphasizes the role of Azcapotzalco in the selection of the Tenochca ruler, but this is not commonly accepted. Based on *Codex Azcatitlan* (Graulich 1975), Zantwijk sees in the overall constellation the beginning of accepted coexistence and power-political alliance between the old population groups of Toltec heritage and the Chichimec Tenochca. The highest noble families of later times derive from Acamapichtli's union with the daughters of Mexica leaders of migration groups (*calpulli*), as his marriage to Ilancueitl apparently was childless (most extensive: Monjarás-Ruiz 1980:93–102; also: Zantwijk 1985:57–93, who emphatically points out that the original migration groups were not egalitarian but already stratified in their organization). Dates mentioned here in connection with the early rulers of the Mexica have been taken from the reconstruction by Davies (1973a:193–210), which was arrived at by historical plausibility, but the additional acceptance of differing calendar styles has not been unanimously approved.

PERIOD OF DEPENDENCY ≡ The sources of the Mexica describe the dependency from Azcapotzalco in the period before the accession of Huitzilihuitl as a time of privations and trying tribute demands, without doubt a subsequent interpretation from an imperial viewpoint. In fact, the positive aspects seem to have outweighed the negative ones. At what time during this period the economically decisive construction of *chinampas* (land gain in shallow areas of the lake by constructing raised beds of high fertility) was started in Mexico cannot be exactly determined. The sources do not show if the early conquests of the

Mexica were executed in the name of Azcapotzalco (as Hassig has it: 1988:132) or based on their own initiative. This is also true for the first wars with Chalco, which happened during the rule of Acamapichtli (overview of the early history of the war against Chalco: Davies 1973:100–107). It is possible that after Acamapichtli's death there was an interregnum of a few years, until his son Huitzilihuitl was elected as his successor (Monjarás-Ruiz 1980:1–3); Huitzilihuitl's mother was a daughter of Acacitli or Cuauhtlequetzqui, or in any event of one of the prominent leaders of the period of land taking.

XALTOCAN ≡ Carrasco P. (1950:259) has attributed an extensive territory to Xaltocan in the northern part of the Valley of Mexico, founded in the thirteenth century by immigrants speaking Otomí; the size of this territory has been doubted by Jiménez Moreno (1954–55:230). According to the thorough source analysis by Trautmann (1968:44–48), Xaltocan ruled only one part of the northeastern Valley of Mexico. Assisted by Huitzilihuitl, the Tepanecs achieved the conquest of a substantial part of the Xaltocan territory (Hassig 1988:134).

ACOLHUACAN ≡ The main indigenous source for the history of the eastern part of the Valley of Mexico, especially for the immigration of Chichimec groups and the establishment of the dynasty, are the writings of the descendant of the ruling house of Tetzcoco, Alva Ixtlilxochitl (O'Gorman 1975–77). Within his works his statements often contradict each other. Also a comparison with the details of his important pictorial prototype, *Códice Xolotl* (Dibble's commentary in 1980, vol. 1:11–123; Offner 1979), shows both mistaken interpretations as well as influences from other traditions. A critical review is still outstanding; summaries can be found in works with other emphases (Offner 1983:1–46; Zantwijk 1973; Nicholson 1972:179–90; Davies 1980:114–33; about Techotlalatzin: Offner 1979).

TEPANEC EMPIRE ≡ The expansion of the Tepanec Empire had started after the fall of Colhuacan and had reached a first pinnacle in the beginning of the second half of the fourteenth century with the conquest of this important city. Carrasco P.'s (1950:116–19, 168–272) opinion that the empire had extended to relatively far-removed areas especially in the west of the Valley of Mexico (Valley of Toluca, Tlachco) under the rulership of Tezozomoc has been countered with good arguments (Trautmann 1968:58–60; Davies 1980:243–44). The generally accepted equation of Cuauhnahuac, conquered by Acamapichtli, with modern Cuernavaca (Morelos) has been challenged (Kelly 1952:282). The discovery of an unknown petition of 1561, containing further clues of Tepanec properties, has moved Carrasco P. (1984b) to address the subject again and confirm his thesis. Understanding this petition and related writings is made difficult by the fact that they were composed in Latin, and in the translation specific terms of Nahuatl or Spanish have become indistinct. Based on a source statement (*Relación de la genealogía*, in García Icazbalceta 1941a), already in

1950 Carrasco P. had seen Coatlichan, Amaquemecan, Huexotzinco (Puebla), and Cuauhnahuac (Cuernavaca, Morelos) as rulerships allied to the Tepanecs. This view is further supported by the listing of Quecholac, Totomihuacan, and Oztoticpac (all in southern Puebla), as cities to which daughters of Tezozomoc had been given in marriage. Such Tepanec interests in the region of southern Puebla would also better explain the conquest of Cuauhtinchan by Tlatelolco under Cuacuauhpitzahuac in 1398, which has so far been an isolated piece of news. (The temporal placement of this, contradictory in the sources, is based on Barlow [1948c].) If one uses another calendar style for the Indian year numbers, this event had occurred later (1438 according to the Mixtec calendar), at the time of the early Triple Alliance (Jiménez Moreno 1953). In the internal order of the Tepanec Empire into family member rulerships, areas directly paying tribute, and allies, Carrasco P. (1984b) recognizes a model that was taken over in later times by the Aztec Triple Alliance.

TEZOZOMOC OF AZCAPOTZALCO ≡ Apparently it is a Mexico-centric topos that the sources describe Tezozomoc as a tyrant. According to Zantwijk (1973: 46–47), although he is alone with this opinion, the military and economic power of the sister cities Tenochtitlán and Tlatelolco was already so significant that Tezozomoc was forced to recognize extensive political concessions and combine them in a Triple Alliance in later times.

CHIMALPOPOCA ≡ The ruler of the Mexica, Chimalpopoca, was presumably a son of Huitzilihuitl and Ayauhcihuatl, a daughter of Tezozomoc, and thus Tezozomoc's grandson. This form of relationship connections between dependent *tlatoani* and the supreme ruler was also practiced in Tlatelolco and other states dependent on the Tepanecs. Some sources say that immediately after Chimalpopoca's birth the tribute payments were lowered. Later, opposing attitudes toward the Mexica were revealed in Azcapotzalco, when the Mexica requested building materials for the construction of an aqueduct for bringing drinking water from the mainland (Chapultepec). The death of Chimalpopoca can possibly be traced back to the machinations of a faction in Tenochtitlán who wanted to eliminate the hardly warlike ruler, who was devoted to the Tepanecs. Reports on this subject and the remaining prehistory of the Tepanec war are most thoroughly discussed by Davies (1973a; abbreviated: 1973b; of interest also: Monjarás-Ruiz 1980:108–11; Zantwijk [1985: 19, 109] sees in these events a rebellion of the Mexica under Itzcoatl).

TEPANEC WAR ≡ The sequence of events in the war of the Mexica against the Tepanecs and the participation of the different rulers is discussed by Davies (1973a:171–90; Barlow 1949b; Hassig 1988:143–45). The exact role of Tlacopan and the circumstances of Maxtla's death remain unclear; the Tetzcocan author Alva Ixtlilxochitl (1975–77, vol. 1:444–46, vol. 2:80) reports that Nezahualcoyotl personally executed Maxtla as a warmonger.

LEGITIMATION OF LAND DISTRIBUTION ≡ The uneven land distribution undertaken in Tenochtitlán after the victory over the Tepanecs is often seen as the reason for the formation of a land-owning, respectively land-using, nobility and the end of an egalitarian society (starting with Moreno 1931:61, 62; reservations already by Katz 1966:38, 39). Against this opinion is the argument that the Mexica had gained land and tribute already under Tezozomoc after their victorious military campaigns. At the latest a more differentiated distribution of property had started at that time. In other areas as well land distribution after conquests customarily favored only the nobility or equally high-ranked warriors, for example in the valley of Atlixco, which belonged to Huexotzinco (Dyckerhoff 1976:161), in Tlaxcallan (Muñoz Camargo 1984), and in southern Puebla (Reyes García 1977).

Among the Mexica the members of Acamapichtli's kin group, who were preferred in the distribution of lands and titles, formed a new elite, differentiated from other nobles and the descendants of leaders of the land-gain period. Now they occupied decisive positions in the military structure as well (Hassig 1988:147). The anecdotal description of a pact between the nobility and fearful commoners can be explained as a (later) justification of the material differences between these property-owning nobles and the people, and from the ideohistorical background prevailing at the time of composition for the specific source (the still unpublished analysis of the ideological Franciscan background of early sources about the *calpulli* by Reyes García [*El término calpulli . . .*] can also be utilized for this situation).

MODELS FOR THE AZTEC EMPIRE ≡ The innovations after the victory over the Tepanecs are regarded as decisive in the development of the political-social system of the Mexica from the beginnings to a centralized state. However, to see in this development a general example for the formation of early historical states is only partially justified. Some time ago Kirchhoff (1948; *1966) pointed out that the Aztec development was stimulated from the outside. Bray (1978) proceeds from this and calls the Aztec development a conscious copy of contemporary situations. Calnek (1982:49–50) characterizes the development in Tenochtitlán within the framework of a general political history in the Valley of Mexico in these words: "The Aztecs of Tenochtitlán (but not Tlatelolco) were unique in resisting neo-Toltec ideologies of legitimate rule as late as 1426, when they too were forced to capitulate to regional trends."

THE PERIOD OF THE TRIPLE ALLIANCE

HISTORY CORRECTIONS ≡ In the indigenous tradition written by Bernardino de Sahagún (Anderson and Dibble 1950–1982, book 10, chap. 29, section "The Mexica") it is stated that under Itzcoatl the leaders of the Mexica had burned the historical archives because their contents had been unsuitable for the simple people. If this (isolated) statement is true, then the Mexica had completed an ideologically motivated break with their previous history, for which different reasons are assumed today: creation of an ideological base for a new directive of economic, political, social, and religious institutions (Conrad and Demarest 1984:32, 37–38), the integration of the basically insignificant tribal deity of the Mexica, Huitzilopochtli, into the group of Toltec creator gods (León-Portilla 1980a:294), the legitimization of the new ruling group around Itzcoatl at the expense of Chimalpopoca's descendants, and the historical connection of the Mexica to the Toltecs (Zantwijk 1985:19), or to place the responsibility for the murder of Chimalpopoca, perpetrated by orders of the Itzcoatl faction, on Maxtla (Rounds 1982:69).

NEZAHUALCOYOTL ≡ Nezahualcoyotl, whose long ruling period (1433–1472) decisively influenced the Acolhuacan state, was one of the most important rulers of Precolumbian Mexico. He made a lasting name for himself not only as a lawgiver, but also as a builder, poet, and philosopher. Religious-philosophical thoughts are attributed to him that gave the polytheistic religious system a monotheistic direction. His life and works became the model for a remarkable historical novel and a biographical text collection (Gillmor 1949; Martínez 1972, as well as other biographies).

TETZCOCO AND TENOCHTITLÁN ≡ It is not justified to evaluate Nezahualcoyotl as a weak ruler, retreating from the Mexica since the beginning of the Alliance. The obscure statement of one source, on which Padden (1967:28–30) based his opinion about an armed dispute between both states after the accession of Moteuczoma I, is understood by other authors quite differently (López Austin 1961:35; Offner 1983:93).

TLACAELEL ≡ The Cihuacoatl Tlacaelel is described as the central figure of the fifteenth century in sources specifically oriented toward Tenochtitlán (group of "Crónica X"); according to some versions he reached an age of one hundred years and was advisor and decision maker to rulers from Moteuczoma I to Axayacatl. Tlacaelel is described as the true creator of all that is intrinsically Mexica or refers to their political organization. Many authors, especially recently, have adopted this view (particularly detailed: Zantwijk 1962). On the other side, early authors like Torquemada questioned the mere existence of this person, because several sources skip him entirely. Even a high-profile historian like Jiménez Moreno (in Jiménez Moreno, Miranda, and Fernández 1965:120–26) does not mention Tlacaelel in his history. In the meantime his existence is confirmed by the fact that independent sources show him and his descendants recorded in genealogies and as landowners especially in the area of Chalco (Colston 1974; Zantwijk 1986a; a narrative biography by Zantwijk 1992).

CIHUACOATL ≡ The office of Cihuacoatl ("female twin") in Tenochtitlán was derived most likely from a priestly office, because Cihuacoatl is also the name of a goddess especially venerated in Colhuacan. The function of the Cihuacoatl was important in interior politics, but did not manifest itself to the outside, so that details remain obscure. Rounds (1982:78–83; about this function: Tschohl 1987:205–19) assumes that the main function of a Cihuacoatl was to preside in an interregnum after the death of a ruler. Until the Spaniards arrived, the office of Cihuacoatl was handed down from father to son in Tlacaelel's family. A generalization that cannot be supported by the sources is the assumption that there was an applicable office title and a dual form of rulership as in other states (Tetzcoco: Offner 1983:151, 184).

FAMINE AND HUMAN SACRIFICE ≡ In presentations of recent years the Aztec development often has been attributed to a consciously formed plan after the victory over Azcapotzalco, leading the way to the empire and including the increase of human sacrifices, which reached eventually very high numbers (Conrad and Demarest 1984:38–54; they talk about an "imperialistic cosmology"). This can be countered by the following: an event such as the great famine of 1451–1455, which caused many Mexica to die in often degrading circumstances, must have left deep impressions in the minds of rulers and subjects and have done more than just motivate them to step up agricultural efforts. In the religious realm one tried to prevent a repetition of the famine by raising the numbers of human sacrifices, as reported in the sources (Jiménez Moreno 1954–55:236). Accordingly, the number of warriors who had the pivotal task of attacking and bringing in the future victims increased.

FLOWERY WAR ≡ It is not correct to see the "Flowery Wars," presumably "ritual" wars, as an invention of Moteuczoma I or Tlacaelel. Even earlier in the Valley of Mexico wars called by that name had been fought by the Chalca against different enemies. Although they were undertaken rather in a form of warlike sports with the goal of making prisoners, they could easily turn into real wars (Hicks 1976:87–92; Isaac 1983b). The Indian sources differ widely in their attempts to explain and justify the introduction of "Flowery Wars" in the time of the Triple Alliance in the fifteenth century. The numbers of the encounters and the participants are not always clear, but they differ from regular conquest wars by the fact that only warriors of a single political unit opposed each other (Davies 1968:111–50; Dyckerhoff 1978:25–27). Hassig (1988:129) emphasizes that the function of Flowery Wars lay in the demonstration of warrior strength. The goal was to gain supremacy alone and without involvement of all military might. Another opinion is held by Zantwijk (1986b): In the late Flowery Wars combatants were provinces of the Triple Alliance with a special status, which encompassed participation in regular wars as a tribute duty.

CONQUEST WARS ≡ The conquests of the Triple Alliance can be seen according to different viewpoints. Subjugations were not always a result of wars, but at least in less remote areas presumably more often the outcome of internal disputes within city-states, independent to begin with, where Tenochtitlán or another power in the Triple Alliance took sides for one faction or one of several rulers either politically (by marriage alliances) or with military force. Then Tenochtitlán would fill the available local ruling position, which in consequence gained in political weight (Hicks 1994). The economic importance of political dominance is undisputed, because it was used predominantly to gain goods for no returns. The military hierarchy gained political weight through conquests; this was cemented additionally by a military ideology stating that sacrificial victims gained in a war were needed to nourish the gods (Lameiras 1985).

SUCCESSION OF MOTEUCZOMA I ≡ In the succession of Moteuczoma I for unknown reasons the still very young Axayacatl was chosen over his two older brothers and all other men in suitable positions. Davies (1973b:124–26) emphasizes the resistance caused by this election. The father of Axayacatl and of his brothers Tizoc and Ahuitzotl was Tezozomoc, a son of Itzcoatl; their mother Atotoztli was a daughter of Moteuczoma I Ilhuicamina. Atotoztli is mentioned in several early sources, written by Franciscans, as ruler after Moteuczoma I. This version has to be rejected, because it was used in early Colonial times to support demands of Doña Isabel Tecuichpoch, a daughter of Moteuczoma II, against the Spaniards (Duverger 1983; 1987). Zantwijk (1978), who cannot clear up the events surrounding the succession of Moteuczoma, shows in a broad historical context basic similarities and suspects that the Mexica could have based their dynastic history on a structural model that does not have a base in history per se. In a more recent work (1985:187–91) he assumes that Atotoztli ruled from 1466 to 1472.

TENOCHTITLÁN AND TLATELOLCO ≡ The position of Tlatelolco, seat of an autonomous or half-autonomous *tlatoani* and situated on the same group of islands as Tenochtitlán, is controversial during the first decades of the Triple Alliance. Tlatelolco had participated in the war against the Tepanecs, but had been overlooked during the founding of the Triple Alliance. Barlow (1948a) considers Tlatelolco an independent political unit until the later subjugation by Axayacatl; opposing accounts are taken to be imperial statements influenced by the viewpoint of Tenochtitlán.

WAR AGAINST TLATELOLCO ≡ Despite very successful military endeavors especially in the southeastern part of the highlands, which Tlatelolco pursued independent of Tenochtitlán, it was first of all a city of merchants. Reasons for growing tension between the neighbors cannot be determined exactly; they may have been caused by losses in trade due to the encroachment of the armies of the Triple Alliance, or loss of influence in the region, or envy by Tenochtitlán because of growing wealth. The rivalry culminated obviously in the time of Moquihuix. Hernández Rodríguez (1961) sees these events as a fight for dominance. Litvak King (1971b) in turn sees the war under Moquihuix merely as the rebellion of a long dependent *tlatoani* (about the war: Davies 1973b:128–33; McAfee and Barlow 1946). After its subjugation, Tlatelolco was ruled by military governors from Tenochtitlán, who were replaced by civil rulers only after several decades (Barlow 1946b). This method of administration in subjugated areas was also chosen for Chalco, but otherwise it was rare.

THE TARASCANS ≡ The most important source about the Tarascans west of the central Mexican area is the early Colonial *Relación de Michoacán* (Tudela 1977). Other sources about the Precolumbian period are missing, because the Tarascans had no indigenous writing tradition that could enable us to follow political developments more closely. Despite general similarities in the area of social structure and material culture—Tarascan language is not related to any other—in many areas of life there were basic differences from central Mexico (overview: Pollard 1993; detail studies: García Alcaraz 1976; López Austin 1981 compares both cultures in an anthology; a very detailed comparison is also in a chapter by Zantwijk 1967b:23–72; overview of Tarascan political history in Warren 1985:3–23). The Tarascan Empire in Michoacán was divided into several parts and at the time of the Spanish conquest it comprised the modern federal state of Michoacán and parts of Jalisco and Guanajuato (about border markers and the question of political membership of individual places: Brand 1971, especially pp. 643–48; Gorenstein 1985:3–18; about the wars with the Mexica: Herrejón Paredo 1978).

The Tarascans were famous for making copper tools. Conrad and Demarest (1984:70–83) suspect that the victory over the Aztecs was decided by the use of metal weapons. Axayacatl had depended on the advice of the *cuauhhuehuetque* ("Eagle elders"), old and meritorious warriors, in his campaign against the Tarascans. Their mistaken evaluations contributed to the loss at Tajimaroa, so that afterwards they no longer had a role to play (Dyckerhoff 1970:47–51).

TIZOC ≡ Only very few places, most of them west of Tenochtitlán, are conquests of the ruler Tizoc. Erdheim (1978), who understands rulership as legitimized by political success, sees a parallel between Chimalpopoca, Tizoc, and Moteuczoma II; he claims that they were all killed by their subjects because of incompetence.

TEMPLE CONSECRATION ≡ For logistic reasons the large number of 80,400 war prisoners from the Zapotec area, from Huexotzinco, Tlappan, and Tziuhcoac, who were sacrificed on the occasion of the consecration of the main temple of Tenochtitlán in 1486, as mentioned in several sources, seems to be hardly credible (Haberland 1986:80–82), even if one takes into consideration the statement that the prisoners were not only kept in Tenochtitlán until the last moment, but were also guarded in other cities. An argument can be made that the high number of sacrificial victims was confused with the number of workers employed for the construction of the temple (Reyes García 1979a and Rojas Rabiela 1979b). The religious justification of human sacrifice (León-Portilla 1986) does not demand such an excess. It is certain that the basic necessity of human sacrifices was accepted not only in the society of the Triple Alliance, but also in all other states.

DEMONSTRATION OF POWER ≡ For the Mexica, festivities connected to grand sacrifices presented a chance to ostentatiously demonstrate their power to strangers, their own elite, and the entire people (Broda 1979; 1978b: 247–51).

CONQUESTS AT THE ISTHMUS OF TEHUANTEPEC ≡ Today there is no question that only under Ahuitzotl (1486–1502) did Aztec campaigns take place in the region of the Isthmus of Tehuantepec (Hassig 1988:200–218). Marcus (1983d) and Flannery (1983) examine the military events in the Valley of Oaxaca and in Tehuantepec by including Zapotec sources. The sites of Ayutla and Mazatlán in Xoconochco belonged to the empire of the Quiché before they were conquered by the Aztecs (Carmack 1981:142).

RESETTLEMENT ≡ The group of settlers destined for the border region to the Tarascans (Alahuiztlan, Teloloapan, and Oztoman) was supposed to be comprised of two thousand people, but in the final analysis there probably were fewer. A dispatching of settlers to Oaxaca is mentioned in the sources for the time of Moteuczoma I, but as the conquests of this ruler took place only in the north of Oaxaca, the statement seems to fit better the time of Ahuitzotl (Davies 1974; *1978).

WARS BETWEEN TLAXCALLAN AND HUEXOTZINCO ≡ At the time of Moteuczoma II the wars between Tlaxcallan, Huexotzinco, and Tenochtitlán and the events connected with them can hardly be disentangled in the sources, as well as the presumably changing positions of Cholollan, but the desperate situation of Huexotzinco is clear (Dyckerhoff 1978:27–33; Barlow 1948b; Davies 1968: 114–39). The entire region fell into a state of such instability that Tlaxcallan alone could no longer afford a lengthy resistance against the Aztecs. Recognition of this made Tlaxcallan a natural ally of the Spaniards.

MOTEUCZOMA II ≡ The sources describe the reforms of Moteuczoma as acts of despotism, and this ruler as oppressive, but at the same time very religious. The religious anchor of the office of ruler is generally accepted (Hippel 1955:76–82; Sullivan 1980; Reyes García 1979b: 34–37; López Austin 1976 discusses this subject for all of Mesoamerica). The exclusion of commoners is seen as a measure to strengthen the position of the birth nobility, necessary because the nobles by merit had enlarged their ranks substantially, especially under

Ahuitzotl (e.g., Vázquez Chamorro 1981b), or because the polygamous marriages of the birth nobility caused a substantial rise of their numbers (Padden 1967:83–87 calls the measures, described in an exaggerated way, "cleaning action"). The effect was in any case a limitation of social mobility (Conrad and Demarest 1984:65–67). However, it can be imagined as well that in the palace the replacement of *macehualli* with nobles fit the emphasis of the ruler as the deputy of a deity, because all nobles were thought to be basically able to rule, and the *macehualli* were not (Sullivan 1980:237). The relief sculptures of rulers showing them in divine attire in Chapultepec are described by Alcocer (1935) and Nicholson (1959).

NEZAHUALPILLI ≡ The last great ruler of Tetzcoco, Nezahualpilli, is celebrated even today as a wise and strictly just ruler and a poet. This evaluation corresponds to the sources belonging to the "Crónica X" tradition and neglects the precarious statements of earlier authors. The ambiguity of the source statements—not even the name of his mother is clearly transmitted—leaves room for multiple possible interpretations (Höhl 1983). In his youth, Nezahualpilli achieved remarkable success in war, but overall there were only few conquests attributed to him—Ahuitzotl clearly had taken the initiative in this area (Offner 1983:228–42). In the time of Nezahualpilli, Tetzcoco had lost sovereign tribute rights to Tenochtitlán in a number of places, but also in Acolhuacan (Hicks 1984b:239). Sources from Tetzcoco say that Moteuczoma even went as far as terminating his membership in the Triple Alliance in opposition to Nezahualpilli.

SUCCESSION DISPUTE IN TETZCOCO ≡ The dispute about the succession of Nezahualpilli was restricted to the sons of two women from Tenochtitlán. The winner, Cacama, obviously was a nephew of Moteuczoma II. This conflict and the subsequent division of the territory ruled by Tetzcoco was one of the reasons for the quick success of the Spaniards, who received decisive logistic and military support against Moteuczoma from Ixtlilxochitl, who had remained general of the united armies of Acolhuacan, despite his loss in the succession dispute. After Cacama had been killed by the Spaniards in Tenochtitlán, Cohuanacoch became ruler of Alcolhuacan. He stood on the side of Tenochtitlán in the fight against the Spaniards as well (Offner 1983:238–41).

THE CONQUISTA ≡ Although no new facts have become known about the history of the conquest of Mexico by the Spaniards, a modern analysis of the subject and evaluation of sources is missing. The most important sources are the reports by conquerors, first among them the letters of Hernán Cortés (Hernández Sánchez-Barba 1963), and from the Indian side Book 12 of the works of Bernardino de Sahagún (an anthology of Indian authors: León-Portilla and Garibay K. 1959; about the conquest of western Mexico there is a more recent work: Warren 1985).

EVALUATION OF MOTEUCZOMA II ≡ The person of Moteuczoma II Xocoyotzin as the central figure of the Mexican conquest was viewed with particular interest. Especially his unusually hesitant if not passive attitude (in today's Western opinion) toward the Spaniards needed explanation. In this the evaluation of one author often depends on whom he blames for the violent death of Moteuczoma in the course of the Spanish conquest, one side or the other, described differently by Spanish and Indian sources (about the different versions: Romero Giordano 1986). It is also decisive how an author evaluates the tradition that Moteuczoma's actions were determined by his conviction that the arrival of the Spaniards was really the return of the god Quetzalcoatl as prophesied. In this way Burland (1973) describes the life of Moteuczoma II in the framework of a sensitive characterization of Aztec life, which is not always concordant with modern knowledge. He sees the ruler torn between a life as a priest and as a ruler, between the religious schools of the deities Quetzalcoatl and Huitzilopochtli, and feels that his wavering actions in the decisive moments of the Conquista were caused by the expectation of Quetzalcoatl (similar tendency in Padden 1967:116–202, and numerous others. Wasserman 1983 rather thinks of an identification of Cortés with Tezcatlipoca). Krickeberg (1952) recognizes in the attitude of Moteuczoma II a fluctuation between fear based on the prophecy and arrogant defiance in the knowledge of his supremacy, together with an inability to face the inevitable. Haberland (1973) on the other hand evaluates the ruler as a statesman who was certainly bound by his religion, but who faced the opponent with skillfully planned actions; lack of information about the new opponent and his culturally determined behavior, which was apparent in the politics of Cortés, and the supremacy of Spanish weapons made success impossible. According to Davies (1973b:258–69), Moteuczoma's actions were determined by fear and an inadequate appraisal of the Spaniards.

In any of these considerations it should not be overlooked that the often described frightful omens of the sources represent retrospective explanation attempts for the Conquest, which toppled the Indian world view; in consequence they cannot have influenced the actions of the time (Prem 1996:105).

FORMS OF SOCIAL AND POLITICAL ORGANIZATION

Numerous examinations have shown in recent decades that in the Aztec area in the Valley of Mexico as well as in the neighboring regions of central Mexico (and beyond to the Isthmus of Tehuantepec) a very similar basic model of economic, social, and political structures existed, where regional differences were only gradual in character.

EGALITARIAN TRIBAL SOCIETY? ≡ Aztec social organization, especially that of the Triple Alliance or its member Tenochtitlán, has absorbed scholars intensively during almost a hundred years. At the end of the last century Aztec society had been understood by Bandelier (1878; 1880), based on Morgan (1877), as a tribal gentile organization, where the democratic and egalitarian *calpulli* formed by patrilinear descent groups were the exclusive owners of land, and the basic structure was described as an equally egalitarian tribal society under a chief-like leader. The existence of a state and of private landowners was denied by Bandelier. Bandelier's opinion created interest and was adopted up until the 1940s. Influenced by him, the importance given to the Precolumbian organizational form of the *calpulli* became a political factor in Mexico, specifically in the laws of the agrarian reforms of 1917: the newly formed village lands, gained from disowning large estates, were called *ejido* ("public land" in Spanish) but derived their mode of usage from the Precolumbian *calpulli.* Bandelier's opinion was in a conscious opposition to earlier presentations and caused in its time in the United States a heated discussion, which Keen (1985, especially pp. 380–410) has summarized. Bandelier found less of an echo in German Americanist circles.

CALPULLI ≡ Like most of the deviant interpretations, Bandelier's also was based on the description of the egalitarian organization of *calpulli* in the report of the Spanish administrator Alonso de Zorita (1891), which is accorded only regional significance today. The model of a democratic Aztec tribal society was attacked in 1931 by Moreno, who saw a theocratic-military oligarchy with a tendency toward monarchy as the government form of the Aztecs. Social relationships were political and had created a class society. The *calpulli* had multiple functions and was marked more by territorial than by kin concerns.

Later authors tried to combine these opposite positions. Monzón (1949) saw the *calpulli,* based on kinship but socially strongly layered, as the foundation of Aztec society, which in its overall mass of political-economic relationships despite their complexity rested on common descent in the final analysis. The study by Katz (1966), and the more limited subject of Kirchhoff's work (1954–55), examined Aztec institutions from the viewpoint of historical development, where the *calpulli,* organized democratically and along kin lines, was only an early phase of a development that later led to the state. A thorough analysis, today a little outdated, of structure and function of the state institutions of Tenochtitlán is given by López Austin (1961, especially pp. 129–31), where he assumes different meanings for the Mexica term *calpulli,* depending on the temporal and local context. Caso (1958–60; *1963) divides landownership—private landownership was one of the core subjects of the discussion—into public and private property.

REORIENTATION OF RESEARCH ≡ Toward the end of the 1960s there was a reorientation directed by Carrasco P. (1970), who rejected a general meaning of the term *calpulli* after he completed local case studies and determined that the term appeared in different levels of organization with correspondingly different significance, and could be applied to almost any constituted group that felt united. Castillo Farreras (1972:69–84, 132), staying close to the sources, saw a complex society but avoided a final decision on the controversial question "private ownership of land" by pointing out that in the framework of Aztec society the relevant feature was not ownership (in the European sense) of the production medium land, but the right to gain and use it. Meanings of terms for the complex landownership, often not noticed, regionally different and frequently overlapping, were evaluated by Dyckerhoff and Prem (1978, with a critical overview of previous presentations).

Numerous localized and partially quantified ethnohistorical examinations have contributed to make the general picture, which previously relied almost exclusively on statements in the usually generalized Colonial reports, more precise and differentiated; these examinations show a differentiated picture of the social and economic reality in Precolumbian Mesoamerica, based on early Colonial data (a collection of regional studies [Carrasco P. 1976b] offers detailed examinations for several areas, also outside of the Valley of Mexico).

In the area of today's Morelos the term *calpulli* could be applied to units of a different organizational level; in the extreme it means no more than a house group with inhabitants of different classes (Carrasco P. 1970:363). In Cuauhtinchan the term applies to an ethnic group of Toltec descent (Reyes García 1977). In Tetzcoco *calpulli* is the smallest territorial organizational unit in the countryside, first of all characterized by shared tribute duties (Hicks 1982). The *calpulli* also occupies an important place in Offner's (1983:124–47) examination of social and judicial structures of Tetzcoco. After examining kin terminology and relationships he concludes that the *calpulli* was the lowest legal level, where no kin terms were relevant.

The role of the nobility as the politically significant social rank, which commanded the main production factors, is not controversial today. Differing opinions prevail in interpretations of late central Mexican societies according to a theoretical model or ideal type, which is often influenced by European concepts. Here Marxist models are especially frequent: the "oriental society" or the "asiatic production mode," which was based on a centralized society (besides authors already mentioned: Palerm 1972; Bartra 1974; López Austin 1974b; *1985). Mercedes Olivera (1978) is a rare exception by presenting an examination of detail based on prime source data. Corona Sánchez (1986) tries to relieve the model-fixated and unicausal socioeconomic classification of Mesoamerican societies by seeing them as multifaceted transition forms on the road to form a state (see on this also Vázquez Chamorro 1986, who shows that in Marx's works Indian civilizations are not uniformly characterized).

NOBLE HOUSES ≡ The configuration of central Mexican noble lineages in main- and sidelines reminds one of European structures, but it is indigenous without a doubt. Each noble house was a lineage in the anthropological sense, descended from one common ancestor and structured in a hierarchy (Carrasco P. 1976b; 1979). The best visual representation of Indian noble lines can be found in the *Matrícula de Huexotzinco*, an early Colonial inhabitant list (Prem 1974), the *Genealogy of Tlatzcantzin* from Tlaxcala (Kutscher 1962b), and the *Elecciones de Calpan* (Bibliothèque Nationale Paris, Fonds mexicain No. 73).

Carrasco P.'s (1978; 1976a) view that the noble houses and the different corporations of commoners form the basic political-territorial segments of which the central Mexican society was composed results from the most convincing analysis of the complex social structure of late Postclassic Mexico that has been presented so far. His presentation is a little vague about the decidedly necessary difference between a noble house either as a unit based on descent or one based on economy. He advances from the conjecture, substantiated in many cases, that the peasants dependent on a noble house trace their origin to the members of the corresponding lineage, which had declined socially. The group of persons tied together economically in a *teccalli* therefore is not congruent with one tied together by common descent, if dependent peasants and artisans of other ethnic origin have been subjugated and joined to noble houses (Dyckerhoff 1976:161; Muñoz Camargo 1984, vol. 1:175). On the other hand it should be noted that important and possibly decisive questions about the integration of dependent people are open in noneconomic areas, such as place of residence, religion, and others, for whose answer the source situation offers only little data.

DISPERSED LANDS OF NOBLES ≡ Property of nobles situated far apart, as Prem (1978) has examined in Huexotzinco, was a phenomenon prevailing all over Mexico. The spatial-geographic presentation of a small noble property is the subject of an area map from Tlaxcala (Kutscher 1962a, interpreted differently).

TEUCTLI ≡ Part of the titles bestowed in Tenochtitlán after the victory over the Tepanecs contained the term *teuctli*, which is documented for the heads of numerous noble houses outside of the Triple Alliance and was bestowed there with a lavish ceremony. The titles themselves often have an ethnic component and were also held in other places where Nahuatl was spoken. However, there were obviously important differences in position and function of a *teuctli* within the political structure of the Triple Alliance, its member states, and other areas, which have not yet been examined. A discussion like that of Rounds (1977) about function, office, rank, and origin of *teuctli* obscures all possible and real differences, by not sufficiently differentiating the place of origin of the sources and examinations, within the large, Nahuatl-speaking area comprised of states with differently organized centralizations.

COMMONERS ≡ The often-used German term *Gemeinfreie* for members of common, often land-owning, corporations is not applicable, because of its typical European connotation. Corporate units of commoners have been called by the ambiguous term *calpulli.* The term *calpule',* derived from it, was used sometimes for members, sometimes for heads, due to confusing information by Zorita (1891).

Summary terms for dependents of a noble house are similarly difficult. The often-used word for them, *mayeque* (only as a plural), or *tlalmaitl,* was taken also from Zorita (1891), and occurs only rarely; the use of these terms was mainly restricted to today's Morelos. In Colonial sources commonly the Spanish term *terrazguero* is used.

In the literature the term *macehuales* (from Nahuatl *macehualli,* Spanish *vasallo,* meaning vassal, retainer) for commoners is frequently used, but it is not entirely correct, because it expresses "dependency" regardless of the social level, and in some regions (e.g., south Puebla) it was used in this very sense for local rulers in their relationship to the Aztec Empire. In religion *macehualli* expressed the subordination of man to the deities (León-Portilla 1986).

DEPENDENT AND INDEPENDENT COMMONERS ≡ In Nahuatl there is no terminological category of commoners as dependents and independents, which suggests that the differentiation, relevant in modern view, did not play a significant role in Indian society. Therefore, Hicks (1976) concluded that the way of life of both groups could not have been significantly different. Early Colonial observers also did not differentiate when they described the peasant population as generally exploited and their life-style deplorable. The classification of peasants directly dependent on noble houses as a separate, socially lower, class, from peasants with land from collective property thus is not justified. Collectively owned land did not exist at all in some areas; where it did, it was due to historical developments, just as dependents were (Dyckerhoff 1976; Olivera 1977).

TENANTS ≡ In Spanish-language sources a group of persons appear by the name *rentero* ("tenant"), who worked the land of others for part of its yield, but their social order or a regional connection are not elucidated. Calnek (1975:45–47) is of the opinion that after the land distribution by Itzcoatl and gaining new land because of the dams, the tenant system was introduced in Tenochtitlán as a new legal form for the usage both of land belonging to the urban elite and administrators, and the collective property of temples and city quarters.

LABOR ORGANIZATION ≡ For large building projects, where a mass of people had to replace the nonexistent beasts of burden, wagons, and technical equipment, the entire male population of a territory was put to forced labor. They were organized for such projects in groups of twenty, which in turn were combined into larger units (Rojas Rabiela 1979a:41–66; Gibson 1956). The group leaders of the upper levels were nobles. Labor efforts occurred in lengthy periods of changing shifts. Tools and food were supplied by the government.

LONG-RANGE MERCHANTS ≡ No other group of the Precolumbian Indian society of central Mexico has been accorded so much attention in the literature as the merchants, especially the long-range merchants (*pochteca*) (about trade routes and ports of trade: Chapman 1957; *1959; *1975; Berdan 1978c; *1978a; Feldman 1976; *1978a; about internal organization and religion: Acosta Saignes 1954; *1975; Zantwijk 1970; 1985:125–76; Lanczkowski 1962; León-Portilla 1962; *1975; slightly modified: *1980b). Nevertheless, there has not yet been a complete monograph, and many questions are still open or have been treated only in a controversial manner.

SOCIAL POSITION ≡ The standing of long-range merchants was determined by wealth and collaboration with the rulers. That is why the *pochteca* are regarded today as a sort of intermediate rank between nobles and commoners, although opinions are divided on the question which of the two groups they were closer to. The position of merchants obviously became a problem in the time of Moteuczoma II, because the sources (first of all Sahagún, Book 9 [1950–1982] with information from long-range merchants from Tlatelolco) emphasize not only the high regard of the ruler, but also his admonitions, and allow the recognition of their precarious position *vis à vis* the warriors. Among modern interpretations of these texts there is a wide spectrum of controversial opinions. In general it is assumed that the special position of the *pochteca* in society was the result of the most recent developments that occurred only after the conquest of Tlatelolco. Isaac (1986) wants to see the manifold cooperation between the ruler and the *pochteca* limited to the period of Ahuitzotl. Lanczkowski (1962) feels that the sharp separation of society into nobility and *macehualli* was severely disturbed by the rise of the *pochteca.* Bittmann Simons and Sullivan (1972; *1978) ask if the *pochteca* became dangerous for the nobility and the ruler himself. Berdan (1978c; *1978a) emphasizes the confrontation with the nobility by birth. Erdheim (1972:107), who studied the question in the most thorough manner of all, recognizes in the attitude of the warriors a reaction toward their rising dependency on the merchants, who became steadily more powerful as providers of luxury goods and status symbols. The spectrum of diverging opinions shows that important historical developments still lack scholarly penetration.

We can add to this discussion the following: in the Valley of Puebla-Tlaxcala a similar inner stratification and status gain can be determined for the merchants as in the Valley of Mexico, which can be derived from a Toltec-associated origin. This shows that generally merchants had a special standing and customs that differentiated them from other commoners. The increasingly strict rules for luxury in the Triple Alliance and the coupling of many luxury goods as status symbols to specific war events also emphasizes a basic special status of merchants. After Moteuczoma II had limited the opportunities of commoners to rise in society and thus had restricted their access to luxury goods, the *pochteca* and their lavish customs appeared provocative to both social strata, which became increasingly antagonistic toward each other.

SLAVES ≡ The fact that none of the social classes of Precolumbian central Mexico can be designated by the term "slaves" (as ownership of human beings who can be bought and sold) is one that chroniclers of the sixteenth and seventeenth centuries such as Torquemada (León-Portilla 1983) have noted already, but a better word seems to be missing in all languages used by scholars. After Bosch-García (1944) had published his thorough treatment of debt- and pledge slavery in ancient Mexico, it was Yolotl González Torres (1979; 1976) who dealt with the subject again in the framework of a new evaluation of Aztec society. Based on assertions about purchases and sales of slaves and about prisoners of war, who were not sacrificed, she turns against the narrow views of Bosch García, and supposes that there had been a small number of slaves of both genders who had their origin outside of the Aztec groups, but who were economically without significance.

PORTERS ≡ Tightly interwoven with the subject "slaves" is the question of the social position of the porters. The Spanish language sources mix terms like *tamemes* (porters), *esclavos* (slaves), *prisioneros* (captives), or also *pobres macehuales* (poor man of the people) rather indiscriminately, when full of pity they speak of porters. Therefore, many authors see the porters as a separate social category. Castillo Farreras (1972:110–13) regards the porters of Tenochtitlán as a socially low professional group without opportunities to rise, but he emphasizes that the sources have not been sufficiently exhausted on the details. Hassig (1985:28–39) follows him in the compilation of data about employment and origin of porters. It is likely that here, as elsewhere, there was a substantial difference between the metropolis Mexico and the rural areas. Early single data come from the area of today's Morelos (Hinz, Hartau, and Heimann-Koenen 1983).

KINSHIP AND MARRIAGE ≡ The Aztecs recognized the side of the woman as equal to that of the male in questions of kinship and descent. The basic examination of kinship terms in Nahuatl was presented by Rammow (1964; more recent works on the subject: Gardner 1982; Díaz Rubio 1986; with a component analysis: Offner 1983:175–201) and has not been substantially enlarged since. A local study on the lowest organizational level could not determine a clear endogamous or exogamous marriage rule (Carrasco P. 1961). Within local political units, as was proven for Tecali, endogamous marriage rules seem to have predominated among commoners (Olivera 1978:136–42). Dynastic marriages obeyed strict rules, which were different in Tetzcoco and Tenochtitlán (Carrasco P. 1984a). Through marriage alliances with members of ruling dynasties, even in dependent states, a strong common interest, transcending former borders, had been developed, which created political stability (Smith 1986). The rulers did not form marriage alliances with their traditional enemies in the Valley of Puebla. These were restricted to exceptions outside of the Nahuatl-speaking area. It was common that the newlywed couple lived close to the house of the groom's father.

FAMILY AND HOUSEHOLD ≡ Information about the size of households, or the amount of tribute and work owed by farms, can be gleaned only from the early Colonial sources. A detailed census from the area of Tepoztlan and Cuernavaca shows a very complex composition of a household with 7.0 to 8.3 persons per unit, which comes closest to the temporal and factual Precolumbian reality. Although households with one or two couples are in the majority, households with three couples are comparatively frequent, but there are only a few with four couples (Carrasco P. 1964b; Nahuatl texts and translations of this and other census efforts are by Hinz, Hartau, and Heimann-Koenen 1983). Similar conditions were found by Calnek (1974) for Tenochtitlán. However, in rural Tepetlaoztoc in the sixteenth century, households composed of the nuclear family of a married or widowed male, including stepchildren or adopted children, were in the majority (Offner 1984). A summary of size of households, composition of families, and marriage rules can be found in Carrasco P. (1970:367–71).

WOMEN ≡ Our knowledge of women among the Indian peoples of Precolumbian Mexico is based on Colonial reports written by men for men about a male-dominated society. It is correspondingly paltry. Added to this is the fact that the gender-determined division of labor corresponded to what Spaniards felt was common practice for the most part, and therefore was not deemed "worthy of note" (Sachse 1963). There are only a few examinations especially of women (Seler-Sachs 1919, 2nd ed. 1984; Vázquez Chamorro 1981a; Hellbom 1982; about sexuality: López Austin 1982; Clendinnen 1991:163–84). More attention has been commanded by the marriage alliances of Indian women of high noble birth, which were of substantial political importance (Carrasco P. 1984a; Schroeder 1992).

YOUTH ≡ A good presentation of Spanish-language source passages and an ideological-critical overview of literature about the educational system can be found in Hauck (1968). The old-fashioned terminology he employs for social structures is not detrimental, because he correctly recognizes the Aztecs as a strongly classified society. Although his thesis that the *telpochcalli* was meant only for the military education of young nobles cannot be upheld quite this way (it was obviously formulated without knowledge of the terminologically better differentiated Nahuatl texts by Sahagún), he is right to question the customarily accepted "general compulsory education," because even in Tenochtitlán, from where most of the information is derived, it is not known for certain exactly which youths went to a *telpochcalli,* and whether the sons of artisans could learn to be warriors, or if craft apprenticeship had precedence.

RHETORIC ≡ The more extensive work by Berdan (1976a) describes public education, but also the rearing of young people in their parents' houses through examples, punishments, and rhetoric (traditional speeches containing admonishments: *huehuetlatolli*) (León-Portilla 1980c:190–204; an overview of educational speeches: Sullivan 1974). An anthology published by Escalante (1985) contains texts about the formal and informal education in different ethnic groups of civilized Mesoamerica, as well as of nomadic tribes living to the north of them.

CITY-STATES ≡ In the Valley of Mexico alone, the large number of tiny political units has been recognized in its totality only through the work of Gibson (1964b:32–57) and is documented best there (overview of Precolumbian political units in today's federal state of Morelos: Gerhard 1970). The Spanish conquerors took pre-Aztec political conditions of city-states as the basis for the early Colonial administrative organization, and these jealously guarded their local, historically founded independence. It can no longer be determined if the cities truly had an urban character. Both in Tetzcoco (whose estimated population was 12,500 to 25,000) and in the smaller Huexotzinco, the former status of a "capital" was not characterized by dense building, but consisted rather of a loose conglomerate of partly sprawling palaces and other buildings (Offner 1983:7; Hicks 1984a; Schmidt 1979:171). General models of origin and interaction of city-states in the Valley of Mexico are described by Calnek (1982; 1978c). An overview beyond the Valley of Mexico, which includes archaeological evidence as well, is given by Bray (1972). The minor significance of archaeological data for cultural reconstructions is deplored by Rojas (1994).

POLYETHNIC SOCIETIES ≡ Although a polyethnic composition has to be assumed for all Postclassic state units of central Mexico, and beyond that for the period predating the Toltecs, which is not covered by the sources, the examination of this important subject leaves much to be desired. Zantwijk (1973) made a contribution by describing in a theoretical framework the growth of the state of Tetzcoco and the attempt by the ruler Techotlalatzin to counter the disruptive tendencies of ethnic plurality by his settlement policy and distribution of offices. Also he discussed the prerequisites of the failure later on. A more recent work has pointed out mistakes in his primary material and necessitates certain revisions; however, these are not basic (Offner 1979). Zantwijk's monograph of the Aztecs (1985) is a very detailed presentation of ethnic integration in Tenochtitlán; the book was written with a structuralistic perspective and is hard to follow. It is to his special credit to have worked out the ethnic stratification of the Aztec capital as well, because this point is often left out and instead the metropolis Mexico is seen as a community in which only Tlatelolco tried to find a separate way. There are several works that deal with this subject in the Valley of Puebla (Reyes García 1977; Carrasco P. 1971; Olivera and Reyes 1969).

PARALLEL RULERS ≡ Often there were two to four rulers (*tlatoani*) at the head of the states, who belonged to different places or quarters, and of them only one appeared as "the ruler" to the outside. Colonial documents from Xochimilco show that each of the three *tlatoani* there was supported in his office by three to four high-ranking officials (Carrasco P. 1977), and each *tlatoani* had his own territory. Tlaxcallan was called a "republic" in early sources because it was ruled by four *tlatoani* (Gibson 1967:1–15; Angiano and Chapa 1976:135). In Huexotzinco the capital was supposed to have shifted between three places (Lehmann, Kutscher, and Vollmer 1981:222). It can be suspected that three different lines of *tlatoani* represented the government of Huexotzinco, taking turns, to the outside. In neighboring Cholollan there existed besides the double rulers with the titles *aquiach* and *tlalchiach* four or six additional local rulers (Carrasco P. 1971:17–22).

DYNASTIC SEQUENCE ≡ The father-son sequence dominated in the succession of rulers. However, it can be doubted that this was the custom in the early period of Tenochtitlán, as is assumed most of the time today, because the source statements about the kinship of early rulers differ from each other. In later times the Tenochca avoided a direct father-son sequence in the election of rulers. A similar procedure is recorded for Colhuacan (in García Icazbalceta 1941a, 2nd ed. vol. 3:267) and for the Matlatzinca in the Valley of Toluca. According to Zorita (1891; *1941) they had three "lords" in each case: The oldest had the title *tlatoani*, and the two younger ones had other high titles. When the *tlatoani* died, the second titleholder took his place, and the third official moved up. For the now empty position a suitable son or brother of the first was elected. There was a similar procedure observed upon the death of the second, so that a son never succeeded his father directly. Zorita also mentions that the Quiché, a Mayan people in the highlands of Guatemala, had a similar procedure. The handling of this succession rule and its anchoring in a ruling group in Tenochtitlán was an important step in centralizing and stabilizing the ruling system (Rounds 1982).

ACCESSION CEREMONIES ≡ Tizoc was the first ruler for whom the sources describe in detail the customary sequence from election to coronation. Before his election he was one of the most prominent generals and probably had served as a priest in the temple for some time. The election proper was conducted by a large but not closely defined group, which determined his successor in the council of four at the same time. After an inauguration ritual in the temple, which also confirmed the election, the newly elected ruler started on his first military campaign. The captives he made were then sacrificed during the following coronation ceremony (León-Portilla 1980a; meaning and background of these ceremonies: Broda 1978b).

THE AZTEC EMPIRE

TRIPLE ALLIANCE ≡ The foundation of the Triple Alliance tied in with an organizational form rich in traditions. Only the political constellation of previous triple alliances is securely known, so it cannot be determined how much of the contents of older forms has been adopted (López Austin 1961:33–39). Each of the member states had a preferred area of influence, where it dominated in conquests (details in Offner 1983:89–91). A reason for the expansive thrust of the Aztec Triple Alliance is often seen in Mexica ideology, which "successfully integrated religious, economic, and social systems into an imperialistic war machine" (Conrad and Demarest 1984:37). The widely spread opinion that the Triple Alliance had military-economic goals (gain of more tribute), is opposed by the view that it was formed first of all because of a political purpose, the pacification of a large area; additional tribute and labor payments had come as a consequence (Monjarás-Ruiz 1980:147). A political reason for the Alliance was surely that the expansion of one member did not happen at the cost of a partner, but of third parties. The Pax Azteca, at first limited to the Valley of Mexico, encompassed an ever-increasing area in time.

LEGAL SYSTEM ≡ Nezahualcoyotl is considered to be the creator of the legal system of Acolhuacan, which was examined by Offner (1983) in a modern work within the anthropology of law. Much less is known about the legal system of Tenochtitlán; the territorial responsibility of judicial officials remains obscure. Here, as well as in Tetzcoco, nobles were punished more harshly for specific misdeeds than commoners. There was a probably comparable legal organization in Tlacopan as well, about which hardly anything is known (López Austin 1961:97–109). An overview of numerous source passages about legal questions, offenses, and punishments, structured according to Roman legal categories, was presented quite early (Kohler 1895; 1924, still not outdated).

Another, older work ties in with this one and treats the origin of ancient American legal systems from a diffusionist viewpoint (Wintzer 1930). Property law is the subject of a specialized examination by Freund (1946; a short summary by catchwords: Durand-Forest 1963).

TETZCOCO ≡ The political and legal reorganization of Acolhuacan after the formation of the Triple Alliance was intended to level the different ethnic and power-political interests by tying them into a centralized organizational structure, which was focused completely on the ruler and his seat in Tetzcoco. The fourteen *tlatoani* formed the state council together with the heads of the four council boards. The statements about the number of *tlatocayotl* vary between fourteen and fifteen, depending on whether Tetzcoco is counted as well or not (Corona Sánchez 1976). Offner (1983:87–120) thinks that despite great power over the dependent *tlatoani* the head ruler of Acolhuacan's freedom of decisions was always limited by the interests and political intrigues of the dependent rulers. The Precolumbian organizational system for the general labor efforts stayed intact until the early Colonial period (Gibson 1956). The *calpixqui,* governors of an area not ruled by a dependent *tlatoani,* were preferably meritorious men of common descent (Hicks 1978).

GOVERNMENT OF TENOCHTITLÁN ≡ Zantwijk (1980) characterizes the mode of government in Tenochtitlán as paternalistic. Much remains equivocal about the separate office functions in the government of Tenochtitlán because of insufficient sources (López Austin 1961:87–97). Even the council of four is controversial (see an indication in Rounds 1982:85, note 8; about the highest ranks also Piho 1972). The inner structure of Tenochtitlán and the relationship of titles of high functionaries with specific city quarters and temples is discussed thoroughly by Zantwijk (1985; 1986b): instead of a Triple Alliance, he sees a unified state with tasks distributed among the three occupants of the throne.

HINTERLAND OF TENOCHTITLÁN ≡ Organizational relationships beyond the political dominion between the island city Mexico and the conquered surrounding areas have hardly been studied so far. *Codex Mendoza* (Berdan and Anawalt 1992: folio 69) shows that the rulers of Tenayocan, Chicnauhtla, and Colhuacan each had a special room in the palace as "friends and allies" of Moteuczoma, just as did the other two Triple Alliance rulers, without there being a reason for this except for the historical significance of Colhuacan. The property scattered everywhere in the neighborhood guaranteed an indirect bond and economical integration (about tribute organization in the surrounding areas: Barlow 1949a:126–33).

TLACOPAN ≡ Tlacopan, the junior partner of the Aztec Triple Alliance, is relatively sparsely documented and has not been examined fully (Barlow 1952; Zantwijk 1969; Gibson 1964a; Carrasco P. 1950; Trautmann 1968:69–77; the literature is summarized and completed by Pérez-Rocha 1982:13–29). It is amazing that the separation of the two ethnic groups in the Azcapotzalco area of influence can be traced to this century (Barrios E. 1952).

EMPIRE? ≡ The term "empire" or "state" for the political entity created by the Aztec Triple Alliance has often been questioned, but it is still used by most of the modern authors, who do not fully adopt the old-world connotations (e.g., Smith 1986). In order to bring more precision to the question, Hassig (1984:16–17) has contrasted the old-world territorial empire with the hegemonical empire of the Aztecs, which was controlled only politically, and for which he found corresponding features in the early phases of the Roman Empire (in the interpretation of Luttwack [1976], also used by other authors in comparisons with Mesoamerica). Much more precisely than can be done on the basis of such a superficial comparison, Carrasco P. (1991:95–96), differentiates four different categories of political dependency and tribute duty, on the basis of data from Tetzcoco and Tlacopan: (1) subjugated areas with their own ruler, (2) the immediate rural surroundings of Tetzcoco and Tlacopan (and most likely also of Tenochtitlán), (3) areas without their own ruler, governed by an official of the central power, and (4) remote conquered places, which paid tribute to all three members of the Triple Alliance.

ARMY ≡ A part of the nobility, whose livelihood was secured by dependent peasants on their property, and who were not involved in other public offices, most likely were available unconditionally for military service. The same is true for nobles by merit, who were given the use of land for their exploits in war. Most likely the elite troops called "warrior orders" were formed by such quasi-professional warriors, while the mass of the soldiers were called up in each case in a general mobilization (not very analytical: Piho 1976). Cook (1946) supposes that the Triple Alliance could command overall one hundred thousand men, and when necessary even three hundred thousand. The most important piece of equipment was a wooden sword, which became a deadly weapon because of inserted obsidian blades, and a slight, but effective, cotton armor. During long-range war expeditions additional weapons and dry rations were taken along, but the brunt of the care for the passing army was carried by the population of the transit areas (Monjarás-Ruiz 1976; Harvey 1984:83–102).

CONDUCT OF WAR ≡ In contrast to the Flowery Wars, the Aztec procedure in conquest wars was aimed at extermination of the enemy. This difference has been pointed out again (Isaac 1983). This does not preclude seeing war basically as a sacred act (Canseco Vincourt 1966). The entire subject is treated thoroughly and in detail in the monograph by Hassig (1988).

FORTRESSES ≡ The "fortresses" often mentioned in the Spanish conquest reports are really civil-religious building complexes in hard-to-reach places, which were sometimes also fortified, but rarely had primarily military assignments (Armillas 1948 presents reports on fortresses and describes the fortress Oztoman; Gorenstein 1973 examines a fortified site conquered in 1503 by the Triple Alliance). Such forts, more than real fortresses, complied with the war conduct and with the fact that during skirmishes in cities the temples were used as bastions, and when they fell the definitive defeat was indicated.

COLONIES, GARRISONS ≡ Statements about intentional measures to secure conquered provinces are rare, except for the two well-documented resettling actions by Ahuitzotl, and any fortified garrisons or similar institutions beyond that are a matter of debate, where their number and effect are concerned (Zantwijk 1967a; Bittmann Simons and Sullivan 1972; *1978:207–8). Military installations manned by troops of the Triple Alliance were certainly an exception (Davies 1974; *1978). Carrasco P. (1991:105) determines that there were eleven garrisons known by name.

EXPANSION OF THE EMPIRE ≡ The basic overview of the Aztec expansion in time and space is by Gibson (1971), who also refers to unsolved questions. In order to determine the extent of the Aztec Empire there are two categories of sources: the conquest lists, which attribute a series of conquests to each ruler (preserved in a part of the pictorial manuscript *Codex Mendoza*, but also integrated into some sources written by Indians in European script), and the various tribute lists and registers of places, which relay a temporally fixed inventory of dependent places (often to the time of the Spanish conquest). Other sources can be consulted as well.

CONQUEST LISTS ≡ The hieroglyphically written place names next to stereotypical pictures or texts of conquest lists hardly allow the identification of details, but just announce "victory over . . ." or, without differentiation, "fall of. . . ." These lapidary statements can cover anything in a broad range of event types, from a successful raid of Mexican troops to a final subjugation with ensuing regular tribute payments and installation of a tribute administrator. The confusion is heightened by the fact that at times a conquest is attributed to a ruler when in fact he may have achieved it as a general under his predecessor. The naming of the same place in the lists of two or more rulers, which can be traced back to such events, may have been reinterpreted in more extensively written reports as "rebellion." On the other hand there are documented cases when a real secession of a tribute-paying region needed the renewed intervention of Aztec troops. Moreover, it remains an open question, when there was a common conquest by the Triple Alliance, and when it was a lone effort by one of the member states. A reconstruction is further hindered by the many homonymous (in the writing system, homographic) place names in Mexico (overview: Barlow 1946a) and a large number of mistaken readings in the various lists (Prem 1992). An overview of the most important conquest lists ordered by rulers, with localizations, has been prepared by Kelly (1952; on the same subject but with major reservations: Holt 1976).

TRIBUTE LISTS ≡ The main category of sources for the reconstruction of the actual territorial extent of the Aztec Empire at the time of the Spanish conquest are the tribute lists. A few Barlow (1949a) evaluated in a work that is still fundamental. However, in many details Barlow's book urgently needs to be supplemented and corrected, which has happened for only a few regions at this time (part of the Gulf Coast: Kelly 1952; state of Guerrero: Harvey 1971). Tschohl (1964, the most thorough approach to the analysis of the Conquest sources) has corrected the supposition by Barlow that the route to Oaxaca and Xoconochco went through Tochtepec, and has shown that the equation of some places beyond the Isthmus of Tehuantepec with conquests was wrong, but he too could not finalize his statements in all cases. Although they do not refer to Barlow, Ball and Brockington (1978) also suggest a route through Tochtepec. The individual military thrusts and the resulting conquests are analyzed by Hassig (1988), but his treatment of sources is highly defective and his conclusions are not always convincing.

BEYOND THE ISTHMUS OF TEHUANTEPEC ≡ To this day the exact extent of Aztec dominance in the southern areas, in the region of the Isthmus of Tehuantepec, remains unknown. The official tribute records in the Codex Mendoza contain only Xoconochco (Socunusco at the border to Guatemala) on the Pacific Coast as a tribute-paying province beyond the Valley of Oaxaca. Although the conquest lists for Ahuitzotl and Moteuczoma II name places on the way there, especially on the Pacific Isthmus coast, no continuous dominance can be shown to have existed. Sources on the Quiché of Utatlán report details that caused Carmack (1981:142) to state that they paid tribute to the Aztecs after 1510, and in consequence the region generally settled down. Other details quoted by Carmack, and the fact that parallel statements are missing in Aztec tribute sources, suggest that this was rather a voluntary recognition and peaceful coexistence. Also statements about the advance of the Aztecs into Chiapas and even into Nicaragua are probably just insinuations that there was a sporadic presence of merchants or ambassadors who asked for tribute (Köhler 1978). In the case of conquest lists and of inventories a revision may yield numerous corrections, once other sources and detailed maps are incorporated into the research.

INDEPENDENT AREAS ≡ Regions in central Mexico that were explicitly mentioned in the written sources as independent of the Aztecs have been examined by Davies (1968, outdated in some details). He pays special attention to the course of borders, but these are very difficult to determine clearly, because permanent borderline demarcations between states were practically unknown. Between independent areas and those dominated by the Aztecs there were commonly only lands either thinly populated or empty, due to natural phenomena. The independent states did not form a coherent or continuous block; indeed, disputes among them were frequent and their political relationship with the Triple Alliance was by no means uniform. The statement that the existence of independent areas constituted a perpetual danger for the Mexican economic structure (Vázquez Chamorro 1981b:209) seems to be acceptable only in singular cases. Barlow (1946:map) implied that the Señorío de Teotitlan del Camino was independent but allied, which was accepted by most of the subsequent authors; however, this was the result of selective source usage and can be seen now as refuted. On the other hand, areas in the eastern basin of Puebla and on the upper Río Balsas surely were not secured under Aztec rule (see map "Aztec Empire").

DEPENDENT PROVINCES ≡ The term "tribute provinces" is an arbitrarily established but commonly accepted expression designating the units that formed the Aztec Empire's divisions for the purpose of tribute deliveries. Each tribute province was headed by a *calpixqui*, who had a "counterpart" in the central organization in the capital (general presentation about the organization of the tribute administration among others in Gibson 1971:389–92; Licate 1980; Berdan 1976b). There are indications that most provinces were created under Moteuczoma I. The borderlines of tribute provinces did not at all coincide with those of the regions of dependent rulers (Hicks 1992) and also did not correspond to those of the originally independent political units, as the seat of the specific head *calpixqui* was not in the traditional capital. The administrative organization of provinces that delivered to Tenochtitlán into five regional groups (center, north, west, south, east) corresponded to the cosmological concept of four world directions and a center (Reyes García 1979b). Agricultural produce intended for tribute was grown on special fields. Further details, also about the manufacture of other tribute goods and the organization of labor details (per capita, per group) are not sufficiently known and may have varied from region to region (individual data in Hinz, Hartau, and Heimann-Koenen 1983; Hicks 1978). Specific raw materials had to be acquired by the tribute payers, sometimes through trade.

INTERIOR CHANGES ≡ The concrete conditions and changes within conquered areas have only recently become subjects of scholarly examinations: Mary Hodge (1984) tries to determine the changes in power-political and economical terms of five city-states in the Valley of Mexico after the conquest by the Aztecs (Amecameca, Cuauhtitlan, Xochimilco, Coyohuacan, Teotihuacán). The different forms of Aztec intrusion could be traced back to different initial conditions of the five city-states, in addition to other factors, but everywhere the intrusion had led to a change in command hierarchies. Hodge's analysis may be criticized for her indiscriminate, eclectic, or seemingly careless utilization of sources; however, it cannot be said that a better differentiation would have added any important perspective.

POLITICAL DEPENDENCE AND TRIBUTE DUTY ≡ Political dependence was separated everywhere from tribute duty, where overlapping interests of the partners in the Triple Alliance were institutionalized. Hicks (1984b) has examined the complex circumstances in the case of Temascalapan in the northeastern part of the Valley of Mexico. The town of Temascalapan did not have its own *tlatoani*, but was politically dependent on Tepechpan, twenty-eight kilometers away, whose *tlatoani* was one of fourteen local rulers who formed the high council of Acolhuacan under the leadership of Tetzcoco. The inhabitants provided workers for the *tlatoani* of Tepechpan according to the common rotation system, and brought him goods as appreciation gifts. Military service and public works (*coatequitl*) were owed to superimposed Tetzcoco. But at the same time, Temascalapan and ten other towns delivered tribute to Tenochtitlán, whose *tlatoani* owned property with peasants in the region for some time. This tribute fell into the competence of a Mexican *calpixqui* in Cempoallan, which was not the seat of a *tlatoani* but was governed by a noble official, who had *macehualli* for the work in his fields and for other services. Hicks regards this specific local tribute dependence, which surmounts political borders, as a measure to discombobulate ethnic loyalties within the Triple Alliance and achieve further consolidation. It cannot be recognized which persons from Acolhuacan had to relinquish hereditary rights in the transfer of tribute to Tenochtitlán, but these could have been recompensed by other advantages from conquests of the Triple Alliance. The same picture can be found in areas that were dependent on Tenochtitlán (Hodge 1991).

SOUTHERN PUEBLA ≡ In Cuauhtinchan, in the southern part of the present federal state of Puebla (from where the important source *Historia Tolteca-Chichimeca*, among others, has come), the changes can be recognized somewhat more clearly: both the conquest by Tlatelolco and the later one by the Tenochca occurred after a request for help from a group of *pilli* from Cuauhtinchan, who felt disadvantaged due to some local developments. After the conquest by the Mexica, Cuauhtinchan lost not only its independence but also its function as a rulership center, because the capitals of areas up until then dependent on it were politically upgraded.

In the capitals Tecali and Tepeaca, and in Cuauhtinchan itself, the changes caused by the Triple Alliance within the local power structure of noble lineages and within the economic system and the shift of territorial borders can be traced. There also was an added burden on commoners through doubled tribute duties (Reyes García 1977; Olivera 1978 possibly sees the conditions before the Chichimec conquest a little too positively; Martínez 1984; about specific tribute provinces see also Litvak King 1971a).

EXPANSION OF NAHUATL ≡ The spread of Nahuatl at the time of the Triple Alliance was not deliberate. New settlements by Nahuatl-speaking peasants extended and intensified the Aztec language area in these regions, as they occurred in the garrison colonies of Ahuitzotl or after the victories of Axayacatl in the Valley of Toluca, where the Otomí-speaking inhabitants had fled from the armed conflict and had to be replaced on property given to the victors (Hernández Rodríguez 1952; Quezada Ramírez 1972). In large areas with a population speaking another language, Nahuatl had become the language of the elite (for the Popoloca in southern Puebla: Jäcklein 1978:5). Linguistic uniformity and the spread of Nahuatl as a *lingua franca* were also furthered by the manifold marriage alliances within the nobility of the Triple Alliance, mentioned above.

AMOUNT OF TRIBUTE ≡ Today, three main questions about the determination of the entire amount of tribute deliveries are not answered: which areas exactly had to deliver tribute; how often tribute was delivered; and how much tribute was delivered. An overview of the discussion of these subjects can be found in Hassig (1985:276–80; about questions of transport: pp. 28–40), who circumvents the equally important question, if the discussed delivery lists pertain to tribute, which was divided among the partners according to different (which?) keys, or if they contained deliveries exclusively destined for Tenochtitlán (Bittmann Simons and Sullivan 1972; *1978; Offner 1983:88–90; Gibson 1971). It seems to be certain that the distribution key and the responsibility for tribute changed in the course of time in Tenochtitlán's favor. Origin and amount of specific goods or groups of products were examined frequently (Anderson and Barlow 1943; Molins Fabrega 1954; Broda 1978a; Berdan 1987; Rojas 1986:249–75), and depending on the source situation almost all examinations refer to Tenochtitlán. The mentioned important open questions aggravate the answers to further questions, among them the one about how tribute was used in particular, which is decisive for statements about the demography and economy in receiving areas.

THE METROPOLIS AS A CENTER OF ECONOMICS

Today, knowledge is determined in many ways by the fact that Mexico was the most important city of the Aztec Empire. As the capital of the later Colonial Spanish Vice-Monarchy Nueva España (New Spain) and the modern United Mexican States, it initiated a rich documentation and numerous publications as well. On the other hand its continuity has aggravated local archaeological examinations substantially.

POPULATION AND EXPANSE ≡ The city was comprised of greater Tenochtitlán in the south and Tlatelolco in the northwest and covered at least 12.5 square kilometers. Only parts of the city were situated on the more or less firm islands; at least half of that area consisted of house lots to which backyard gardens in the form of *chinampas* were attached, raised from the lake bottom (mostly based on documents: Calnek 1974; 1972b; *1978c:315–26). An extension of 13.5 square kilometers and a population number of at least 200,000 is the conclusion of Rojas (1986:39–43, 65–92) after a thorough discussion of the pertinent literature and modern evidence. Around 300,000 for the population was estimated by Sanders (1970:430; but on p. 449 more conservatively ca. 120,000 to 200,000; *1976). Such a dense population had not been created by the natural growth of the once-immigrated Mexica, but, rather, the center of power and trade had attracted numerous settlers from outside. The percentage of the population comprised of the elite of all kinds (nobles, foreign lords and their retinue, functionaries, priests), and of the specialized artisans who had been brought in, must have been extremely high. But in the surrounding areas as well the population density reached a maximum that could barely be fed (Williams 1989:730). The specialization in manufacture and marketing of consumer goods was more advanced in Mexico than elsewhere. A large part of the population worked in the service industry (Calnek 1972; *1978b; population structure by professions is thoroughly discussed in Rojas 1986:127–248).

INFRASTRUCTURE ≡ The city of Mexico was permeated by an almost regular net of canals, based on natural waterways, sometimes with streets next to them. The main traffic axes, oriented to the four cardinal directions and emanating from the main temple precinct, divided Tenochtitlán into four not quite equal-sized quarters. The most important transport and traffic vehicle was the log canoe. Roads on dams connected the city with the mainland, from which water was brought in by aqueducts (reconstruction by thorough evaluation of Colonial sources: Palerm 1973).

A symptomatic overinterpretation, possibly based on the importance of constructed roads in modern civilization, was undertaken by Santley (1986) with the help of a network analysis. The basis of his analysis was a reconstructive map, only partly based on modern reference points, of settlements and their connecting roads in the Valley of Mexico (González Aparicio 1973). From the dendritic organization of the road network he reconstructed, he concludes that there was a similarly constructed political economy, in which goods were moved by administrative intervention according to the hierarchy of the settlements. Santley himself reduces the reliability of his statements, because the dominant traffic taking place on the Lake of Mexico is excluded, which shows the distance from reality of his approach.

WATER CONTROL MEASURES ≡ In order to prevent the floods that constantly threatened the island city, an approximately fourteen-kilometer-long dam had been built, one of the great Aztec engineering feats in the highlands. It separated the dangerous saltwater lake of Tetzcoco from the adjoining sweetwater lake of Chalco, where the city was situated (Palerm 1973). The dam also allowed better agricultural yields through *chinampas* (Calnek 1975:44–46).

PALACES ≡ On the south side of the ceremonial center of Tenochtitlán, there were the palaces of the elite around a large plaza. Among them on the western side was the palace built for Moteuczoma I Ilhuicamina (1440–1468), also known as Axayacatl's (1468–1481) palace, because he had repaired it after the 1475 earthquake caused some damage. On the eastern side was the "new palace" built by Moteuczoma II, which had a sprawling private part with houses for wives and children, a zoo, and gardens, and in another part housed the state institutions: the courts of law, meeting halls for the council, warriors, tribute collectors, and other rooms for official occasions (Alcocer 1935).

CITY QUARTERS ≡ A second city center was situated in Tlatelolco, separated from Tenochtitlán only by a narrow canal. Here there was the main market place next to the ceremonial center. Subcenters with a temple, market, and other public buildings were in each of the four quarters of Tenochtitlán as well. They were divided in turn into smaller units (*tlaxilacalli*) or living quarters. The position of the Aztec city quarters was reconstructed by Caso (1956a) on the basis of a thorough evaluation of Colonial reports and documents; Calnek (1972a) was able to supplement this and add precision. The internal organization of the quarters and their relationship with specific temples, deities, etc. has been dealt with by Zantwijk in several articles and a concluding monograph (1985), using a structural approach.

LIVING QUARTERS ≡ The commoners lived in complexes, separated from the street, consisting of several one- or two-room houses around a courtyard; depending on its size and their social status, two to six nuclear families lived there. Houses on platforms, two-story houses, and observation towers were reserved for the nobility, whose property also contained flower gardens (Calnek 1974; 1972b; *1978b; 1976).

The center of the city was densely built up. Toward the edges of town more and more *chinampas* were attached to the living complexes, but only in the southeast were they large enough to feed the inhabitants. Most of the time the *chinampas* served as house gardens for fresh corn and vegetables. The *chinampas* can be studied well through archaeological and documentary examinations (Calnek 1972a). The plan and treatise by González Aparicio (1973) reconstructs the position of the city and its ties to its environment correctly in general, but is hypothetical in details. Lombardo de Ruiz (1973) describes the historical development under the different rulers.

ECONOMY ≡ In the economy of central Mexico land and work force were not freely exchangeable production factors. Their availability was determined by political events and their use was allocated to the individual according to his position and status. The distribution of manufactured goods was undertaken according to different institutionalized systems, which were intertwined.

Analyses of the subject economy, which agree basically in their presentation, come from Carrasco P. and Frances Berdan (1978b). Berdan's unpublished dissertation *Trade, tribute and market in the Aztec Empire* formed the base for numerous publications on economy (among others Berdan 1977). Systems of the circulation of goods are described by Carrasco P. (1978) against the background of the society (the part dealing with the "market" with minor changes: Carrasco P. 1980).

TRIBUTE ≡ The deliveries of goods, fixed by amount, to the state's central power are called tribute by the sources and modern authors. The redistribution of these surplus goods shows up the dual economic functions of the state (Carrasco P. 1978:47). As a representative of the entire population it passes on a part of the goods to different groups, or uses them as investments in their favor. As an organ of rulership it uses the possibilities of a selective distribution for itself and keeps a large part of these goods for the elite. A concrete and illuminating example for redistribution is mentioned by Carrasco P. (1978:53; 1977:234): Nobles from Xochimilco received as tribute from their subjects, who lived in a forest, log canoes that were passed on to other subjects to be used in an area of *chinampas*. According to Broda (1978b:252), the public and ceremonial form of distributing goods underlines the prestige of rulers and expresses the political relationship of ruler and subject, which makes it an ideological instrument of rulership. The mechanics of redistribution show a lessening of intensity from the core to the periphery; in remote tribute provinces the political relationship with the Triple Alliance was reduced to a one-sided delivery of goods. Closed local systems were functioning next to it. It depends on one's theoretical views, if the tasks of the central state, such as maintenance of precautions for military defense, provisions in times of need, execution of the rituals on a nonindividual level in order to transcendentally secure the very existence, can be taken as a nonmaterial return for tribute.

RECIPROCITY ≡ Carrasco P. (1978:53) emphasizes the reciprocity of many exchanges. Where property went from one owner to another, he understands it as a symmetrical relationship between members of the same rank or group. It furthered integration, such as on the occasion of gift exchanges on the highest political level. Contrary to Andean studies, reciprocity in Mesoamerica has not become the subject of anthropological inquiry.

TRADE ≡ The circulation of goods outside of tribute is divided by Berdan (1977:96–99) into export trade and exchange in markets. The export trade, mostly import of raw materials for luxury items, was a group activity, undertaken by the long-range merchants (*pochteca*) in international ports of trade. This monopoly had been given to the merchants by the ruler. The *pochteca* took along the ruler's goods on commission, which probably originated in tribute, and they also sold their own merchandise. The extent of trade possibilities, left to the merchants within the realm of the Triple Alliance after tribute had been extracted, is still a matter of dispute. Most of the time the *pochteca* exchanged finished products for raw materials. Carrasco P. (1978:62–63) recognizes that long-range trade offered the best opportunity to accumulate wealth and create a modest trading capital, the accretion of which was curtailed by the duty to produce lavish ceremonies in order to gain status and climb socially.

MARKETS ≡ Trading in local or regional markets (*tianquiztli*) served the regional traffic in goods. Participants in the roles of consumers, middlemen, or producers sold their work directly and often in tiny amounts. The *pochteca* also participated in the sale of private goods as individuals, but abided by the rules of their association; as members they also supervised the markets. All merchants paid a market fee to the state or to the *tlatoani*—apparently in goods. A free interplay of supply and demand to determine prices most likely did not exist: prices were subject to some administrative regulations. As a standardized exchange unit there were cacao beans and a special type of white cotton cloth (*cuachtli*), which also had merchandise value and whose significance is seen as negligible by Berdan (1978b:85; about local markets, see also 1980; about measures of value, Durand-Forest 1967; 1971; with inclusion of origin, Rojas 1986:249–75; Durand-Forest 1962, with an early Colonial sketch of the market at Tenochtitlán; a reconstruction of it by Feldman 1978b). Hassig (1982) examined periodicity and market hierarchies and points out the important difference of functional and ritual markets; Berdan (1985) describes the different significance of markets in the central area of the Triple Alliance and in the border regions.

TENOCHTITLÁN—ECONOMICALLY NOT SELF-SUFFICIENT ≡ Molins Fabrega (1954–55; contents supplemented by Calnek 1975; Parsons 1976) has described through quantifying concepts the stratified economy of the city of Mexico, which was by no means self-sufficient, but depended to a large extent on incoming tribute, which in turn flowed into the trade and had to be supplemented by imported goods. In all examinations of the degree of dependence of Mexico City on incoming tribute, all those goods cannot be included (due to a lack of source material) that flowed into local noble residences from their private or office-related lands; according to data from other areas these were anything but meager.

ECONOMIC SIGNIFICANCE ≡ The decision is still not made, which basic model describes the economy of the Precolumbian societies of the central highlands in the least controversial manner. In recent years attention has been concentrated especially on the significance of the institutionalized economic systems of tribute and trade in the overall economy of the Aztec state, which is taken as an indicator for the developmental stage of the state at the same time. The fact that the discussion is still determined by not explicitly stated basic attitudes has become clear during the dispute between Carrasco P. and Offner (in *American Antiquity* 46 [1981]:43–74), which was futile in the last analysis. Added to this is the fact that in conclusions it is often not properly taken into account that Tenochtitlán may not be regarded as exemplary, due to its special situation, its size, and its political circumstances.

Therefore, Berdan (1983) suggests a function model, which has to take regional and political variables into account in a better way. In a similar way Smith (1983) argues against distinctly unilinear explanation models and for a multicausal view (in the sense of systems theory), where the reciprocal influences of core and periphery, marked by feedback, allow for a more differentiated picture of events.

MINOR SIGNIFICANCE OF MARKETS ≡ In a source-critical paper, which incomprehensibly overlooks Sahagún, Martínez Garnica (1984–85) came to the extraordinary conclusion that markets had a function only within religious ceremonies. Based on her archaeological data from Huexotla, a second-ranked center in Acolhuacan, Brumfiel (1980) recognizes an economy in which tribute goods coming in because of Aztec expansion politics overlap the original distribution functions of the markets for craft products. In it the city population gave the rural population tribute goods in exchange for food.

Susan Evans (1980) is of the opinion (like Berdan) that one has to differentiate between local market transactions and the long-range trade, dependent on transport. In the economy, which she sees overall as fragmented and politically controlled, she rejects the influence of supply and demand on the distribution of goods and hence on the settlement patterns, which were determined in her eyes by political and ecological factors. The statements on economical subjects by authors such as Evans and Smith, who are archaeologists, are naturally more model oriented and go further into the past than ethnohistorical works. They explicitly or implicitly use ethnohistorical evidence, and don't question if it can be transposed into a distant past.

MARKET-ORIENTED ECONOMY ≡ Smith (1979; 1980) represents the position, opposed to the one by Evans, that profit-oriented decisions had formed the basis of the development of a highly commercialized, market-integrated economic system in the Valley of Mexico, which had profited from the *Pax Azteca* and had contributed to the formation of the settlement pattern. Here, as in other statements, there is a suspicion or even certainty that there is no precise differentiation between markets, trade activities, and abstract market principles. Kurtz (1974) characterizes Mexican markets as an intermediate stage between peripheral markets and a market economic system, influenced by Bohannan and Dalton (1962), and emphasizes the difference between capital and rural hinterland. Tying in with this, Hicks (1987) describes the economy in the Valley of Mexico as being on the road to an integrated market economy, for which state measures had created the prerequisites.

STATE-CONTROLLED MARKETS ≡ As one of only few authors, Carrasco P. (1983) has clearly defined his concept of "market" as an abstract system of price and economy design. To make the discussion more precise and the reconstruction more flexible he suggests the necessity of being conscious of the degree of political control. The market principle did not have a major role in Precolumbian Mexico, despite the well-developed markets, and the economy was politically controlled to a large extent, on the one hand, because land was not a trade commodity, and the transactions in markets were of little significance in their overall bulk—often only small amounts for daily use were traded—and on the other hand, because possibilities of free transfer of goods were restricted by the Aztec state through luxury laws, status emblems, and the like.

ECONOMY OF THE METROPOLIS ≡ According to the calculations of Calnek (1978a; 1975), food and goods for daily use, which came into Tenochtitlán as tribute, were sufficient at best for one third of the city population. A large number of people had to purchase these things in the market. Tribute receivers as well, especially the elite, appeared in the markets as buyers of goods not contained in tribute deliveries, and as sellers of tribute products they did not need themselves. From this Calnek concludes that the organizational form of the state's redistribution system had required a free market system and decides that the traffic of goods outside of tribute was a relatively well-developed market economic system, especially outside of the metropolis Mexico. According to Calnek the fact that standardized value gauges were not subjected to any controls also argues against a state-controlled economy. Rojas (1986), who analyzed the profession-specific sources thoroughly for his voluminous monograph, represents the same line of thought and sees a rising use of the standardized value gauges. The tribute had to even out the asymmetry between supply and demand that was rising daily. The fundamental significance of trade for the metropolis Mexico is emphasized by other authors as well (Bittmann Simons and Sullivan 1972; *1978).

RELIGION

Religion is one of the best-known areas of central Mexican culture. The most and the grandest archaeological and pictorial legacies come from it. The pantheon was marked by the different cultural and ethnic traditions that came together in the states. The deities were seen as responsible for the creation and maintenance of the present, the fourth world, and the beings and objects in it. In exchange man was responsible for a symbolic maintenance of the gods. A greatly stratified priesthood performed the rituals, whose high points were religious feasts in the eighteen calendar months of the year, and on several other occasions. At the center of many of the feasts was a sacrificial ceremony where a human being, as the earthly representative of the deity, was ritually killed.

SOURCE PROBLEMS ≡ On the question of religion the problems of source interpretation appear more pronounced than in any other area of Precolumbian culture. Reports by Colonial authors are almost all marked regularly by a Christian's fearful aversion to a heathen faith, in which he could see nothing but deception and seduction of the devil, and in consequence the names of Indian deities were replaced or supplemented in the texts by *"diablo."* Added to this is the repugnance numerous ritual practices inspired, especially the bloody self-castigations and human sacrifices. Other authors, among them most of the Indian ones, had a tendency to see in indigenous religion a connection to or prophecy of Christianity: the Aztec Quetzalcoatl was readily identified with the apostle Thomas (Lafaye 1974; *1977), or the Andean composite Tunupa-Viracocha was created (Rostworowski de Diez Canseco 1983:29–30). This strategy intrinsically goes along with making the all-too-heathenish religious activities sound harmless. In all events the sources reflect the official religion of the elite, while the concepts and activities of the majority of the population cannot be found at all. Their religious customs, which continued after the mission efforts in a hard-to-fathom measure, can be reconstructed only vaguely from documents about individual criminal prosecutions of heathenish practices. Recent customs and concepts, especially of the rural population, can be utilized as a source for Precolumbian times only with major constraints, because in them the sixteenth-century folk catholicism of the Iberian Pensinsula has melded almost indivisibly with indigenous Indian concepts.

GENERAL PRESENTATIONS ≡ For the knowledge of Precolumbian religion in Mesoamerica the works of Seler (partially contained in 1902–1923; reprint and index 1967), written around the turn of the century and in details often outdated, are basic. The literature about Mexican religion deals mainly with its best-documented appearance in the Valley of Mexico in the time just before the Spanish conquest (summaries with different emphases: Caso 1954; *1956b; Nicholson 1971; in the form of a dictionary: Miller and Taube 1993; other overviews: Brundage 1979; Carrasco 1987; with a larger scope: Nicholson 1987b). The German presentation by Lanczkowski (1984) leaves something to be desired, despite a very good description of some religious subjects, because there is only a very narrow data base and almost the entire analytical literature written overseas after the 1960s is ignored, among others the work of León-Portilla and the important source-critical evaluation of the myth of the return of the god Quetzalcoatl by Stenzel (1982; 1980), who could prove convincingly that the expectation of a return of Quetzalcoatl as the "white god," which plays a major role in the descriptions and in the evaluation of events during the conquest of Mexico by the Spaniards, is missing in the indigenous tradition and appeared only retrospectively after the Conquest.

GROUPS OF DEITIES ≡ In all descriptions of late Postclassic religions in central Mexico two large complexes of different importance become evident, which, depending on regionally formed culture, complement each other: the belief system around the rain god Tlaloc and other vegetation deities of the agrarian population, and the rituals for martial creator gods connected with the sun and Venus of the Tezcatlipoca group, followed mainly by the nobility and the warriors (Broda 1976). The patron deities of groups who immigrated in the late Postclassic as well as those of the later city-states of central Mexico belonged to the latter group.

HUITZILOPOCHTLI ≡ The origin of the tribal god of the Mexica, Huitzilopochtli, is described in the mythical section of their migration period. This kind of description, wavering at first between god and leader, can also be found in central Mexico for other deities of the post-Toltec period. In the myths about Huitzilopochtli numerous overlaps and parallels can be found with the patron deities of other Chichimec immigration groups (González Torres 1966; very close to the sources: López Austin 1973; Uchmany 1978; Graulich 1983; Eschmann 1976:162–68, 179–90). A symposium at the Americanist Congress in Paris (Davies, coordinator, 1979) has examined especially the dichotomy "God-Hero" among the patron deities, such as Huitzilopochtli, Mixcoatl, Quetzalcoatl, and Tezcatlipoca, but in the final analysis numerous questions remained unanswered.

MARTIAL-RELIGIOUS COMPLEX ≡ Numerous modern authors see in the prophecies of future power attributed to Huitzilopochtli during the migration of the Mexica, and his later transformation into an astral deity, the trigger of subsequent Aztec expansion, because "The Aztecs, the people of Huitzilopochtli, were the chosen people of the Sun. They were charged with the duty of supplying him with food. For that reason war was a form of worship and a necessary activity" (Caso 1956b:13). Origin, development, and political effect of this martial-religious faith have been discussed often with different viewpoints. While many authors recognize a special development of the Mexica going back to a personal initiative by Tlacaelel or other persons (Padden 1967; Conrad and Demarest 1984:37; León-Portilla 1959:249–57), Anncharlott Eschmann (1976:162–68) puts the event into an overall Mexican context of similar traditions, and Kerkhoff (1964) in the framework of the space-time perception of the Aztecs. Davies (1979a) describes the sojourn of the Mexica and their defeat in Chapultepec as the historically significant period of this development. Bernal (1957) recognizes from the beginning of the migrations onward a small, fearless group of Mexica leaders, which successfully carried out an extremely realistic, even if cruel, policy with a genial political-religious idea without regard for losses of their own or others. In the expansion politics of Tetzcoco a comparable religious propaganda has played a relatively small role (Offner 1983:284).

HUMAN SACRIFICE ≡ In all ancient American civilizations, although to a different extent, human beings were sacrificed through ritual acts. Colonial sources have either emphasized and often exaggerated this fact, depending on their goals, or they have rendered it harmless, and even denied it completely (a complete denial has been tried recently, but not very convincingly: Hassler 1992). In central Mexico human sacrifice had a special meaning, which was also expressed in the number of such events. In the meantime, the world view that motivated human sacrifice is more and more understood. León-Portilla (1986) in particular describes the religious-philosophical background of human sacrifice. González Torres (1985) informs us extensively of the manifestations and ceremonial contexts of human sacrifices as practiced in all rituals.

The attitude of the population toward human sacrifices must have been ambivalent. In any event, Demarest (1984:232) explains the legend of Quetzalcoatl opposing human sacrifices in Tollan as an expression of widespread discomfort with the massive human sacrifices, which had been stepped up since the beginning of the Postclassic. Mesoamerican human sacrifices were executed by cutting out the heart (examination on the basis of Mayan visual data and anatomical facts from the viewpoint of a heart surgeon by Robicsek and Hales 1984).

AMOUNT IN NUMBERS ≡ The numbers of victims are estimated very differently. Cook (1946) calculated for central Mexico just before the Conquista fifteen thousand human victims per year, while Harner (1977; *1980), citing Borah, states that one percent of the population per year, meaning two hundred fifty thousand victims, were sacrificed; this number is based on a misunderstanding (Borah, letter to the author, September 2, 1987), and is too high in any event.

RITUAL CANNIBALISM? ≡ Quite a controversy was caused by Harner's (1977; *1980) statement, spread by Harris (1977:153–59), that human sacrifices (which were at least partially consumed) were indispensable in such high numbers for the protein supply of the population, and had been made for this purpose. Both the stated deficit in animal proteins (Ortiz de Montellano 1978; *1979; Conrad and Demarest 1984:165–70) and the asserted innumerable sacrificial victims have been questioned vehemently (Davies 1981; Haberland 1986:80–82).

RITUAL ACTS ≡ The role of warriors and priests and their functions in the bloody rituals are described by Inga Clendinnen (1991), who scrutinizes the grisly details extensively, and includes questionable analogies to North American prairie Indians.

COSMOLOGY AND SOCIAL STRUCTURE ≡ Influence of the world view on organizational forms can be shown for the whole of Aztec culture. Soustelle (1940) in particular deals with cosmology and world view, but all examinations of Aztec religion concern themselves with this subject. A thorough presentation of the subject is offered by Graulich (1987). Influence of number symbolism and cosmological beliefs on the design of sacred building structures has often been stated (among others: Krickeberg 1950), but remains speculative. The main temple of Tenochtitlán and the surrounding ceremonial district were the subject of a great many publications, which have been added to recently after renewed excavations with somewhat exciting evidence that confirmed the close relationship of myths about Huitzilopochtli and the temple area (León-Portilla 1978; Zantwijk 1981; Matos Moctezuma 1987). David Carrasco (1975) is of the opinion that the Mexica understood the overall design of the city as a cosmic symbol, as an adaptation of the real world to the order of the cosmos, in order to coordinate supernatural and social forces. The great temple within the city had been the navel of the Aztec world and of the cosmos at the same time; the four large city quarters had corresponded to the four quadrants of the universe (Calnek 1972b; *1978b). Tichy (1991) sees the orientation of Precolumbian ceremonial centers in their specific deviation from the cardinal directions continued in the rural areas, where they were preserved until today.

The cosmological direction in scholarship can be traced back to Kirchhoff (1947), who had suspected cosmological beliefs and number symbolism in the real political and social structures when he described the Toltec Empire, and other authors had followed him (Zantwijk 1963; 1965; about the structure of the empire: Reyes García 1979b; Broda 1978a; about the internal organization of Tetzcoco: Offner 1980). Zantwijk (1985) sees Aztec society as characterized by a correlation between the world of gods and the world view.

OFFICIAL ART ≡ The official art of Tenochtitlán is devoted exclusively to religion. The essential work has been done by Pasztory (1982:141–43). The emphasis on monumental art in the capital as opposed to that in other regions reproduces the concept of opposition of the middle and the periphery in Mexica thought, which can also be traced in religion and organization (Townsend 1979).

EVALUATION OF THE AZTEC EMPIRE

REASONS FOR AZTEC EXPANSION ≡ The rapid rise of the Aztec Empire after the formation of the Triple Alliance, and the fall after the arrival of the Spaniards, have led to questions about the reasons. As a superficial goal of the expansion the gain of tribute in the form of goods and services from a subjugated population is seen. Beyond this, numerous hypotheses have been formed about the motivation for the imperial expansion of the Triple Alliance.

RELIGIOUS MISSION ≡ According to a religious explanation, Mexica religion demanded frequent human sacrifices to keep the world functioning. This duty, for which the Mexica saw themselves chosen, necessitated war campaigns, justified the subjugation of other peoples, and legitimized the state (Caso 1954; *1956b; Broda 1979). A mandate to spread the faith in the Mexican national deity Huitzilopochtli cannot be proven convincingly, even if Padden (1967:30) cites as proof the Huitzilopochtli temple in Tetzcoco, because this sanctuary goes back to a much earlier migration of the Mexica, according to the Colonial Tetzcoco author Pomar (1891; *1941). On the other hand, Nicholson (1971:426) recognizes in the course of imperial expansion also a spread of Huitzilopochtli's cult. Generally, religious tolerance is emphasized: since Moteuczoma II established a temple for the deities of subjugated peoples in the main temple district of Tenochtitlán, it is taken as a sign of polytheistic and political integration.

POPULATION EXPLOSION ≡ Other explanations for the expansion use ecological models, which are determined by the interdependence between environment, feeding potential, and population development; this interdependence pushed the development of state and society in the Valley of Mexico toward a rising urbanization and population explosion, which made necessary ever larger imports of food from other regions and therefore enforced expansion. Conrad and Demarest (1984) base a persuasive analysis of the Aztec state on this concept, which has, however, not managed to overcome the numerous discrepancies, increasing through the expansion, between the overpopulated, consuming, and ruling center and the underpopulated, ruled, and delivering periphery. In their view, which regards details often quite eclectically, the Aztec state was already in a crisis by the time the Spaniards conquered it.

WEAK STATE STRUCTURE ≡ The fall of the Aztec Empire during the Conquista is often blamed on the failure to fully assimilate the incorporated subject societies into the state (Kurtz 1978). Conrad and Demarest (1984) also regard the considerable independence of local rulers as a weak point of the empire, because of the constant danger of rebellions.

A differentiated view cannot be satisfied with catchwords and global notions of reasons, such as lack of "integration." The attitude of the Indian political units toward the Spaniards was not at all uniform and also had different causes. Thus the support the Totonacs, who were only recently conquered by the Aztecs, gave to the Spaniards on the Gulf Coast—they were the first to give food and porters—was short-lived, and the taking of sides of some political units in the Valley of Mexico was really not more than a passive waiting around. Indian support that was much more decisive for the Spaniards came from states not yet conquered by the Aztecs, but in fear of them: from Tlaxcallan, which became almost a home base for the Spaniards, and which supplied large and forceful troop contingents together with Huexotzinco, or from Michoacán, whose *cazonci* refused to assist the threatened city of Mexico, as requested. The fact that Ixtlilxochitl of Tetzcoco placed himself on the side of the Spaniards is also not a sign of a lack of integration of the empire, but rather a consequence of the attempt by Moteuczoma to broaden and strengthen his power by intervening in the succession disputes of Tetzcoco. The example of the Inca state, which forced all parts of the empire into a much stricter economic and political integration, but could not resist the Europeans either, also contradicts this view.

ADVANTAGES OF A LOOSE STRUCTURE ≡ In recent years opinions have gained support that recognize advantages in a loose structure of the empire, or regard other linking structures as more important. Thus Calnek (1982:60) believes that due to the indirect rule the Triple Alliance saved on the organization of a complete bureaucracy. Michael Smith (1986), Brumfiel (1983), and Calnek (1982:60) emphasize the cohesive effect of kin ties and the common interests of the nobility, which gained by the expansion politics even in dependent areas. Hassig (1985) based his thorough analysis of the Aztec state on transport possibilities and comes to the conclusion that in the final analysis the expansion is a successful social adaptation to strong ecological and technical pressures. In his view the loose structure of the empire had substantial advantages for the supply of Tenochtitlán; by comparison the danger of rebellions appeared less of a problem. The system was effective as long as there was no comparatively powerful competition. This was provided by the advent of the Spaniards, which could not have been foreseen, who used previously irrelevant weaknesses to their advantage.

WRITTEN HISTORY OF THE AZTECS ≡ In descriptions of Mexica history and of the Aztec Triple Alliance different, often controversial, tendencies can be found since the last century that still appear in the scholarly and popular literature; they are presented in various combinations and affect the description of other subjects according to their points of departure.

The previously described different evaluation of the Aztec state at the time of the Spanish conquest is not new and can be reduced to two opposing views: (1) The decapitation development: the Aztec Empire, on the way to achieve a high point (unknown until that time in Mesoamerica) of political-structural power was destroyed in full bloom—or even before it had achieved its high point. (2) The shaking state: problems in the interior and exterior had brought about a precarious state of instability even before the Spaniards landed; the Conquista merely preempted the inevitable collapse.

Two opposing views can be determined as well about the development of the Mexica Empire: (1) The followers: the immigrating Mexica are seen as a nomadic group with the simplest possible culture, who seized the achievements of peoples who had settled in the Valley of Mexico long before them. (2) The initiators: the Mexica, settling under deplorable conditions, are themselves the creators of the situation encountered by the Spaniards, which was marked by a hierarchical society, peasants dependent on the nobility, conquest wars, tribute empire, and excessive human sacrifices.

By comparison, two opinions are expressed about the evaluation of the achievements of Aztec culture as well as overall Indian cultures: (1) The Spanish view, which describes Precolumbian situations as less lustrous than (2) the indigenous view, which in turn underlines the dark sides of the Conquest and Colonization.

All these directions depend on often even "fashionable" trends of research and are reciprocal to political currents of modern Mexico and her state-forming national ideology, which selects and reinterprets according to topical-political needs.

15

The Andean Cultures in Archaeology

EARLY CULTURES IN THE ANDES

CHAVÍN ≡ The stylistic influence that emanated from the center Chavín de Huantar in northern Peru reaching large parts of the Andes constitutes the Early Horizon. Opinions about the nature of this influence vary greatly (Pozorski and Pozorski 1987:45). They depend indivisibly on the degree of political integration assumed for Chavín. If Chavín is seen as a chiefdom, the area open to a direct political control must have been small, and the larger zone of influence can only have been the result of the spread of a powerful and attractive ideological-religious complex. Opposed to this is a view that in the case of Chavín a state-directed expansion already took place (with the goals and methods of the Inca Empire: Lorandi 1978; *1986). This thesis is rejected in the very detailed and thorough, contemporary description of Chavín (excavation and style) by Burger (1992).

The research at Cerro Sechín and this site's relationship to Chavín is summarized by Bischof (1987; monograph: Tello 1960; architecture: Maldonado 1992). Contrary to the almost exclusive attention to early ceremonial centers (Donnan 1985), Tellenbach (1987) describes a hierarchically structured, planned settlement. As a reason for the cultural and sociopolitical innovations that become manifest in the Early Horizon, Pozorski and Pozorski (1987) see an invasion from the highlands, whose reflection can also be discovered in the iconography of Cerro Sechín.

Exemplary not only for the interpretation of visual conventions in the style of Chavín, Rowe (1962b) proposed the idea that a visual encoding had taken place, comparable to the kennings in ancient Icelandic poetry. This way, the depicted motifs should not be taken as realistic renderings, but as corresponding to a verbal metaphor, which could possibly express attributes of deities otherwise not graphically communicable. It seems that such metaphors became independent and turned into a general convention. This way it became common to depict every mouth as the open jaw of a catlike animal; originally the teeth of a jaguar obviously were meant to denote nonhuman beings. How little the religious-ideological area of archaeological evidence is open to interpretations of a secure nature is shown by the hard to explain conscious and extremely careful covering of religious structures with earth ("temple entombment" [Shimada 1986]).

MOCHE ≡ In the coastal valleys, by moving settlements a strategy with local differences was followed in order to maximize arable land and minimize the effort, yet still maintain administrative control (Conrad 1978).

The incredible richness in the contents of vase paintings and of three-dimensional decorations has challenged interpreters. At first the depicted (and the neglected) subjects of scenes and their contents are informative (with a misleading title, which is derived from an older terminology: Kutscher 1950; 1983; Donnan 1978). Hocquenghem (1978) found thought-provoking arguments against older interpretations of depictions of fights on Moche vessels as pictures of real events and defeated warriors as members of another ethnic group; so did Schuler-Schömig (1979). Benson (1972) formed groups of the supernatural beings and characterized them by their depicted activities and associations.

THE MIDDLE HORIZON IN THE ANDES

Lately authors explain the close ties of the three centers and their domains in the Middle Horizon more and more by trade relations (summary: Browman 1978:331–34).

HUARI ≡ The examination of the sprawling ruins of the administrative-political center Huari near Ayacucho is still in its beginning. Peruvian archaeology understands Huari as acting as a selective mediator and transformer of the stylistic complex and ideology emanating from the Bolivian Tiahuanaco (Moseley 1983; Lumbreras 1980; Bennett 1953 was the first to describe the nature of the relationship Huari-Tiahuanaco). One remarkable difference from the structure of Tiahuanaco is the lack of ceremonial architecture for the most part, both in Huari proper and in its provincial centers. Another peculiarity are chambers built of large stone blocks, which might have been burial places of high-ranked persons and their retinue or family. The economic aspect of Huari was obviously more important than the ceremonial one, as is attested by the workshop areas for the manufacture of semiprecious stones (Isbell 1984). The central problem of interpretation is whether or not Huari can be called a "pristine state." The special burial sites are understood as evidence of the existence of an elite (Isbell 1987). Now that the urban character of Huari (with an estimated population of ten to twenty thousand) seems to be confirmed (Isbell 1986), the stratification of the settlements and the administrative architecture (Isbell and Schreiber 1978) could be seen as another indicator for the presence of a state. However, the primarily political interpretation of the stylistic influence of

Huari is just one of the possibilities (Schreiber 1987; trade as alternative: Shady and Ruiz 1979:683). An explanation for the sudden end of Huari, for which ecological or violent reasons cannot be recognized, is still missing.

TIAHUANACO ≡ Tiahuanaco on the shore of Lake Titicaca was not only a religious-administrative center with a massive, specialized, and characteristic architecture, but also a large settlement with substantial surroundings used for agriculture. A large number of dependent provincial centers in the Titicaca basin have been discovered in the meantime. A discovery in the coastal area of the Moquegua valley that sheds light on internal conflicts is still an isolated incident (Goldstein 1993). On this basis, Kolata (1993:205) understands Tiahuanaco as a dynamic, expansive state. After its fall the extremely fertile fields were amazingly expanded, possibly to allow an extensive llama-grazing economy (Graffam 1992). An odd combination of trustworthy archaeological recording and wild speculation characterizes the work of Posnansky (1945; 1957) in Tiahuanaco. The influence of Tiahuanaco is interpreted as analogous to the exploitation of different elevation zones by one ethnic group, which can be proven historically for the Late Horizon (Kolata 1983:263). The question remains whether interpretations of archaeological evidence of the Middle Horizon on the basis of institutions known from the Inca period are legitimate or not.

THE LATE INTERMEDIATE PERIOD

CHIMÚ ≡ Knowledge about Chimú comes from the results of archaeological work as well as from a few brief reports of the Colonial period. A summary of the culture is presented by Rowe (1948; *1970). Of special historical importance is the question of the nature and extent of the political-administrative institutions that the Inca Empire took over from Chimú. In this case, the written sources yield little, so the main emphasis is on the interpretation of archaeological evidence. A special danger, which obviously is not always recognized as such, is that of circular conclusions, when an interpretation is prompted by facts known from the Inca Empire. In this vein, the function of the conspicuous walled complexes (*ciudadelas*) in Chan Chan has been interpreted beyond their undoubtedly administrative nature (Day 1982) as rulers' seats and tombs kept up by the royal families, analogous to the Inca *panaca* and the cult of dead rulers in Cuzco (Conrad 1981; comments by Isbell 1981; and by Paulsen 1981; reply by Conrad 1982). Other than these remarkable complexes, Chan Chan had extensive living quarters with an internal stratification (Klymyshyn 1982; Topic 1982) that allows no doubt about its nature as a city. The fact that Chimú was a state seems to be supported by building complexes in the surroundings that have structural similarities with the walled complexes of Chan Chan, and are viewed accordingly as administrative sub-centers (Keatinge 1974).

16

History of the Andes

GENERAL PROBLEMS

Indigenous descriptions of historical facts do not attempt a characterization that is as realistic as possible, but serve to substantiate and justify a contemporary situation. To achieve this goal neither a chronologically exact (linear) nor a thematically balanced treatment was required. The adoption of such indigenous traditions into the works of authors with a European concept of history has to lead to incompatibilities.

Modern history can refer to written sources from early Colonial times only for the Late Horizon. But even these statements by the mainly Spanish authors who report on Precolumbian history are contradictory and hardly abundant in contents, especially for the early period (Wedin 1966:41–97). In such a situation the work of modern authors usually occupies extreme positions. On one hand there is an uncritical, mostly additive repeating of statements from the reports, which does not neutralize their historical conditioning and internal dependency. For these authors the texts of Colonial histories contain mainly correct statements (Brundage 1963; review by Zuidema 1965; reply by Brundage and answer by Zuidema 1966; conditions on the eve of the Conquest: Brundage 1967).

On the other hand are those modern authors whose skeptical approach can be best summarized by the words of Zuidema (1965; see Brundage 1963), their most prominent interpreter: "The only positive thing we know about the history of these peoples is the date when the Inca were conquered by the Spaniards; everything else is speculation." They view the oral traditions used by the Spanish authors as an expression of mythical explanations and justifications of historical situations, which do not allow access to past events. Spanish authors, misunderstanding the nature of these traditions on the basis of their own image of history, took these descriptions as historical reports and have represented them as such.

A third position understands indigenous historical traditions as a conscious transformation with the long-range goal of cementing the central political role of the Incas also by a corresponding blueprint of the transmitted history (Espinoza Soriano 1987:475–82).

Another dichotomy on the part of modern authors can be recognized in the evaluation of the moving factors. While traditionally, just as in early historical descriptions, an outstanding person, such as Pachacutec, is given an important, if not decisive, role, the process-oriented historical research puts events in the social sphere in the foreground. Archaeologists naturally feel a greater affinity to this type of thinking, because in archaeological evidence one finds not the activity of an individual but rather long-range material changes, which can be correlated with their counterparts in social, economic, or religious areas. The question is if the incompatibility of the archaeological picture of the time before the appearance of the Incas in the Cuzco area with the descriptions in the sources, as found by Bauer (1992), is not primarily determined by source- and research-specific causes.

CHIMÚ EMPIRE ≡ The unfortunate source situation regarding the history of the Chimú Empire is the result of several factors. The empire had ceased to exist about seventy years prior to the Spanish Conquista, and its centers with possible informants were situated outside the sphere of Spanish authors. An overview of the few available sources and the insights they allow is given by Rowe (1948; *1970). All other political units existing before the Inca Empire and contemporaneous with it are mentioned in the Colonial reports only in a superficial way. Research into these units depends on the evaluation of early Colonial administrative and judicial documents and the extrapolations into the past that these allow.

INCA EMPIRE ≡ A historical-critical literature on the history of the Inca Empire is missing almost entirely. The possibilities for this are shown by Rostworowski de Diez Canseco (1953) in her monograph on the Inca ruler Pachacutec. Summaries of the actual state of research are also rare (Patterson 1991; from a materialistic viewpoint: Espinoza Soriano 1987; Millones 1987 tries for a compassionate interpretation).

THE INCA EMPIRE

RULER DYNASTIES ≡ Deviating from the majority of the sources, contrary to the majority of modern authors (e.g., Espinoza Soriano 1987) and the sequence described here, Zuidema (1964:126–27, followed by Duviols 1980) recognizes two parallel ruler sequences, based on the Colonial authors Polo de Ondegardo (1916b), Acosta (O'Gorman 1940), who was influenced by him, and Cieza de León (Cantú 1985). Both sequences had started with Manco Capac and each had belonged either to the city half Hurin Cuzco or to Hanan Cuzco. The first sequence was comprised of the rulers Sinchi Roca, Capac Yupanqui, Lloque Yupanqui, Mayta Capac, and (otherwise not mentioned) Tarco Huaman, the second Yahuar Huacac, Viracocha Inca, Pachacutec, Tupac

Yupanqui, Huayna Capac, and Huascar. Zuidema follows here his concept of the strictly mythical-explanatory nature of early history descriptions. On the other hand his and Duviols's arguments for the existence of parallel rulers cannot be rejected out of hand. A dual system as a mirror of universal dichotomies has been accepted in the meantime by other authors (Rostworowski de Diez Canseco 1983:130–88) and can also be shown for other areas.

The sources attribute to specific rulers a transformation of historical traditions for prevalent political reasons. On one of these occasions the Inca rulers not enumerated by the majority of Colonial authors, Urco, Tarco Huaman, and Sapaca (Rostworowski de Diez Canseco 1983:179; 1953:84–86), could have been eliminated from the traditions. The fact that historical events, especially of the early period, were often rendered mythical is explained by Espinoza Soriano (1987:38–48) in the legendary migration story of the Incas and Manco Capac.

PACHACUTEC ≡ The most important personality of Inca history is without a doubt the ruler Pachacutec (his authenticity is questioned by Pease G. Y. 1972:21–23). The change from a small and unimportant chiefdom to an expansive state is attributed to him (Schaedel 1978a:291). Pachacutec also initiated the expansion politics that were continued by his immediate successors.

EXPEDITIONS ≡ Among the puzzling episodes of the empire's expansion is a raft voyage by Inca Tupac Yupanqui, which had been suggested by local merchants and proceeded from the Ecuadorian coast into the Pacific, in order to visit remote islands, from which he brought back gold, silver, and dark-skinned people. Like other such trips, this one also started numerous speculations. The discoverer of the Galapagos, Pedro Sarmiento de Gamboa (Pietschmann 1906), was convinced that the raft journey had reached these islands, which is not consistent with the items that were brought back. Technically, the inhabitants of the coasts were able to travel on the high seas and did so (very informative: Oberem and Hartmann 1982:128–49). The theory of Heyerdahl (1952) that Polynesia was at least partially settled from America belongs in this context.

HUASCAR AND ATAHUALPA ≡ Most of the time the conflict between the ambiguously designated successor of Huayna Capac, Huascar, and his half brother Atahualpa is seen as a dispute about inheriting the rulership between the legitimate son and the illicit hopeful. Pease G.Y. (1972; *1991) emphasizes the conflict between Cuzco and its religious elite on the side of Huascar, and Tomebamba near Quito, represented by Atahualpa.

THE END OF THE INCA EMPIRE ≡ The events of the Conquest, described by contemporary sources in detail and partly as eyewitness reports, are beyond the scope of this book. The preceding fraternal war between Huascar and

Atahualpa, which made the Conquest so much easier, is of decisive importance (a summary: Ballesteros Gaibrois 1982).

Of interest is the attempt over a long period of time after the Conquest by a part of the Inca family to drive the Spaniards out of the country by laying siege to Cuzco and Lima; after that failed they tried to keep their independence in an area the Spaniards could not reach (the complementary descriptions: Kubler 1944; 1947 [these are standard, and also highlight the cultural conflict]; 1946). The relationship with the millenarian rebellion movement Taqui Onco is examined by Wachtel (1971; *1976; *part 3 chap. 1 published separately in 1973). The location of Vilcabamba, the center of this area, discussed for a long time, was confirmed by Lee (1989) to be situated on the middle section of the Río Pampaconas.

RULERSHIP IN THE ANDES

EXPANSION ≡ The fast and efficient expansion of the Inca Empire within two generations has generated many questions. On one hand the time span as given in the early Colonial sources has been questioned (Wedin 1963), on the other hand it has been pointed out that the empire created by the Inca rulers out of Cuzco was not the first of its kind. Centuries earlier large states around the centers of Huari and Tiahuanaco existed according to archaeological evidence; however, it has to be asked if the structural similarities are not at least in part the result of interpretations of the archaeological evidence according to the model of the Inca Empire. The model of Chimú is much clearer. It is attributed to a mainly military expansion, like the Inca Empire.

For the Inca expansion some ecologically determined explanations have been offered. In a period of favorable (relatively moist) climatic conditions a spiral of population growth and enlargement of arable lands had been set in motion. A climatic change starting in A.D. 1400 intensified conflicts about food resources in the form of land, and finally led to the expansion of the Inca Empire (Paulsen 1976). The reality, extent, and date of the climatic change have been doubted with vehemence, as well as the practicality of military expansion as a counter measure (Conrad 1981; review by Isbell 1981; and by Paulsen 1981; Trigger 1978; Conrad and Demarest 1984:84–230). Instead, Conrad (1992:172) and Rowe (1948; *1970) see the beginning of the expansion rather as a coincidental and unplanned result of the victory over Cajamarca.

INTEGRATION ≡ Control and integration of an empire created in such a short time was possible only on the basis of indirect rule, which confirmed local leaders in their positions and at the same time tied them to the Inca family, through marriages and in other ways. Rostworowski de Diez Canseco (1978b; 1977a) also recognizes in the beginning expansion of the Inca Empire the old pan-Andean structure of hierarchically ordered political units. The Inca ruler was able to achieve a hegemonical position in relation to other *curacas* by reciprocal associations and redistribution of goods. The rise of the Incas was not caused by military success in neighboring areas alone, but by the skillful use of resources. According to Schaedel (1978b), the indirect rule in the beginning was supplemented in the last fifty years before the Conquista by a rise of responsibilities and activities directly answering to the central power. Thus for Chimú a continuation of interior political structures can be deduced especially through archaeological evidence, but at the same time the territory shrank in the attractive higher regions of the valleys (Netherly 1988). The northern border of the empire also shows more complex structures than was previously suspected. Ethnic/linguistic separations can be expressed in dichotomous patterns as well (analysis of territorial organization on the basis of a statistical examination of personal names: Salomon 1988; 1980:255).

Archaeological evidence shows that the elite in the conquered areas quickly adopted Inca luxury goods, while this aspect of a conquest naturally did not affect the common people (Salomon 1980:255; *1986). Despite the advantages presented by the *Pax Incaica* local rulers liked to use the opportunity for rebellions when the central power and the army were occupied elsewhere (Murra 1978a:929–30; *1986). The Inca goal of politically integrating local rulers into the empire often met with only superficial success. This also became apparent during the Spanish conquest, when the resentment of local rulers against the Incas was expressed in their readiness to collaborate with the Spaniards (Espinoza Soriano 1973). It is important for the interpretation of Colonial evidence that Inca institutions (at least their names) were still spread or enforced after the Conquista (Salomon 1986:257).

ARMY ≡ In the Inca Empire the warriors were selected according to their accomplishments among the adolescent young men and specially trained. In the early period of the Inca Empire military service was carried out within the rotating *mit'a* duties under leaders from their own group. Later whole ethnic groups (such as the Charca and even later the resettled Cañari) were relieved of other regular duties and were exclusively allocated for military service (Murra 1978a:932–33; *1986). The standing army was obviously divided in decimal and semidecimal units and it was supplied out of granaries destined for its use that were spread all over the empire. The armament consisted of bow and arrow, lance and spear thrower, sling-shot balls and club (superficially: Bram 1941; *1977). In important operations the commander in chief was often the Inca himself, or members of his family. They were assisted by experienced army leaders from the nobility.

POLYETHNIC STRUCTURE ≡ The expanse of the Inca Empire overlaid a large number of ethnic groups, which were organized partly in small political units. Although they shared basic cultural traits, they were by no means homogenous. This is apparent in the linguistic disposition: while Quechua was spoken only in a comparatively small area around Cuzco of 150 kilometers at most, the speakers of Aymara lived in a much larger area around Lake Titicaca and especially to the south of it. The largest area of the Inca Empire by far was populated by numerous other language groups. The goal of a cultural unification of the empire was sought to be achieved by the politics of the Incas through the establishment of a formal conformity between small structures (on a local and regional level) and large structures (state level). In this they were successful even with those ethnic groups who displayed structures much different from those of the Inca central Andes area, such as the ones in the north (Salomon 1978; *1986), although these are hardly known yet in their particulars. Where the economic and political structures were already in compliance with the uniform model of vertical resource control and sociological hierarchy, only the military independence was removed (Pease G. Y. 1979; *1982).

SUCCESSION RULES ≡ Most authors differentiate between succession rules for pre-Inca lords in the Andes and those for the developing and consolidating Inca rulers. According to Rostworowski de Diez Canseco (1953:230–40), local rulers (*curaca*) elected their successors in pre-Inca times from the most capable in their groups, without regarding a specific rank or family. In the early period of the Incas, government was passed normally to the son of the main wife. This rule was later amended in such a way that during the lifetime of the father that son of the main wife who was best suited for the office was elected co-regent. However, if his capabilities were not confirmed, this could be revoked (Rowe 1946, different opinion based on the conflict Huascar-Atahualpa; Pease G. Y. 1972:79–100; *1991). However, this succession rule was so unstable that factions within the high nobility had the opportunity to engage in power intrigues (Rostworowski de Diez Canseco 1990; 1993).

Inheritance rules within the Inca family differentiated between the throne and the material possessions, including land, that remained (at least since Pachacutec) in the hands of the heirs (*panaca*). This came to bear on the need for rulers to construct each time a new palace; according to Conrad (1981:18–21; comment by Isbell 1981; and by Paulsen 1981), each new ruler was forced to acquire new property especially in the form of land, and for this purpose he enlarged the empire, which finally led to its collapse. Conrad (1981:10; comment by Isbell 1981; and by Paulsen 1981) recognizes corresponding succession rules in the Chimú Empire, based on the spatial organization of the palace complexes with associated burial platforms in Chan Chan.

PRIVILEGES OF THE NOBILITY ≡ Polygyny as practiced by the high nobility in Cuzco and by the Inca himself was also common among the local *curaca.* Colonial documents help to elucidate detailed questions such as the laws of inheritance and succession (Espinoza Soriano 1977).

ORGANIZATION OF THE EMPIRE ≡ The designation of the Inca Empire as Tahuantinsuyu refers to an organization into four quarters (*suyu*), as Guamán Poma de Ayala (1980) depicted it in a schematic map. A more precise localization of borders in the vicinity of Cuzco was achieved by Zuidema and Poole (1981), who investigated statements from a document of 1577 in the field. Rostworowski de Diez Canseco (1990; 1993) questions this schematic organization by showing that in the southern part of the empire there existed three other *suyu.*

DECIMAL ORGANIZATION ≡ The notion of a totally organized and centrally regulated state of the Incas corresponds to the conviction that there existed a system of strict decimal organization that encompassed many sections of life. Wedin (1965) criticizes the selective data base of such statements, which led to a neglect of accounts about the lower levels of organization; he considers the assumption of a more or less firm number of ten thousand men for a "province" nonsensical, because it cannot be maintained as a constant and the historical origin of a "province" as the area of an ethnic group contradicts a fixed numerical quantity. He is of the opinion that the decimal organization system, reported by many Colonial authors, was applied mainly in the military. On the other hand, Zuidema (1964) comes to the conclusion that the decimal organization was an adaptation, a combination of a local system on the basis of "5" with the decimal system of the Chimú, and that categories called by multiples of ten were not reflecting exact numbers, but have to be taken rather as aids for classifications.

Catherine Julien (1982) does not build on global descriptions, but uses a *visita,* whose data base is a *quipu* made just before the Conquest. The numbers classifying the tribute payers seem to confirm the existence of a decimal system on the highest level. However, parallel to it there existed locally different, nondecimal organizations.

SOCIAL AND ECONOMIC ORGANIZATION

The social, economic, and political institutions of the late period in the Inca Empire are the result of a directed alteration of older, pre-Inca forms, according to the congruous views of many modern authors (Murra 1975a; *1981a; 1980; *1978; Godelier 1973a; *1974:63–69; 1973b; Golte 1978; Wachtel 1973b; *1981). The Inca state changed the functions of these institutions according to its needs, and by doing so it undermined their original character so much that eventually they represented new contents in old forms. This process of newly defining institutions like *ayllu, yana, mitmac,* as well as rules for land acquisitions for the nobility, seems to have just begun when it was interrupted by the Spanish conquest. Colonial sources therefore show institutions in different phases of this process, which creates contradictions that impede their interpretation.

SOCIAL GENDER RELATIONS ≡ Knowledge of the social relations of men and women is necessarily one-sided and incomplete due to the fact that informants as well as Colonial authors were male (Zuidema 1977a:254; *1980b). On one hand the Inca form of gender relations contained the principle of symmetrical, balanced associations; on the other hand there were asymmetrical, hierarchical relations. For instance, the male-dominated sun cult is complemented in a balanced way by an emphatically female moon cult; both genders had parallel access to economical resources and had social and religious rights and duties. On the other hand, women were excluded almost completely from political power. The institution of *aclla* and the polygenic households, which were reserved for the nobility, show that being in charge of women was both means and expression of political power (Silverblatt 1976; 1987; Rostworowski de Diez Canseco 1986).

AYLLU ≡ The term *ayllu* denotes social groupings, not unlike the Mexican *calpulli,* of very different size, composition, and hierarchic category. Units called *ayllu* had functions in the social, economic, religious, and political-judicial areas. Colonial sources added to the confusion by using various terms, including *ayllu,* for different Indian terms with different meanings. In addition to the numerous meanings for *ayllu* a single one was picked as an administrative term, especially after the administration reforms under Viceroy Toledo, and adapted for Colonial needs.

Modern authors have developed very controversial notions of *ayllu,* depending on the sources they use and their theoretical positions. Authors under the influence of classical culture evolutionism have interpreted regional differences or coexisting structures of a controversial nature as a development sequence (Saavedra 1913). According to their understanding, *ayllu* was a localized group defined by kinship ("market co-operative," "blood association") (Cunow 1891; Cunow 1937:97–112, 135–39), an exogamous, matrilinear, totemic clan (Trimborn 1923–24; 1925), later a "totemic phratry" (among others Urteaga 1931:32–36). The notion of a totemic clan has been opposed by Rowe (1946); basically it is a kinship group with endogamy, only if there is a deviation from this rule, the affiliation with the male line is determined. The origin is traced back to a common ancestor, who can be a human being, but can also be an animal or a natural object. Rowe found no sufficient grounds to state the existence of a totemic group.

Numerous authors speak of unilinear kinship and endogamy (Karsten 1938; title misleading: *1949:111; Kirchhoff 1949; Castro Pozo 1946, vol. 2:484). It has been stated often that in the north of the Andes matrilinearity dominated, and in the south patrilinearity, but recently much more differentiated conditions are proposed (Zuidema 1977a; *1980b; Lounsbury 1986). Zuidema's statement that there was an incest taboo for four generations is most likely a misinterpretation of a Colonial mission instruction (Cock Carrasco 1981).

The territory that was defined by the living quarters of the *ayllu* members was not necessarily the same as the one they had the right to use. Examinations of Colonial administrative documents have shown that both territories need not have been rounded out, as Cunow had assumed (Pease G. Y. 1980, vol. 2:242–44; 1981; Martínez 1981; Cock Carrasco 1978; Rostworowski de Diez Canseco 1985). The aspect of territoriality recedes in some regions, for instance on the coast, in favor of collectively executed undertakings (fishing, getting salt) (Rostworowski de Diez Canseco 1981). Cock Carrasco (1981) points out that there were differently comprehensive categories of *ayllu*: an *ayllu mayor*, which served social classification, contained several *ayllu* of a lower category. Since these levels of *ayllu* are determined by different categories of membership and different functions, the demand for a completely new view of *ayllu* has not been met at this time.

YANA ≡ A dogmatic evaluation of *yana* (the word may come from the Chimú language) (Rowe 1948:47; *1970) as slaves is opposed by Murra (1966; *1975c) on the basis of Colonial *visitas*. In his discussion of the different possibilities of the word's origin he may not have come to a generally accepted conclusion, but he does prove a pre-Inca origin of this social category, based on a *visita* of the Lupaqa. A special aspect of *yana* is emphasized by Rostworowski de Diez Canseco (1976:346–48). Their efforts meant substantial advantages to the Incas in their desire for acquisition of power and goods, because they did their work without compensation in a complicated rule of reciprocal relations. The category *yana* was not at all homogenous (Murra 1980 [written in 1955]; *1978c; Rowe 1982:96–105). The unusually high segment of 10 percent *yana* of the total population in a Colonial census in Ecuador may be traced back to the incorporation of another local group into this Inca category (Salomon 1980:200; English original 1986). Without data other than a constantly belabored analogy to Germanic institutions (which he doesn't cite properly), Trimborn (1923–24:999; 1925; 1927:338–43) assumes that the *yana* he calls "rechtlose Leibeigene (serfs without rights)" were mostly prisoners of war, convicted criminals and conscripted members of *ayllu*.

ACLLA ≡ In the case of *aclla* the different origin and function of the women combined in this social category leads to difficulties of evaluation as well.

Rostworowski de Diez Canseco (1986:12–13) emphasizes that the state used these women mainly as a work force. But the ruler did give them to men he wanted to place under an obligation, or he took them as wives for himself, if such a union created or strengthened a political alliance. Within these facts, Alberti Manzanares (1985) sees the role of women as much more unconstrained. The religious function of the *aclla* is discussed by Gareis (1987).

MITMAC ≡ Numerous questions that resulted from the inaccurately drawn picture of the *mitmac* by Colonial authors can be elucidated by the evaluation of new sources. According to Rowe (1982), the terms *mitmac* and *yana* do not denote two different groups of persons, but two different stations, which can even coincide in one person. The status of a *mitmac* expresses only that a man is not living permanently in his ethnic place of origin. At the same time he could be attached to the ruler, his family, or persons favored by him, or religious institutions, and hence be *yana*. Which status was emphasized in each case—especially in an early Colonial situation—depended on the context.

The major dissimilarities of those called *mitmac*, in terms both of their incorporation into the provincial administrative structures of their new settlement and of their activities, are shown by Espinoza Soriano (1982; 1978; 1975a; 1969–70) through several local studies. The example of a resettlement in the Cochabamba valley, well documented in a Colonial legal dispute (Wachtel 1981b; *1982), allows insights into land distribution methods and land working techniques. The *mitmac* settled there to grow corn for the Inca army were helped in their work by people from their former home rendering *mit'a*, which contributed to the preservation of a close link. There were constantly more than fourteen thousand people at work. In this case, it was uncommon that besides land given to *mitmac* households for their own use, the *curaca* of their original groups had been given land-use rights as well. In this way, not only was the state able to profit from the resettlement, but also the original group had access to the much-valued corn fields, as Wachtel (1978; *1986) shows for the Uru.

Mitmac had to take care of themselves. They were fed from the granaries of the state only in the first phase of their resettlement (Lalone and Lalone 1987). An example of *mitmac* in the area of Titicaca shows that the state placed at their disposal resources compatible with their traditional expectations: they received land in a much-desired location of lower altitude and sent members of their group to work it (Saignes 1978; *1986).

AGRICULTURAL LAW ≡ The complex distribution of land and the access to its use on the part of institutions as well as individuals cannot be understood in the Andes as elsewhere by adopting European legal notions, such as the difference between "ownership" and "possession" (Latcham 1927; Murra 1980 [written in 1955]; *1978c), nor by a leveling view of the whole empire. Rather, the different categories of access to land have to be seen in conjunction with agricultural methods and political power positions (Falk Moore 1958).

AYLLU LANDS ≡ Modern examinations do not unanimously evaluate collective and private access rights to land of tribute payers. The majority of authors seem to be of one opinion, namely that land and animal herds, at least in small, independent political units prior to the expansion of the Inca Empire, basically belonged to the entire village or the *ayllu*, often identical with it, and that this rule was kept intact in Inca times for the most part (for example: Trimborn 1923–24; 1925:580–93). Latcham (1927:230–36) places more emphasis on the creation of personal ownership, based on modern ethnographic reports. There had been a category of private land that belonged to the house(hold), and another category, the *ayllu* land, consisting of several large sectors adapted to the local conditions of crop and fallow rotation, where each category was distributed to single families. In the second category the *ayllu* made all decisions. These parcels could be inherited under the supervision of the *ayllu*.

Other authors also cite modern ethnographic reports in order to clear up Polo de Ondegardo's (1916b) report that every year land was "redistributed." This obvious misunderstanding refers to the yearly ceremonial pacing of land and confirmation of family land parcels, also a periodic adaptation of available land to household sizes by redistribution and the opening of new sections (Murra 1979; Falk Moore 1958:21–23; Rowe 1946, vol. 2:266). The administrative and legal documents of the Colonial period also show that access to land in the Precolumbian *ayllu* was governed by a meshing of individual and collective agricultural laws.

PRIVATE LAND OF NOBLES ≡ Colonial land disputes confirm the hints of early Colonial authors that members of the nobility had a special access to land (Rostworowski de Diez Canseco 1966; 1962). Not only the ruling Inca, his principal wife (*coya*), and the *panaca* of his predecessor, but also the local *curaca* owned quite extensive lands, which were worked by *yana*.

The extreme opposite cannot be upheld, which says that private ownership of land was not only reserved for the nobility, but also could be in the hands of the commoners (Benayas 1951, with a very selective bibliography), and that all involvement of the *ayllu* was denied, at least for the largest part of the empire.

INSTITUTION LANDS ≡ The land of institutions was comprised of very different types, which were differentiated by those working on them, as well as by those who profited from the yields. The largest part of these lands was worked by tribute-paying *ayllu* members. The yields were collected in granaries and were used mainly for redistribution in state projects. Other state land was worked by *yana, aclla,* or *mitmac* for state purposes. A part of the harvest was kept for their own provision (Murra 1979). In areas conquered by the Inca Empire some land in addition to existing institutional land (for local deities) was partitioned off for the central state and religion ("land of the sun"). Its size varied. As criteria for the determination of its size the circumstances of the Conquest (evidence from the coast: Rostworowski de Diez Canseco 1978–80:168) and additional ecological considerations were taken into account (Murra 1979).

OTHER LAND ACCESS ≡ Examinations of deviant conditions in the different regions of the Inca Empire become important: at least in some valleys of the northern coast there were partial tenant relations between the land-owning nobility and the rest of the population (Rostworowski de Diez Canseco 1972; *1977d:39–41; Falk Moore, 1958:28, talks about the possibility of a "feudal arrangement"). A noble could also have a tenant agreement with the subjects of another noble (Ramírez 1985).

LAND AND WORK ≡ Only the utilization of a sufficient work force made land productive and therefore rights of access valuable; both cannot be examined in isolation (Murra 1979:282–83). While single households of the *ayllu* organized the communal labor on their own land, local authorities called on members of the group for regular work on land parcels, whose yields were destined for the political overlords and the religious institutions, both for the local units and for the central state (forms of work as defined by entries in a Colonial Quechua dictionary: Golte 1974).

TRIBUTE ≡ All tribute payments were basically defined as contribution of work. Only the delivery of products of a collective economy (gathering, hunting) were determined by quantity (Murra 1958). An interesting glance at type and quantity of tribute is given by Murra (1982b), who examines an early Colonial administrative document. However, his derivation of ethnocategories from this document seems to be an overinterpretation.

MINING ≡ The same classification as for landed property was used for mining: silver and gold mines "of the Inca" yielded the raw material for the needs of the state, for the ruling family, and for the public religious institutions. Other mines were at the disposal of local rulers. The work force was recruited in a set percentage in the form of *mit'a* from the inhabitants (Berthelot 1978; *1986). There were also some *mitmac* employed. The techniques involved consisted of washing gold and mining it in simple tunnels; the gold contained in the earth was then also washed out.

ECONOMY ≡ The evaluation of source groups (only recently made accessible), especially of *visitas*, which allow insights into a narrowly defined complex of facts about Colonial-period tribute relations that reach back into Precolumbian times, created the prerequisite for an analysis of economic systems in the Andes, going far beyond the original scope of the *visitas*. The dominant model for the interpretation of the Precolumbian economy in the Andes is the principle of ecological zones, which is used in other mountain regions of the world as well.

"VERTICAL CONTROL" ≡ Murra (1972; *1975b) carefully formulated an idea causing a continuous wave of examinations ever since, that "el control vertical de un máximo de pisos ecológicos (vertical control of a maximal number of ecological levels)" was an ideal valid in the entire Andes in all periods. It meant an optimal usage of agricultural zones, which were situated in the distinctly segmented relief of the Andes' vertical levels, often closely together, but subject to different climates (Troll 1943). This was achieved by giving a population outside of their original territory further living grounds, which were scattered like islands ("archipelago"), some quite a distance away. This distribution of their property, including the people who worked there, meant that the different ethnic groups or smaller units had direct access ("control") to different production zones, without the intervention of a middleman or a trade system. This setup also allowed a rational usage of the available work force, because agricultural activities in these zones occur at different times (Golte 1978; 1980). A characteristic feature is that the population in the peripheral settlement islands remained full members of their original ethnic group, which caused sometimes a polyethnic structure in the desirable cultivated regions.

As described by Murra the basic model was adapted by the Inca state according to its requirements. It can be recognized as "structural verticality" if one thinks of the large number of *mitmac* who were resettled not only for agricultural purposes, but also in military garrisons or as artisans in regions farther and farther away.

SPATIAL VALIDITY ≡ Evidence that the principle of "verticality" was realized in the form of production archipelagos with polyethnic enclaves mainly comes from central Peru down to and including Bolivia (Ortiz de Zúñiga 1967–72; Murra 1968; enlarged: *1975e). Rostworowski de Diez Canseco (1981:120; 1978b:75–80) feels that Murra's concept of vertical archipelagos is geared too much toward the region south of central Peru. Only there existed the political prerequisites for the archipelago structure in the form of a hegemony of ethnic groups in the Altiplano, covering the entire region. Enclaves outside the core area of these groups in consequence were an expression of a political power configuration, which was not as distinct in the Andes farther north. Moreover, in southern Peru and Bolivia the larger horizontal distance between lands of different altitude levels was also detrimental to the application of the principle.

TEMPORAL VALIDITY ≡ A large part of the works on "verticality" is concentrated on recent conditions or archaeological evidence (Shimada 1982). However, evidence that a population uses goods from different ecological zones cannot be interpreted as evidence for political control in these zones. The possibilities of proving anything for periods that can be studied only through archaeology are severely limited (methods of archaeological evaluations: D.E. Thompson 1968; *1970).

SOURCE SITUATION ≡ The structure of vertical control has not been demonstrated in Colonial reports, but mainly in administrative documents of the Colonial period. Since the original condition as postulated by Murra, the system had endured the two fundamental changes of the Inca expansion and the Conquista. Moreover, the system was so alien to the Spanish administrators that their descriptions are only sparse and not very precise. In consequence, interpretation of them demands substantial effort.

VARIANTS ≡ An additional variant of ecological correspondence is tied to suitable situations with large altitude differences. It allowed an ethnic group to utilize a substantial number of different altitude levels within their territory, despite the fact that the territory was not extensive ("micro-verticality" [Webster 1971; Oberem 1978]). Micro-verticality appears to be the result of production techniques well adapted to spatial conditions (recent example: Orlove 1977). The resources of different zones can be exploited by one ethnic group in a cyclical sequence (Rostworowski de Diez Canseco 1978a:167–77).

LIMITS OF THE VERTICALITY MODEL ≡ The multiple changes during the early Colonial period are a warning against uncritical backward projections. The example of the Lupaqa, chosen by Murra, was shown by Catherine Julien (1985) to contain differentiated spatial-temporal forms of resource control and had a connection with political-administrative constellations. Saignes (1981) also emphasizes a difference between permanently settled *mitmac* and inhabitants of the ethnic core area for the Lupaqa, who appeared only for seasonal work. Another variant of interpretation was suggested by Golte (1970): inhabitants of the highlands worked for a time in the areas where coca was grown and had taken in exchange for this effort half of the harvest. However, this particular piece of Colonial evidence can actually reflect a very early Spanish introduction.

RECIPROCITY ≡ According to the presently favored classification by Polanyi, Arensberg, and Pearson (1957) there are three types of economical integration within societies, which he calls reciprocity, redistribution, and market exchange. For descriptions of the economic, sociological, and political organizations in the Andes the concept of reciprocity has been used ever since ca. 1967 (influenced earlier: Murra 1980 [written 1955]; *1978). Despite divergences of detail, reciprocity is understood to reflect the exchange of goods and services as mutual; symmetric and asymmetric relations are distinguished.

LEVELS OF RECIPROCITY ≡ According to Wachtel (1971; *1976; *1977) there are three levels of reciprocal relations: *ayllu* members among each other, between *ayllu* members and local rulers, and between *ayllu* members and the state. While there is symmetrical reciprocity on the first level, this changes in relationships to central institutions such as local rulers and eventually the state to become more and more asymmetrical reciprocity, and finally exploitation. A much more complex concept of reciprocal relationships is suggested by Rostworowski de Diez Canseco (1976:342). Criteria of symmetry are also discussed: Are the delivered goods in symmetry with the service of a local ruler who not only organizes the production and distribution of goods, but also the relationship to the gods, which ensures the existence of the community, or with the service of the state, which secures peace inside and outside of the realm (positive: Murra 1981c)? In the Inca state the visible, traditional form of reciprocal relationships appears to mask really novel institutions (Wachtel 1973b; *1981a; skeptical: Meillassoux 1981).

REDISTRIBUTION ≡ Redistribution is seen as an asymmetrical form of reciprocity between *ayllu* members and their local rulers, and later the Inca state, which had, according to Murra (1980:121, 139 [written in 1955]; *1978c) the function of a kind of market, by allowing an exchange of products from different regions and services of different groups of people. This is contradicted by Morris (1986) on the basis of archaeological work; he sees almost no signs of inter-regional transfers between the large storage centers. While the simple subsistence products (especially corn and potatoes) were hoarded in large quantities near their production locale in special storage rooms (Morris 1992) and distributed from there to people who had served the state either temporarily or permanently, it was almost exclusively the luxury and ceremonial goods that were brought to Cuzco from the provinces, and were distributed from there. The fact that the state depended so much on its supply reserves, as demonstrated by the huge capacity of the granaries, revealed its inability to continuously secure its need of goods through long-term productive investments (Morris 1986:67, contrary to current opinion).

TRADE ≡ There are contrary positions on the existence and the role of a market trade in the Andes on the basis of controversial source statements. The interpretation of Andean economy through verticality (dominating at present), which allows an extensive economic self-sufficiency, hardly leaves room for a transfer of goods in markets, because the production of all necessary goods was either in the hands of the consumers (micro-verticality), or in the sphere of influence of a redistributing local ruler (archipelago-verticality). In consequence, Murra (1980:139–50 [written in 1955]; *1978c) has questioned the existence of markets (regular market events), and sees in the few early Colonial source clues about them (the market in Cuzco) a description of misunderstood redistribution activity.

It has to be mentioned here that even in sources that were used to formulate the thesis of verticality, trade relations are mentioned (Fonseca Martel 1983–85:307). Lalone (1982) sharply argues against the existence of markets and of commercial trade as an economic regulative; the entire economy of the Inca Empire is understood by him as politically determined.

MARKETS ≡ Nevertheless, even in the opinion of Murra there was a local exchange trade, mainly for foodstuffs and a few raw materials, especially from the tropics. The statement of Colonial authors against the existence of markets, quoted by Murra, that volume and value of the individual trade agreements was very minor, is recognized by Hartmann (1968:214–18; 1971) in a modern situation as well. As opposed to a purely economic viewpoint, she rightfully emphasizes the strong social function of a market visit. Despite the paltry source conditions, she found that there was a "developed market system" everywhere in the central Andes of a pre-Inca or non-Inca origin, which was replaced to an extent not exactly ascertainable by Inca tribute and gift exchange relationships. Indeed, the statements about trade and markets are clearly more pronounced in Ecuador, which was incorporated into the Inca Empire at a comparatively late date. Most likely the use of the central Mexican term *tiangues* (instead of the local *catu*) by early Colonial authors is not an argument against the existence of markets, because elsewhere the transfer of terms from areas where the Spaniards first came into contact with a distinctive matter can be determined (specifically first the Caribbean, then central Mexico).

MONEY ≡ A generally accepted, standardized value measure did not exist. For individual regions the following surrogates are mentioned: small bones, called *carato* by Colonial authors, which were strung up twenty-four at a time (Oberem 1981b:81), small disks of salmon-colored shell (*spondylus*) (Murra 1975d; *1982a; the possibility of imports from as far away as Mesoamerica: Marcos 1980), or the excavated copper axes, which were impractical to use as tools. These precious objects, which could be transported over long distances, contrary to food and other consumer goods, eased the flow of state income especially in the border zones of the empire ("wealth finance" [D'Altroy and Earle 1985]), and allowed for the storage of collected riches.

UNITS OF MEASURE ≡ Scales, albeit with a small load capacity, have been found in archaeological contexts and were mentioned in early reports. The units to measure lengths and volume were regionally very different (Rostworowski de Diez Canseco 1964). Caution is necessary for all units mentioned in Colonial documents that seem to coincide exactly with Spanish measures.

PROFESSIONAL MERCHANTS ≡ It seems that professional merchants were limited to the border regions of the Inca Empire. A large number of professional land and sea merchants seems to have existed in some sections of the coast.

Rostworowski de Diez Canseco (in the Chincha Valley: 1970; *1977e; 1975b; *1977b; *1977c) emphasizes the importance of "longitudinal" trade exchanges that ran down the Peruvian coast. In the northern border regions of today's Ecuador, which were conquered late, merchants (*mindalaes*) formed their own social group and depended directly on the local rulers, for whom they provided tribute in goods, but no work services. They enjoyed a certain political autonomy under a *primus inter pares* and settled near places convenient for traffic, which developed market functions; in Quito it was directly next to the central market (Salomon 1978:974–75, 977; *1986; 1980:163–69).

A question hard to answer from the sources is whether or not the function of these merchants was mainly their participation in local redistributions directed by the state, through which their ethnic group gained access to goods they could not get within their own vertical access area (Murra 1975d; *1982a), or whether it was an adaptation of the redistribution organization to permeable political borders of small political units (Salomon 1980:304–14; 1986). Contrary to opinions dominated by Murra, some authors adopt the view that there was a commercially determined trade, specially based on source material from Ecuador (Oberem 1978; *1981a; Hartmann 1968). The existence of specific marketplaces in the core area of the Inca Empire has to be doubted on the basis of archaeological examinations. The thorough excavations of the regional center Huánuco Pampa with its substantial storage capacities showed that there was no market area (Morris 1978a:323; *1978b; *1978c).

ENGINEERING FEATS

ROADS ≡ The lavishly built roads that cross the entire Inca Empire commanded the attention of Colonial authors, who used them in part themselves. The technical achievement has also attracted travelers of the nineteenth century and even inspired novelists (especially T. Wilder, *The Bridge of San Luis Rey*, Boni, New York, 1927). A reconstruction of the main roads on the basis of a minute evaluation of early sources and later statements was prepared by Regal (1936). So far, the archaeological verification has been restricted merely to following a few courses of roads here and there. Hagen (1955) presented the results of his research only in an adventure-type travelogue. Solely in the most recent, thorough study, which reflects past work adequately in the bibliography and contains comments on some (Hyslop 1984), were long road sections documented exactly, and the presently manifest total network was estimated to be twenty-four thousand kilometers long, a number that will be much enlarged by possible future examinations.

PRE-INCA ROADS ≡ If any of these roads ran through deserts or uninhabited mountain regions, they were possibly first laid out during the Inca expansion.

Otherwise, existing trail connections were improved. In part, the roads left by past empires (Huari, possibly using another building technique) were taken over and improved here and there. The system of roads lends itself to the clear recognition of a shift of orientation toward important centers (Huari and Inca Empire) (Schreiber 1984).

IRRIGATION WORKS ≡ Next to roads the extensive irrigation works in the form of canals running along slopes is seen as one of the superb engineering feats of the Inca Empire. Indeed, large canal systems, especially in the coastal valleys, go back in time much further, at least to the Early Intermediate period. Their archaeological investigation is still in its preliminary stages (the scholarly results of a large survey have not been completely published because of the death of Kosok; the book that has been brought out for the general public contains amazing photographs: Kosok 1965; exemplary for a modern detail study: Moseley and Deeds 1982). The role that irrigation is thought to play occasionally in the origin of states has been mentioned already. Faced with supra-regional irrigation works, which even connected some valleys on the Peruvian coast, one cannot overlook a mutual dependency of canal construction and political organization.

PLANNED SETTLEMENTS ≡ Living quarters and settlements of all sizes, which had been constructed according to plans in the last decades of the Inca Empire, were closely connected with the system of roads, both in space and in function. The large urban settlements of this type had extensive ceremonial and elite areas, but small resting places along the roads, called *tampu,* also contained living quarters for persons of elevated rank. The extensive granaries described by Colonial authors have been discovered in archaeological excavations, but for the most part they seem to have been used to support settlements situated in areas unsuitable for farming. Stylistic features foreign to the specific region underline the intrusive character of the structures (Morris projected for the Inca Empire a storage capacity of over one million cubic meters [1978a:321; *1978b; *1978c; 1972]). The fact that they were quickly abandoned after the Conquista documents that their commissioning was intricately connected with the Inca Empire.

BORDER FORTIFICATIONS ≡ The expansion of the Inca Empire never went beyond the eastern edge of the mountains; the historical reports of the disastrous military campaigns into the woodlands are an expression of a situation not mastered properly. The threatened instability of the border is also attested to by a mass of small fortresses, especially in the southeast and the south (summary of archaeological evidence in Chile and northwestern Argentina: Raffino 1981), but the entire eastern border had such installations; important places such as Quito were protected by a ring of fortresses.

EXPANSION ≡ For the expansion period the archaeological evidence is less significant than the historical, and therefore it is evaluated under the individual subject headings. Archaeological examinations are concentrated on areas neglected by Colonial authors. Therefore the administrative centers in the provinces have generated much interest for a while now; in part they were completely reconstructed according to a plan (Menzel 1959; Schjellerup 1984; Morris and D.E. Thompson 1970). Another concern is the recording of settlement patterns and cultivation zones (Kendall 1984, as well as other papers about this project in this book; Lerche 1986).

INCA ARCHITECTURE ≡ The examination of Inca architecture is still in its beginnings. A broad survey was done by Gasparini and Margolies (with extensive and often exquisite illustrations of rarely mentioned places: 1977; *1980). The formal, and by including the reports also the functional, classification, and the composition of a sequence of stylistic developments (seriation), led Kendall (1985) to propose a series of three or four phases in architecture. An instructive study by Protzen (1993) deals especially with the construction and planning details. Besides the monumental stone architecture that has been the chief focus of attention for a long time, there were also many buildings or construction segments put up in adobe (Moorehead 1978). With very few exceptions all roofs were constructed of beams and covered with grass.

RELIGION AND RITUALS

When discussing religion in central Mexico, problems with the sources were mentioned already; they afflict a reconstruction of all areas of religion and ritual life. Although hardly anything is known about the daily customs, numerous summaries deal especially with the official definition of religion in the Inca Empire (Kauffmann Doig 1987; Duviols 1987). In addition there are monographs about the most important deities (Demarest 1981; Benson 1987b; Benson 1987a). By comparison there was only little attention paid to the female deities (Mariscotti de Görlitz 1978). The regional origin of deities, their amalgamation within the Inca Empire, and interpretation problems because of Colonial reinterpretations are the subjects of Rostworowski de Diez Canseco (1983:21–96), who was clearly influenced by Levi-Strauss' structuralism. The official religion of Cuzco and the relationship to regional and local cults was used by the Incas as a means to integrate and strengthen their empire (Gareis 1987).

HUMAN SACRIFICES ≡ The apologetic defusion or negation of human sacrifice was much more clearly expressed in the Andes than in Mesoamerica, although it had a much less important role there and never reached the numbers reported for the Aztecs. In the Inca Empire predominantly children were sacrificed; their number never exceeded two hundred, even on special occasions (Rowe 1946, vol. 2:305–6; Duviols 1976).

CEQUE SYSTEM ≡ Thanks to a favorable source situation it was possible to reconstruct an area of the religious system in Cuzco that may not be restricted to this place alone. From the center of town radiating imaginary lines lead to a large number of shrines in the immediate vicinity. The analysis is based foremost on remarks preserved in Cobo's (1956) short version of a thorough report (Rowe 1979; Zuidema [1964] takes the ceque system as the focal point of his overall reconstruction of Andean culture).

EVALUATION OF THE INCA EMPIRE

Unlike that of the Aztecs, the Inca Empire has generated global, often idealizing, characterizations. In the interest of the history of thought it might be valuable to follow up on the roots of these views.

GENERAL CHARACTERIZATION ≡ The controversy between the extremes of a positive-admiring evaluation of the structure of the Inca Empire and a negative-repudiating view of its institutions, which are tied to the writings of Garcilaso de la Vega (1960) on one hand and authors in the environment of the Viceroy Toledo on the other, continued until the present time. An example for a modern, almost rapturous, and in any event most idealizing view is presented by Valcárcel (1966): The centralized rule had been executed with restraint; the general planning "por objeto el bienestar de todos los seres humanos (with the goal to benefit all)" had "la mayor aproximación al concepto científico del planeamiento (reached the greatest approximation to the scientific concept of planning)" and at the same time realized "el más alto sentido de humanidad y justicia (the highest regard for humanity and justice)." He even assumes that the conquests of the Incas have been called by that term in error, and instead speaks of integration approaches ("misiones de integración"). Other authors have spoken in a similarly uncritical and exalted fashion (e.g., Hanstein 1923:25).

SOCIAL STATE? ≡ During their attempts to characterize state organization of the Inca Empire in a more precise way, European authors again and again brought up the term socialism, which they each defined differently. Martens (1895), based almost exclusively on Garcilaso, saw the state as socialistic and centralistic. In contrast, Cunow (1896), who did not accept Garcilaso as a dependable source because of his bias, saw the Inca state as clearly based on rulership and exploitation, an example of a general level of human development, according to evolutionary thoughts of his time. A similar, differentiated view came from Rosa Luxemburg (1975, vol. 5:656–64), who recognized in the Inca Empire "zwei übereinandergelagerte soziale Schichten, die, beide kommunistisch im Innern organisiert, zueinander in einem Verhältnis der Ausbeutung und Knechtschaft standen (two social levels one atop the other, which were both communistically organized within, and had a relationship of exploitation of and subservience to each other)."

Several authors also called Inca state organization communist, one of them Valcárcel (1925:169), who sees the entire social structure aiming for the greatest possible contentment of the people, and Karsten (1938; *[title misleads] 1949)—speaking of agrarian communism—who sees the principle of socialization of work achieve the goal of mutual support. Trimborn (1923–24; 1925) views the high social care attributed to the Inca Empire in a more utilitarian light: it had allowed the state military to expand in the first place. Any economic activity had been in the hands of local communities, hence one had to speak of a local collectivism.

The discussion saw the largest expansion with *L'Empire socialiste des Inka* by the French economist Baudin (1928). He thought that an older agrarian collectivism had coexisted with a state socialism introduced by the Incas, and had shadowed all life with a monotonous *tristesse.*

Especially in view of Baudin, Wedin (1966:21) characterized the socialism debate aptly: "Lo que han buscado en las fuentes (los historiadores) no ha sido la verdad objetiva, sino más bien un apoyo a sus propias políticas, un argumento para el debate político (What historians looked for in the sources was not the objective truth, but support for their own political views, an argument for the political debate)." On the same line Murra (1975a; 1981a; compare also: Métraux 1961) criticizes the use of categories from European economical and social history.

Asiatic Production? ≡ In the center of a fairly new turn of this debate is the classification of Inca production mode as "asiatic" (Espinoza Soriano 1987:485, who prefers the term "modo de producción comunal-tributario"). This discussion inevitably means an explanation of the term "asiatic production mode," which Marx had not coined as precisely as that (Eich 1983:34–66). Golte (1978) thinks that the Inca state became part of the production conditions of the *ayllu* and ethnic units by providing infrastructural measures, resources, and products, so that one cannot speak any more of a self-sufficient village community. This contradicts Godelier (1973a; 1973b), who sees the technical and administrative measures of the state exclusively as well disguised ways to exploit and suppress the self-sufficient community.

If one looks for the one singular event that most determined the fate of ancient American cultures, the answer is never in doubt: the conquest by the Europeans and the incorporation into the Spanish Colonial empire. This not only meant the end of cultural autonomy, of political self-determination and economic autarchy, and the subordination to the interests of a power engaged primarily in Europe; almost immediately contact with the Europeans meant first of all physical death for nine tenths of the Indian population due to foreign diseases. Even if this physical demise was not intentional—and in any event only a fraction of it was intentionally perpetrated—it was largely sanctioned by the Spaniards, because it created the scope needed to take over the land. This occurrence is reflected in a change of term and the shift of focus of historical attention: instead of ancient America, in the future one will speak of Latin America, where the Indian component increasingly is granted only a marginal role.

Bibliography

Citations marked in the text with an asterisk are republications or translations of journal articles or contributions to collections.

Acosta, J. R. 1964. *El Palacio del Quetzalpapalotl.* Memorias del Instituto Nacional de Antropología e Historia 10, México.

Acosta, José de. 1940. *Historia natural y moral de las Indias,* edited by E. O'Gorman. Fondo de Cultura Económica, México.

———. 1976. Los toltecas. In *Los señoríos y estados militaristas,* edited by Noguera A., pp. 137–58. Instituto Nacional de Antropología e Historia, México.

Acosta Saignes, M. 1945. Los pochteca: Ubicación de los mercaderes en la estructura social tenochca. *Acta Americana* 1(1):1–92.

———. 1946. Migraciones de los Mexica. *Memorias de la Academia Mexicana de la Historia* 5:177–85.

———. 1954. Los pochteca: Ubicación de los mercaderes en la estructura social tenochca. México.

———. 1975. Los pochteca: Ubicación de los mercaderes en la estructura social tenochca. In *El comercio en el México prehispánico,* edited by E. Florescano, pp. 19–61. Instituto Mexicano de Comercio exterior de México, México.

Acuña, R., ed. 1981–88 *Relaciones Geográficas del siglo XVI.* Universidad Nacional Autónoma de México, Instituto de Investigaciones Antropológicas, México. (The volumes are 1: Guatemala; 2, 3: Antequera; 4, 5: Tlaxcala; 6–8: México; 9: Michoacan; 10: Nueva Galicia.)

Adams, R. E. W. 1973. Maya collapse: Transformation and termination in the ceramic sequence at Altar de Sacrificios. In *The classic Maya collapse,* edited by T. P. Culbert, pp. 133–63. University of New Mexico Press, Albuquerque.

———. 1977. *Prehistoric Mesoamerica.* Little, Brown, Boston.

Adelhofer, O., ed. 1963. *Codex Vindobonensis Mexicanus 1.* Akademische Druck- und Verlagsanstalt, Graz.

Adorno, R. 1981. Current research on Waman Puma and his Nueva Corónica. *Latin American Literatures* 5:9–15.

———. 1986. *Guaman Poma, writing and resistance in colonial Peru.* University of Texas Press, Austin.

Aguilar, Francisco de. 1977. *Relación breve de la conquista de la Nueva España,* edited by J. Gurría Lacroix, 7th ed., Universidad Nacional Autónoma de México, Instituto de Investigaciones Históricas, México.

Alberti Manzanares, P. 1985. La influencia económica y política de las acllacuna en el incanato. *Revista de Indias* 45, No. 176:557–85.

Albornoz, C. de. 1967. Instrucción para descubrir todos los guacas del Perú y sus camayos y haziendas, edited by P. Duviols. *Journal de la Société des Américanistes de Paris, N.S.* 56:7–39.

Alcina Franch, J. 1975. Juan de Torquemada, 1564–1624. In *Guide to Ethnohistorical Sources,* edited by H. F. Cline, pp. 256–75. Handbook of Middle American Indians, vol. 13. R. Wauchope, general editor. University of Texas Press, Austin.

Alcocer, I. 1935. Estátuas de reyes aztecas en el cerro de Chapultepec. In *Apuntes sobre la antigua México-Tenochtitlán,* edited by I. Alcocer. Publicaciones de Instituto Panamericano de Geografía e Historia 14:91–98, Tacubaya/México.

Alden, J. R. 1974. A reconstruction of Toltec period political units in the Valley of Mexico. In *Transformations: Mathematical approaches to culture change,* edited by C. Renfrew and K. L. Cooke, pp. 169–200. Academic Press, New York.

Alva Ixtlilxochitl, Fernando de. 1975–77. *Obras históricas,* edited by E. O'Gorman, 2 vols., 3rd ed. Universidad Nacional Autónoma de México, Instituto de Investigaciones Históricos, México.

Alvarado, Pedro de. 1954. *Relación,* edited by J. Valero Silva. José Porrúa e Hijos, México.

Alvarado Guinchard, M., ed. 1976. *El Códice de Huichapan, I relato otomí del México prehispánico y colonial.* Instituto Nacional de Antropología e Historia, México.

Alvarado Tezozomoc, Hernando. 1878 (1598). *Crónica Mexicana,* edited by M. Orozco y Berra. Biblioteca Mexicana, México.

Anders, F. 1963. *Das Pantheon der Maya.* Akademische Druck- und Verlagsanstalt, Graz.

Anders, F., ed. 1967. *Codex Tro-Cortesianus (Codex Madrid).* Akademische Druck- und Verlagsanstalt, Graz.

———. 1968. *Codex Peresianus (Codex Paris).* Akademische Druck- und Verlagsanstalt, Graz.

Anders, F. (introduction, summary). 1972. *Codex Vaticanus 3773.* Akademische Druck- und Verlagsanstalt, Graz.

Anders, F., and H. Deckert, eds. 1975. *Codex Dresdensis.* Akademische Druck- und Verlagsanstalt, Graz.

Anders, F., and N. P. Troike (introduction). 1987. *Codex Zouche-Nuttall,* Akademische Druck- und Verlagsanstalt, Graz.

Anderson, E., and R. H. Barlow. 1943. The maize tribute of Moctezuma's empire. *Annals of the Missouri Botanical Garden* 3:413–18.

Anderson, L. B. 1993. The writing system of La Mojarra and associated monuments. Ecological Linguistics, Washington.

Andrews, G. F. 1975. *Maya cities: Placemaking and urbanization.* University of Oklahoma Press, Norman.

———. 1985. Chenes-Puuc architecture: Chronology and cultural interaction. In *Arquitectura y arqueología* (Collection Etudes Mésoaméricaines II–8), coordinated by P. Gendrop, pp. 11–39. Centre d'Études Mexicaines et Centreaméricaines, México.

———. 1986. *Los estilos arquitectónicos del Puuc: Una nueva apreciación.* Colección Cientifica, Serie Arqueología 150, México.

Andrews IV, E. Wyllys. 1965. Archaeology and prehistory in the northern Maya lowlands: An introduction. In *Archaeology of Southern Mesoamerica*, edited by G. R. Willey, pp. 288–330. Handbook of Middle American Indians, vol. 2. R. Wauchope, general editor. University of Texas Press, Austin.

Andrews V, E. Wyllys. 1990. The early ceramic history of the lowland Maya. In *Vision and revision in Maya studies*, edited by F. S. Clancy and P. D. Harrison, pp. 1–20. University of New Mexico Press, Albuquerque.

Andrews V, E. Wyllys, and J. A. Sabloff. 1985. Classic to postclassic: A summary discussion. In *Late lowland Maya civilization: Classic to postclassic*, edited by J. A. Sabloff and E. W. Andrews V, pp. 433–56. University of New Mexico Press, Albuquerque.

Andrews V, E. Wyllys, and N. Hammond. 1990. Redefinition of the Swasey Phase at Cuello, Belize. *American Antiquity* 55:570–84.

Angiano, M., and M. Chapa. 1976. Estratificación social en Tlaxcala durante el siglo XVI. In *Estratificación social en la Mesoamérica prehispánica*, edited by P. Carrasco P., and J. Broda, pp. 118–56. Centro de Investigaciones Superiores, Instituto Nacional der Antropología e Historia, México.

Anonymous. 1968. Relación de las costumbres antiguas de los naturales del Perú. In *Crónicas peruanas de interés indígena*, edited by F. Esteve Barba, pp. 151–90. Atlas, Madrid.

Anonymous. 1973 (1681). *Recopilación de Leyes de los Reynos de las Indias* . . . , 4 vols., facsimile edition. Ediciones Cultura Hispánica, Madrid.

Arguedas, J. M., and P. Duviols, eds. 1966. *Dioses y hombres de Huarochirí*: Edición bilingüe; Narración quechua recogida por Francisco de Avila. Museo Nacional de Historia y el Instituto de Estudios Peruanos, Lima.

Armillas, P. 1948. Fortalezas mexicanas. *Cuadernos Americanos* 41:143–63.

Ascher, M., and R. Ascher. 1981. *Code of the quipu: A study in media, mathematics, and culture.* University of Michigan Press, Ann Arbor.

Aveni, A. 1978. The pecked cross symbol in ancient Mesoamerica. *Science* 202:267–79.

Avila, Francisco de. 1939. *Dämonen und Zauber im Inkareich*, edited by H. Trimborn and G. Friederici. Quellen und Forschungen zur Geschichte der Geographie und Völkerkunde, Band 4. F. K. Köhler, Leipzig.

Ball, H. G., and D. L. Brockington. 1978. Trade and travel in prehispanic Oaxaca. In *Mesoamerican communication routes and cultural contacts*, edited by T. A. Lee, Jr., and C. Navarrete, pp. 107–14. University of Utah Press, Salt Lake City.

Ball, J. W. 1979. Ceramics, culture history, and the Puuc tradition: Some alternative possibilities. In *The Puuc: New perspectives*, edited by L. Mills, pp. 18–35. Central College, Pella.

———. 1985. Campeche, the Itza, and the postclassic: A study in ethnohistorical archaeology. In *Late lowland Maya civilization: Classic to postclassic*, edited by J. A. Sabloff and E. W. Andrews V, pp. 379–408. University of New Mexico Press, Albuquerque.

Ballesteros Gaibrois, M. 1982. *La caída del imperio de los Incas.* Forja, Madrid.

Bandelier, A. F. 1878. On the distribution and tenure of land and the customs with respect to inheritance among the ancient Mexicans. In *Eleventh Annual Report of the Peabody Museum of American Archaeology and Ethnology.* Harvard University, Cambridge.

———. 1880. On the social organizations and mode of government of the ancient Mexicans. In *Twelfth Annual Report of the Peabody Museum of American Archaeology and Ethnology*, Harvard University, Cambridge.

Bandera, D. de la. 1965. Relación general de la disposición y calidad de la Provincia de Guamanga. In *Relaciones geográficas de Indias-Perú*, edited by M. Jiménez de la Espada, vol. 1:176–80. Atlas, Madrid.

Bardsley, S. N. 1994. Rewriting history at Yaxchilan. Inaugural art of Bird Jaguar IV. In *Seventh Palenque Round Table, 1989,* edited by M. Greene Robertson, pp. 87–94. The Pre-Columbian Art Research Institute, San Francisco.

Barlow, R. H. 1944. Tlatelolco en el período Tepaneca. *Tlatelolco a Través de los Tiempos* 1:23–42, México.

———. 1945a. La Crónica X: Versiones coloniales de la historia de los Mexica Tenochca. *Revista Mexicana de Estudios Antropológicos* 7:65–87.

———. 1945b. Some remarks on the term 'Aztec Empire.' *The Americas* 1:345–49.

———. 1946a. Materiales para una cronología del imperio de los Mexica. *Revista Mexicana de Estudios Antropológicos* 8:207–15.

———. 1946b. Los "cónsules" de Tlatelolco. *Tlatelolco a Través de los Tiempos* 8:412–14.

———. 1948a. Cuauhtlatoa: El apogeo de Tlatelolco. *Tlatelolco a Través de los Tiempos* 10:14–48.

———. 1948b. El derrumbe de Huejotzingo. *Cuadernos Americanos* 7:147–60.

———. 1948c. Un problema cronológico: La conquista de Cuauhtinchan por Tlatelolco. *Tlatelolco a Través de los Tiempos* 10:43–46, México.

———. 1949a. *The extent of the Empire of the Culhua Mexica.* University of California Press, Berkeley.

———. 1949b. La fundación de la Triple Alianza (1427–1433). *Anales del Instituto Nacional de Antropología e Historia* 3:147–55.

———. 1952. Los Tecpanecas después de la caída de Azcapotzalco. *Tlalocan* 3:285–87.

Barrera Vásquez, A., and S. Rendón, translators. 1948. *El libro de los Libros de Chilam Balam.* Fondo de Cultura Económica, México.

Barrientos, C. de. 1967. Visita que hizo . . . 1540. *Revista Peruana de Cultura* 11–12:25–41.

Barrios E., P. M. 1952. Tecpanecos y mexicanos. *Tlalocan* 3:287–88.

Barthel, T. S. 1982. Veritable "texts" in Teotihuacán art? *The Masterkey* 56:4–12.

Bartra, R. 1974. Tributo y tenencia de la tierra en la sociedad azteca. In *El modo de producción asiático,* edited by R. Bartra, pp. 212–31. Ediciones Era, México.

Baudin, L. 1928. *L'Empire socialiste des Inca.* Institut d'Ethnologie, Paris.

———. 1942. *Les incas du Pérou.* Librairie de Médicis, Paris.

Bauer, B. S. 1992. *The development of the Inca state.* University of Texas Press, Austin.

Bauer, B. S., and D. S. P. Dearborn. 1995. *Astronomy and empire in the ancient Andes.* University of Texas Press, Austin.

Benavente, Toribio o Motolinía de. 1971 (1568). *Memoriales o libro de las cosas de la Nueva España y de los naturales de ella,* edited by E. O'Gorman. Universidad Nacional Autónoma de México, Instituto de Investigaciones Históricas, México.

Benayas, J. 1951. *Los mitos comunistas, socialistas y colectivistas del Perú prehispano.* Talleres gráficas de la Editorial Lumen, Lima.

Bennett, W. C. 1953. *Excavations at Wari, Ayacucho, Peru.* Yale University Press, New Haven.

Benson, E. P. 1972. *The Mochica: A culture of Peru.* Praeger, New York.

———. 1987a. Inti. In *Encyclopedia of Religion,* edited by M. Eliade, vol. 7:268. Macmillan, New York.

———. 1987b. Viracocha. In *Encyclopedia of Religion,* edited by M. Eliade, vol. 15:272. Macmillan, New York.

Berdan, F. F. 1976a. Enculturation in an imperial society: The Aztecs of Mexico. In *Enculturation in Latin America: An Anthology,* edited by J. Wilbert, pp. 237–64. Latin American Center Publications, University of California, Los Angeles.

———. 1976b. La organización del tributo en el imperio azteca. *Estudios de Cultura Nahuatl* 12:185–93.

———. 1977. Distributive Mechanism in the Aztec economy. In *Peasant livelihood: Studies in economic anthropology and cultural ecology,* edited by R. Halperin and J. Dow, pp. 91–101. St. Martin's Press, New York.

———. 1978a. Ports of trade in Mesoamerica: A reappraisal. In *Cultural continuity in Mesoamerica,* edited by D. L. Browman, pp. 179–98. Mouton, The Hague.

———. 1978b. Tres formas de intercambio en la economía azteca. In *Economía*

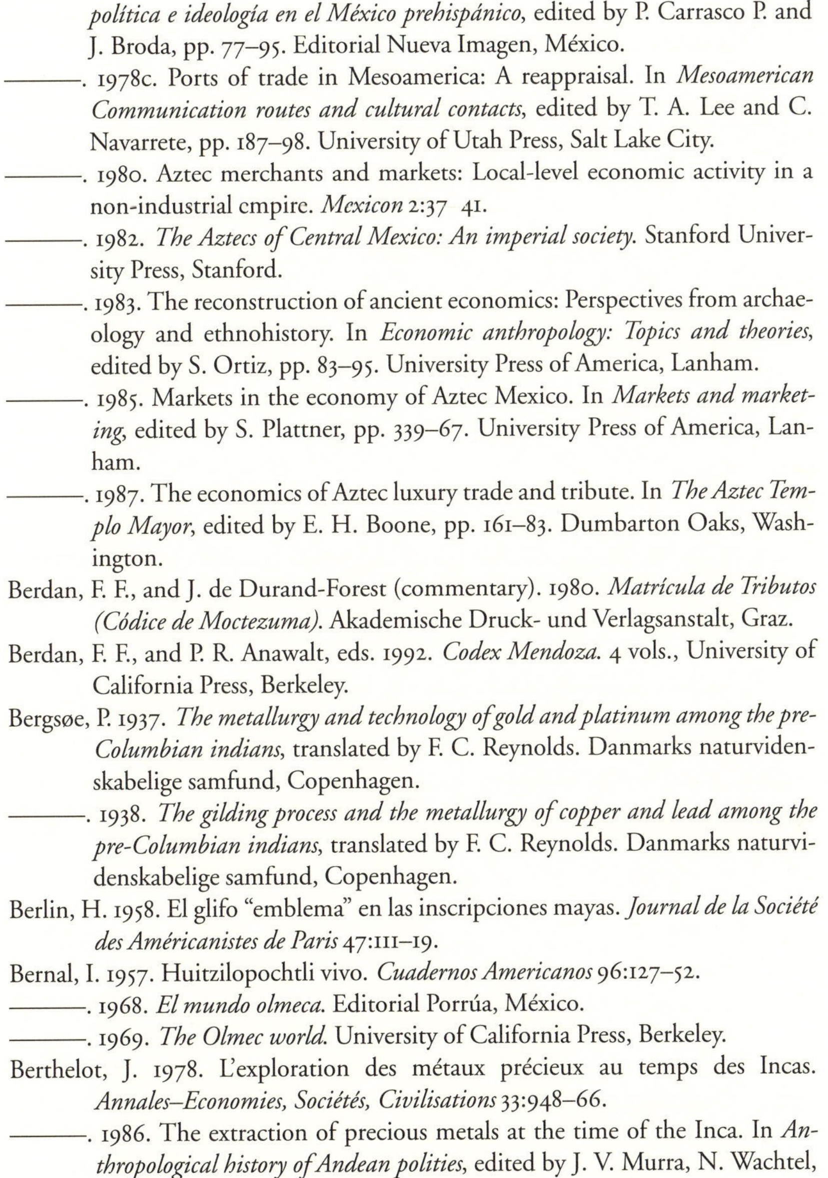

política e ideología en el México prehispánico, edited by P. Carrasco P. and J. Broda, pp. 77–95. Editorial Nueva Imagen, México.

———. 1978c. Ports of trade in Mesoamerica: A reappraisal. In *Mesoamerican Communication routes and cultural contacts*, edited by T. A. Lee and C. Navarrete, pp. 187–98. University of Utah Press, Salt Lake City.

———. 1980. Aztec merchants and markets: Local-level economic activity in a non-industrial empire. *Mexicon* 2:37 41.

———. 1982. *The Aztecs of Central Mexico: An imperial society.* Stanford University Press, Stanford.

———. 1983. The reconstruction of ancient economics: Perspectives from archaeology and ethnohistory. In *Economic anthropology: Topics and theories*, edited by S. Ortiz, pp. 83–95. University Press of America, Lanham.

———. 1985. Markets in the economy of Aztec Mexico. In *Markets and marketing*, edited by S. Plattner, pp. 339–67. University Press of America, Lanham.

———. 1987. The economics of Aztec luxury trade and tribute. In *The Aztec Templo Mayor*, edited by E. H. Boone, pp. 161–83. Dumbarton Oaks, Washington.

Berdan, F. F., and J. de Durand-Forest (commentary). 1980. *Matrícula de Tributos (Códice de Moctezuma).* Akademische Druck- und Verlagsanstalt, Graz.

Berdan, F. F., and P. R. Anawalt, eds. 1992. *Codex Mendoza.* 4 vols., University of California Press, Berkeley.

Bergsøe, P. 1937. *The metallurgy and technology of gold and platinum among the pre-Columbian indians*, translated by F. C. Reynolds. Danmarks naturvidenskabelige samfund, Copenhagen.

———. 1938. *The gilding process and the metallurgy of copper and lead among the pre-Columbian indians*, translated by F. C. Reynolds. Danmarks naturvidenskabelige samfund, Copenhagen.

Berlin, H. 1958. El glifo "emblema" en las inscripciones mayas. *Journal de la Société des Américanistes de Paris* 47:111–19.

Bernal, I. 1957. Huitzilopochtli vivo. *Cuadernos Americanos* 96:127–52.

———. 1968. *El mundo olmeca.* Editorial Porrúa, México.

———. 1969. *The Olmec world.* University of California Press, Berkeley.

Berthelot, J. 1978. L'exploration des métaux précieux au temps des Incas. *Annales–Economies, Sociétés, Civilisations* 33:948–66.

———. 1986. The extraction of precious metals at the time of the Inca. In *Anthropological history of Andean polities*, edited by J. V. Murra, N. Wachtel, and J. Revel, pp. 69–88. Cambridge University Press, New York.

Betanzos, Juan de. 1987 (1576). *Suma y narración de los Incas*, edited by María del Carmen Martín Rubio. Atlas, Madrid.

Beyer, H. 1937. *Studies on the Inscriptions of Chichen Itza.* Carnegie Institution of Washington Publication 483, No. 21:29–175. Washington.

Bierhorst, J. 1992a. *Codex Chimalpopoca: The text in Nahuatl with a glossary and grammatical notes.* University of Arizona Press, Tucson.

———. 1992b. *History and Mythology of the Aztecs, the Codex Chimalpopoca.* University of Arizona Press, Tucson.

Binford, L. R. 1962. Archaeology as anthropology. *American Antiquity* 28:217–25.

———. 1986. In pursuit of the future. In *American archaeology, past and future,* edited by D. J. Meltzer, D. D. Fowler, and J. A. Sabloff, pp. 459–79. Society for American Archaeology by the Smithsonian Institution Press, Washington.

Bird, J., and J. Hyslop. 1985. The preceramic excavations at Huaca Prieta, Chicama Valley, Peru. *Anthropological Papers of the American Museum of Natural History* 62:1–294.

Bischof, H. 1979. San Pedro and Valdivia—Frühe Keramikkomplexe an der Küste Südwest-Ekuadors. *Beiträge zur Allgemeinen und Vergleichenden Archäologie* 1:335–88.

———. 1987. Archäologische Forschungen in Cerro Sechín (Casma): Ikonographische und stilgeschichtliche Aspekte. *Archaeologica Peruana* 1:23–46.

Bittmann Simons, B., and T. Sullivan. 1972. The pochteca. In *Atti del XL Congresso Internazionale degli Americanisti* 4:202–12. Tilgher, Roma-Genova.

———. 1978. The pochteca. In *Mesoamerican Communication routes and cultural contacts,* edited by T. A. Lee and C. Navarrete, pp. 211–18. University of Utah Press, Salt Lake City.

Blanton, R. E. 1978. *Monte Albán: Settlement patterns at the ancient Zapotec capital.* Academic Press, New York.

Blanton, R. E., G. M. Feinman, S. A. Kowalewski, and P. N. Peregrine. 1996. Dual-process theory for the evolution of Mesoamerican civilization. *Current Anthropology* 37:1–14.

Bohannan, P., and G. Dalton, eds. 1965. Introduction, *Markets in Africa.* Northwestern University Press, Evanston.

Bolles, J. S. 1977. *Las Monjas: A major pre-Mexican architectural complex at Chichén Itzá.* University of Oklahoma Press, Norman.

Boone, E. H. 1983. *The Codex Magliabechiano and the lost prototype of the Magliabechiano Group.* University of California Press, Berkeley.

Borah, W., and S. F. Cook. 1963. *The aboriginal population of Central Mexico on the eve of the Spanish Conquest.* University of California Press, Berkeley.

Bosch García, C. 1944. *La esclavitud prehispánica entre los Aztecas.* El Colegio de México, Centro de Estudios Históricos, México.

Bosch-Gimpera, P. 1970. Paralelos transpacíficos de las altas culturas americanas y su cronología. *Anales de Antropología* 7:48–89.

Bram, J. 1941. *An analysis of Inca militarism.* American Ethnological Society, New York.

———. 1977. *Análisis del militarismo incaico.* Universidad Nacional Mayor de San Marcos, Lima.

Brand, D. 1971. Ethnohistoric Synthesis of Western Mexico. In *Archaeology of Northern Mesoamerica*, edited by G. F. Ekholm and I. Bernal, pp. 632–56. Handbook of Middle American Indians, vol. 11. R. Wauchope, general editor, University of Texas Press, Austin.

Bray, W. 1972. The city state in Central Mexico at the time of the Spanish Conquest. *Journal of Latin American Studies* 4:161–85.

———. 1976. From predation to production: The nature of agricultural evolution in Mexico and Peru. In *Problems in economic and social archaeology*, edited by I. H. Longworth, K. E. Wilson, and G. de G. Sieveking, pp. 73–95. Duckworth, London.

———. 1978. Civilizing the Aztecs. In *The evolution of social systems*, edited by M. J. Rowlands, and J. Friedman, pp. 373–98. University of Pittsburgh Press, Pittsburgh.

Bricker, V. R. 1992. Noun and verb morphology in the Maya script. In *Epigraphy*, Handbook of Middle American Indians Supplement, vol. 5:70–81, edited by V. R. Bricker. V. R. Bricker, general editor, University of Texas Press, Austin.

Broda, J. 1976. El carácter diferente de la participación en el ritual: El soberano, el estamento dominante y la gente común. In *La estratificación social en la Mesoamérica prehispánica*, edited by P. Carrasco P. and J. Broda, pp. 39–66. Editorial Nueva Imagen, México.

———. 1978a. El tributo en trajes guerreros y la estructura del sistema tributario mexica. In *Economía política e ideología en el México prehispánico*, edited by P. Carrasco P. and J. Broda, pp. 113–73. Editorial Nueva Imagen, México.

———. 1978b. Relaciones políticas ritualizadas: El ritual como expresión de una ideología. In *Economía política e ideología en el México prehispánico*, edited by P. Carrasco P. and J. Broda, pp. 219–55. Editorial Nueva Imagen, México.

———. 1979. Aspectos socio-económicos e ideológicos de la expansión del estado Mexica. *Revista de la Universidad Complutense* 28:73–94.

Bronson, B. 1977. The earliest farming: Demography as cause and consequence. In *Origins of agriculture*, edited by C. H. Reed, pp. 23–48. Mouton, The Hague.

Browman, D. L. 1978. Toward the development of the Tiahuanaco (Tiwanaku) state. In *Advances in Andean archaeology*, edited by D. L. Browman, pp. 327–49. Mouton, The Hague.

Brown, C. L. 1991. Hieroglyphic literacy in ancient Mayaland, inferences from linguistic data. *Current Anthropology* 32:489–96.

Brumfiel, E. M. 1980. Specialization, market exchange, and the Aztec state: A view from Huexotla. *Current Anthropology* 21:459–78.

———. 1983. Aztec state making: Ecology, structure, and the origin of state. *American Anthropologist* 85:261–84.

Brundage, B. C. 1963. *Empire of the Inca.* University of Oklahoma Press, Norman. (Review: R. T. Zuidema, in *American Anthropologist* 67:176–77 [1965]. Reply: Brundage and answer by Zuidema in *American Anthropologist* 68:229–31.)

———. 1967. *Lords of Cuzco: A history and description of the Inca people in their final days.* University of Oklahoma Press, Norman.

———. 1972. *A rain of darts: The Mexica Aztecs.* University of Texas Press, Austin.

———. 1979. *The fifth sun: Aztec Gods, Aztec World.* University of Texas Press, Austin.

Burger, R. L. 1992. *Chavín and the origins of Andean civilization.* Thames and Hudson, London.

Burland, C. A. 1973. *Montezuma: Lord of the Aztecs.* Putnam, New York.

Burland, C. A. (introduction). 1966. *Codex Laud: Ms. Laud Misc. 678. Bodleian Library.* Akademische Druck- und Verlagsanstalt, Graz.

———. 1971. *Codex Fejérváry-Mayer: Museum of the City of Liverpool.* Akademische Druck- und Verlagsanstalt, Graz.

Bushnell, G. H. S. 1956. *Peru.* Thames and Hudson, London.

Cabello de Balboa, M. 1951. *Miscelánea antárctica.* Universidad Nacional Mayor de San Marcos, Instituto de Etnología, Lima.

Cabrera Castro, R. 1986. La verificación de algunos de los resultados del Mapping Project en recientes excavaciones en Teotihuacán. *Revista Mexicana de Estudios Antropológicos* 32:127–46.

Cabrera Castro, R., I. Rodríguez G. and N. Morelos G., eds. 1982. *Memoria del proyecto arqueológico Teotihuacán 1980–82.* Instituto Nacional de Antropología e Historia, México.

Calancha, Antonio de la. 1981 (1639). *Corónica moralizada del orden de San Agustín en el Perú, con sucesos ejemplares vistos en esta monarquía.* Universidad Nacional Mayor de San Marcos, Lima.

Calnek, E. E. 1972a. Settlement pattern and chinampa agriculture at Tenochtitlán. *American Antiquity* 37:104–15.

———. 1972b. The internal structure of cities in America: Pre-Columbian cities: The case of Tenochtitlan. In *Actas del 39 Congreso Internacional de Americanistas,* vol. 2:347–58. Instituto de Estudios Peruanos, Lima.

———. 1974. Conjunto urbano y modelo residencial en Tenochtitlán. In *Ensayos sobre el desarrollo urbano de México.* SepSetentas 154, pp. 11–59. Secretaría de Educación Pública, México.

———. 1975. Organización de los sistemas de abastecimiento urbano de alimentos: El caso de Tenochtitlán. In *Las ciudades de América Latina y sus áreas de influencia a través de la historia,* edited by J. E. Hardoy and R. P. Schaedel, pp. 41–60. Ediciones SIAP, Buenos Aires.

———. 1976. The internal structure of Tenochtitlán. In *The Valley of Mexico,* edited by E. Wolf, pp. 287–302. University of New Mexico Press, Albuquerque.

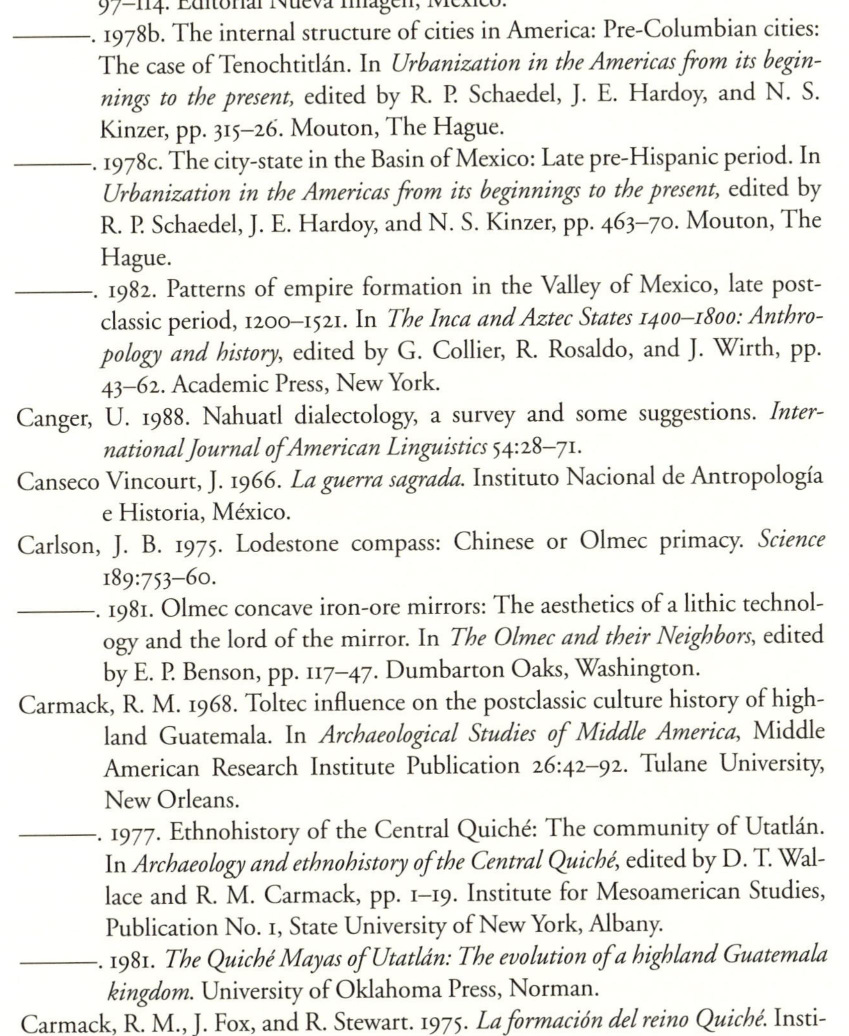

———. 1978a. El sistema de mercado en Tenochtitlán. In *Economía política e ideología en el México prehispánico,* edited by P. Carrasco P. and J. Broda, pp. 97–114. Editorial Nueva Imagen, México.

———. 1978b. The internal structure of cities in America: Pre-Columbian cities: The case of Tenochtitlán. In *Urbanization in the Americas from its beginnings to the present,* edited by R. P. Schaedel, J. E. Hardoy, and N. S. Kinzer, pp. 315–26. Mouton, The Hague.

———. 1978c. The city-state in the Basin of Mexico: Late pre-Hispanic period. In *Urbanization in the Americas from its beginnings to the present,* edited by R. P. Schaedel, J. E. Hardoy, and N. S. Kinzer, pp. 463–70. Mouton, The Hague.

———. 1982. Patterns of empire formation in the Valley of Mexico, late postclassic period, 1200–1521. In *The Inca and Aztec States 1400–1800: Anthropology and history,* edited by G. Collier, R. Rosaldo, and J. Wirth, pp. 43–62. Academic Press, New York.

Canger, U. 1988. Nahuatl dialectology, a survey and some suggestions. *International Journal of American Linguistics* 54:28–71.

Canseco Vincourt, J. 1966. *La guerra sagrada.* Instituto Nacional de Antropología e Historia, México.

Carlson, J. B. 1975. Lodestone compass: Chinese or Olmec primacy. *Science* 189:753–60.

———. 1981. Olmec concave iron-ore mirrors: The aesthetics of a lithic technology and the lord of the mirror. In *The Olmec and their Neighbors,* edited by E. P. Benson, pp. 117–47. Dumbarton Oaks, Washington.

Carmack, R. M. 1968. Toltec influence on the postclassic culture history of highland Guatemala. In *Archaeological Studies of Middle America,* Middle American Research Institute Publication 26:42–92. Tulane University, New Orleans.

———. 1977. Ethnohistory of the Central Quiché: The community of Utatlán. In *Archaeology and ethnohistory of the Central Quiché,* edited by D. T. Wallace and R. M. Carmack, pp. 1–19. Institute for Mesoamerican Studies, Publication No. 1, State University of New York, Albany.

———. 1981. *The Quiché Mayas of Utatlán: The evolution of a highland Guatemala kingdom.* University of Oklahoma Press, Norman.

Carmack, R. M., J. Fox, and R. Stewart. 1975. *La formación del reino Quiché.* Instituto de Antropología e Historia, Guatemala.

Carmack, R. M., and J. L. Mondloch, eds. 1983. *El Título de Totonicapán.* Universidad Nacional Autónoma de México, Instituto de Investigaciones Filológicas, Centro de Estudios Mayas, México.

Carneiro, R. L. 1970. A theory of the origin of the state. *Science* 169:733–38.

———. 1981. The chiefdom, precursor of the state. In *The transition to statehood in the New World,* edited by G. D. Jones and R. R. Kautz, pp. 37–79. Cambridge University Press, New York.

Carrasco, D. 1975. City as symbol in Aztec thought: The clues from the Codex Mendoza. *History of Religions* 19:199–223.

———. 1987. Aztec religion. In *Encyclopedia of Religion*, edited by M. Eliade, vol. 2:23–29. Macmillan, New York.

Carrasco, R., S. Boucher, and A. Peña. 1986. Río Bec, un modelo representativo del patrón de asentamiento regional. *Boletín de la Escuela de Ciencias Antropológicas de la Universidad de Yucatán* 13:20–30.

Carrasco P., P. 1950. *Los otomíes: Cultura e historia prehispánica de los pueblos mesoamericanos de habla otomiana.* Biblioteca Enciclopédica del Estado de México, México.

———. 1961. El barrio y la regulación del matrimonio en un pueblo del Valle de México en el siglo XVI. *Revista Mexicana de Estudios Antropológicos* 17:7–26.

———. 1964a. Tres libros de tributos del Museo Nacional de México y su importancia para los estudios demográficos. In *Actas y Memorias del XXXV Congreso Internacional de Americanistas*, vol. 3:373–78. Editorial Libros de México, México.

———. 1964b. Family Structure of Sixteenth-Century Tepoztlan. In *Process and Pattern in Culture: Essays in honor of Julian H. Steward*, edited by R. A. Manners, pp. 185–210. Aldine Publishing Co., Chicago.

———. 1970. Social Organization of Ancient Mexico. In *Archaeology of Northern Mesoamerica*, edited by G. F. Ekholm and I. Bernal, pp. 349–75. Handbook of Middle American Indians, vol. 10, part 1. R. Wauchope, general editor. University of Texas Press, Austin.

———. 1971. Los barrios antiguos de Cholula. *Estudios y Documentos de la Región Puebla-Tlaxcala* 3:9–88.

———. 1976a. La sociedad mexicana antes de la conquista. In *Historia General de Mexico.* D. Cosío Villegas (Coord.), vol. 1:165–288. El Colegio de México, México. (The first edition has many production mistakes; later editions are preferable.)

———. 1976b. Los linajes nobles del México antiguo. In *Estratificación social en la Mesoamérica prehispánica*, edited by P. Carrasco P. and J. Broda, pp. 19–36. Centro de Investigaciones Superiores, Instituto Nacional de Antropología e Historia, México.

———. 1977. Los señores de Xochimilco en 1548. *Tlalocan* 7:229–65.

———. 1978. La economía del México prehispánico. In *Economía política e ideología en el México prehispánico*, edited by P. Carrasco P. and J. Broda, pp. 15–76. Editorial Nueva Imagen, México.

———. 1979. The chiefly houses (*teccalli*) of ancient Mexico. In *The contact period in nuclear America: Documentary and archaeological evidence,* edited by H. R. Harvey and D. E. Thompson, vol. IX-B:177–85, Actes du XLIIe Congrès International des Américanistes, Société des Américanistes, Musée de l'Homme, Paris.

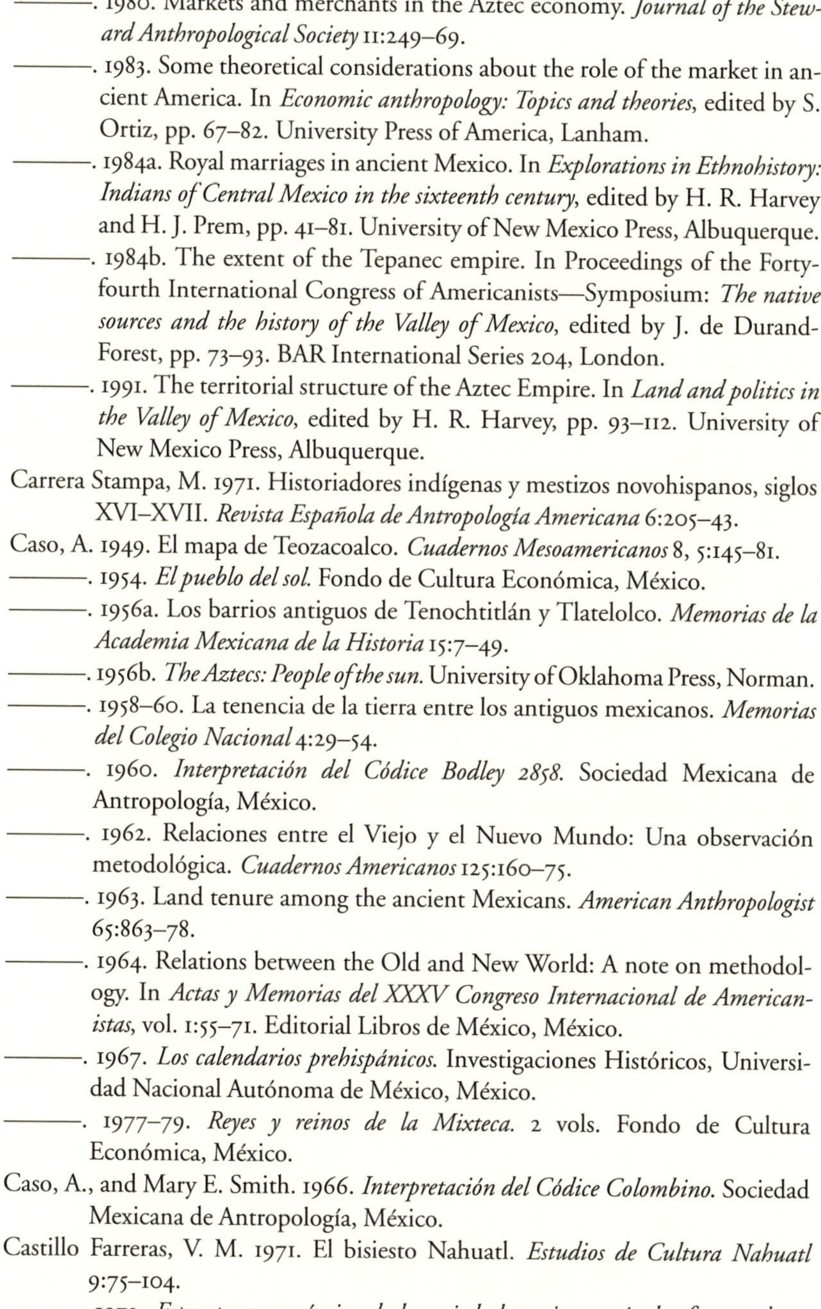

———. 1980. Markets and merchants in the Aztec economy. *Journal of the Steward Anthropological Society* 11:249–69.

———. 1983. Some theoretical considerations about the role of the market in ancient America. In *Economic anthropology: Topics and theories*, edited by S. Ortiz, pp. 67–82. University Press of America, Lanham.

———. 1984a. Royal marriages in ancient Mexico. In *Explorations in Ethnohistory: Indians of Central Mexico in the sixteenth century*, edited by H. R. Harvey and H. J. Prem, pp. 41–81. University of New Mexico Press, Albuquerque.

———. 1984b. The extent of the Tepanec empire. In Proceedings of the Forty-fourth International Congress of Americanists—Symposium: *The native sources and the history of the Valley of Mexico*, edited by J. de Durand-Forest, pp. 73–93. BAR International Series 204, London.

———. 1991. The territorial structure of the Aztec Empire. In *Land and politics in the Valley of Mexico*, edited by H. R. Harvey, pp. 93–112. University of New Mexico Press, Albuquerque.

Carrera Stampa, M. 1971. Historiadores indígenas y mestizos novohispanos, siglos XVI–XVII. *Revista Española de Antropología Americana* 6:205–43.

Caso, A. 1949. El mapa de Teozacoalco. *Cuadernos Mesoamericanos* 8, 5:145–81.

———. 1954. *El pueblo del sol.* Fondo de Cultura Económica, México.

———. 1956a. Los barrios antiguos de Tenochtitlán y Tlatelolco. *Memorias de la Academia Mexicana de la Historia* 15:7–49.

———. 1956b. *The Aztecs: People of the sun.* University of Oklahoma Press, Norman.

———. 1958–60. La tenencia de la tierra entre los antiguos mexicanos. *Memorias del Colegio Nacional* 4:29–54.

———. 1960. *Interpretación del Códice Bodley 2858.* Sociedad Mexicana de Antropología, México.

———. 1962. Relaciones entre el Viejo y el Nuevo Mundo: Una observación metodológica. *Cuadernos Americanos* 125:160–75.

———. 1963. Land tenure among the ancient Mexicans. *American Anthropologist* 65:863–78.

———. 1964. Relations between the Old and New World: A note on methodology. In *Actas y Memorias del XXXV Congreso Internacional de Americanistas*, vol. 1:55–71. Editorial Libros de México, México.

———. 1967. *Los calendarios prehispánicos.* Investigaciones Históricos, Universidad Nacional Autónoma de México, México.

———. 1977–79. *Reyes y reinos de la Mixteca.* 2 vols. Fondo de Cultura Económica, México.

Caso, A., and Mary E. Smith. 1966. *Interpretación del Códice Colombino.* Sociedad Mexicana de Antropología, México.

Castillo Farreras, V. M. 1971. El bisiesto Nahuatl. *Estudios de Cultura Nahuatl* 9:75–104.

———. 1972. *Estructura económica de la sociedad mexica, según las fuentes documentales.* Universidad Nacional Autónoma de México, Mexico.

Castro, C. del, and D. de Ortega Morejón. 1974. Relación y declaración del modo que en este valle de Chincha y sus comarcanos se governaban . . . , edited by J. C. Crespo. *Historia y Cultura* 8:91–104.

Castro Pozo, H. 1946. Social and economico-political evolution of the communities of Central Peru. In *Handbook of South American Indians*, edited by J. H. Steward, vol. 2:483–99. Smithsonian Institution, Bureau of American Ethnology, Bulletin 143, Washington.

Castro Titu Cusi Yupanqui, Diego de. 1916. Relación de la conquista del Perú y hechos del Inca Manco II. In *Colección de libros y documentos referentes a la historia del Perú*, edited by H. H. Urteaga and C. A. Romero, series 1, vol. 2. Sanmartí y ca., Lima.

Chadwick, R. 1971. Native pre-Aztec history of Central Mexico. In *Archaeology of Northern Mesoamerica*, edited by G. F. Ekholm and I. Bernal, pp. 474–504. Handbook of Middle American Indians, vol. 11, part 2. R. Wauchope, general editor. University of Texas Press, Austin.

Chang-Rodríguez, R. 1982. Sobre los cronistas indígenas del Perú y los comienzos de una escritura hispanoamericana. *Revista Iberoamericana* 48:533–48.

Chapman, A. M. 1957. Port of trade enclaves in Aztec and Maya civilization. In *Trade and market in the early empires*, edited by K. Polanyi, C. M. Arensberg, and H. W. Pearson, pp. 114–53. Free Press, Glencoe.

———. 1959. *Puertos de intercambio en Mesoamerica prehispánica.* Instituto Nacional de Antropología e Historia, México.

———. 1975. Puertos de intercambio en Mesoamerica prehispánica. In *El comercio en el México prehispánico*, edited by E. Florescano, pp. 97–153. Instituto Mexicano de Comercio exterior de México, México.

Chase, A. F. 1985. Time depth or vacuum: The 11.3.0.0.0. correlation and the lowland Maya postclassic. In *Late Lowland Maya Civilization*, edited by J. A. Sabloff and E. W. Andrews V, pp. 99–140. University of New Mexico Press, Albuquerque.

Chávez Orozco, L., ed. 1947. *Códice Osuna.* Instituto Indigenista Interamericano, México.

Chiu, B. C., and P. Morrison. 1980. Astronomical origin of the offset street grid at Teotihuacán. *Archaeoastronomy* 2:556–64.

Cieza de León, Pedro de. 1985. Crónica del Perú-segunda parte, edited by F. Cantú. Pontifícia Universidad Católica del Perú, Fondo de Editorial, Academia Nacional de la Historia, Lima.

Clark, J. E. 1986. From mountains to molehills: A critical review of Teotihuacán's obsidian industry. *Research in Economic Anthropology, Supplement* 2:23–74. Greenwich.

Clavijero, Francisco J. 1964. *Historia antigua de México*, edited by M. Cuevas. Editorial Porrúa, México.

Clendinnen, I. 1991. *Aztecs: an interpretation.* Cambridge University Press, New York.

Clewlow, C. W. Jr., 1974. *A stylistic and chronological study of Olmec monumental sculpture.* University of California Press, Berkeley.

Clewlow, C. W. Jr., R. A. Cowan, J. F. O'Conell, and C. Benemann. 1967. *Colossal heads of the Olmec culture.* Contributions of the University of California Archaeological Research Facility No. 4. Department of Anthropology, University of California, Berkeley.

Cline, H. F. 1968. A note on Torquemada's native sources and historiographical method. *The Americas* 25:372–86.

———. 1972a. The Relaciones Geográficas of the Spanish Indies, 1577–1648. In *Guide to Ethnohistorical Sources,* edited by H. F. Cline, pp. 183–242. Handbook of Middle American Indians, vol. 12. R. Wauchope, general editor, University of Texas Press, Austin.

———. 1972b. A census of the Relaciones Geográficas of New Spain, 1579–1612. In *Guide to Ethnohistorical Sources,* edited by H. F. Cline, pp. 324–69. Handbook of Middle American Indians, vol. 12. R. Wauchope, general editor. University of Texas Press, Austin.

———. 1972c. The Relaciones Geográficas of Spain, New Spain and the Spanish Indies: An annotated bibliography. In *Guide to Ethnohistorical Sources,* edited by H. F. Cline, pp. 370–95. Handbook of Middle American Indians, vol. 12. R. Wauchope, general editor. University of Texas Press, Austin.

Cline, H. F., ed. 1975. *Guide to Ethnohistorical Sources.* Handbook of Middle American Indians, vols. 14 and 15. R. Wauchope, general editor. University of Texas Press, Austin.

Closs, M. 1984. The dynastic history of Naranjo: The early period. *Estudios de Cultura Maya* 15:77–96.

———. 1985. The dynastic history of Naranjo: The middle period. In *Fifth Palenque Round Table, 1983,* edited by M. Greene Robertson and V. M. Fields, vol. 7:65–77. The Pre-Columbian Art Research Institute, San Francisco.

———. 1989. The dynastic history of Naranjo: The late period. In *Word and Image in Maya Culture,* edited by W. F. Hanks and D. Rice, pp. 244–54. University of Utah Press, Salt Lake City.

Cobo, Bernabé. 1956. *Historia del Nuevo Mundo.* Atlas, Madrid.

Cock Carrasco, G. 1978. Ayllu, territorio y frontera en los Collaguas. In *Etnohistoria y antropología andina* (Primera Jornada del Museo Nacional de Historia), edited by M. Koth de Paredes and A. Castelli, pp. 29–32. (s.n.), Lima.

———. 1981. El ayllu en la sociedad andina: Alcances y perspectivas. In *Etnohistoria y antropología andina* (Segunda Jornada del Museo Nacional de Historia), edited by A. Castelli, M. Koth de Paredes, and M. Mould de Pease, pp. 231–53. (s.n.), Lima.

Codex Aubin—Lehmann, W., G. Kutscher, and G. Vollmer, transl. 1981. *Geschichte der Azteken: Codex Aubin und verwandte Dokumente.* Gebrüder Mann Verlag, Berlin.

Codex Azcatitlan—Graulich, M. (introduction) 1975. *Codex Azcatitlan.* Bibliothèque Nationale de France, Paris.

Codex Becker—Nowotny, K. A., ed. 1961. *Codices Becker I/II.* Akademische Druck- und Verlagsanstalt, Graz. Also Nowotny, K. A., ed. *El Fragmento de Nochistlan.* Hamburgisches Museum für Völkerkunde, Hamburg.

Codex Borgia—Nowotny, K. A. *Codex Borgia: Biblioteca Apostolica Vaticana—Messicano Riserva 28* (recte: Cod. Borg. Messicano 1). Akademische Druck- und Verlagsanstalt, Graz.

Codex Borgia—Seler, E. 1904–1909. *Codex Borgia: Eine altmexikanische Bilderschrift der Bibliothek der Congregatio de Propaganda Fide.* 3 vols., Verlag A. Asher und Co., Berlin.

Codex Boturini in Corona Núñez, J., ed. 1964:7–29.

Codex Chimalpopoca—Bierhorst, John. 1992. *Codex Chimalpopoca, the text in Nahuatl with a glossary and grammatical notes.* University of Arizona Press, Tucson.

Codex Cospi—Nowotny, K. A. (introduction and summary). 1968. *Codex Cospi: Calendario messicano 4093.* Akademische Druck- und Verlagsanstalt, Graz.

Codex en Cruz—Dibble, C. E., ed. 1981. *Codex en Cruz.* 2 vols., University of Utah Press, Salt Lake City.

Codex Dresdensis—Anders, F., and H. Deckert, eds. 1975. *Codex Dresdensis.* Akademische Druck- und Verlagsanstalt, Graz.

Codex Fejérváry-Mayer—Burland, C. A. 1971. *Codex Fejérváry-Mayer: Museum of the City of Liverpool.* Akademische Druck- und Verlagsanstalt, Graz.

Codex Grolier—Coe, M. D. 1973. *The Maya scribe and his world.* The Grolier Club, New York.

Codex Grolier—Lee, T. A., Jr., ed. 1985. *Los Códices Maya.* Universidad Autónoma de Chiapas, Tuxtla Gutiérrez.

Codex Laud—Burland, C. A. (introduction). 1966. *Codex Laud: Ms. Laud Misc. 678. Bodleian Library.* Akademische Druck- und Verlagsanstalt, Graz.

Codex Madrid—See Codex Tro-Cortesianus.

Codex Magliabechiano—Boone, E. H. 1983. *The Codex Magliabechiano and the lost prototype of the Magliabechiano Group.* University of California Press, Berkeley.

Codex Mariano Jiménez—See Códice de Otlazpan.

Codex Mendoza—Berdan, F. F., and P. R. Anawalt, eds. 1992. *Codex Mendoza.* 4 vols., University of California Press, Berkeley.

Codex Mexicanus—Mengin, E. 1952. Commentaire du Codex Mexicanus No. 23–24 de la Bibliothèque Nationale de Paris. *Journal de la Société des Américanistes de Paris, n.s.* 41:387–498 (with separate facsimile).

Codex Nuttall—See Codex Zouche-Nuttall.

Codex Peresianus (Codex Paris)—Anders, F., ed. 1968. *Codex Peresianus (Codex Paris).* Akademische Druck- und Verlagsanstalt, Graz.

Codex Telleriano-Remensis—Quiñones Keber, Eloise. 1995. *Codex Telleriano-Remensis: Ritual, divination and history in a pictorial Aztec manuscript.* University of Texas Press, Austin

Codex Tro-Cortesianus (Codex Madrid)—Anders, F., ed. 1967. *Codex Tro-Cortesianus (Codex Madrid).* Akademische Druck- und Verlagsanstalt, Graz.

Codex Vaticanus 3773—Seler, E. 1902. *Codex Vaticanus Nr. 3773: Eine altmexikanische Bilderschrift der Vatikanischen Bibliothek.* 2 vols., Verlag A. Asher und Co., Berlin.

Codex Vaticanus 3773—Anders, F. (introduction, summary). 1972. *Codex Vaticanus 3773.* Akademische Druck- und Verlagsanstalt, Graz.

Codex Vaticanus 3738. 1979. *Codex Vaticanus 3738 der Biblioteca Apostolica Vaticana.* Akademische Druck- und Verlagsanstalt, Graz.

Codex Vindobonensis—Adelhofer, O., ed. 1963. *Codex Vindobonensis Mexicanus 1.* Akademische Druck- und Verlagsanstalt, Graz.

Codex Zouche-Nuttall—Anders, F., and N. P. Troike (introduction). 1987. *Codex Zouche-Nuttall,* Akademische Druck- und Verlagsanstalt, Graz.

Códice Bodley—Caso, A. 1960. *Interpretación del Códice Bodley 2858.* Sociedad Mexicana de Antropología, México.

Códice Colombino—Caso, A., and Mary E. Smith. 1966. *Interpretación del Códice Colombino.* Sociedad Mexicana de Antropología, México.

Códice de Huichapan—Alvarado Guinchard, M., ed. 1976. *El Códice de Huichapan, I relato otomí del México prehispánico y colonial.* Instituto Nacional de Antropología e Historia, México.

Códice de Moctezuma—Berdan, F. F., and J. de Durand-Forest (commentary). 1980. *Matrícula de Tributos (Códice de Moctezuma).* Akademische Druck- und Verlagsanstalt, Graz.

Códice Osuna—Chávez Orozco, L., ed. 1947. *Códice Osuna.* Instituto Indigenista Interamericano, México.

Códice de Otlazpan—Leander, B., ed. 1967. *Códice de Otlazpan.* Instituto Nacional de Antropología e Historia, México.

Códice Pérez—Solís Alcalá, E. 1949. *Códice Pérez.* Liga de Acción Social, Mérida.

Códice Pérez—Craine, E. R., and R. C. Reindorp, eds. 1979. *The Codex Pérez and the Book of Chilam Balam of Maní.* University of Oklahoma Press, Norman.

Códice Tudela—Tudela de la Orden, J., ed. 1980. *Códice Tudela.* 2 vols., Ediciones Cultura Hispánica, Madrid.

Códice Xolotl—Dibble, C. E., ed. 1980. *Códice Xolotl,* 2 vols., Universidad Nacional Autónoma de México, Instituto de Investigaciones Históricas, México.

Coe, M. D. 1965. *The jaguar's children: Pre-classic Central Mexico.* Museum of Primitive Art, New York.

———. 1972. Olmec jaguars and Olmec kings. In *The cult of the feline*, edited by E. P. Benson, pp. 1–12. Dumbarton Oaks, Washington.

———. 1973. *The Maya scribe and his world.* The Grolier Club, New York.

———. 1978. *Lords of the Underworld: Masterpieces of Classic Maya Ceramics.* Princeton University Press, Princeton.

———. 1981a. Religion and the rise of Mesoamerican states. In *The transition to statehood in the New World*, edited by G. D. Jones and R. R. Kautz, pp. 157–71. Cambridge University Press, New York.

———. 1981b. San Lorenzo Tenochtitlan. In *Archaeology*, edited by J. A. Sabloff, Handbook of Middle American Indians, Supplement, vol. 1:117–46. V. R. Bricker, general editor, University of Texas Press, Austin.

———. 1992. *Breaking the Maya code.* Thames & Hudson, London.

Coe, M. D., and R. A. Diehl. 1980. *In the land of the Olmec.* 2 vols., University of Texas Press, Austin.

Cohen, M. N. 1977. *The food crisis in prehistory: Overpopulation and the origins of agriculture.* Yale University Press, New Haven.

———. 1981. The ecological basis of New World state formation: General and local model building. In *The transition to statehood in the New World*, edited by G. D. Jones and R. R. Kautz, pp. 105–22. Cambridge University Press, New York.

Cohodas, M. 1978. Diverse architectural styles and the ball game cult: The late middle classic period in Yucatan. In *Middle Classic Mesoamerica, A.D.400–700*, edited by E. Pasztory, pp. 86–107. Columbia University Press, New York.

Colston, S. A. 1974. Tlacaelel's descendants and the authorship of the "Historia Mexicana." *Indiana* 2:69–72.

Conrad, G. W. 1978. Models of compromise in settlement pattern studies: An example from coastal Peru. *World Archaeology* 9:281–97.

———. 1981. Cultural materialism, split inheritance, and the expansion of ancient Peruvian empires. *American Antiquity* 48:3–26. (Comments: W. H. Isbell: Comment on Conrad. *American Antiquity* 48:27–30; A. C. Paulsen: The archaeology of the absurd, comments on Conrad. *American Antiquity* 48:31–37.)

———. 1982. The burial platforms of Chan Chan: Some social and political implications. In *Chan Chan: Andean desert city*, edited by M. E. Moseley and K. C. Day, pp. 87–117. University of New Mexico Press, Albuquerque.

———. 1992. Inca Imperialism and the accident of empire. In *Ideology and precolumbian civilizations*, edited by A. A. Demarest and G. W. Conrad, pp. 159–74. School of American Research Press, Santa Fe.

Conrad, G. W., and A. A. Demarest. 1984. *Religion and empire: The dynamics of Aztec and Inca expansionism.* Cambridge University Press, New York.

Cook, N. D. 1981. *Demographic collapse, Indian Peru, 1520–1620.* Cambridge University Press, New York.

Cook, N. D., A. Málaga Medina, and T. Boyssee-Cassangne, eds. 1975. *Tasa de la visita general de Francisco de Toledo.* Universidad Nacional Mayor de San Marcos, Lima.

Cook, S. F. 1946. Human sacrifice and warfare as factors in the demography of pre-colonial Mexico. *Human Biology* 18:81–102.

———. 1947. The interrelation of population, food supply, and building in pre-conquest Central Mexico. *American Antiquity* 1:45–52.

Cook, S. F., and W. Borah. 1960. *The Indian population of Central Mexico 1531–1610.* University of California Press, Berkeley.

———. 1971. *Essays in population history: Mexico and the Carribean.* Vol. 1. University of California Press, Berkeley.

Corona Núñez, J., ed. 1964. *Antigüedades de México, basadas en la recopilación de Lord Kingsborough.* 2 vols., Secretaría de Hacienda y Crédito Público, México.

Corona Sánchez, E. 1976. La estratificación social en el Acolhuacán. In *Estratificación social en la Mesoamérica prehispánica,* edited by P. Carrasco P. and J. Broda, pp. 88–101. Centro de Investigaciones Superiores, Instituto Nacional de Antropología e Historia, México.

———. 1986. Sobre el nivel de desarrollo de las fuerzas productivas para la caracterización del estado en Mesoamérica. *Revista de Antropología Americana* 16:35–42.

Cortés, Hernando. 1963. *Cartas y documentos,* edited by M. Hernández Sánchez-Barba. Editorial Porrúa, México.

Couch, N. C. C. 1991. The Codex Ramirez: copy or original. *Estudios de Cultura Nahuatl* 21:109–25.

Covarrubias, M. 1961. *Arte indígena de México y Centroamérica.* Universidad Nacional Autónoma de México, Mexico.

Cowgill, G. L. 1979. Teotihuacán, internal militaristic competition, and the fall of the classic Maya. In *Maya archaeology and ethnohistory,* edited by N. Hammond and G. R. Willey, pp. 51–62. University of Texas Press, Austin.

———. 1992. Social differentiation at Teotihuacán. In *Mesoamerican elites, an archaeological assessment,* edited by D. Z. Chase and A. F. Chase, pp. 206–20. University of Oklahoma Press, Norman.

———. 1993. Beyond criticizing New Archaeology. *American Anthropologist* 95:551–73.

Craine, E. R., and R. C. Reindorp, eds. 1979. *The Codex Pérez and the Book of Chilam Balam of Maní.* University of Oklahoma Press, Norman.

Culbert, T. P. 1988. The collapse of Maya civilization. In *The collapse of ancient states and civilizations,* edited by N. Yoffee and G. L. Cowgill, pp. 69–101. University of Arizona Press, Tucson.

Cunow, H. 1891. Das peruanische Verwandtschaftssystem und die Geschlechtsverbände der Inka. *Das Ausland* 64:881–86, 914–19, 934–40, 950–56.

———. 1896. *Die soziale Verfassung des Inkareichs: Eine Untersuchung des altperuanischen Agrarkommunismus.* J. H. W. Dietz, Stuttgart.

———. 1937. *Geschichte und Kultur des Inkareiches.* Elsevier, Amsterdam.

D'Altroy, T. N., and T. K. Earle. 1985. Staple finance, wealth finance, and storage in the Inca political economy. *Current Anthropology* 26:187–206.

Davies, C. Nigel B. 1968. *Los señoríos independientes del imperio azteca.* Instituto Nacional de Antropología e Historia, México.

———. 1973a. *Los mexicas: Primeros pasos hacia el imperio.* Universidad Nacional Autónoma de México, Instituto de Investigaciones Historicas, México.

———. 1973b. *The Aztecs: A history.* Macmillan, London.

———. 1974. The military organization of the Aztec empire. In *Atti del XL Congresso Internazionale degli Americanisti,* vol. 4:213–21. Tilgher, Roma-Genova.

———. 1977. *The Toltecs: Until the fall of Tula.* University of Oklahoma Press, Norman.

———. 1978. The military organization of the Aztec empire. In *Mesoamerican communication routes and cultural contacts,* edited by T. A. Lee and C. Navarrete, pp. 223–30. University of Utah Press, Salt Lake City.

———. 1979a. The Mexica period in Chapultepec: Its influence on their political and religious development. In *Mesoamérica: Homenaje al doctor Paul Kirchhoff,* B. Dahlgren, coord., pp. 97–103. Instituto Nacional de Antropología e Historia, México.

———. 1979b. *Voyagers to the New World: fact or fantasy.* Macmillan, London.

———. 1980. *The Toltec heritage: From the fall of Tula to the rise of Tenochtitlan.* University of Oklahoma Press, Norman.

———. 1986. *Voyagers to the New World.* University of New Mexico Press, Albuquerque.

———. 1991. *Human sacrifice—in history and today.* Morrow, New York.

———. 1995. *The Incas.* University Press of Colorado, Niwot.

Davies, C. Nigel B., coord. 1979. Los dioses titulares étnicos y los héreos deificados. In *Actes du XLIIe Congrès International des Américanistes,* vol. 6:7–68. Société des Américanistes, Musée de l'Homme, Paris.

Day, K. C. 1982. Ciudadelas, their form and function. In *Chan Chan: Andean desert city,* edited by M. E. Moseley and K. C. Day, pp. 55–67. University of New Mexico Press, Albuquerque.

Demarest, A. A. 1978. Interregional conflict and "situational ethics" in Classic Maya warfare. *Human Mosaic* 12:101–11.

———. 1981. *Viracocha: The nature and antiquity of the Andean high god.* Peabody Museum Monographs 6, Peabody Museum of Archaeology and Ethnology. Harvard University, Cambridge.

———. 1984. Overview: Mesoamerican human sacrifice in evolutionary perspective. In *Ritual human sacrifice in Mesoamerica,* edited by E. H. Boone, pp. 227–43. Dumbarton Oaks, Washington.

———. 1992. Ideology in ancient Maya cultural evolution: The dynamics of galactic polities. In *Ideology and pre-columbian civilizations,* edited by

A. A. Demarest and G. W. Conrad, pp. 135–57. School of American Research Press, Santa Fe.

Díaz Cadena, I. 1978. *Libro de tributos del Marquesado del Valle* (Biblioteca Nacional de Antropología e Historia-Cuadernos de la Biblioteca). Biblioteca Nacional de Antropología e Historia, México.

Díaz del Castillo, Bernal. 1960. *Historia verdadera de la conquista de la Nueva España,* edited by J. Ramírez Cabañas, 2 vols., 2nd ed. Editorial Porrúa, México.

Díaz Rubio, E. 1986. Acerca de la terminología de parentesco en el nahuatl clásico: Tlacamecayotl. *Revista Española de Antropología Americana* 16:63–80.

Dibble, C. E. 1971. Writing in Central Mexico. In *Archaeology of Northern Mesoamerica,* edited by G. F. Ekholm and I. Bernal, pp. 322–32. Handbook of Middle American Indians, vol. 10, part 1. R. Wauchope, general editor. University of Texas Press, Austin.

Dibble, C. E., ed. 1980. *Códice Xolotl,* 2 vols. Universidad Nacional Autónoma de México, Instituto de Investigaciones Históricas, México.

———. 1981. *Codex en Cruz.* 2 vols. University of Utah Press, Salt Lake City.

Diehl, R. A. 1981. Tula. In *Archaeology,* edited by J. A. Sabloff, Handbook of Middle American Indians Supplement, vol. 1:277–95. V. R. Bricker, general editor. University of Texas Press, Austin.

———. 1989. A shadow of its former self, Teotihuacán during the Coyotlatelco Period. In *Mesoamerica after the decline of Teotihuacán, A.D. 700–900,* edited by R. A. Diehl and J. C. Berlo, pp. 9–18. Dumbarton Oaks, Washington.

Diehl, R. A., ed. 1974. *Studies of Ancient Tollan.* University of Missouri, Columbia.

Diehl, R. A., and M. D. Mandeville. 1987. Tula, and wheeled animal effigies in Mesoamerica. *Antiquity* 61:239–46.

Dillon, B. J. 1982. Bound prisoners in Maya art. *Journal of New World Archaeology* 5:24–45.

Disselhoff, H. D., and S. Linné. 1960. *Alt-Amerika.* Holle, Baden-Baden.

Dobyns, H. F. 1966. Estimating aboriginal American population: An appraisal of techniques with a new hemispheric estimate. *Current Anthropology* 7:395–449.

———. 1993. Debate: Building stones and paper from Native American historical numbers. *Latin American Population History Bulletin* 24:11–19.

Donnan, C. B. 1973. A precolumbian smelter from northern Peru. *Archaeology* 26:289–97.

———. 1978. *Moche art of Peru.* Museum of Cultural History, University of California, Los Angeles.

Donnan, C. B., ed. 1985. *Early ceremonial architecture in the Andes.* Dumbarton Oaks, Washington.

Drucker, P., R. F. Heizer, and R. J. Squier. 1959. *Excavations at la Venta, Tabasco, 1955.* Bureau of American Ethnology, Washington.

Durán, Diego. 1967 (1588?). *Historia de las Indias de Nueva España e Islas de Tierra Firme*, edited by A. M. Garibay K., 2 vols. Editorial Porrúa, México.

Durand, J. 1976. *El Inca Garcilaso: Clásico de América.* Secretaría de Educación Pública, México.

Durand-Forest, J. de. 1962. De la monnaie chez les Aztèques. *Cahiers de l'Institut de Science Economique Appliquée (Humanités)* 4:63–78.

———. 1963. Les Aztèques & les Mayas. In *Introduction bibliographique à l'histoire du droit et à l'ethnologie juridique*, edited by J. Gilissen. Les Editions de l'Institut de Sociologie, Université Libre de Bruxelles.

———. 1967. El cacao entre los aztecas. *Estudios de Cultura Nahuatl* 7:155–81.

———. 1971. Cambios económicos y moneda entre los aztecas. *Estudios de Cultura Nahuatl* 9:105–24.

Durand-Forest, J. de, transl. 1987. *Troisième relation de Chimalpahin Quauhtlehuanitzin.* L'Harmattan, Paris.

Duverger, C. 1983. *L'Origine des Azteques.* Seuil, Paris.

———. 1987. *El origen de los Aztecas.* Grijalbo, México.

Duviols, P. 1976. La Capachoa. *Allpanchis Phuturinqua* 9:11–57.

———. 1980. Algunas reflexiones acerca de la tesis de la estructura dual del poder incaico. *Historica–Pontificia Universidad Católica del Perú* 4:183–96.

———. 1987. Inca religion. In *Encyclopedia of Religion*, edited by M. Eliade, vol. 7:152–56. Macmillan, New York.

Dyckerhoff, U. 1970. *Die Crónica Mexicana des Hernando Alvarado Tezozomoc: Quellenkritische Untersuchungen.* Klaus Renner Verlag, München.

———. 1976. La estratificación social en Huexotzinco. In *Estratificación social en la Mesoamérica prehispánica*, edited by P. Carrasco P. and J. Broda, pp. 157–80. Centro de Investigaciones Superiores, Instituto Nacional de Antropología e Historia, México.

———. 1978. La región del Alto Atoyac en la historia: La época prehispánica. In *Milpa y hacienda: Tenencia de la tierra indígena y española en la cuenca del alto Atoyac, Puebla, México (1520–1650)*, edited by H. J. Prem, pp. 18–34. Steiner, Wiesbaden.

Dyckerhoff, U., and H. J. Prem. 1978. Der vorspanische Landbesitz. *Zeitschrift für Ethnologie* 103:186–238.

Earle, T. K. 1972. Lurin Valley, Peru: Early intermediate period settlement development. *American Antiquity* 37:467–77.

Eaton, J. 1972. A report on excavations at Chicanna, Campeche, Mexico. *Cerámica de Cultura Maya* 8:42–61.

Edmonson, M. S., 1979. Some postclassic questions about the classic Maya. *Estudios de Cultura Maya* 12:155–78.

———. 1985. Quiché Literature. In *Literatures*, edited by M. S. Edmonson, Handbook of Middle American Indians Supplement, vol. 3:107–132. V. R. Bricker, general editor. University of Texas Press, Austin.

———. 1988. *The book of the year, Middle American calendrical systems.* University of Utah Press, Salt Lake City.

Edmonson, M. S., transl. 1971. *The Book of the Counsel: The Popol Vuh of the Quiché Maya of Guatemala.* Middle American Research Institute, Publication 35, Tulane University, New Orleans.

———. 1982. *The ancient future of the Itza: The Book of Chilam Balam of Tizimin.* University of Texas Press, Austin.

———. 1986. *Heaven born Merida and its destiny: The Book of Chilam Balam of Chumayel.* University of Texas Press, Austin.

Edmonson, M., and V. R. Bricker. 1985. Yucatecan Mayan Literature. In *Literatures,* edited by M. S. Edmonson, Handbook of Middle American Indians Supplement, vol. 3:44–63. V. R. Bricker, general editor. University of Texas Press, Austin.

Eich, D. 1983. *Ayllú und Staat der Inka: Zur Diskussion der asiatischen Produktionsweise.* K. D. Vervuert, Frankfurt/Main.

Erdheim, M. 1972. *Prestige und Kulturwandel: Eine Studie zum Verhältnis subjektiver und objektiver Faktoren des kulturellen Wandels zur Klassengesellschaft bei den Azteken.* Focus-Verlag, Wiesbaden.

———. 1978. Transformación de la ideología Mexica en realidad social. In *Economía política e ideología en el México prehispánico,* edited by P. Carrasco P. and J. Broda, pp. 193–220. Editorial Nueva Imagen, México.

Escalante, P. 1985. *Educación e ideología en el México Antiguo: Fragmentos para la reconstrucción de una historia.* Secretaría de Educación Pública, Ediciones El Caballito, México.

Eschmann, A. 1976. *Das religiöse Geschichtsbild der Azteken.* Gebrüder Mann, Berlin.

Espinoza Soriano, W. 1963. La guaranga y la reducción de Huancayo. *Revista del Museo Nacional, Lima* 32:8–80.

———. 1969–70. Los mitmas yungas de Collique en Cajamarca, siglo XV, XVI y XVII. *Revista del Museo Nacional, Lima* 36:9–57.

———. 1973. *La destrucción del imperio de los incas.* Ediciones Retablo de Papel, Lima.

———. 1975a. Los mitmas Huayacuntu en Quito o guarniciones para la represión armada, siglos XV y XVI. *Revista del Museo Nacional, Lima* 41:351–95.

———. 1975b. Ichoc-Huánuco y el señorío del curaca Huanca en el reino de Huánuco. *Anales Científicos, Universidad Nacional del Centro del Perú (Huancayo)* 4:7–70.

———. 1977. La poliginia señorial en el reino de Caxamarca, siglos XV y XVI. *Revista del Museo Nacional, Lima* 43:399–466.

———. 1978. Los mitmas cañar en el reino de Yaro (Perú), siglos XV y XVI. In *Amerikanistische Studien: Festschrift für Hermann Trimborn,* edited by R. Hartmann and U. Oberem, pp. 153–61. Haus Völker und Kulturen, Anthropos Institut, St. Augustin.

———. 1982. Los chambillas y mitmas incas y chinchaysuyos en territorio lupaca, siglos XV–XX. *Revista del Museo Nacional, Lima* 46:419–506.

———. 1987. *Los incas, economía, sociedad y estado en la era del Tahuantinsuyo.* AMARU, La Victoria/Perú.

Espinoza Soriano, W., ed. 1974. El curacazgo de Conchucos y la visita de 1543. *Bulletin de l'Institut Français d'Etudes Andines* 3:9–31.

———. 1975. El valle de Jayanca y el reino de los Mochica, siglos XV y XVI. *Bulletin de l'Institut Français d'Etudes Andines* 4:243–74.

Estrada, E., and B. Meggers. 1961. A complex of traits of possible transpacific origin on the coast of Ecuador. *American Anthropologist* 63:913–39.

Evans, S. T. 1980. Spatial analysis of Basin of Mexico settlement: Problems with the use of the central place model. *American Anthropologist* 45:866–75.

Falk Moore, S. 1958. *Power and property in Inca Peru.* Columbia University Press, New York.

Farriss, N. M. 1987. Remembering the future, anticipating the past: History, time and cosmology among the Maya of Yucatan. *Comparative Studies in Society and History* 29:566–93.

Feldman, L. H. 1976. Moving merchandise in Protohistoric Quauhtemallan. In *Atti del XL Congresso Internazionale degli Americanisti*, vol. 4:194–97. Tilgher, Roma-Genova.

———. 1978a. Moving merchandise in Protohistoric Quauhtemallan. In *Mesoamerican Communication routes and cultural contacts*, edited by T. A. Lee and C. Navarrete, pp. 7–17. University of Utah Press, Salt Lake City.

———. 1978b. Inside a Mexica market. In *Mesoamerican communication routes and cultural contacts*, edited by T. A. Lee and C. Navarrete, pp. 219–22. University of Utah Press, Salt Lake City.

Feldman, R. A., and M. E. Moseley. 1983. The northern Andes. In *Ancient South Americans*, edited by J. D. Jennings, pp. 139–77. Freeman, San Francisco.

Fernández de Oviedo y Valdes, G. 1959. *Historia general de las Indias*, edited by J. Pérez de Tudela y Bueso, 5 vols. Atlas, Madrid.

Fisher, J. R. 1981. Resources for the Study of Colonial Peru. In *Research guide to Andean History: Bolivia, Chile, Ecuador, and Peru*, edited by J. J. TePaske and J. R. Bakewell, pp. 212–23. Duke University Press, Durham.

Flannery, K.V. 1967. Culture history vs. cultural process: A debate in American archaeology. *Scientific American* 217:119–22.

———. 1968. Archaeological systems theory and early Mesoamerica. In *Anthropological archaeology in the Americas*, edited by B. J. Meggers, pp. 67–87. Anthropological Society of Washington, Washington.

———. 1972a. Culture history vs. cultural process: A debate in American archaeology. In *Contemporary archaeology*, edited by M. P. Leone, pp. 102–7. Southern Illinois University Press, Carbondale.

———. 1972b. Archaeological systems theory and early Mesoamerica. In *Contemporary archaeology*, edited by M. P. Leone, pp. 222–34. Southern Illinois University Press, Carbondale.

———. 1972c. The cultural evolution of civilizations. *Annual Review of Ecology and Systematics* 3:399–426.

———. 1983. Zapotec warfare: Archeaological evidence for the battles of Huitzo and Guiengola. In *The Cloud People: Divergent evolution of the Zapotec and Mixtec civilizations,* edited by K. F. Flannery and J. Marcus, pp. 318–22. Academic Press, New York.

Flannery, K. V., ed. 1986. *Guilá Naquitz: Archaic foraging and early agriculture in Oaxaca, Mexico.* Academic Press, New York.

Flannery, K. V., and J. Marcus. 1983a. The origins of the state in Oaxaca. In *The Cloud People: Divergent evolution of the Zapotec and Mixtec civilizations,* edited by K. V. Flannery and J. Marcus, pp. 79–83. Academic Press, New York.

———. 1983b. Monte Albán and Teotihuacán. In *The Cloud People: Divergent evolution of the Zapotec and Mixtec civilizations,* edited by K. V. Flannery and J. Marcus, pp. 161–66. Academic Press, New York.

Florescano, E. 1963. Tula-Teotihuacán, Quetzalcóatl y la Toltecayótl. *Historia Mexicana* 13:193–234.

———. 1992 (abbreviated). El mito de Quetzalcóatl. *Allpanchis Phuturinqua* 40:11–93.

———. 1993. *El mito de Quetzalcóatl.* Fondo de Cultura Económica, México.

Fonseca Martel, C. 1983–85. El modelo andino de la complementaridad ecológica. *Revista del Museo Nacional, Lima* 48:291–317.

Fowler, M. L. 1968. *Un sistema preclásico de distribución de agua en la zona arqueológica de Amalucan, Puebla.* Instituto Poblano de Antropología e Historia, Puebla.

Fox, J. W. 1978. *Quiché conquest: Centralism and regionalism in highland Guatemalan state development.* University of New Mexico Press, Albuquerque.

———. 1980. Lowland to highland mexicanization process in Southern Mesoamerica. *American Antiquity* 45:43–54.

Freidel, D. A. 1981. Civilization as a state of mind: The cultural evolution of the lowland Maya. In *The transition to statehood in the New World,* edited by G. D. Jones and R. R. Kautz, pp. 188–227. Cambridge University Press, New York.

———. 1986. Maya warfare—an example of peer polity interaction. In *Peer polity interaction and sociopolitical change,* edited by C. Renfrew and J. F. Cherry, pp. 93–108. Cambridge University Press, New York.

Freund, G. 1946. Agrarrecht und Katasterwesen im alten Mexiko. *Ethnos* 11:24–48.

Fried, M. H. 1967. *The evolution of political society.* Random House, New York.

———. 1974. On the evolution of social stratification and the state. In *The rise and fall of civilizations,* edited by J. A. Sabloff and C. C. Lamberg-Karlowsky, pp. 26–39. Cummings Publishing Co., Menlo Park.

Fritz, G. J. 1994. Are the first American farmers getting younger? *Current Anthropology* 35:304–9.

Fuente, B. de la, and N. Gutiérrez Solana. 1973. *Escultura monumental olmeca.* Instituto de Investigaciones Estéticas, Universidad Nacional Autónoma de México, México.

Furst, J. L. 1978a. *Codex Vindobonensis Mexicanus I, a commentary.* Institute for Mesoamerican Studies, Publication No. 4, State University of New York at Albany.

———. 1978b. The year 1 Reed, day 1 Alligator: A Mixtec metaphor. *Journal of Latin American Lore* 4:93–128.

Furst, P. T. 1968. The Olmec were-jaguar motif in the light of ethnographic reality. In *Dumbarton Oaks Conference on the Olmec,* edited by E. P. Benson, pp. 143–74. Dumbarton Oaks, Washington.

Galdos Rodríguez, G. 1977. Visita a Atico y Caraveli. *Revista del Archivo General de la Nación (Lima)* 4-5:55–80.

García Alcaraz, A. 1976. Estratificación social entre los tarascos prehispánicos. In *Estratificación social en la Mesoamérica prehispánica,* edited by P. Carrasco P. and J. Broda, pp. 221–24. Centro de Investigaciones Superiores, Instituto Nacional de Antropología e Historia, México.

García Cook, A. 1981. The historical importance of Tlaxcala in the cultural development of the Central Highlands. In *Archaeology,* edited by J. A. Sabloff, Handbook of Middle American Indians Supplement, vol. 1:244–76. V. R. Bricker, general editor. University of Texas Press, Austin.

García Icazbalceta, J., ed. 1941a. Relación de la genealogía. In *Nueva Colección de documentos para la historia de México,* vol. 3:240–56, 2nd ed. Editorial Salvador Chávez Hayhoe, México.

———. 1941b. Origen de los mexicanos. In *Nueva Colección de documentos para la historia de México,* vol. 3:256–80, 2nd ed. Editorial Salvador Chávez Hayhoe, México.

Gardner, B. 1982. A structural and semantic analysis of classical Nahuatl kinship terminology. *Estudios de Cultura Nahuatl* 15:89–124.

Gareis, I. 1987. *Religiöse Spezialisten des zentralen Andengebietes zur Zeit der Inka und während der spanischen Kolonialherrschaft.* Verlag Klaus Renner, Hohenschäftlarn.

Garibay K., A. M., ed. 1956 (1590). *Historia general de las cosas de Nueva España.* 4 vols., Editorial Porrúa, México.

———. 1964. *Poesía nahuatl,* vol. 1:149–228. Universidad Nacional Autónoma de México, México.

———. 1973. *Teogonía e historia de los mexicanos.* 2nd ed. Editorial Porrúa, México.

Garza, M. de la, M. del Carmen León Cázares, A. L. Izquierdo, and C. Ontiveros, eds. 1983. Relaciones histórico-geográficas de la Gobernación de Yucatán (Mérida, Valladolid, Tabasco). 2 vols. Universidad Nacional Autónoma de México, Instituto de Investigaciones Filológicas, Centro de Estudios Mayas, México.

Gasparini, G., and L. Margolies. 1977. *Arquitectura inca.* Centro de Investigaciones Históricas y Estéticas, Facultad de Arquitectura y Urbanismo, Universidad Central de Venezuela, Caracas.

———. 1980. *Inca architecture.* Indiana University Press, Bloomington.

Gay, C. T. E. 1971. *Chalcatzingo.* Akademische Druck- und Verlagsanstalt, Graz.

Gendrop, P. 1983. *Los estilos Río Bec, Chenes y Puuc en la arquitectura Maya.* Universidad Nacional Autónoma de México, División de Estudios de Posgrado Facultad de Arquitectura, México.

Gerhard, P. 1970. A method of reconstructing pre-columbian political boundaries in Central Mexico. *Journal de la Société des Américanistes de Paris, N.S.* 59:27–41.

Gibson, C. 1956. Llamamiento General: Repartimiento and the Empire of Acolhuacan. *Hispanic American Historical Review* 36:l–27.

———. 1964a. The pre-conquest Tepanec zone and the labor drafts of the sixteenth century. *Revista de Historia de América* 57/58:136–45.

———. 1964b. *The Aztecs under Spanish rule: A history of the Indians of the Valley of Mexico, 1519–1819.* Stanford University Press, Stanford.

———. 1967. *Tlaxcala in the sixteenth century.* Stanford University Press, Stanford.

———. 1971. Structure of the Aztec Empire. In *Archaeology of Northern Mesoamerica,* edited by G. F. Ekholm and I. Bernal, pp. 376–94. Handbook of Middle American Indians, vol. 10, part 1. R. Wauchope, general editor. University of Texas Press, Austin.

Gifford, J. C. 1976. *Prehistoric pottery analysis and the ceramics of Barton Ramie in the Belize Valley.* Peabody Museum of Archaeology and Ethnology, Harvard University, Cambridge.

Gillespie, S. D. 1989. *The Aztec kings, the construction of rulership in Mexican history.* University of Arizona Press, Tucson.

Gillmor, F. 1949. *Flute of the smoking mirror: A portrait of Nezahualcoyotl—poet king of the Aztecs.* University of New Mexico Press, Albuquerque.

Godelier, M. 1973a. Der Begriff der ökonomischen Gesellschaftsformation: Das Beispiel der Inka. In *Ökonomische Anthropologie: Untersuchungen zum Begriff der sozialen Struktur primitiver Gesellschaften,* edited by M. Godelier, pp. 92–100. Rowohlt, Reinbek.

———. 1973b. Die Nichtentsprechung zwischen Formen und Inhalten sozialer Beziehungen: Erneute Reflexion über das Beispiel der Inka. In *Ökonomische Anthropologie: Untersuchungen zum Begriff der sozialen Struktur primitiver Gesellschaften,* edited by M. Godelier, pp. 281–92. Rowohlt, Reinbek.

———. 1974. The concept of 'social and economic formation': The Inca example. In *Perspectives in Marxist Anthropology.* Cambridge University Press, New York.

Goldstein, P. 1993. Tiwanaku temples and state expansion: A Tiwanaku sunken-court temple in Moquegua, Peru. *Latin American Antiquity* 4:22–47.

Golte, J. 1970. Algunas consideraciones acerca de la producción y distribución de la coca en el estado inca. In *Verhandlungen des XXXVIII Internationalen Amerikanistenkongresses,* vol. 2:471–78. Verlag Klaus Renner, Stuttgart.

———. 1974. El trabajo y la distribución de bienes en el runa simi del siglo XVI. In *Atti del XL Congresso Internazionale degli Americanisti*, vol. 2:489–505. Tilgher, Roma-Genova.

———. 1978. La economía del estado Inca y la noción del modo de producción asiático. In *Los modos de producción en el imperio de los Incas*, edited by W. Espinoza Soriano, pp. 285–97. Editorial Mantaro, Lima.

———. 1980. *La racionalidad de la organización andina.* Instituto de Estudios Peruanos, Lima.

González Aparicio, L. 1973. *Plano reconstructivo de la región de Tenochtitlán.* Instituto Nacional de Antropología e Historia, México.

González Torres, Y. 1966. El dios Huitzilopochtli en la peregrinación Mexica. *Anales del Instituto Nacional de Antropología e Historia* 19:175–90.

———. 1976. La esclavitud entre los Mexica. In *Estratificación social en la Mesoamérica prehispánica*, edited by P. Carrasco P. and J. Broda, pp. 78–87. Centro de Investigaciones Superiores, Instituto Nacional de Antropología e Historia, México.

———. 1979. La esclavitud en la época prehispánica. In *Mesoamérica, Homenaje al Dr. Paul Kirchhoff*, edited by B. Dahlgren and W. Jiménez Moreno, pp. 87–96. Instituto Nacional de Antropología e Historia, México.

———. 1985. *El sacrificio humano entre los Mexicas.* Instituto Nacional de Antropología e Historia, Fondo de Cultura Económica, México.

Gorenstein, S. 1973. *Tepexi el Viejo: A postclassic fortified site in the Mixteca-Puebla region of Mexico.* American Philosophical Society, Philadelphia.

Gorenstein, S., ed. 1985. *Acámbaro: Frontier settlement on the Tarascan-Aztecan border.* Vanderbilt University, Nashville.

Graffam, G. 1992. Beyond state collapse, rural history, raised fields, and pastoralism in the South Andes. *American Anthropologist* 94:905–25.

Graham, I. 1975–present. *Corpus of Maya hieroglyphic inscriptions.* Harvard University Press, Cambridge (16 vols. published to date).

Graham, J. A., R. F. Heizer, and E. M. Shook. 1978. Abaj Takalik 1976: Exploratory investigations. *Contributions of the University of California Archaeological Research Facility* 36:85–110.

Graulich, M. (introduction) 1975. *Codex Azcatitlan.* Bibliothèque Nationale de France, Paris.

———. 1983. La peregrinación azteca y el ciclo de Mixcoatl. *Estudios de Cultura Nahuatl* 11:311–45.

———. 1987. *Mythes et rituels du Mexique ancien préhispanique.* Palais des Académies, Brussels.

———. 1990. *Mitos y rituales del México antiguo.* Editorial Istmo, Madrid.

Greene Robertson, M. 1983. *The Sculpture of Palenque*, vol. 1: The Temple of Inscriptions. Princeton University Press, Princeton.

———. 1985a. *The Sculpture of Palenque*, vol. 2: The early buildings of the Palace and the wall paintings. Princeton University Press, Princeton.

———. 1985b. *The Sculpture of Palenque*, vol. 3: The late buildings of the Palace. Princeton University Press, Princeton.

———. 1991. *The Sculpture of Palenque*, vol. 4: The Cross Group, the North Group, the Olvidado, and other pieces. Princeton University Press, Princeton.

Grove, D. C. 1970. *Los murales de la cueva de Oxtotitlán, Acatlán, Guerrero.* Instituto Nacional de Antropología e Historia, México.

———. 1981. Olmec monuments: Mutilation as a clue to meaning. In *The Olmec and their Neighbors*, edited by E. P. Benson, pp. 49–68. Dumbarton Oaks, Washington.

Grube, N. 1986. Untersuchungen zur dynastischen Geschichte von Naranjo. *Zeitschrift für Ethnologie* 111:47–118.

———. 1990. *Die Entwicklung der Mayaschrift, Grundlagen zur Erforschung des Wandels der Mayaschrift von der Protokolassik bis zur spanischen Eroberung.* Acta Mesoamericana 3. Verlag von Flemming, Berlin.

———. 1996. Palenque in the Maya World. In *Eighth Palenque Round Table, 1993*, edited by M. Greene Robertson, pp. 1–14. The Pre-Columbian Art Research Institute, San Francisco.

Guamán Poma de Ayala, Felipe. 1980. *El primer nueva corónica y buen gobierno*, edited by J. V. Murra and R. Adorno. Siglo Veintiuno, México.

Gutiérrez Solana, N., and D. Schávelzon. 1980. *Corpus bibliográfico de la cultura olmeca.* Universidad Nacional Autónoma de México, México.

Haas, J. 1982. *The evolution of the prehistoric state.* Columbia University Press, New York.

Haberland, W. 1973. Moctezuma II. In *Die Grossen der Weltgeschichte*, edited by K. Fassmann, pp. 614–29. Kindler, Zürich.

———. 1986. Das Hochtal von Mexiko. In *Glanz und Untergang des Alten Mexiko: Die Azteken und ihre Vorläufer*, edited by A. Eggebrecht, pp. 19–86. Philip von Zabern, Mainz.

Hagen, V. W. von. 1955. *Highway of the sun.* Little Brown and Company, Boston and Toronto.

Hamblin, R. L., and B. L. Pitcher. 1980. The classic Maya collapse: Testing class conflict hypothesis. *American Antiquity* 45:246–67. (Review: Lowe, J. W. G., 1981. On mathematical models of the classic Maya collapse: The class conflict hypothesis reexamined. *American Antiquity* 47:643–51.)

Hammond, N. 1977. Ex oriente lux: A view from Belize. In *The origins of Maya civilization*, edited by R. E. W. Adams, pp. 45–76. University of New Mexico Press, Albuquerque.

———. 1980. Early Maya ceremonial at Cuello, Belize. *Antiquity* 54:176–89.

———. 1982. *Ancient Maya civilization.* Cambridge University Press, New York.

Hammond, N., and C. H. Miksicek. 1981. Ecology and Economy of a Formative site at Cuello, Belize. *Journal of Field Archaeology* 8:259–69.

Hanstein, O. von. 1923. *Die Welt des Inka: Ein Sozialstaat der Vergangenheit.* Carl Reißner, Dresden.

Hardoy, J. E. 1973. *Pre-Columbian Cities,* translated by J. Thorne. Walker, New York (revised translation of 1954, *Ciudades precolombinas.* Buenos Aires).

Harner, M. 1977. The ecological basis for Aztec sacrifice. *American Ethnologist* 4:117–35.

———. 1980. Bases ecologicas del sacrificio azteca. *Historia* "16" año 5, no. 45:94–105.

Harris, M. 1977. *Cannibals and kings.* Random House, New York.

Harrison, P. D. 1977. The rise of the bajos and the fall of the Maya. In *Social process in Maya prehistory,* edited by N. Hammond, pp. 469–508. Academic Press, New York.

Harrison, P. D., and B. L. Turner II, eds. 1978. *Pre-hispanic Maya agriculture.* University of New Mexico Press, Albuquerque.

Hartmann, R. 1968. *Märkte im alten Peru.* Rheinische Friedrich-Wilhelms-Universität, Bonn.

———. 1971. Mercado y ferias prehispánicas en el area andina. *Boletín de la Academia Nacional de Historia* 54:214–35.

———. 1981. El texto quechua de Huarochirí: Una evaluación crítica de las ediciones a disposición. *Historica–Pontificia Universidad Católica del Perú* 5:167–208.

Hartung, H. 1971. *Die Zeremonialzentren der Maya.* Akademische Druck- und Verlagsanstalt, Graz.

Harvey, H. R. 1971. Ethnohistory of Guerrero. In *Archaeology of Northern Mesoamerica,* edited by G. F. Ekholm and I. Bernal, pp. 603–18. Handbook of Middle American Indians, vol. 11. R. Wauchope, general editor. University of Texas Press, Austin.

———. 1984. Aspects of land tenure in ancient Mexico. In *Explorations in ethnohistory: Indians of Central Mexicon in the sixteenth century,* edited by H. R. Harvey and H. J. Prem, pp. 83–102. University of New Mexico Press, Albuquerque.

Hassan, F. A. 1981. *Demographic archaeology.* Academic Press, New York.

Hassig, R. 1982. Periodical markets in precolumbian Mexico. *American Antiquity* 47:346–55.

———. 1984. The Aztec empire: A reappraisal. In *Five centuries of law and politics in Central Mexico,* edited by R. Spores and R. Hassig, pp. 15–24. Vanderbilt University, Nashville.

———. 1985. *Trade, tribute and transportation: The sixteenth-century political economy of the Valley of Mexico.* University of Oklahoma Press, Norman.

———. 1988. *Aztec warfare: Imperial expansion and political control.* University of Oklahoma Press, Norman.

Hassler, P. 1992. *Menschenopfer bei den Azteken.* Verlag Lang, Bern.

Hauck, D. 1968. *La educación pública entre los Aztecas: Una crítica de las fuentes y de la bibliografía secundaria.* Publicaciones del Instituto Tecnológico y de Estudios Superiores de Monterrey, Serie: Historia 8, Monterrey, N. L.

Healan, D. M., J. M. Kerley, and G. J. Bey III. 1983. Excavation and preliminary analysis of an obsidian workshop in Tula, Hidalgo, Mexico. *Journal of Field Archaeology* 10:127–45.

Heine-Geldern, R. von. 1954. Die asiatische Herkunft der südamerikanischen Metalltechnik. *Paideuma* 5:347–423.

———. 1966. The problem of transpacific influences in Mesoamerica. In *Archaeological Frontiers and External Connections,* edited by G. F. Ekholm and G. R. Willey, pp. 277–95. Handbook of Middle American Indians, vol. 4. R. Wauchope, general editor. University of Texas Press, Austin.

Heizer, R. F., and J. E. Gullberg. 1981. Concave mirrors from the site of La Venta, Tabasco: Their occurrence, mineralogy, optical description, and function. In *The Olmec and their neighbors,* edited by E. P. Benson, pp. 109–16. Dumbarton Oaks, Washington.

Helfrich, K. 1973. *Menschenopfer und Tötungsrituale im Kult der Maya.* Monumenta Americana 9. Gebrüder Mann, Berlin.

Hellbom, A.-B. 1982. The life and role of women in the Aztec culture. *Cultures* (UNESCO) 8:55–65.

Helmer, M. 1955. La visitación de los yndios Chupachos; Inca et encomendero, 1549. *Travaux de L'Institut Français d'Etudes Andines* 5:3–50.

Henige, D. 1992. Native American population at contact, standards of proof and styles of discourse in the debate. *Latin American Population History Bulletin* 22:2–24.

Hernández Rodríguez, R. 1952. El Valle de Toluca, su historia: Epoca prehispánica y siglo XVI. *Boletín de la Sociedad Mexicana de Geografía y Estadística* 74:1–124.

———. 1961. Moquihuix. *Anuario de Historia* 1:69–73.

Herrejón Paredo, C. 1978. La pugna entre mexicas y tarascos. *Cuadernos de Historia* 1:9–47.

Heyden, D. 1975. An interpretation of the cave underneath the pyramid of the Sun in Teotihuacán, Mexico. *American Antiquity* 40:131–46.

———. 1987. Mesoamerican religions: Classic cultures. In *Encyclopedia of Religion,* edited by M. Eliade and C. J. Adams, vol. 9:409–19. Macmillan, New York.

Heyerdahl, T. 1952. *American Indians in the Pacific: The theory behind the Kon-Tiki expedition.* Allen & Unwin, London.

———. 1971. *The Ra-expeditions.* Allen & Unwin, London.

Hicks, F. 1976. Mayeque y calpuleque en el sistema de clases del México antiguo. In *Estratificación social en la Mesoamérica prehispánica,* edited by P. Carrasco P. and J. Broda, pp. 67–77. Centro de Investigaciones Superiores, Instituto Nacional de Antropología e Historia, México.

———. 1978. Los calpixque de Nezahualcóyotl. *Estudios de Cultura Nahuatl* 13:129–52.

———. 1979. "Flowery war" in Aztec history. *American Ethnologist* 6:87–92.

———. 1982. Tetzcoco in the early 16th century: The state, the city and the calpolli. *American Ethnologist* 9:230–49.

———. 1984a. Rotational labor and urban development in prehispanic Tetzcoco. In *Explorations in Ethnohistory*, edited by H. Harvey and H. J. Prem, pp. 147–74. University of New Mexico Press, Albuquerque.

———. 1984b. La posición de Temascalapan en la Triple Alianza. *Estudios de Cultura Nahuatl* 17:235–60.

———. 1987. First steps toward a market-integrated economy in Aztec Mexico. In *Early State Dynamics. Studies in Human Society*, edited by H. J. M. Claessen and P. van de Velde, vol. 2:91–197. E. J. Brill, New York.

———. 1992. Subject states and tribute provinces, the Aztec empire in the northern Valley of Mexico. *Ancient Mesoamerica* 3:1–19.

———. 1994. Alliance and intervention in Aztec imperial expansion. In *Factional competition and political development in the New World*, edited by E. M. Brumfiel and J. W. Fox, pp. 111–16. Cambridge University Press, New York.

Hinz, E., C. Hartau, and M. L. Heimann-Koenen. 1983. *Aztekischer Zensus: Zur indianischen Wirtschaft und Gesellschaft im Marquesado um 1540*. 2 vols. Verlag für Ethnologie, Hannover.

Hippel, E. von. 1955. *Geschichte der Staatsphilosophie an Hauptkapiteln*. A. Hain, Meisenheim.

Hocquenghem, A. M. 1978. Les combats Mochicas: Essai d'interprétation d'un matériel archéologique à l'aide de l'iconologie, de l'ethno-histoire et de l'ethnologie. *Baessler Archiv, Neue Folge* 26:127–57.

Hodge, M. G. 1984. *Aztec city-states* (Studies in American Ethnohistory & Archaeology 3). Museum of Anthropology, University of Michigan, Ann Arbor.

———. 1991. Land and lordship in the Valley of Mexico: The politics of Aztec provincial administration. In *Land and politics in the Valley of Mexico, a two thousand year perspective*, edited by H. R. Harvey, pp. 113–40. University of New Mexico Press, Albuquerque.

Höhl, M. 1983. Ensayo de biografía de un soberano de Tezcoco: Nezahualpilli. *Revista española de Antropología Americana* 13:59–94.

Hole, F. 1983. Changing directions in archeological thought. In *Ancient South Americans*, edited by J. D. Jennings, pp. 1–23. Freeman, San Francisco.

Holt, H. B. 1976. The extent of the dominance of Tenochtitlan during the reign of Mocteuczoma Ilhuicamin. In *Middle American Research Institute, Publications* 22:49–62. Tulane University, New Orleans.

Hopkins, J. W., III. 1984. *Irrigation and the Cuicatec ecosystem: A study of agriculture and civilization in North Central Oaxaca*. University of Michigan, Museum of Anthropology, Ann Arbor.

Hosler, D., J. A. Sabloff, and D. Runge. 1977. Simulation model development: A case study of the classic Maya collapse. In *Social process in Maya prehistory*, edited by N. Hammond, pp. 553–90. Academic Press, New York.

Houston, S. D. 1992. Classic Maya history and politics in Dos Pilas, Guatemala. In *Epigraphy*, edited by V. R. Bricker. Handbook of Middle American Indians Supplement, vol. 5:110–27. V. R. Bricker, general editor. University of Texas Press, Austin.

Houston, S. D., and P. Mathews. 1985. *The dynastic sequence of Dos Pilas, Guatemala.* Pre-Columbian Art Research Institute, Monograph 1, San Francisco.

Houston, S. D., and D. Stuart. 1992. On Maya hieroglyphic literacy. *Current Anthropology* 33:589–93.

Hyslop, J. 1984. *The Inca road system.* Academic Press, New York.

Icaza, F. A. de, ed. 1923. *Diccionario autobiográfico de conquistadores y pobladores de Nueva España.* 2 vols. Impr. de "El Adelantado de Segovia," Madrid, 2nd ed. Aviña Levy, Guadelajara.

Ingstad, H. 1969. *Westward to Vinland: The discovery of pre-Columbian Norse house-sites in North-America,* translated by E. J. Friis. Cape, London.

Irving, W. N. 1985. Context and chronology of early man in the Americas. *Annual Review of Anthropology* 14:529–55.

Isaac, B. L. 1983a. Aztec warfare: Goals and battlefield comportment. *Ethnology* 22:121–31.

———. 1983b. The Aztec "flowery war": A geopolitical explanation. *Journal for Anthropological Research* 39:415–31.

———. 1986. Obsidian, pochteca, and Tlatelolco in the Aztec Empire. In *Economic aspects of prehispanic highland Mexico,* edited by B. L. Isaac, pp. 319–43. JAI Press, Greenwich/London.

Isbell, W. H. 1981. Comment on Conrad (Cultural materialism, split inheritance, and the expansion of ancient Peruvian empires). *American Antiquity* 48:27–30.

———. 1984. Huari urban prehistory. In *Current archaeological projects in the Central Andes: Some approaches and results* (Proceedings of the Forty-fourth International Congress of Americanists), edited by A. Kendall, pp. 95–131. BAR International Series 210, Oxford.

———. 1986. Emergence of city and state at Wari, Ayacucho, Peru, during the Middle Horizon. In *Andean archaeology,* edited by R. Matos M., S. A. Turpin, and H. H. Eling, Jr., pp. 189–200. Institute of Archaeology, University of California, Los Angeles.

———. 1987. State origins in the Ayacucho Valley, central highlands, Peru. In *The origins and development of the Andean state,* edited by J. Haas, S. Pozorski, and T. Pozorski, pp. 83–90. Cambridge University Press, New York.

Isbell, W. H., and K. J. Schreiber. 1978. Was Huari a state? *American Antiquity* 43:372–89.

Jäcklein, K. 1978. *Los Popolocas de Tepexi (Puebla): Un estudio ethnohistórico.* Steiner, Wiesbaden.

Jansen, M. 1992. Mixtec pictography: Conventions and contents. In *Epigraphy,* edited by V. R. Bricker. Handbook of Middle American Indians Supplement, vol. 5:20–33. V. R. Bricker, general editor. University of Texas Press, Austin.

Jett, S. C. 1983. Precolumbian transoceanic contacts. In *Ancient South Americans,* edited by J. D. Jennings, pp. 337–93. Freeman, San Francisco.

Jiménez de la Espada, M., ed. 1881–97. *Relaciones geográficas de Indias.* 4 vols. M. G. Hernández, Madrid.

Jiménez Moreno, W. 1940. Signos cronográficos del Códice y calendario mixteco. In *Códice de Yanhuitlán,* edited by W. Jiménez Moreno and S. Mateos Higuera, pp. 69–76. Instituto Nacional de Antropología e Historia, México.

———. 1941. Tula y los toltecas según las fuentes históricas. *Revista Mexicana de Estudios Antropológicos* 5:79–83.

———. 1953. Cronología de la historia de Veracruz. *Revista Mexicana de Estudios Antropológicos* 13:312–13.

———. 1954-55. Síntesis de la historia precolonial del Valle de México. *Revista Mexicana de Estudios Antropológicos* 14:219–36.

———. 1958. Diferente principio del año entre diversos pueblos y sus consecuencias para la cronología prehispánica. *El México Antiguo* 9:137–52.

———. 1966a. Horizonte Postclásico. In *Compendio de Historia de México,* edited by W. Jiménez Moreno, J. Miranda, and M. T. Fernández, pp. 97–171. Editorial E. C. L. A. L. S. A., México.

———. 1966b. Mesoamerica before the Toltecs. In *Ancient Oaxaca: Discoveries in Mexican Archeology and History,* edited by J. Paddock, pp. 3–82. Stanford University Press, Stanford.

Jiménez Moreno, W., J. Miranda, and M. T. Fernández. 1965. *Historia de México.* Instituto Nacional de Antropología e Historia, México.

Johnston, K. 1985. Maya dynastic territorial expansion: Glyphic evidence from Classic centers of the Pasión river, Guatemala. In *Fifth Palenque Round Table, 1983,* edited by M. Greene Robertson and V. M. Fields, vol. 7:49–56. The Pre-Columbian Art Research Institute, San Francisco.

Jones, C., and L. Satterthwaite. 1982. *The monuments and inscriptions of Tikal: The carved monuments.* Tikal Report 33, Part A. The University Museum, University of Pennsylvania, Monograph 44, Philadelphia.

Joralemon, D. 1971. *A study of Olmec iconography.* Dumbarton Oaks, Washington.

Josserand, J. K., and N. A. Hopkins. 1991. The Inscriptions of Yaxchilán. In *A Handbook of Classic Maya Inscriptions,* Part 1: The Western Lowlands. Final Performance Report, National Endowment for the Humanities Grant RT-21090-89.

Julien, C. J. 1982. Inca decimal administration in the Lake Titicaca region. In *The Inca and Aztec states 1400–1800,* edited by G. A. Collier, R. I. Rosaldo, and J. D. Wirth, pp. 119–51. Academic Press, New York.

———. 1985. Guano and resource control in sixteenth century Arequipa. In *Andean ecology and civilization: An interdisciplinary perspective on Andean ecological complementarity,* edited by S. Masuda, I. Shimada, and C. Morris, pp. 185–231. University of Tokyo Press, Tokyo.

Justeson, J. S., and T. Kaufman. 1993. A decipherment of epi-Olmec hieroglyphic writing. *Science* 259:1703–11.

Justeson, J. S., W. M. Norman, L. Campbell, and T. Kaufman. 1985. *The foreign impact on lowland Mayan language and script.* Middle American Research Institute, Publication 53. Tulane University, New Orleans.

Karsten, R. 1938. *Inkariket och dess kultur i det forna Peru.* Helsinki.

———. 1949. *A totalitarian state of the past: The civilization of the Inca empire in ancient Peru.* Serie Commentationen humanorum litterarum, Helsinki.

Katz, F. 1966. *Situación social y económica de los aztecas durante los siglos XV y XVI.* Instituto de Investigaciones Históricos, México.

———. 1972. *Pre-Columbian Civilizations.* Weidenfeld & Nicholson, London.

Kauffmann Doig, F. 1983. *Manual de arqueología peruana.* 8th ed. Peisa, Lima.

———. 1987. South American Indians—Indians of the Andes. In *Encyclopedia of Religion,* edited by M. Eliade, vol. 13:465–72. Macmillan, New York.

Keatinge, R. W. 1974. Chimú rural administrative centres in the Moche valley, Peru. *World Archaeology* 6:66–82.

———. 1981. The nature and role of religious diffusion in the early stages of state formation: An example from Peruvian prehistory. In *The transition to statehood in the New World,* edited by G. D. Jones and R. R. Kautz, pp. 172–87. Cambridge University Press, New York.

Keen, B. 1985. *The Aztec image in western thought.* 2nd ed. Rutgers University, New Brunswick.

Kelley, D. H. 1968. Kakupacal and the Itzas. *Estudios de Cultura Maya* 7:255–68.

———. 1976. *Deciphering the Maya script.* University of Texas Press, Austin.

Kelly, I. 1952. The Mexican conquests. In *The Tajin Totonac,* part 1, History, subsistence, shelter and technology, appendix B, edited by I. Kelly and A. Palerm, pp. 264–318. Smithsonian Institution, Institute of Social Anthropology, Washington.

Kendall, A. 1984. Archaeological investigations of Late Intermediate Period and Late Horizon Period at Cusichaca, Peru. In *Current archaeological projects in the Central Andes: Some approaches and results* (Proceedings of the Forty-fourth International Congress of Americanists), edited by A. Kendall, pp. 247–90. BAR International Series 210, Oxford.

———. 1985. *Aspects of Inca architecture: Description, function and chronology.* 2 vols., BAR International Series 242, Oxford.

Kerkhoff, M. 1964. Orientierung über die Philosophie der Nahua-Völker. *Zeitschrift für Philosophische Forschung* 18:185–223.

Kirchhoff, P. 1947. Prólogo, in *Historia Tolteca-Chichimeca: Anales de Quauhtinchan,* pp. xix–lxiv. Antiqua Librería Robredo, de J. Porrúa e Hijos, México.

———. 1948. Civilizing the Chichimecs: A chapter in the culture history of ancient Mexico. In *Some Educational and Anthropological Aspects of Latin America,* vol. 5:80–85. University of Texas Press, Austin.

———. 1949. The social and political organization of the Andean people. In *Handbook of South American Indians,* edited by J. H. Steward, vol. 5:293–311. Smithsonian Institution, Bureau of American Ethnology, Washington.

———. 1950. The Mexican calendar and the founding of Tenochtitlan-Tlatelolco. In *Transaction of the New York Academy of Science* 1, 12:126–32.

———. 1952. Mesoamerica, its geographic limits, ethnic composition and cultural characteristics. In *Heritage of Conquest*, edited by S. Tax, pp. 17–30. Glencoe Free Press, Chicago.

———. 1954. Calendarios Tenochca, Tlatelolca y otros. *Revista Mexicana de Estudios Antropológicos* 14:257–67.

———. 1954-55. Land tenure in ancient Mexico. *Revista Mexicana de Estudios Antropológicos* 14:351–59.

———. 1955. Quetzalcoatl, Huemac y el fin de Tula. *Cuadernos Americanos* 14:164–96.

———. 1958. La ruta de los tolteca-chichimeca entre Tula y Cholula. In *Miscellanea Paul Rivet Octogenario dicata*, vol. 1:485–94. Universidad Nacional Autónoma de México, México.

———. 1959. Las dos rutas de los colhua entre Tula y Culhuacán. *Mitteilungen aus dem Museum für Völkerkunde Hamburg* 25:75–81.

———. 1960. Los pueblos de la Historia Tolteca Chichimeca: Sus migraciones y parentesco. *Revista Mexicana de Estudios Antropológicos* 4:77–104.

———. 1961. ¿Se puede localizar Aztlán? *Anuario de Historia* 1:59–67.

———. 1962. Das Toltekenreich und sein Untergang. *Saeculum* 12:248–65.

———. 1966. Civilizing the Chichimecs: A chapter in the culture history of ancient Mexico. In *Ancient Mexico: Selected readings*, edited by J. A. Graham, pp. 273–78. Peek Publications, Palo Alto.

———. 1985. El Imperio Tolteca y su caída. In *Mesoamérica y el centro de México*, edited by J. Monjarás-Ruiz, R. Brambila, and E. Pérez-Rocha, pp. 249–72. Instituto Nacional de Antropología e Historia, México.

Kirchhoff, P., L. Odena Güemes, and L. Reyes García, eds. 1976. *Historia Tolteca Chichimeca*. Instituto Nacional de Antropología e Historia, México.

Kirkby, A. V. T. 1973. *The use of land and water resources in the past and present, Valley of Oaxaca, Mexico*. Museum of Anthropology, University of Michigan, Ann Arbor.

Klymyshyn, Ulana A. M. 1982. Elite compounds in Chan Chan. In *Chan Chan: Andean desert city*, edited by M. E. Moseley and K. C. Day, pp. 119–44. University of New Mexico Press, Albuquerque.

Knorozov, Y. V. 1967. *Selected chapters from the writing of the Maya indians*, translated by Sophie D. Coe. Chapters 1, 6, 7, and 9 of YK 1963. Russian Translation Series No. 4. Peabody Museum, Harvard University, Cambridge.

Kohler, J. 1895. Das Recht der Azteken. *Zeitschrift für vergleichende Rechtswissenschaft* 11:1–111.

———. 1924. *El derecho de los Aztecas*. Edición de la Revista Jurídica de la Escuela Libre de Derecho, México.

Köhler, U. 1978. Reflections on Zinacantan's role in Aztec trade with Soconusco. In *Mesoamerican communication routes and cultural contacts*, edited by T. A. Lee and C. Navarrete, pp. 67–73. University of Utah Press, Salt Lake City.

———. 1985. Olmeken und Jaguare: Zur Deutung von Mischwesen in der präklassischen Kunst Mesoamerikas. *Anthropos* 80:15–52.

Kolata, A. L. 1983. The southern Andes. In *Ancient South Americans*, edited by J. D. Jennings, pp. 241–85. Freeman, San Francisco.

———. 1993. Understanding Tiwanaku: Conquest, colonization and clientage in the south central Andes. In *Latin American horizons*, edited by D. S. Rice, pp. 193–224. Dumbarton Oaks, Washington.

Kosok, P. 1965. *Life, land and water in ancient Peru.* Long Island University Press, New York.

Krickeberg, W. 1950. Bauform und Weltbild im alten Mexico. *Paideuma* 4:295–333.

———. 1952. Moctezuma II. *Saeculum* 3:255–76.

———. 1956. *Altmexikanische Kulturen.* Safari Verlag, Berlin.

Kubler, G. 1944. A Peruvian chief of state: Manco Inca (1515–1545). *Hispanic American Historical Review* 24:253–76.

———. 1946. The Quechua in the colonial world. In *Handbook of South American Indians*, edited by J. H. Steward, vol. 1:331–410. Smithsonian Institution, Bureau of American Ethnology, Washington.

———. 1947. The Neo-Inca state (1537–1572). *Hispanic American Historical Review* 27:189–203.

———. 1961. Chichén Itzá y Tula. *Estudios de Cultura Maya* 1:47–80.

———. 1980. Eclecticism at Cacaxtla. In *Third Palenque Round Table, 1978* (part 2, 1980), edited by M. Greene Robertson, Part 2:163–72. University of Texas Press, Austin.

———. 1984. *The art and architecture of ancient America; the Mexican, Maya and Andean peoples.* Revised 3rd ed. The Pelican History of Art, Penguin Books, Harmondsworth.

Kurbjuhn, K. 1989. *Maya. The complete catalogue of glyph readings.* Schneider und Weber, Kassel.

Kurtz, D. V. 1974. Peripheral and transitional markets: The Aztec case. *American Ethnologist* 1:685–705.

———. 1978. The legitimation of the Aztec state. In *The early state*, edited by H. J. M. Claessen and P. Skalník, pp. 169–89. Mouton, The Hague.

———. 1987. The economics of urbanization and state formation at Teotihuacán. *Current Anthropology* 28:329–53.

Kurtz, D. V., and M. C. Nunley. 1993. Ideology and work at Teotihuacán: a hermeneutic interpretation. *Man* (n.s.) 28:761–78.

Kutscher, G. 1950. *Chimú, eine altindianische Hochkultur.* Gebrüder Mann, Berlin.

———. 1962a. Die Flurkarte des Chiquatzin Tecuihtli: Postkolumbische Bilddokumente aus Mexiko im Berliner Museum für Völkerkunde 2. *Baessler Archiv, Neue Folge* 10:129–44.

———. 1962b. Die Genealogie des Tlatzcantzin: Postkolumbische Bilddokumente aus Mexiko im Berliner Museum für Völkerkunde 4. *Baessler Archiv, Neue Folge* 10:319–37.

———. 1983. *Nordperuanische Gefäßmalereien des Moche-Stils.* C. H. Beck, München.

Lafaye, J. 1974. *Quetzalcóatl et Guadalupe: la formation de la conscience nationale au Mexique.* Gallimard, Paris.

———. 1977. *Quetzalcóatl y Guadalupe: la formación de la conciencia nacional en México.* Fondo de Cultura Económica, México.

Lalone, D. E. 1982. The Inca as a nonmarket economy: Supply on command versus supply and demand. In *Contexts for prehistoric exchange,* edited by J. E. Ericson and T. K. Earle, pp. 291–316. Academic Press, New York.

Lalone, M. B., and D. E. Lalone. 1987. The Inca state in the southern highlands; state administration and production enclaves. *Ethnohistory* 34:47–62.

Lameiras, J. 1985. *Los déspotas armados: Un espectro de la guerra prehispánica.* Colegio de Michoacán, Zamora.

Lanczkowski, G. 1962. Die religiöse Stellung der aztekischen Großkaufleute. *Saeculum* 13:346–62.

———. 1984. *Götter und Menschen im alten Mexiko.* Walter Verlag, Freiburg i. Br.

Landa, Diego de. 1959. *Relación de las cosas de Yucatán,* edited by A. M. Garibay K. Editorial Porrúa, México.

Langley, J. C. 1986. *Symbolic notation of Teotihuacán: Elements of writing in a Mesoamerican culture of the Classic period.* BAR International Series 313, Oxford.

Lanning, E. P. 1967. *Peru before the Incas.* Prentice-Hall, Inc., Englewood Cliffs.

Las Casas, Bartolomé de. 1967. *Apologética historia sumaria,* edited by E. O'Gorman, 2 vols., 3rd ed. Universidad Nacional Autónoma de México, Instituto de Investigaciones Historicas, México.

Latcham, R. 1927. El dominio de la tierra y el sistema tributario en el antiguo imperio de los Incas. *Revista Chilena de Historia y Geografía* 52:201–57.

Leander, B., ed. 1967. *Códice de Otlazpan.* Instituto Nacional de Antropología e Historia, México.

Lee, T. A., Jr., ed. 1985. *Los Códices Maya.* Universidad Autónoma de Chiapas, Tuxtla Gutiérrez.

Lee, V. R. 1989. *Chanansuyu, the ruins of Inca Vilcabamba.* (Privately printed.) Wilson.

Lehmann, W. 1938. *Die Geschichte der Königreiche von Colhuacan und Mexiko.* Verlag W. Kohlhammer, Stuttgart.

Lehmann, W., and G. Kutscher, transl. 1958. *Das Memorial breve acerca de la fundación de la Ciudad de Culhuacan.* Verlag W. Kohlhammer, Stuttgart.

Lehmann, W., G. Kutscher, and G. Vollmer, transl. 1981. *Geschichte der Azteken: Codex Aubin und verwandte Dokumente.* Gebrüder Mann Verlag, Berlin.

León, A., transl. 1949 (1598). *Crónica Mexicayotl.* Impr. Universitaria, Mexico.

León-Portilla, M. 1959. *La filosofía nahuatl.* 2nd ed. Universidad Autónoma de México, Instituto de Histórica, Seminario de Cultura Nahuatl, México.

———. 1962. La institución cultural del comercio. *Estudios de Cultura Nahuatl* 3:23–54.

———. 1975. La institución cultural del comercio. In *El comercio en el México prehispánico*, edited by E. Florescano, pp. 69–96. Instituto Mexicano de Comercio exterior de México, México.

———. 1978. *México-Tenochtitlan: Su espacio y tiempo sagrados.* Instituto Nacional de Antropología e Historia, México.

———. 1980a. Tlacaelel y el sistema electoral de los Mexicas. In *Toltecayotl, aspectos de la cultura nahuatl*, edited by M. León-Portilla, pp. 293–99. Fondo de Cultura Económica, México.

———. 1980b. La institución cultural del comercio. In *Toltecayotl, aspectos de la cultura nahuatl*, edited by M. León-Portilla, pp. 309–42. Fondo de Cultura Económica, México (in slightly changed form).

———. 1980c. *Toltecayotl, aspectos de la cultura Nahuatl.* Fondo de Cultura Económica, México.

———. 1986. Die Religion. In *Das Alte Mexico*, edited by H. J. Prem and U. Dyckerhoff, pp. 236–58. Bertelsmann Verlag, München.

———. 1992. *The Aztec image of self and society, an introduction to Aztec culture.* University of Utah Press, Salt Lake City.

León-Portilla, M., and A. M. Garibay K. 1959. *Visión de los vencidos: Relaciones indígenas de la Conquista.* Universidad Nacional Autónoma de México, México.

León-Portilla, M., and R. Heuer, eds. 1962. *Rückkehr der Götter: Die Aufzeichnungen der Azteken über den Untergang ihres Reiches.* F. Middelhauve, Köln.

Lerche, P. 1986. *Häuptlingstum Jalca: Bevölkerung und Ressourcen bei den vorspanischen Chachapoya, Peru.* Reimer, Berlin.

Levillier, R. 1924. Libro de la visita general del virrey Don Francisco de Toledo, 1570–1575. *Revista Histórica* 7:113–216.

———. 1925. *Gobernantes del Perú, cartas y papeles, siglo XVI*, vol. 9:114–230. Sucesores de Rivadeneyra, Madrid.

Levillier, R., ed. 1940. Informaciones que mandó levantar el virrey Toledo sobre los Incas. In *Don Francisco de Toledo, supremo organizador del Peru.* vol. 2:1–204. Espasa Calpe, Buenos Aires.

Licate, J. A. 1980. The forms of Aztec territorial organization. *Geoscience and Man* 21:27–45.

Lincoln, C. E. 1986. The chronology of Chichén Itzá: A review of the literature. In *Late lowland Maya civilization: Classic to postclassic*, edited by J. A. Sabloff and E. W. Andrews V, pp. 141–96. University of New Mexico Press, Albuquerque.

Litvak King, J. 1971a. *Cihuatlan y Tepecoacuilco: Provincias tributarias de México en el siglo XVI.* Universidad Nacional Autónoma de México, Instituto de Investigaciones Históricos, México.

———. 1971b. Las relaciones entre México y Tlatelolco antes de la conquista de Axayacatl: Problemática de la expansión Mexica. *Estudios de Cultura Nahuatl* 9:17–21.

———. 1974. Algunas observaciones acerca del clásico de Xochicalco, México. *Anales de Antropología* 11:9–18.

Locke, L. L. 1923. *The ancient quipu or Peruvian knot record.* The American Museum of Natural History, New York.

Lombardo de Ruiz, S. 1973. *Desarrollo urbano de México-Tenochtitlán según las fuentes históricas.* Instituto Nacional de Antropología e Historia, Departamento de Investigaciones Históricos, México.

Lombardo de Ruiz, S., and A. Barrera Rubio, eds. 1987. *La pintura mural en Quintana Roo.* Instituto Nacional de Antropología e Historia, México.

López Austin, A. 1961. *La constitución real de México-Tenochtitlán.* Universidad Nacional Autónoma de México, Seminario de Cultura Nahuatl, México.

———. 1973. *Hombre-Dios: Religión y política en el mundo Nahuatl.* Universidad Nacional Autónoma de México, Instituto de Investigaciones Históricas, México.

———. 1974a. The research method of Fray Bernardino de Sahagún, the questionnaires. In *Sixteenth-century Mexico; the work of Sahagún,* edited by M. S. Edmonson, pp. 111–49. University of New Mexico Press, Albuquerque.

———. 1974b. Organización política en el altiplano central de Mexico durante el posclásico. *Historia Mexicana* 4:515–50.

———. 1976. El fundamento mágico-religioso del poder. *Estudios de Cultura Nahuatl* 12:197–240.

———. 1981. *Tarascos y mexicas.* Fondo de Cultura Económica, México.

———. 1982. La sexualidad entre los antiguas nahuas. In *Familia y sexualidad en Nueva España,* Memoria del Primer Simposio de Historia de las Mentalidades: "Familia, matrimonio y sexualidad en Nueva España." Instituto Nacional de Antropología e Historia, pp. 141–76. Fondo de Cultura Económica, México.

———. 1985. Organización política en el altiplano central de Mexico durante el posclásico (with "Addenda"). In *Mesoamérica y el centro de México,* edited by J. Monjarás-Ruiz, R. Brambila, and E. Pérez-Rocha, pp. 197–247. Instituto Nacional de Antropología e Historia, México.

López de Gómara, Francisco. 1954. *Historia general de Indias, "Hispania Victrix,"* edited by P. Guibelalde, vol. 2. Editorial Iberia, Barcelona.

López de Molina, D. 1981. Un informe preliminar sobre la cronología de Cacaxtla. In *Interacción cultural en México Central,* edited by E. C. Rattray, J. Litvak K., and C. Díaz O., pp. 169–73. Universidad Nacional Autónoma de México, México.

Lorandi, A. M. 1978. Les "horizons" andins: Critique d'un modèle. *Annales–Economies, Sociétés, Civilisations* 33:921–25.

———. 1986. Horizons in Andean archaeology. In *Anthropological history of Andean polities,* edited by J. V. Murra, N. Wachtel, and J. Revel, pp. 35–45. Cambridge University Press, New York.

Lothrop, S. K. 1951. Peruvian metallurgy. In *The civilizations of Ancient America: Selected papers of the Twenty-ninth International Congress of Americanists*, edited by Sol Tax, pp. 219–23. University of Chicago Press, Chicago.

Lounsbury, F. G. 1973. On the Derivation and Reading of the 'Ben-ich' Prefix. In *Mesoamerican Writing Systems*, edited by E. P. Benson, pp. 99–143. Dumbarton Oaks, Washington.

———. 1984. Glyphic Substitutions: Homophonic and Synonymic. In *Phoneticism in Mayan Hieroglyphic Writing*, edited by J. S. Justeson and L. Campbell, pp. 167–84. Institute for Mesoamerican Studies, Publication No. 9, State University of New York at Albany, Albany.

———. 1986. Some aspects of the Inca kinship system. In *Anthropological history of the Andean polities*, edited by J. V. Murra, N. Wachtel, and J. Revel, pp. 121–36. Cambridge University Press, New York.

———. 1992. Derivation of the Maya-to-Julian calendar correlation from the Dresden Codex venus chronology. In *The sky in Mayan literature*, edited by A. F. Aveni, pp. 184–206. Oxford University Press, New York/Oxford.

Lovell, W. G. 1985. *Conquest and survival in colonial Guatemala: A historical geography of the Chuchumatanes Highlands 1500-1821.* McGill-Queens University Press, Kingston.

Lowe, G. W. 1978. Eastern Mesoamerica. In *Chronologies in New World archaeology*, edited by R. E. Taylor and C. W. Meighan, pp. 331–94. Academic Press, New York.

Lowe, J. W. G. 1981. On mathematical models of the classic Maya collapse: The class conflict hypothesis reexamined. *American Antiquity* 47:643–51.

———. 1985. *The dynamics of apocalypse: A systems simulation of the classic Maya collapse.* University of New Mexico Press, Albuquerque.

Lumbreras, L. G. 1980. El imperio Wari. In *Historia del Perú*, edited by J. M. Baca, vol. 2:11–91. Pontificia Universidad Católica del Perú, Fundación Volkswagenwerk Alemania, Lima.

———. 1981. *Arqueología de la América Andina.* Editorial Mille Batres, Lima.

Luttwack, E. N. 1976. *The Grand Strategy of the Roman Empire.* Johns Hopkins University Press, Baltimore.

Luxemburg, R. 1975. Einführung in die Nationalökonomie. In *Gesammelte Werke*, vol. 5:524–778. Dietz Verlag, Berlin.

Lynch, T., ed. 1980. *Guitarrero Cave: Early man in the Andes.* Academic Press, New York.

MacNeish, R. S. 1973. The scheduling factor in the development of effective food production in the Tehuacan Valley. In *Variation in anthropology: Essays in honour of John McGregor*, edited by D. W. Lathrap, pp. 75–89. Illinois Archaeological Survey, Urbana.

———. 1977. The beginning of agriculture in Central Peru. In *Origins of agriculture*, edited by C. H. Reed, pp. 753–802. Mouton, The Hague.

———. 1981. Tehuacan's accomplishments. In *Archaeology*, edited by J. A. Sabloff,

Handbook of Middle American Indians Supplement, vol. 1:31–47. V. R. Bricker, general editor. University of Texas Press, Austin.

Maldonado, E. 1992. *Arqueología de Cerro Sechín. Tomo 1-Arquitectura.* Pontífica Universidad Católica del Perú, Lima.

Marcos, J. 1980. Intercambio a larga distancia en América: El caso del spondylus. *Boletín de Antropología Americana* 1:124–29.

Marcus, J. 1976a. *Emblem and state in the Classic Maya lowlands: An epigraphic approach to territorial organization.* Dumbarton Oaks, Washington.

———. 1976b. The iconography of militarism at Monte Albán and neighboring sites in the Valley of Oaxaca. In *Origins of religious art and iconography in preclassic Mesoamerica,* edited by H. B. Nicholson, pp. 125–39. University of California, Latin American Studies Series 31, Los Angeles.

———. 1983a. The conquest slabs of Building J, Monte Albán. In *The Cloud People: Divergent evolution of the Zapotec and Mixtec civilizations,* edited by K. V. Flannery and J. Marcus, pp. 106–8. Academic Press, New York.

———. 1983b. Teotihuacán visitors on Monte Albán monuments and murals. In *The Cloud People: Divergent evolution of the Zapotec and Mixtec civilizations,* edited by K. V. Flannery and J. Marcus, pp. 175–81. Academic Press, New York.

———. 1983c. Changing patterns of stone monuments after the fall of Monte Albán, A.D. 600–900. In *The Cloud People: Divergent evolution of the Zapotec and Mixtec civilizations,* edited by K. V. Flannery and J. Marcus, pp. 191–97. Academic Press, New York.

———. 1983d. Aztec military campaigns against the Zapotecs: The documentary evidence. In *The Cloud People: Divergent evolution of the Zapotec and Mixtec civilizations,* edited by K. F. Flannery and J. Marcus, pp. 314–18. Academic Press, New York.

———. 1993. Ancient Maya political organization. In *Lowland Maya civilization in the eighth century A.D.,* edited by J. A. Sabloff and J. S. Henderson, pp. 111–84. Dumbarton Oaks, Washington.

Mariscotti de Görlitz, A. M. 1978. *Pachamama Santa Tierra: Contribución al estudio de la religión autóctona en los Andes centro-meridionales.* Gebrüder Mann Verlag, Berlin.

Marschall, W. 1972. *Transpazifische Kulturbeziehungen: Studien zu ihrer Geschichte.* Klaus Renner Verlag, München.

Martens, O. 1895. *Ein sozialistischer Großstaat vor 400 Jahren.* 2nd ed. Emil Streisand, Berlin.

Martínez, G. 1981. Espacio Lupaqa: Algunas hipótesis de trabajo. In *Etnohistoria y antropología andina* (Segunda Jornada del Museo Nacional de Historia), edited by A. Castelli, M. Koth de Paredes, and M. Mould de Pease, pp. 263–80. Museo Nacional de Historia, Lima.

Martínez, H. 1984. *Tepeaca en el siglo XVI.* Centro de Investigaciones y Estudios Superiores en Antropología Social, México.

Martínez, J. L. 1972. *Nezahualcoyotl.* Fondo de Cultura Económica, México.

Martínez Donjuán, G. 1986. Teopantecuanititlán. In *Primer Coloquio de Arqueología y Etnohistoria del Estado de Guerrero,* edited by R. Cervantes-Delgado, pp. 55–80. Instituto Nacional de Antropología e Historia, México.

Martínez Garnica, A. 1984–85. De la metáfora al mito: La visión de las crónicas sobre el tianguis prehispánico. *Historia Mexicana* 34:685–700.

Martínez Marín, C. 1964. La cultura de los mexica durante la migración: Nuevas ideas. In *Actas y Memorias del 35 Congreso Internacional de Americanistas,* vol. 2:113–23. México.

———. 1971. La cultura de los mexica durante la migración: Nuevas ideas. In *De Teotihuacán a los aztecas: Antología de fuentes e interpretaciones históricas,* edited by M. León-Portilla, pp. 247–60. Universidad Nacional Autónoma de México, México.

Mason, J. A. 1957. *The ancient civilization of Peru.* Penguin Books, Harmondsworth.

Mastache F., A. G., and R. H. Cobean. 1985. Tula. In *Mesoamérica y el centro de México,* edited by J. Monjarás-Ruiz, R. Brambila, and E. Pérez-Rocha, pp. 273–307. Instituto Nacional de Antropología e Historia, México.

Mathews, P. 1985. Maya Early Classic monuments and inscriptions. In *A consideration of the Early Classic period in the Maya lowlands,* edited by G. R. Willey and P. Mathews, pp. 5–54. Institute for Mesoamerican Studies, Publication No. 10, State University of New York at Albany, Albany.

———. 1988. *The Sculpture of Yaxchilán.* Unpublished Ph.D. diss. Yale University, New Haven.

Matos Moctezuma, E. 1987. Symbolism of the Templo Mayor. In *The Aztec Templo Mayor,* edited by E. H. Boone, pp. 185–209. Dumbarton Oaks, Washington.

McAfee, B., and R. H. Barlow. 1946. La guerra entre Tlatelolco y Tenochtitlán, según el Códice Cozcatzin. *Tlatelolco a Través de los Tiempos* 7:44–55.

Means, P. A. 1928. *Biblioteca Andina.* Connecticut Academy of Arts and Science, New Haven.

Meggers, B. J. 1966. *Ecuador.* Praeger, New York.

———. 1975. The transpacific origin of Mesoamerican civilization; a preliminary review of the evidence and its theoretical implications. *American Anthropologist* 77:1–27.

Meggers, B. J., and C. Evans. 1966. A transpacific contact in 3000 B.C. *Scientific American* 214:28–35.

Meillassoux, C. 1981. Discussion. In *Research in economic anthropology,* edited by G. Dalton, vol. 4:60–62. JAI Press, Greenwich.

Méluzin, S. 1987. The Tuxtla statuette: An internal analysis of its writing system. In *The periphery of the southeastern classic Maya realm,* edited by G. W. Pahl, pp. 68–113. UCLA Latin American Center Publications, Los Angeles.

Mendieta, Gerónimo de. 1860 (1945). *Historia eclesiástica indiana, obra escrita a fines del siglo XVI*, edited by J. García Icazbalceta. Editorial Salvador Chávez Hayhoe, México.

Mengin, E., transl. 1939. Unos annales históricos de la Nación mexicana. *Baessler Archiv, Neue Folge* 22:67–168.

———. 1940. Unos annales históricos de la Nación mexicana. *Baessler Archiv, Neue Folge* 23:115–39.

———. 1950. *Diferentes historias originales de los reynos de Culhuacan, y Mexico, y de otras provincias. . .* Cram, Hamburg.

Menzel, D. 1959. The Inca occupation of the south coast of Peru. *Southwestern Journal of Anthropology* 15:125–42.

Métraux, A. 1961. Despotism or socialism. *Diogenes* 35:78–98.

Michels, J. W. 1977. Political organization at Kaminaljuyu: Its implications for interpreting Teotihuacán influence. In *Teotihuacán and Kaminaljuyu: A study in prehistoric culture contact*, edited by W. T. Sanders and J. W. Michels, pp. 455–67. Pennsylvania State University Press, University Park.

Milbrath, S. 1979. *A study of Olmec sculptural chronology*. Dumbarton Oaks, Washington.

Miller, A. G. 1973. *The mural painting of Teotihuacán*. Dumbarton Oaks, Washington.

———. 1982. *On the edge of the sea: Mural painting at Tancah-Tulum*. Dumbarton Oaks, Washington.

Miller, M. E., and K. Taube. 1993. *The gods and symbols of ancient Mexico and the Maya, an illustrated dictionary of Mesoamerican religion*. Thames and Hudson, London.

Millon, R. 1973. *The Teotihuacán map*. University of Texas Press, Austin.

———. 1981. Teotihuacán: City, state, and civilization. In *Archaeology*, edited by J. A. Sabloff, Handbook of Middle American Indians Supplement, vol. 1: 198–243. V. R. Bricker, general editor. University of Texas Press, Austin.

———. 1988. The last years of Teotihuacán dominance. In *The collapse of ancient states and civilizations*, edited by N. Yoffee and G. L. Cowgill, pp. 102–64. University of Arizona Press, Tucson.

———. 1992. Teotihuacán studies: from 1950 to 1990 and beyond. In *Art, ideology, and the city of Teotihuacán*, edited by J. C. Berlo, pp. 339–401. Dumbarton Oaks, Washington.

Millones, L. 1987. *Historia y poder en los Andes centrales*. Alianza, Madrid.

Molina Montes, A. 1982. Archaeological buildings: Restoration or misrepresentation. In *Falsifications and misreconstruction of pre-columbian art*, edited by E. H. Boone, pp. 125–41. Dumbarton Oaks, Washington.

Molins Fabrega, N. 1954–55. El Códice Mendocino y la economía de Tenochtitlán. *Revista Mexicana de Estudios Antropológicos* 14:303–35.

Monjarás-Ruiz, J. 1976. Panorama general de la guerra entre los aztecas. *Estudios de Cultura Nahuatl* 12:241–64.

———. 1980. *La nobleza Mexica: Surgimiento y consolidación*. Edicol, México.

Monzón, A. 1949. *El calpulli en la organización política y social de los tenochca.* Publicaciones del Instituto de Historia, México.

Moorehead, E. L. 1978. Highland Inca architecture in adobe. *Ñawpa Pacha* 16:65–94.

Moreno, M. M. 1931. *La organización política y social de los aztecas.* Sección editorial, México.

Morgan, L. H. 1877. *Ancient Society.* Henry Holt and Company, New York.

Morley, S. G. 1915. *An introduction to the study of the Maya hieroglyphs.* Smithsonian Institution Bureau of American Ethnology, Bulletin 57, Washington.

———. 1920. *The Inscriptions at Copán.* Carnegie Institution of Washington Publication 219, Washington.

———. 1937–38. *The Inscriptions of Petén.* Carnegie Institution of Washington Publication 437, 5 vols., Washington.

Morley, S. G., and G. W. Brainerd. 1956. *The ancient Maya.* 3rd ed. Stanford University Press. Stanford.

Morris, C. 1972. State settlements in Tawantinsuyu; A strategy of compulsory urbanism. In *Contemporary Archaeology,* edited by M. P. Leone, pp. 393–401. Southern Illinois University Press, Carbondale.

———. 1978a. The archaeological study of Andean exchange systems. In *Social archaeology: Beyond subsistence and dating,* edited by C. L. Redman, W. T. Langhorne, Jr., M. J. Berman, N. M. Versaggi, E. V. Curtin, and J. C. Wanser, pp. 315–27. Academic Press, New York.

———. 1978b. The archaeological study of Andean exchange systems. In *Organización social y complementaridad económica en los Andes centrales,* coordinated by J. A. Flores Ochoa, vol. 4:19–30. Actes du XLIIe Congrés International des Américanistes, Société des Américanistes, Musée de l'Homme, Paris.

———. 1978c. L'etude archéologique de l'échange dans les Andes. *Annales–Economies, Sociétés, Civilisations* 33:936–47.

———. 1986. Storage, supply and redistribution in the economy of the Inca state. In *Anthropological history of Andean polities,* edited by J. V. Murra, N. Wachtel, and J. Revel, pp. 59–68. Cambridge University Press, New York.

———. 1992. Huánuco pampa and Tunsukancha: Major and minor nodes in the Inca storage network. In *Inca storage systems,* edited by T. Y. LeVine, pp. 151–75. University of Oklahoma Press, Norman.

Morris, C., and D. E. Thompson. 1970. Huánuco Viejo: An Inca administrative center. *American Antiquity* 35:344–62.

Moseley, M. E. 1983. Central Andean civilizations. In *Ancient South Americans,* edited by J. D. Jennings, pp. 179–239. Freeman, San Francisco.

Moseley, M. E., and E. E. Deeds. 1982. The land in front of Chan Chan: Agrarian expansionism, reform, and collapse in the Moche valley. In *Chan Chan: Andean desert city,* edited by M. E. Moseley and K. C. Day, pp. 25–54. University of New Mexico Press, Albuquerque.

Müller-Beck, H. 1966. Paleohunters in America: Origins and diffusion. *Science* 152:1191–1210.

Mundkur, B. 1978. The alleged diffusion of Hindu divine symbols into pre-Columbian Mesoamerica: A critique. *Current Anthropology* 19:541–83.

———. 1979. The alleged diffusion of Hindu divine symbols into pre-Columbian Mesoamerica: A critique. *Current Anthropology* 20:167–71.

Muñoz Camargo, Diego. 1984. Descripción de la ciudad y provincia de Tlaxcala. In *Relaciones geográficas del siglo XVI: Tlaxcala,* edited by R. Acuña, vol. 1:25–286. Universidad Nacional Autónoma de México, México.

Murra, J. V. 1958. On Inca political structure. In *Systems of political control and bureaucracy in human societies,* edited by V. F. Ray, pp. 30–41. American Ethnological Society, Seattle.

———. 1964. Una apreciación etnológica de la visita. In *Visita hecha a la provincia de Chucuito por Garci Diez de San Miguel en el año 1567,* edited by W. Espinoza Soriano, pp. 419–44. Casa de la Cultura del Perú, Lima.

———. 1966. New data on retainer and servile population in Tawantinsuyu. In *Actas y Memorias del XXXVI Congreso Internacional de Americanistas,* vol. 2:35–45. Sevilla.

———. 1968. An Aymara kingdom in 1567. *Ethnohistory* 15:115–51. *([enlarged] 1975. Un reino aymara en 1567. In *Formaciones económicas y políticas del mundo andino,* edited by J. V. Murra, pp. 193–223. Instituto de Estudios Peruanos, Lima.)

———. 1970. Current research and prospects in Andean ethnohistory. *Latin American Research Review* 5:3–36.

———. 1972. El control vertical de un máximo de pisos ecológicos en las sociedades andinas. In *Visita de la provincia de León de Huánuco,* edited by I. Ortiz de Zúñiga, vol. 2:429–68. Universidad Nacional Hermilio Valdizán, Facultad de Letras y Educación, Huánuco.

———. 1975a. En torno a la estructura política de los Inca. In *Formaciones económicas y políticas del mundo andino,* edited by J. V. Murra, pp. 23–43. Instituto de Estudios Peruanos, Lima.

———. 1975b. El control vertical de un máximo de pisos ecológicos en las sociedades andinas. In *Formaciones económicas y políticas del mundo andino,* edited by J. V. Murra, pp. 59–116. Instituto de Estudios Peruanos, Lima.

———. 1975c. Nueva información sobre las poblaciones yana. In *Formaciones económicas y políticas del mundo andino,* edited by J. V. Murra, pp. 225–42. Instituto de Estudios Peruanos, Lima.

———. 1975d. El tráfico de mullu en la costa del Pacífico. In *Formaciones económicas y políticas del mundo andino,* edited by J. V. Murra, pp. 255–67. Instituto de Estudios Peruanos, Lima.

———. 1975e. Current research and prospects in Andean ethnohistory. In *Formaciones económicas y políticas del mundo andino,* pp. 275–312. Instituto de Estudios Peruanos, Lima.

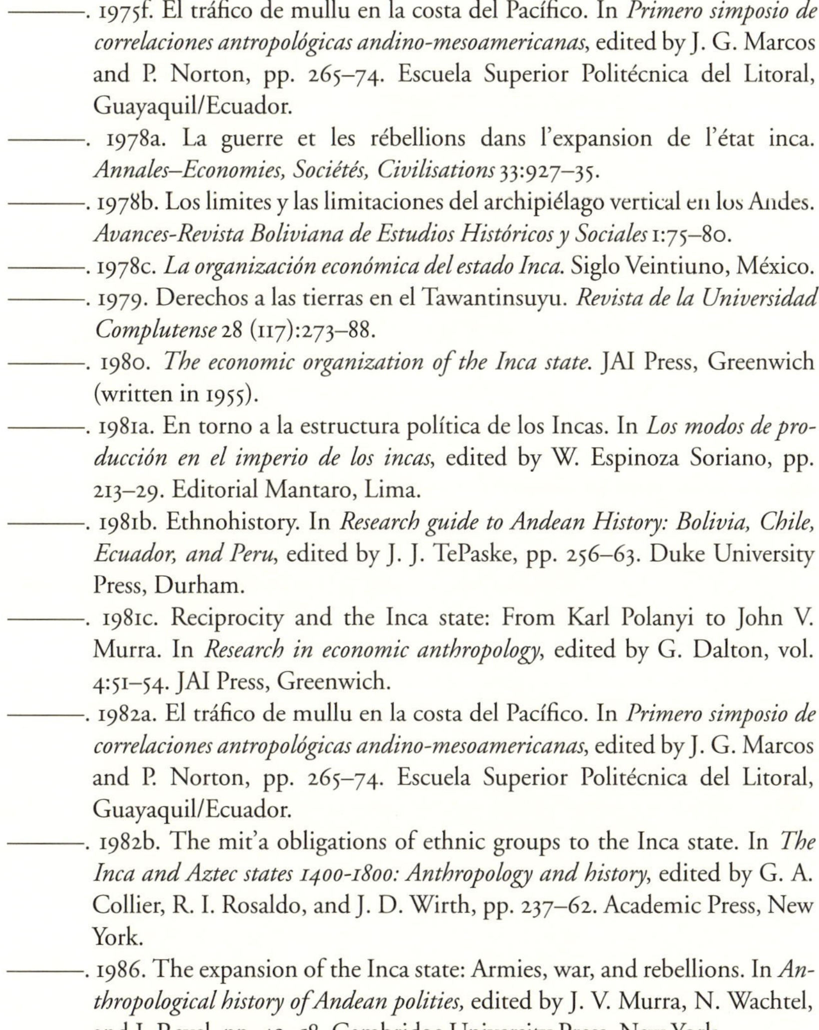

———. 1975f. El tráfico de mullu en la costa del Pacífico. In *Primero simposio de correlaciones antropológicas andino-mesoamericanas*, edited by J. G. Marcos and P. Norton, pp. 265–74. Escuela Superior Politécnica del Litoral, Guayaquil/Ecuador.

———. 1978a. La guerre et les rébellions dans l'expansion de l'état inca. *Annales–Economies, Sociétés, Civilisations* 33:927–35.

———. 1978b. Los limites y las limitaciones del archipiélago vertical en los Andes. *Avances-Revista Boliviana de Estudios Históricos y Sociales* 1:75–80.

———. 1978c. *La organización económica del estado Inca.* Siglo Veintiuno, México.

———. 1979. Derechos a las tierras en el Tawantinsuyu. *Revista de la Universidad Complutense* 28 (117):273–88.

———. 1980. *The economic organization of the Inca state.* JAI Press, Greenwich (written in 1955).

———. 1981a. En torno a la estructura política de los Incas. In *Los modos de producción en el imperio de los incas*, edited by W. Espinoza Soriano, pp. 213–29. Editorial Mantaro, Lima.

———. 1981b. Ethnohistory. In *Research guide to Andean History: Bolivia, Chile, Ecuador, and Peru*, edited by J. J. TePaske, pp. 256–63. Duke University Press, Durham.

———. 1981c. Reciprocity and the Inca state: From Karl Polanyi to John V. Murra. In *Research in economic anthropology*, edited by G. Dalton, vol. 4:51–54. JAI Press, Greenwich.

———. 1982a. El tráfico de mullu en la costa del Pacífico. In *Primero simposio de correlaciones antropológicas andino-mesoamericanas*, edited by J. G. Marcos and P. Norton, pp. 265–74. Escuela Superior Politécnica del Litoral, Guayaquil/Ecuador.

———. 1982b. The mit'a obligations of ethnic groups to the Inca state. In *The Inca and Aztec states 1400-1800: Anthropology and history*, edited by G. A. Collier, R. I. Rosaldo, and J. D. Wirth, pp. 237–62. Academic Press, New York.

———. 1986. The expansion of the Inca state: Armies, war, and rebellions. In *Anthropological history of Andean polities,* edited by J. V. Murra, N. Wachtel, and J. Revel, pp. 49–58. Cambridge University Press, New York.

Murra, J. V., ed. 1991. *Visita de los valles de Sonqo en los yunka de coca de la Paz (1568–1570).* Instituto de Cooperación Iberoamericana, Madrid.

Murra, J. V., and C. Morris. 1976. Dynastic oral tradition: Administrative records and archaeology in the Andes. *World Archaeology* 7:269–79.

Nelson, B. A. 1990. Observaciones acerca de la presencia tolteca en La Quemada, Zacatecas. In *Mesoamérica y el Norte de México, siglo IX–XII.* F. Sodi Miranda (Coord.), vol. 2:521–539. Instituto Nacional de Antropología e Historia, México.

Netherly, P. J. 1988. El reino de Chimor y el Tawantisuyu. In *La fronteras incas con el reino de Chimor.* 45 Congreso Internacional de Americanistas, Arqueología de las Américas, edited by T. D. Dillehay and P. Netherly, pp. 105–29. Fondo de Promoción de la Cultura, Bogotá.

Nichols, D. L. 1982. A middle formative irrigation system near Santa Clara Coatitlan in the Basin of Mexico. *American Antiquity* 47:133–44.

Nicholson, H. B. 1959. The Chapultepec cliff sculpture of Motecuhzoma Xocoyotzin. *El Mexico Antiguo* 9:379–423.

———. 1960. The Mixteca-Puebla concept in Mesoamerican archaeology; a reexamination. In *Men and Cultures.* Selected papers, Fifth International Congress of Anthropological and Ethnological Sciences, edited by A. F. C. Wallace, pp. 612–18. University of Pennsylvania Press, Philadelphia.

———. 1971. Religion in pre-Hispanic Central Mexico. In *Archaeology of Northern Mesoamerica,* edited by G. F. Ekholm and I. Bernal, pp. 395–446. Handbook of Middle American Indians, vol. 10, Part 1. R. Wauchope, general editor, University of Texas Press, Austin.

———. 1972. The problem of the historical identity of the Cerro Portezuelo/San Antonio archaeological site: An hypothesis. In *Teotihuacán,* edited by A. Ruz L., vol. 2:157–200. XI Mesa Redonda, Sociedad Mexicana de Antropología, México.

———. 1978. Western Mesoamerica: A.D. 900–1520. In *Chronologies in New World archaeology,* edited by R. W. Taylor and C. W. Meighan, pp. 285–329. Academic Press, New York.

———. 1987a. Iconography–Mesoamerican Iconography. In *Encyclopedia of Religion,* edited by M. Eliade and C. J. Adams, vol. 7:21–27. Macmillan, New York.

———. 1987b. Mesoamerican religions: Postclassic cultures. In *Encyclopedia of Religion,* edited by M. Eliade, vol. 9:419–28. Macmillan, New York.

Nicolau d'Olwer, L., H. F. Cline, and H. B. Nicholson. 1973. Bernardino de Sahagún, 1499–1590. In *Guide to Ethnohistorical Sources,* edited by H. F. Cline, pp. 186–239. Handbook of Middle American Indians, vol. 13. R. Wauchope, general editor. University of Texas Press, Austin.

Nowotny, K. A. 1961. *Tlacuilolli: die mexikanischen Bilderhandschriften.* Monumenta Americana 3. Gebrüder Mann, Berlin.

Nowotny, K. A., ed. 1961. *Codices Becker I/II.* Akademische Druck- und Verlagsanstalt, Graz.

———. 1975. *El Fragmento de Nochistlan.* Hamburgisches Museum für Völkerkunde, Hamburg.

———. 1976. *Codex Borgia: Biblioteca Apostolica Vaticana—Messicano Riserva 28* (recte: Cod. Borg. Messicano 1). Akademische Druck- und Verlagsanstalt, Graz.

Nowotny, K. A. (introduction and summary). 1968. *Codex Cospi: Calendario messicano 4093.* Akademische Druck- und Verlagsanstalt, Graz.

Nuñez A., L. 1978. Northern Chile. In *Chronologies in New World archaeology,* edited by R. E. Taylor and C. W. Meighan, pp. 483–512. Academic Press, New York.

Oberem, U. 1978. El acceso a recursos naturales de diferentes ecologías en la sierra ecuatoriana (siglo XVI). In *Organización social y complementaridad económica en los Andes centrales.* Coordinated by J. A. Flores Ochoa, vol. 4:51–64. Actes du XLIIe Congrès International des Américanistes, Société des Américanistes, Musée de l'Homme, Paris.

———. 1981a. El acceso a recursos naturales de diferentes ecologías en la sierra ecuatoriana (siglo XVI). In *Contribución a la etnohistoria ecuatoriana,* edited by S. Moreno Y. and U. Oberem, pp. 45–71. Instituto Otavaleño de Antropología, Otavalo/Ecuador.

———. 1981b. Los Caranquis de la sierra norte del Ecuador y su incorporación al Tahuantinsuyu. In *Contribución a la etnohistoria ecuatoriana,* edited by S. Moreno Y. and U. Oberem, pp. 73–101. Instituto Otavaleño de Antropología, Otavalo/Ecuador.

Oberem, U., and R. Hartmann. 1982. Zur Seefahrt in den Hochkulturen Altamerikas. In *Zur geschichtlichen Bedeutung der frühen Seefahrt,* edited by H. Müller-Karpe, pp. 121–57. C. H. Beck, München.

O'Brien, M. J., D. E. Lewarch, R. D. Mason, and J. A. Neely. 1980. Functional analysis of water control features at Monte Albán, Oaxaca, Mexico. *World Archaeology* 11:342–55.

Offner, J. A. 1979. A reassessment of the extent and structuring of the empire of Techotlalatzin, fourteenth century ruler of Texcoco. *Ethnohistory* 26:231–41.

———. 1980. Aztec political numerology and human sacrifice: The ideological ramifications of the number six. *Journal of Latin American Lore* 6:205–15.

———. 1983. *Law and politics in Aztec Texcoco.* Cambridge University Press, New York.

———. 1984. Household organization in the Texcocan heartland: The evidence of the Codex Vergara. In *Explorations in ethnohistory: Indians of Central Mexico in the sixteenth century,* edited by H. R. Harvey and H. J. Prem, pp. 127–46. University of New Mexico Press, Albuquerque.

Olivera, M. 1977. Papel de los pillis de Tecali en la sociedad prehispánica del siglo XVI. *Anales de Antropología* 14:257–80.

———. 1978. *Pillis y macehuales: Las formaciones sociales y los modos de producción de Tecali del siglo XII al XVI.* Centro de Investigaciones Superiores del Instituto de Antropología e Historia, México.

Olivera, M., and C. Reyes. 1969. Los choloques y los cholultecas: Apuntes sobre las relaciones étnicas en Cholula hasta el siglo XVI. *Anales del Instituto Nacional de Antropología e Historia* 1:247–74.

Olvia, J. A. 1895. *Historia del reino y provincias del Perú, de sus Incas reyes, decubrimiento y conquista por los españoles . . . ,* edited by J. F. Pazos Varela and L. Varela y Orbegoso. Imprenta y Libraría de S. Pedro, Lima.

Orellana, S. 1984. *The Tzutujil Maya: Continuity and change, 1250–1630.* University of Oklahoma Press, Norman.

Orlove, B. S. 1977. Integration through production: The use of zonation in Espinar. *American Ethnologist* 4:84–101.

Ortiz de Montellano, B. R. 1978. Aztec cannibalism: An ecological necessity. *Science* 200:611–17.

———. 1979. El canibalismo azteca ¿una necesidad ecológica? *Anales de Antropología* 16:155–82.

Ortiz de Zúñiga, I. 1967–1972. *Visita de la provincia de León de Huánuco*, edited by J. V. Murra. 2 vols. Universidad Nacional Hermilio Valdizán, Facultad de Letras y Educación, Huánuco/Perú.

Pachacuti Yamqui Salcamayhua, Joan de Santa Cruz. 1968. Relación de antigüedades deste reyno del Peru. In *Crónicas peruanas de interés indígena*, edited by F. Esteve Barba, pp. 279–319. Atlas, Madrid.

Padden, R. C. 1967. *The hummingbird and the hawk: Conquest and sovereignty in the Valley of Mexico, 1503–1541.* Ohio State University Press, Columbus.

Paddock, J. 1966. Mixtec ethnohistory and Monte Albán V. In *Ancient Oaxaca: Discoveries in Mexican Archeology and History*, edited by J. Paddock, pp. 367–85. Stanford University Press, Stanford.

———. 1982. Confluence in Zapotec and Mixtec ethnohistory: The 1580 Mapa de Macuilxochitl. *Papers in Anthropology-University of Oklahoma* 23:345–57.

———. 1983a. The Oaxaca barrio at Teotihuacán. In *The Cloud People: Divergent evolution of the Zapotec and Mixtec civilizations*, edited by K. V. Flannery and J. Marcus, pp. 170–75. Academic Press, New York.

———. 1983b. Mixtec impact on the postclassic Valley of Oaxaca. In *The Cloud People: Divergent evolution of the Zapotec and Mixtec civilizations*, edited by K. V. Flannery and J. Marcus, pp. 272–77. Academic Press, New York.

Padilla Bendezú, A. 1979. *Huamán Poma; El Indio cronista dibujante.* Fondo de Cultura Económica, México.

Palerm, A. 1972. La teoría de la sociedad oriental aplicada: Mesoamérica. In *Agricultura y sociedad en Mesoamérica*, edited by A. Palerm, pp. 160–95. Secretaría de Educación Pública, México.

———. 1973. *Obras hidráulicas prehispánicas en el sistema lacustre del Valle de México.* Instituto de Antropología e Historia, Seminario de Etnohistoria del Valle de México, México.

Parsons, J. R. 1974. The development of a prehistoric complex society: A regional perspective from the Valley of Mexico. *Journal of Field Archaeology* 1:81–108.

———. 1976. The role of chinampa agriculture in the food supply of Aztec Tenochtitlan. In *Cultural change and continuity: Essays in honor of James Bennett Griffin*, edited by C. E. Cleland, pp. 233–62. Academic Press, New York.

Parsons, L. A. 1969. *Bilbao, Guatemala: An archaeological study of the Pacific coast Cotzumalhuapa Region.* Milwaukee Public Museum Publications in Anthropology, Nos. 11, 12. Milwaukee.

———. 1981. Post-Olmec stone sculpture: The Olmec-Izapan transition on the southern Pacific coast and highlands. In *The Olmec and their neighbors,* edited by E. P. Benson, pp. 257-88. Dumbarton Oaks, Washington.

Paso y Troncoso, F. del, ed. 1905. *Suma de visitas, in Papeles de Nueva España: Segunda serie, geografía y estadistica.* Vol. 1. Est. Tipográfico "Sucesores de Rivadeneyra," Madrid.

Pasztory, E. 1982. *Aztec Art.* H. N. Abrams, New York.

Patterson, T. C. 1991. *The Inca empire: The formation and disintegration of a pre-capitalist state.* St. Martin's Press, New York.

Paulsen, A. C. 1976. Environment and empire, climatic factors in prehistoric Andean culture change. *World Archaeology* 8:121–32.

———. 1977. Patterns of maritime trade between south coastal Ecuador and Western Mesoamerica, 1500 B.C.–A.D. 600. In *The sea in the pre-columbian world,* edited by E. P. Benson, pp. 140–66. Dumbarton Oaks, Washington.

———. 1981. The archaeology of the absurd, comments on Conrad (Cultural materialism, split inheritance, and the expansion of ancient Peruvian empires). *American Antiquity* 48:31–37.

Pease G. Y., F. 1972. *Los últimos incas del Cuzco.* Ediciones P. L. V., Lima.

———. 1978. Las fuentes del siglo XVI y la formación del Tawantinsuyu. In *Del Tawantinsuyu a la historia del Perú,* edited by F. Pease G. Y., pp. 31–114. Instituto de Estudios Peruanos, Lima.

———. 1979. La formación del Tawantinsuyo: Mecanismos de colonización y relación con unidades étnicas. *Historica–Pontificia Universidad Católica del Perú* 3:79–120.

———. 1980. Los Incas. In *Historia del Perú,* coordinated by F. Silva Santisteban, vol. 2:187–293. Editorial J. Mejaía Baca, Lima.

———. 1981. Ayllu y parcialidad: Reflexiones sobre el caso de Collaguas. In *Etnohistoria y antropología andina* (Segunda Jornada del Museo Nacional de Historia), edited by A. Castelli, M. Koth de Paredes, and M. Mould de Pease, pp. 15–33. (s.n.), Lima.

———. 1982. The formation of Tawantinsuyu: Mechanisms of colonization and relationship with ethnic groups. In *The Inca and Aztec states 1400–1800: Anthropology and history,* edited by G. A. Collier, R. I. Rosaldo, and J. D. Wirth, pp. 173–98. Academic Press, New York.

———. 1984. Cieza de León y la tercera parte de la Crónica del Perú. *Revista Interamericana de Bibliografía* 34:403–20.

———. 1988a. Las crónicas y los andes. *Revista de Crítica Literaria Latinoamericana (Lima)* 14:117–58.

———. 1988b. Nota sobre una nueva edición de la suma y narración de los incas. *Historica–Pontificia Universidad Católica del Perú* 12:183–92.

———. 1991. *Los últimos incas del Cuzco.* Alianza Editorial, Madrid.

Pérez-Rocha, E. 1982. *La tierra y el hombre en la Villa de Tacuba durante la época colonial.* Instituto Nacional de Antropología e Historia, México.

Phillips, P. 1966. The role of transpacific contacts in the development of New World pre-Columbian civilizations. In *Archaeological Frontiers and External Connections*, edited by G. F. Ekholm and G. R. Willey, pp. 296–315. Handbook of Middle American Indians, vol. 4. R. Wauchope, general editor. University of Texas Press, Austin.

Piho, V. 1972. Tlacatecutli, tlacochtecutli, tlacatecatl y tlacochcalcatl. *Estudios de Cultura Nahuatl* 10:315–28.

———. 1976. Esquema provisional de la organización militar mexica. In Actas del 41 Congreso Internacional de Americanistas, *Historia e Historiografía precolombinas*, coordinated by R. van Zantwijk, vol. 2:169–78. Instituto Nacional de Antropología e Historia, México.

Piña Chan, R., M. Covarrubias, and L. Covarrubias. 1964. *El pueblo del jaguar: Los olmecas arqueológicos.* Consejo para la Planeacion e Instalacion del Museo Nacional de Antropología, México.

Polanyi, K., 1957. The economy as instituted process. In *Trade and market in the early empires*, edited by K. Polanyi, C.M. Arensberg and H.W. Pearson, pp. 243–70. Free Press, Glencoe.

Pollard, H. P. 1993. *Taríacuri's legacy, the prehispanic Tarascan state.* University of Oklahoma Press, Norman.

Pollock, H. E. D. 1980. *The Puuc, an architectural survey of the hill country of Yucatan and northern Campeche, Mexico.* Memoirs of the Peabody Museum of Archaeology and Ethnology 19, Harvard University, Cambridge.

Polo de Ondegardo, J. 1916a. Los errores y supersticiones de los Indios, sacadas del tratado y averiguaciones que hizo el licenciado . . . In *Colección de libros y documentos referentes a la historia del Perú*, edited by H. H. Urteaga and C. A. Romero, series 1, vol. 3:1–43. Sanmartí y ca., Lima.

———. 1916b. Del linage de los Ingas y como extendieron sus conquistas. In *Colección de libros y documentos referentes a la historia del Perú*, edited by H. H. Urteaga and C. A. Romero, series 1, vol. 4:45–138. Sanmartí y ca., Lima.

———. 1917. Relación de los adoratorios de los Indios en los cuatro caminos (zeques) que salían del Cuzco. In *Colección de libros y documentos referentes a la historia del Perú*, edited by H. H. Urteaga and C. A. Romero, series 1, vol. 4:3–44. Sanmartí y ca., Lima.

Pomar, Juan Bautista. 1891. Relación de Texcoco. In *Nueva colección de documentos para la historia de Mexico*, edited by Joaquín García Icazbalceta, Bd. 3, 1–69. México.

———. 1941. Relación de Texcoco. In *Nueva colección de documentos para la historia de Mexico*, edited by Joaquín García Icazbalceta, vol. 3:1–64. Editorial Salvador Chávez Hayhoe, México.

Porras Barrenechea, R. 1986. *Los cronistas del Perú (1528–1650) y otros ensayos.* Edición, prologo y notas de F. Pease G. Y., 2nd revised ed. Banco Crédito del Perú: Ministerio de Educación, Lima.

Posnansky, A. 1945. *Tiahuanacu: The cradle of American man.* Vol. 1–2, J. J. Augustin, New York.

———. 1957. *Tiahuanacu: The cradle of American man.* Vol. 3–4, translated by J. F. Shearer, edición bilingue ingles-castellano. Ministerio de Educación, La Paz.

Potter, D. F. 1977. *Maya architecture of the Central Yucatan Peninsula.* Middle American Research Institute, Publication No. 44. Tulane University, New Orleans.

Pozorski, S., and T. Pozorski. 1987. *Early settlement and subsistence in the Casma Valley, Peru.* University of Iowa Press, Iowa City.

Pozorski, T., and S. Pozorski. 1987. Chavín, the Early Horizon and the Initial Period. In *The origins and development of the Andean state,* edited by J. Haas, S. Pozorski, and T. Pozorski, pp. 36–46. Cambridge University Press, New York.

Prem, H. J. 1974. *Matrícula de Huexotzinco.* Akademische Druck- und Verlagsanstalt, Graz.

———. 1977. Was hielt Teotihuacán am Leben? Folgerungen aus der ökonomischen Situation der ältesten Metropole Mesoamerikas. *Lateinamerika-Studien* 3:100–119.

———. 1978. *Milpa y Hacienda: La tenencia de la tierra indígena y española en la cuenca del Alto Atoyac, Puebla, México, (1520–1650).* Steiner, Wiesbaden.

———. 1979a. Methodische Forderungen an den Nachweis transpazifischer Kulturkontakte. *Archiv für Völkerkunde* 33:7–14.

———. 1979b. Aztec writing considered as a paradigm for Mesoamerican scripts. In *Mesoamérica,* edited by B. Dahlgren, pp. 104–18. Instituto Nacional de Antropología e Historia, México.

———. 1983. Das Chronologieproblem in der autochthonen Tradition Zentralmexikos. *Zeitschrift für Ethnologie* 108:133–61.

———. 1984a. Die Herrscherfolge von Colhuacan (Chronologische Miszellen IV). *Mexicon* 6:86–89.

———. 1984b. The chronological dilemma. In Proceedings of the Forty-fourth International Congress of Americanists—Symposium: *The native sources and the history of the Valley of Mexico,* edited by J. de Durand-Forest, pp. 5–25. BAR International Series 204, London.

———. 1988. *Milpa y Hacienda: La tenencia de la tierra indígena y española en la cuenca del Alto Atoyac, Puebla, México, (1520–1650).* CIESAS, México.

———. 1991 ¿Conceptos cosmológicos o racionalidad política en la organización territorial del México Central? In *América; religión y cosmos,* edited by J. A. Muñoz Mendoza, pp. 215–39. Diputación Provincial de Granada, Granada.

———. 1992. Aztec writing. In *Epigraphy,* edited by V. R. Bricker. Handbook of Middle American Indians Supplement, vol. 5:53–69. V. R. Bricker, general editor. University of Texas Press, Austin.

———. 1996. *Die Azteken, Geschichte, Kultur, Religion.* Verlag C. H. Beck, München.

Prem, H. J., and U. Dyckerhoff, eds. 1986a. *Das alte Mexiko.* Bertelsmann Verlag, München.

———. 1986b. *El Antiguo México.* Plaza y Janés, Esplugues de Llobregat.

———. 1987. *Le Mexique Ancien.* Bordas, Paris.

Price, B. J. 1974. Prehispanic chiefdoms in the Americas: Implications for urban development. In *Atti del XL Congresso Internazionale degli Americanisti,* edited by E. Cerulli, vol. 4:69–78. Tilgher, Roma-Genova.

———. 1980. The truth is not in accounts but in account books; on the epistemological status of history. In *Beyond the myths of culture, essays in cultural materialism,* edited by E. B. Ross, pp. 155–80. Academic Press, New York.

Proskouriakoff, T. 1950. *A study of classic Maya sculpture.* Carnegie Institution of Washington Publication 593, Washington.

———. 1960. Historical implications of a pattern of dates at Piedras Negras, Guatemala. *American Antiquity* 25:454–75.

———. 1961. The lords of the Maya realm. *Expedition* 4:14-21.

———. 1963. Historical data in the inscriptions of Yaxchilán. *Estudios de Cultura Maya* 3:149–69.

———. 1964. Historical data in the inscriptions of Yaxchilán. *Estudios de Cultura Maya* 4:177–202.

Protzen, J.-P. 1993. *Inca architecture and construction at Ollantaytambo.* Oxford University Press, New York.

Puleston, D. E. 1977. The art and archaeology of hydraulic agriculture in the Maya lowlands. In *Social process in Maya prehistory,* edited by N. Hammond, pp. 449–67. Academic Press, New York.

———. 1982. The role of ramón in Maya subsistence. In *Maya subsistence,* edited by K. V. Flannery, pp. 353–66. Academic Press, New York.

Puleston, D. E., and O. S. Puleston. 1974. An ecological approach to the origins of Maya civilization. *Archaeology* 24:33–37.

Quezada Ramírez, M. N. 1972. *Los Matlatzincas: Epoca prehispánica y época colonial hasta 1650.* Instituto Nacional de Antropología e Historia, México.

Quiñones Keber, E. 1995. *Codex Telleriano-Remensis: Ritual, Divination, and History in a Pictorial Aztec Manuscript.* University of Texas Press, Austin.

Radicati di Primeglio, C. N.d. *El sistema contable de los incas.* Librería Studium, Lima.

Raffino, R. A. 1981. *Los Incas del Kollasuyu: Origen, naturaleza y transfiguraciones de la ocupación Inca en los Andes meridionales.* Ramos Americana, La Plata/Buenos Aires.

Ramírez, S. 1985. Social frontiers and the territorial base of curacazgos. In *Andean ecology and civilization: An interdisciplinary perspective on Andean ecological complementarity,* edited by S. Masuda, I. Shimada, and C. Morris, pp. 423–42. University of Tokyo Press, Tokyo.

Ramírez Horton, S. E. 1978. Cherrepe en 1572: un analisis de la visita general del virrey Francisco de Toledo. *Historia y Cultura* 11:79–121.

Rammow, H. 1964. *Die Verwandtschaftsbezeichnungen im klassischen Aztekischen.* Im Selbstverlag des Hamburgischen Museums für Völkerkunde und Vorgeschichte, Hamburg.

Ramos Gavilán, Alonso. 1976 (ca. 1570). *Historia del celebre santuario de Nuestra Señora de Copacabana,* edited by J. Muñoz Reyes, Academia Boliviana de la Historia, La Paz.

Ramusio, G. B. 1556. Relatione di alcune cose della Nuovo Spagna . . . fatta per uno gentil'huomo del signor Fernando Cortese. In *Terzo volume della navigationi et viaggi* . . . . Nella Stamperia de Giunti, Venezia.

Rathje, W. L. 1971. The origins and development of lowland classic Maya civilization. *American Antiquity* 36:275–85.

———. 1972. Praise the gods and pass the metates: A hypothesis of the development of lowland rainforest civilizations in Mesoamerica. In *Contemporary archaeology,* edited by M. P. Leone, pp. 365–92. Southern Illinois University Press, Carbondale.

———. 1973. Classic Maya development and denouement: A research design. In *The classic Maya collapse,* edited by T. P. Culbert, pp. 405–54. University of New Mexico Press, Albuquerque.

———. 1977. The Tikal connection. In *The origins of Maya civilization,* edited by R. E. W. Adams, pp. 373–82. University of New Mexico Press, Albuquerque.

Recinos, A. 1957. *Crónicas indígenas de Guatemala.* Editorial Universitaria, Guatemala.

Recinos, A., ed. 1950. *Memorial de Sololá: Anales de los Cakchiqueles, Título de los señores de Totonicapán,* translated by Dionisio José Chonay. Fondo de Cultura Económica, México.

Recinos, A., and D. Goetz, transl. 1953. *The Annals of the Cakchiquels/Title of the Lords of Totonicapán.* University of Oklahoma Press, Norman.

Redmond, E. M. 1983. *A fuego y sangre: Early Zapotec imperialism in the Cuicatlán Cañada, Oaxaca.* University of Michigan, Museum of Anthropology, Ann Arbor.

Regal, A. 1936. *Los caminos del Inca en el antiguo Perú.* Sanmartí y ca., Lima.

Regalado de Hurtado, L. 1981. La relación de Titu Cusi Yupanqui: Valor de un testimonio tardío. *Historica–Pontificia Universidad Católica del Perú* 5:45–61.

Rendón, S., transl. 1965. *Relaciones originales de Chalco Amaquemecan, escritas por don Francisco de San Antón Muñón Chimalpahin Cuauhtlehuanitzin.* Fondo de Cultura Económica, México.

Renfrew, C. 1986. Introduction: Peer polity interaction and sociopolitical change. In *Peer polity interaction and sociopolitical change,* edited by C. Renfrew and J. F. Cherry, pp. 1–18. Cambridge University Press, New York.

———. 1994. Towards a cognitive archaeology. In *The ancient mind, elements of cognitive archaeology,* edited by C. Renfrew and E. B. W. Zubrow, pp. 3–12. Cambridge University Press, Cambridge.

Reyes García, L. 1977. *Cuauhtinchan del siglo XII al XVI: Formación y desarrollo histórico de un señorío prehispánico.* Steiner, Wiesbaden.

———. 1979a. Comentarios. In *El trabajo y los trabajadores en la historia de México*—Ponencias y comentarios presentados en la V Reunión de Historiadores Mexicanos y Norteamericanos, Pátzcuaro, 12 a 15 de octubre de 1977, edited by E. C. Frost, M. C. Meyer, and J. Z. Vázquez, pp. 41–66. Colegio de México, México.

———. 1979b. La visión cosmológica y la organización del imperio mexica. In *Mesoamérica: Homenaje al doctor Paul Kirchhoff,* edited by B. Dahlgren, pp. 34–40. Instituto Nacional de Antropología e Historia, México.

Rice, D. S. 1976. Middle preclassic Maya settlement in the central Maya lowland. *Journal of Field Archaeology* 3:425–45.

Rice, D. S., and P. M. Rice. 1981. Muralla de Leon: A lowland Maya fortification. *Journal of Field Archaeology* 8:271–88.

Riese, B. 1982. Kriegsberichte der klassischen Maya. *Baessler Archiv, Neue Folge* 30:255–321.

———. 1986a. Die Maya. In *Das alte Mexiko,* edited by H. J. Prem and U. Dyckerhoff, pp. 154–89. Bertelsmann Verlag, München.

———. 1986b. Late classic relationship between Copán and Quiriguá: Some epigraphic evidence. In *The southeast Maya periphery,* edited by P. A. Urban and E. M. Schortmann, pp. 94–101. University of Texas Press, Austin.

———. 1986c. *Ethnographische Dokumente aus Neuspanien im Umfeld der Codex Magliabechi-Gruppe.* F. Steiner Verlag, Stuttgart.

———. 1992. The Copán dynasty. In *Epigraphy,* edited by V. R. Bricker. Handbook of Middle American Indians Supplement, vol. 5:128–53. V. R. Bricker, general editor. University of Texas Press, Austin.

Rindos, D. 1984. *The origins of agriculture: An evolutionary perspective.* Academic Press, New York.

Rivera Dorado, M. 1982. *Los Mayas, una sociedad oriental.* Universidad Complutense, Madrid.

Robicsek, F., and D. Hales. 1984. Maya heart sacrifice, cultural perspective and surgical technique. In *Ritual human sacrifice in Mesoamerica,* edited by E. H. Boone, pp. 49–90. Dumbarton Oaks, Washington.

Rojas, J. L. de. 1986. *México Tenochtitlán: Economía y sociedad en el siglo XVI.* Fondo de Cultura Económica, México.

———. 1994. Los aztecas ¿cultura arqueológica o cultura con arqueología? *Revista Española de Antropología Americana* 24:75–92.

Rojas Rabiela, T. 1979a. *El trabajo y los trabajadores en la Historia de México.* Colegio de México, México.

———. 1979b. La organización del trabajo para las obras públicas: El coatequitl y las cuadrillas de trabajadores. In *El trabajo y los trabajadores en la historia de México*—Ponencias y comentarios presentados en la V Reunión de Historiadores Mexicanos y Norteamericanos, Pátzcuaro, 12 a 15 de octubre de 1977, edited by E. C. Frost, M. C. Meyer, and J. Z. Vázquez, pp. 41–66. Colegio de México, México.

Romero Galván, J. R. 1977. Las fuentes de las diferentes historias originales del Chimalpahin. *Journal de la Société des Americanistes* 64:51–56.

Romero Giordano, C. 1986. *Moctezuma II: El misterio de su muerte.* 2nd ed. Panorama Editorial, México.

Roosevelt, A. C. 1984. Population, health, and the evolution of subsistence: Conclusions from the conference. In *Paleopathology and the origins of agriculture,* edited by M. N. Cohen and G. J. Armelagos, pp. 559–83. Academic Press, New York.

Rostworowski de Diez Canseco, M. 1953. *Pachacutec Inca Yupanqui.* Lima.

———. 1962. Nuevos datos sobre tenencia de tierras reales en el Incario. *Revista del Museo Nacional, Lima* 31:130–64.

———. 1964. Nuevos aportes para el estudio de la medición de tierra en el virreynato e incario. *Revista del Archivo Nacional del Perú* 28:31–58.

———. 1966. Las tierras reales y su mano de obra en el Tahuantinsuyu. In *Actas y Memorias del XXXVI Congreso Internacional de Americanistas,* vol. 2:31–34. Sevilla.

———. 1970. Mercaderes del Valle de Chincha en la época prehispánica: Un documento y unos comentarios. *Revista Española de Antropología Americana* 5:135–62.

———. 1972. Las etnías del valle del Chillón. *Revista del Museo Nacional, Lima* 38:250–314.

———. 1975a. La "visita" a Chinchaycocha de 1549. *Anales Científicos, Universidad Nacional del Centro del Perú (Huancayo)* 4:73–88.

———. 1975b. Pescadores, artesanos y mercaderes costeños en el Perú prehispánico. *Revista del Museo Nacional, Lima* 41:311–49.

———. 1976. Reflexiones sobre la reciprocidad andina. *Revista del Museo Nacional, Lima* 42:341–54.

———. 1977a. La estratificación social y el hatun curaca en el mundo andino. *Historica–Pontificia Universidad Católica del Perú* 1:249–86.

———. 1977b. Pescadores, artesanos y mercaderes costeños en el Perú prehispánico. In *Etnía y sociedad: Costa peruana prehispánica,* edited by M. Rostworowski de Diez Canseco, pp. 211–71. Instituto de Estudios Peruanos, Lima.

———. 1977c. Coastal fishermen, merchants, and artisans in pre-hispanic Peru. In *The sea in the pre-columbian world,* edited by E. P. Benson, pp. 167–88. Dumbarton Oaks, Washington.

———. 1977d. Las etnías del valle del Chillón. In *Etnía y sociedad: Costa peruana prehispánica,* edited by M. Rostworowski de Diez Canseco, pp. 21–95. Instituto de Estudios Peruanos, Lima.

———. 1977e. Mercaderes del Valle de Chincha en la época prehispánica: Un documento y unos comentarios. In *Etnía y sociedad: Costa peruana*

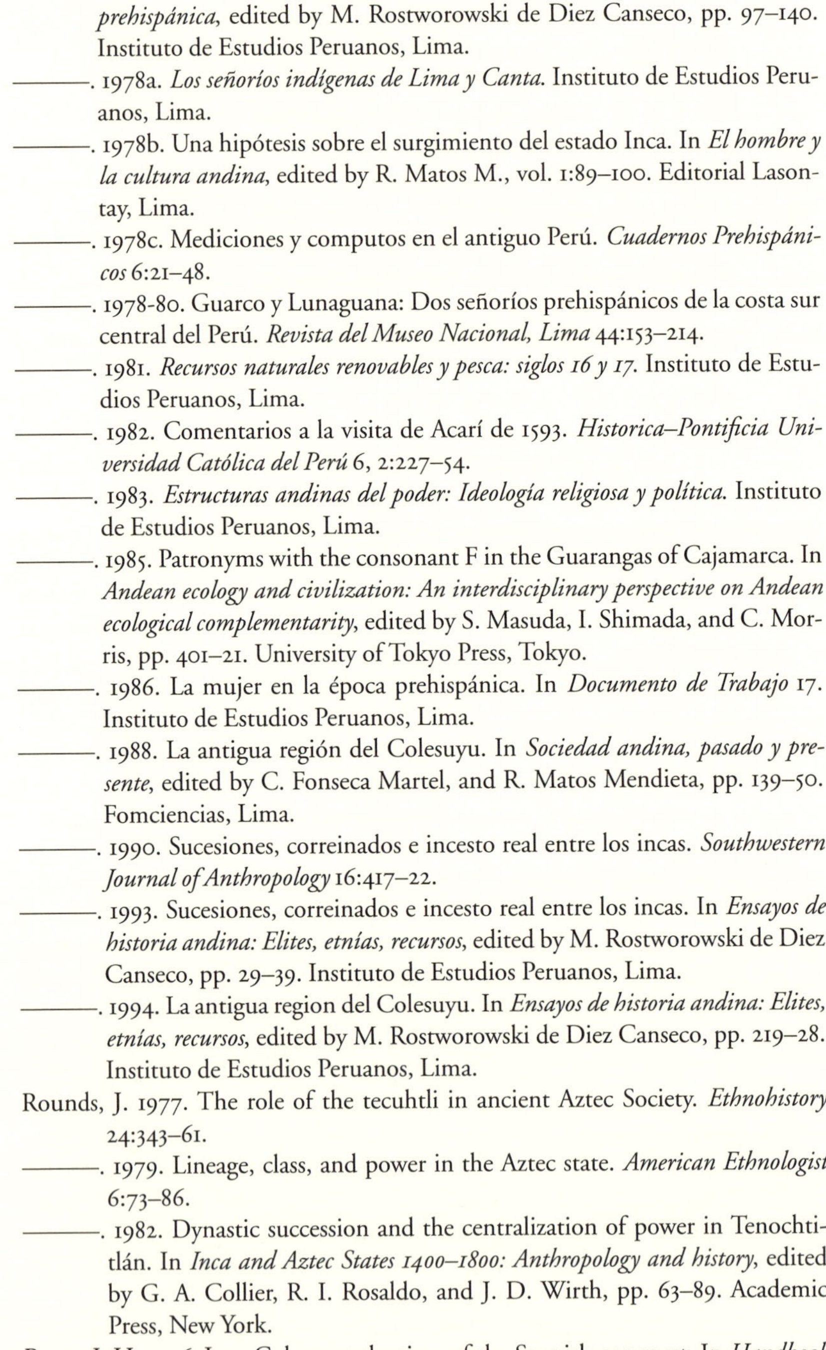

prehispánica, edited by M. Rostworowski de Diez Canseco, pp. 97–140. Instituto de Estudios Peruanos, Lima.

———. 1978a. *Los señoríos indígenas de Lima y Canta.* Instituto de Estudios Peruanos, Lima.

———. 1978b. Una hipótesis sobre el surgimiento del estado Inca. In *El hombre y la cultura andina*, edited by R. Matos M., vol. 1:89–100. Editorial Lasontay, Lima.

———. 1978c. Mediciones y computos en el antiguo Perú. *Cuadernos Prehispánicos* 6:21–48.

———. 1978-80. Guarco y Lunaguana: Dos señoríos prehispánicos de la costa sur central del Perú. *Revista del Museo Nacional, Lima* 44:153–214.

———. 1981. *Recursos naturales renovables y pesca: siglos 16 y 17.* Instituto de Estudios Peruanos, Lima.

———. 1982. Comentarios a la visita de Acarí de 1593. *Historica–Pontificia Universidad Católica del Perú* 6, 2:227–54.

———. 1983. *Estructuras andinas del poder: Ideología religiosa y política.* Instituto de Estudios Peruanos, Lima.

———. 1985. Patronyms with the consonant F in the Guarangas of Cajamarca. In *Andean ecology and civilization: An interdisciplinary perspective on Andean ecological complementarity*, edited by S. Masuda, I. Shimada, and C. Morris, pp. 401–21. University of Tokyo Press, Tokyo.

———. 1986. La mujer en la época prehispánica. In *Documento de Trabajo* 17. Instituto de Estudios Peruanos, Lima.

———. 1988. La antigua región del Colesuyu. In *Sociedad andina, pasado y presente*, edited by C. Fonseca Martel, and R. Matos Mendieta, pp. 139–50. Fomciencias, Lima.

———. 1990. Sucesiones, correinados e incesto real entre los incas. *Southwestern Journal of Anthropology* 16:417–22.

———. 1993. Sucesiones, correinados e incesto real entre los incas. In *Ensayos de historia andina: Elites, etnías, recursos*, edited by M. Rostworowski de Diez Canseco, pp. 29–39. Instituto de Estudios Peruanos, Lima.

———. 1994. La antigua region del Colesuyu. In *Ensayos de historia andina: Elites, etnías, recursos*, edited by M. Rostworowski de Diez Canseco, pp. 219–28. Instituto de Estudios Peruanos, Lima.

Rounds, J. 1977. The role of the tecuhtli in ancient Aztec Society. *Ethnohistory* 24:343–61.

———. 1979. Lineage, class, and power in the Aztec state. *American Ethnologist* 6:73–86.

———. 1982. Dynastic succession and the centralization of power in Tenochtitlán. In *Inca and Aztec States 1400–1800: Anthropology and history*, edited by G. A. Collier, R. I. Rosaldo, and J. D. Wirth, pp. 63–89. Academic Press, New York.

Rowe, J. H. 1946. Inca Culture at the time of the Spanish conquest. In *Handbook of South American Indians*, edited by J. H. Steward, vol. 2:183–330. Smithsonian Institution, Bureau of American Ethnology, Washington.

———. 1948. The kingdom of Chimor. *Acta Americana* 6:26–59.

———. 1962a. Stages and periods in archaeological interpretation. *Southwestern Journal of Anthropology* 18:1–27.

———. 1962b. *Chavín art: An inquiry into its form and meaning.* Museum of Primitive Art, New York.

———. 1970. El reino de Chimor. In *100 años de arqueología en el Perú*, edited by R. Ravines, pp. 321–55. Instituto de Estudios Peruanos, Lima.

———. 1979. An account of the shrines of ancient Cuzco. *Ñawpa Pacha* 17:1–80.

———. 1982. Inca policies and institutions relating to the cultural unification of the empire. In *The Inca and Aztec states 1400–1800: Anthropology and history*, edited by G. A. Collier, R. I. Rosaldo, and J. D. Wirth, pp. 93–118. Academic Press, New York.

Roys, R. L., transl. 1967. *The Book of Chilam Balam of Chumayel.* University of Oklahoma Press, Norman.

Rust, W. F., III. 1992. New ceremonial and settlement evidence at La Venta, and its relation to preclassic Maya cultures. In *New Theories on the Ancient Maya*, edited by E. C. Danien and R. J. Sharer, pp. 123–29. University Museum Monograph 77. The University Museum, University of Pennsylvania, Philadelphia.

Ruz Lhuillier, A. 1962. Chichén Itzá y Tula: Comentarios a un ensayo. *Estudios de Cultura Maya* 2:205–20.

———. 1973. *El templo de las inscripciones: Palenque.* Collección Cientifica Arqueología 7, Instituto Nacional de Antropología e Historia, México.

Saavedra, B. 1913. *El ayllu: Estudios sociológicos sobre América.* P. Ollendorf, Paris.

Sabloff, J. A. 1973. Continuity and disruption during terminal late classic times at Seibal: Ceramic and other evidence. In *The classic Maya collapse*, edited by T. P. Culbert, pp. 107–31. University of New Mexico Press, Albuquerque.

———. 1977. Old myths, new myths: The role of sea traders in the development of ancient Maya civilization. In *The sea in the pre-columbian world*, edited by E. P. Benson, pp. 67–88. Dumbarton Oaks, Washington.

Sachse, U. 1963. Zum Problem der zweiten gesellschaftlichen Arbeitsteilung bei den Azteca: Historische Quellen und sprachliche Analysen. *Wissenschaftliche Zeitschrift der Humboldt-Universität Berlin, Ges.-Sprachw. Reihe* 12:851–79.

Sahagún, B. de. 1950–1982. *Florentine Codex: General history of the things of New Spain*, edited by A. J. O. Anderson and C. E. Dibble, 13 vols., Monographs of the School of American Research, Santa Fe.

———. 1956 (1590) *Historia general de las cosas de Nueva España*, edited by A.M. Garibay K., 4 vols. Editorial Porrúa, México

Saignes, T. 1978. De la filiation a la résidence: Les ethnies dans les vallées de Larecaja. *Annales–Economies, Sociétés, Civilisations* 33:1160–81.

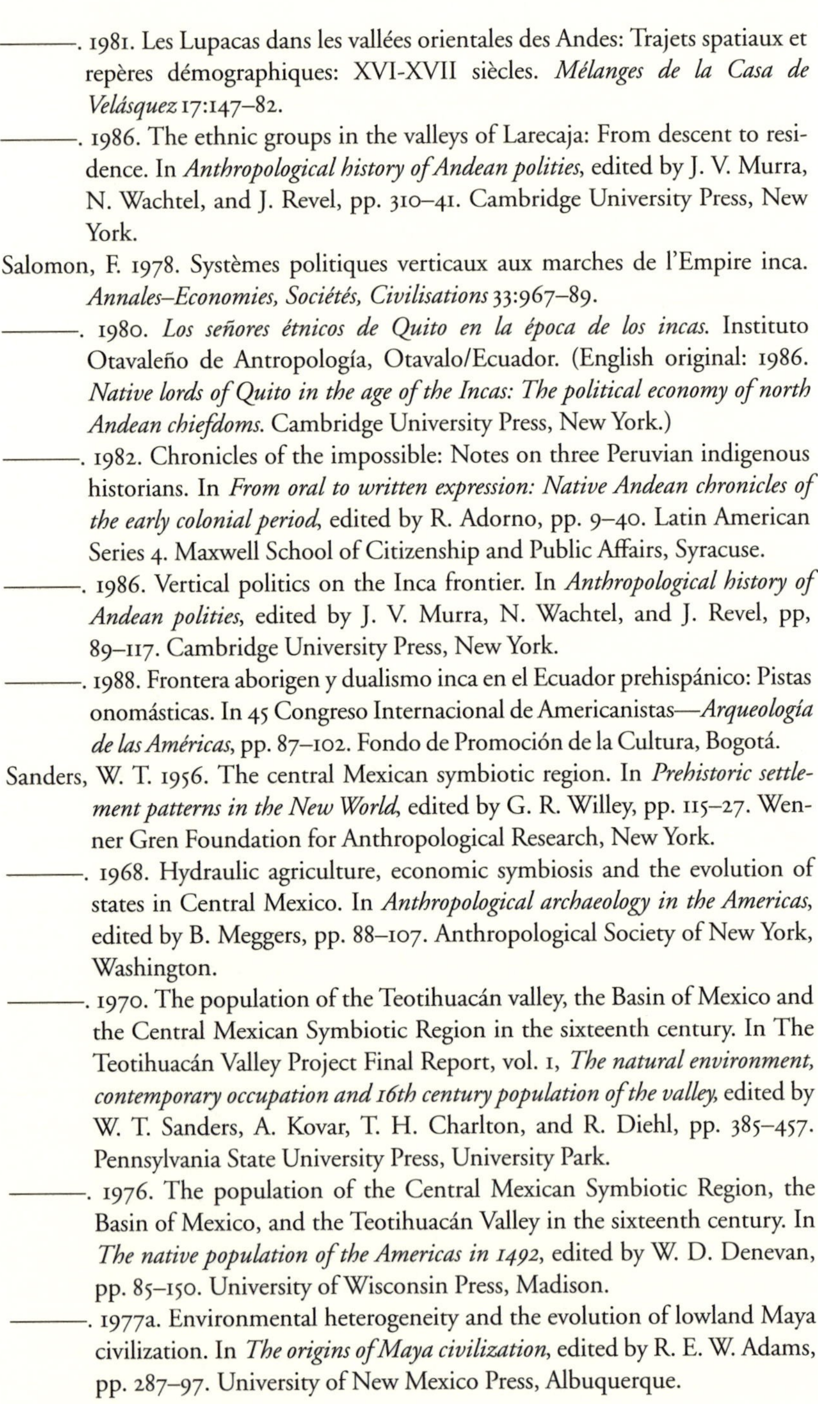

———. 1981. Les Lupacas dans les vallées orientales des Andes: Trajets spatiaux et repères démographiques: XVI-XVII siècles. *Mélanges de la Casa de Velásquez* 17:147–82.

———. 1986. The ethnic groups in the valleys of Larecaja: From descent to residence. In *Anthropological history of Andean polities*, edited by J. V. Murra, N. Wachtel, and J. Revel, pp. 310–41. Cambridge University Press, New York.

Salomon, F. 1978. Systèmes politiques verticaux aux marches de l'Empire inca. *Annales–Economies, Sociétés, Civilisations* 33:967–89.

———. 1980. *Los señores étnicos de Quito en la época de los incas.* Instituto Otavaleño de Antropología, Otavalo/Ecuador. (English original: 1986. *Native lords of Quito in the age of the Incas: The political economy of north Andean chiefdoms.* Cambridge University Press, New York.)

———. 1982. Chronicles of the impossible: Notes on three Peruvian indigenous historians. In *From oral to written expression: Native Andean chronicles of the early colonial period*, edited by R. Adorno, pp. 9–40. Latin American Series 4. Maxwell School of Citizenship and Public Affairs, Syracuse.

———. 1986. Vertical politics on the Inca frontier. In *Anthropological history of Andean polities*, edited by J. V. Murra, N. Wachtel, and J. Revel, pp, 89–117. Cambridge University Press, New York.

———. 1988. Frontera aborigen y dualismo inca en el Ecuador prehispánico: Pistas onomásticas. In 45 Congreso Internacional de Americanistas—*Arqueología de las Américas*, pp. 87–102. Fondo de Promoción de la Cultura, Bogotá.

Sanders, W. T. 1956. The central Mexican symbiotic region. In *Prehistoric settlement patterns in the New World*, edited by G. R. Willey, pp. 115–27. Wenner Gren Foundation for Anthropological Research, New York.

———. 1968. Hydraulic agriculture, economic symbiosis and the evolution of states in Central Mexico. In *Anthropological archaeology in the Americas*, edited by B. Meggers, pp. 88–107. Anthropological Society of New York, Washington.

———. 1970. The population of the Teotihuacán valley, the Basin of Mexico and the Central Mexican Symbiotic Region in the sixteenth century. In The Teotihuacán Valley Project Final Report, vol. 1, *The natural environment, contemporary occupation and 16th century population of the valley*, edited by W. T. Sanders, A. Kovar, T. H. Charlton, and R. Diehl, pp. 385–457. Pennsylvania State University Press, University Park.

———. 1976. The population of the Central Mexican Symbiotic Region, the Basin of Mexico, and the Teotihuacán Valley in the sixteenth century. In *The native population of the Americas in 1492*, edited by W. D. Denevan, pp. 85–150. University of Wisconsin Press, Madison.

———. 1977a. Environmental heterogeneity and the evolution of lowland Maya civilization. In *The origins of Maya civilization*, edited by R. E. W. Adams, pp. 287–97. University of New Mexico Press, Albuquerque.

———. 1977b. Ethnographic analogy and the Teotihuacán horizon style. In *Teotihuacán and Kaminaljuyú: A study in prehistoric culture contact,* edited by W. T. Sanders and J. W. Michels, pp. 397–410. Pennsylvania State University Press, University Park.

———. 1979. The Jolly Green Giant in tenth century Yucatán, or fact and fancy in classic Maya agriculture. *Reviews in Anthropology* 6:493–506.

Sanders, W. T., and B. J. Price. 1968. *Mesoamerica: The evolution of a civilization.* Random House, New York.

Sanders, W. T., and D. Webster. 1978. Unilinealism, multilinealism, and the evolution of complex societies. In *Social archaeology: Beyond subsistence and dating,* edited by C. E. Redman, W. T. Langhorne, Jr., M. J. Berman, N. M. Versaggi, E. V. Curtin, and J. C. Wanser, pp. 249–302. Academic Press, New York.

Sanders, W. T., J. F. Parsons, and R. S. Santley. 1979. *The Basin of Mexico: Ecological processes in the evolution of a civilization.* Academic Press, New York.

Santillán, F. de. 1879. Relación. In *Tres relaciones de antigüedades peruanas,* edited by M. Jiménez de la Espada, pp. 3–133. M. Tello, Madrid.

Santillán, G. de. 1976. Visita . . . al pueblo de Coyoacán y su sujeto Tacubaya. In *Colección de documentos sobre Coyoacán,* vol. 1, edited by P. Carrasco P. and J. Monjarás-Ruiz. Centro de Investigaciones Superiores, Instituto Nacional de Antropología e Historia, México.

Santley, R. S. 1984. Obsidian exchange, economic stratification, and the evolution of complex society in the basin of Mexico. In *Trade and exchange in early Mesoamerica,* edited by K. G. Hirth, pp. 43–86. University of New Mexico Press, Albuquerque.

———. 1986. Prehispanic roadways, transport network geometry, and Aztec politico-economic organization in the Basin of Mexico. In *Economic aspects of prehispanic highland Mexico,* edited by B. I. Isaac, pp. 223–44. JAI Press, Greenwich.

Santley, R. S., P. Ortiz Ceballos, and C. A. Pool. 1987. Recent archaeological research at Matacapan, Veracruz; a summary of the results of the 1982 to 1986 field season. *Mexicon* 9:41–48.

Sarmiento de Gamboa, Pedro. 1906. *Geschichte des Inkareichs,* edited by R. Pietschmann. Weidmann, Berlin.

Scarborough, V. L. 1983. A Preclassic Maya water system. *American Antiquity* 48:720–44.

Schaedel, R. P. 1978a. Early state of the Incas. In *The early state,* edited by H. J. M. Claessen and P. Skalník, pp. 289–320. Mouton, The Hague.

———. 1978b. Formation of the Inca state. In *El hombre y la cultura andina,* edited by R. Matos M., vol. 1:112–56. Editorial Lasontay, Lima.

———. 1978c. The city and the origins of the state in America. In *Urbanization in the Americas from its beginnings to the present,* edited by R. P. Schaedel, J. E. Hardoy, and N. S. Kinzer, pp. 31–49. Mouton, The Hague.

Schele, L. 1982. *Maya glyphs: The verbs.* University of Texas Press, Austin.

———. 1984. Human Sacrifice among the Classic Maya. In *Ritual human sacrifice in Mesoamerica,* edited by E. H. Boone, pp. 7–48. Dumbarton Oaks, Washington.

———. 1992. A new look at the dynastic history of Palenque. In *Epigraphy,* edited by V. R. Bricker. Handbook of Middle American Indians Supplement, vol. 5:82–109. V. R. Bricker, general editor. University of Texas Press, Austin.

Schele, L., and D. Freidel. 1990. *A forest of kings—the untold story of the ancient Maya.* William Morrow & Company, New York.

Schele, L. and P. Mathews. 1991. Royal visits and other intersite relationships among the Classic Maya. In *Classic Maya political history: Hieroglyphic and archaeological evidence,* edited by T. P. Culbert, pp. 226–52. Cambridge University Press, Cambridge.

Schjellerup, I. 1984. Cochabamba—an Incaic administrative centre in the rebellious province of Chachapoyas. In *Current archaeological projects in the Central Andes: Some approaches and results* (Proceedings of the Forty-fourth International Congress of Americanists), edited by A. Kendall, pp. 161–87. BAR International Series 210, Oxford.

Schmidt, P. J. 1979. Investigaciones arqueológicas en la región de Huejotzingo, Puebla. *Comunicaciones Proyecto Puebla-Tlaxcala* 16:169–82.

Scholes, F. V., and R. L. Roys. 1948. *The Maya Chontal indians of Acalan-Tixchel.* University of Oklahoma Press, Norman.

Schreiber, K. J. 1984. Prehistoric roads in the Carahuarazo valley, Peru. In *Current archaeological projects in the Central Andes: Some approaches and results* (Proceedings of the Forty-fourth International Congress of Americanists), edited by A. Kendall, pp. 75–94. BAR International Series 210, Oxford.

———. 1987. From state to empire: The expansion of Wari outside the Ayacucho Basin. In *The origins and development of the Andean state,* edited by J. Haas, S. Pozorski, and T. Pozorski, pp. 91–96. Cambridge University Press, New York.

Schroeder, S. 1992. Noblewomen of Chalco. *Estudios de Cultura Nahuatl* 22:45–86.

Schuler-Schömig, I. von. 1979. Die "Fremdkrieger" in Darstellungen der Moche-Keramik. *Baessler Archiv, Neue Folge* 27:135–213.

Schultze-Jena, L. (transl. and commentary). 1944. *Popol Vuh. Das heilige Buch der Quiché-Indianer von Guatemala.* Verlag W. Kohlhammer, Stuttgart.

Séjourné, L. 1954. Teotihuacán, la ciudad sagrada de Quetzalcóatl. *Cuadernos Americanos* 13:177–205.

Seler, E. 1894. Wo lag Aztlan, die Heimath der Azteken? *Globus* 65:317–24.

———. 1898. Quetzalcouatl-Kulkulcan in Yucatán. *Zeitschrift für Ethnologie* 30:377–410.

———. 1902. Quetzalcouatl-Kulkulcan in Yucatán. In *Gesammelte Abhandlungen,* vol. 1:668–705. Verlag A. Asher und Co., Berlin.

———. 1902–1923. *Gesammelte Abhandlungen zur amerikanischen Sprach- und Alterthumskunde,* 5 vols., Verlag A. Asher und Co., Berlin. Reprint and Index: 1967, Akademische Druck- und Verlagsanstalt, Graz.

———. 1904. Wo lag Aztlan, die Heimath der Azteken? In *Gesammelte Abhandlungen zur Amerikanischen Sprach- und Altertumskunde,* vol. 2:31–48. Verlag A. Asher und Co., Berlin.

Seler, E. (commentary). 1901. *Codex Fejérváry-Mayer: Eine altmexikanische Bilderhandschrift des Free Public Museums in Liverpool.* Verlag A. Asher und Co., Berlin.

———. 1902. *Codex Vaticanus Nr. 3773: Eine altmexikanische Bilderschrift der Vatikanischen Bibliothek.* 2 vols., Verlag A. Asher und Co., Berlin.

———. 1904–1909. *Codex Borgia: Eine altmexikanische Bilderschrift der Bibliothek der Congregatio de Propaganda Fide.* 3 vols., Verlag A. Asher und Co., Berlin.

Seler-Sachs, C. 1919. *Frauenleben im Reiche der Azteken: Ein Blatt aus der Kulturgeschichte Alt-Mexikos.* Reimer, Berlin; 2nd ed., 1984.

Service, E. R. 1975. *Origins of the state and civilization: The process of cultural evolution.* Norton, New York.

Shady, R., and A. Ruiz. 1979. Evidence for interregional relationship during the Middle Horizon on the north-central coast of Peru. *American Antiquity* 44:676–84.

Shea, D. E. 1976. A defense of small population estimates for the Central Andes in 1520. In *The native population of the Americas in 1492,* edited by W. D. Denevan, pp. 157–80. University of Wisconsin Press, Madison.

Sheets, P. D. 1976. *Ilopango Volcano and the Maya protoclassic.* Southern Illinois University Press, Carbondale.

Shimada, I. 1982. Horizontal archipelago and coast-highland interaction in North Peru: Archaeological models. In *El hombre y su ambiente en los Andes Centrales,* edited by L. Millones, and H. Tomoeda, pp. 137–210. Museo Nacional de Etnología, Osaka.

———. 1986. Batán Grande and cosmological unity in the prehistoric Central Andes. In *Andean archaeology,* edited by R. Matos Mendieta, S. A. Turpin, and H. H. Eling, Jr., pp. 163–88. Institute of Archaeology, University of California, Los Angeles.

Shuman, M. K. 1977. Archaeology and ethnohistory: The case of the lowland Maya. *Ethnohistory* 24:1–18.

Siemens, A. H., and D. E. Puleston. 1972. Ridged fields and associated features in Southern Campeche: New perspectives on the lowland Maya. *American Antiquity* 37:228–39.

Silverblatt, I. M. 1976. Principios de organización femenina en el Tahuantinsuyu. *Revista del Museo Nacional, Lima* 42:299–340.

———. 1987. *Moon, sun and witches: Gender ideologies and class in Inca and colonial Peru.* Princeton University Press, Princeton.

Smith, C. T. 1970. Depopulation in the Central Andes in the Sixteenth Century. *Current Anthropology* 11:453–64.

Smith, Mary E. 1973. *Picture writing from ancient southern Mexico: Mixtec place signs and maps.* University of Oklahoma Press, Norman.

Smith, Michael E. 1979. The Aztec marketing system and settlement pattern in the Valley of Mexico: A central place analysis. *American Antiquity* 44:110–25.

———. 1980. The role of the marketing system in Aztec society and economy: Reply to Evans. *American Antiquity* 45:878–83.

———. 1983. El desarrollo económico y la expansión del imperio Mexica: Una perspectiva sistémica. *Estudios de Cultura Nahuatl* 16:134–64.

———. 1984. The Aztlan migrations of the Nahuatl chronicles: Myth or history. *Ethnohistory* 31:153–86.

———. 1986. The role of social stratification in the Aztec empire: A view from the provinces. *American Anthropologist* 88:70–91.

———. 1994. Hernán Cortés on the size of Aztec cities. *Latin American Population History Bulletin* 25:25–27.

Soisson, P., and J. Soisson. 1978. *Life of the Aztecs in Ancient Mexico.* Productions Liber, Barcelona.

Solís Alcalá, E. 1949. *Códice Pérez.* Liga de Acción Social, Mérida.

Soustelle, J. 1940. *La pensée cosmologique des anciens Méxicains.* Hermann & Cie., Paris.

———. 1955. *La vie quotidienne des Aztèques.* Hachette, Paris.

———. 1979. *Les Olmèques.* Arthaud, Paris.

Spence, M. W. 1981. Obsidian production and the state in Teotihuacán. *American Antiquity* 46:769–87.

———. 1984. Craft production and polity in early Teotihuacán. In *Trade and exchange in early Mesoamerica,* edited by K. G. Hirth, pp. 87–114. University of New Mexico Press, Albuquerque.

———. 1992. Tlailotlacan, a Zapotec enclave in Teotihuacán. In *Art, ideology, and the city of Teotihuacán,* edited by J. C. Berlo, pp. 59–88. Dumbarton Oaks, Washington.

Spencer, C. S. 1982. *The Cuicatlan cañada and Monte Albán: A study of primary state formation.* Academic Press, New York.

Spencer, H. 1880–96. *The principles of sociology.* 3 vols., D. Appleton and Company, New York.

Spinden, H. 1924. *The reduction of Maya dates.* Papers of the Peabody Museum of Archaeology and Ethnology, vol. 6, number 4. Harvard University, Cambridge.

Spores, R. 1967. *The Mixtec kings and their people.* University of Oklahoma Press, Norman.

———. 1984. *The Mixtecs in ancient and colonial times.* University of Oklahoma Press, Norman.

Stenzel, W. 1980. Quetzalcoatl von Tula: Die Mythogenese einer postkortesischen Legende. *Zeitschrift für Lateinamerika* 18. Wien.

———. 1982. Orígen y elementos del mito del regreso de dios blanco Quetzalcoatl. In *International Colloquium: The Indians of México in pre-Columbian and modern times*, edited by M. E. Jansen and T. J. Leyenaar, pp. 170–75. Rutgers, Leiden.

Stephens, J. L. 1841. *Incidents of travel in Central America, Chiapas and Yucatan.* 1st ed., Harper and Brothers, New York.

———. 1843. *Incidents of travel in Yucatan.* 1st ed., Harper and Brothers, New York.

Steward, J. H., and L. C. Faron. 1959. *Native peoples of South America.* McGraw-Hill, New York.

Stuart, D. 1993. Historical Inscriptions and the Maya Collapse. In *Lowland Maya civilization in the eighth century A.D*, edited by J. A. Sabloff and J. S. Henderson, pp. 321–54. Dumbarton Oaks, Washington.

Stuart, G. E. 1992. Quest for decipherment, a historical and biographical survey of Maya hieroglyphic investigation. In *New Theories on the Ancient Maya*, edited by E. C. Danien and R. J. Sharer, pp. 1–63. University Museum Monograph 77. University Museum, University of Pennsylvania, Philadelphia.

Stuiver, M. P., and J. Reimer. 1993. Extended ^{14}C data base and revised Calib 3.0 ^{14}C age calibration program. *Radiocarbon* 35:215–30.

Sullivan, T. D. 1974. The rhetorical orations, or huehuetlatolli, collected by Sahagún. In *Sixteenth century Mexico: The Work of Sahagún*, edited by M. S. Edmonson, pp. 79–109. University of New Mexico Press, Albuquerque.

———. 1980. Tlatoani and tlatocayotl in the Sahagún manuscripts. *Estudios de Cultura Nahuatl* 14:225–38.

Tapia, Andrés de. 1866. Relación. In *Colección de documentos para la historia de México*, edited by J. García Icazbalceta, vol. 2:554–94. J. M. Andrade, México.

Taylor, G. 1982. Las ediciones del manuscrito quechua de Huarochirí. *Historica–Pontificia Universidad Católica del Perú* 6:255–78.

Taylor, G., ed. 1980. *Rites et traditions de Huarochirí: Manuscrit quechua du début du 17e siècle.* L'Harmattan, Paris.

———. 1987. *Ritos y tradiciones de Huarochirí del siglo XVII.* Instituto de Estudios Peruanos: Instituto Frances de Estudios Andinos, Lima.

Tedlock, D., transl. 1985. *Popol Vuh: The Maya book of the dawn of life.* Simon and Schuster, New York.

Teeple, J. E. 1927. Maya inscriptions: The lunar calendar and its relation to Maya history. *American Anthropologist* 29:391–407.

Tellenbach, M. 1987. Grabungen im Jequetepeque-Tal, Nordperu: Ein Beitrag zur andinen Siedlungsarchäologie. *Archaeologica Peruana* 1:47–60.

Tello, J. 1960. *Chavín: Cultura matriz de la civilización andina.* Universidad Nacional Mayor de San Marcos, Lima.

Tena, R. 1992. *El calendario mexica y la cronografía.* Instituto Nacional de Antropología e Historia, México.

Thompson, D. E. 1968. An archaeological evaluation of ethnohistoric evidence on Inca culture. In *Anthropological Archaeology in the Americas,* edited by B. J. Meggers, pp. 108–20. The Anthropological Society of Washington, Washington.

———. 1970. Una evaluación arqueológica de las evidencias etnohistóricas sobre la cultura incaica. In *100 años de arqueología en el Perú,* edited by R. Ravines, pp. 565–82. Instituto de Estudios Peruanos, Lima.

Thompson, J. E. S. 1935. Maya Chronology, the correlation question. Contributions to American Archaeology 14. Carnegie Institution, Washington.

———. 1950. *Maya hieroglyphic writing: An introduction.* University of Oklahoma Press, Norman.

———. 1954. *The rise and fall of Maya civilization.* University of Oklahoma Press, Norman; 2nd revised ed.: 1967.

———. 1964. Trade relations between Maya highlands and lowlands. *Estudios de Cultura Maya* 4:13–50; slightly enlarged in 1970, pp. 124–58.

———. 1970. *Maya history and religion.* University of Oklahoma Press, Norman.

———. 1972. *A commentary on the Dresden Codex, a Maya hieroglyphic book.* Memoirs of the American Philosophical Society 93, Philadelphia.

Tichy, F. 1991. *Die geordnete Welt indianischer Völker.* F. Steiner, Stuttgart.

Tolstoy, P. 1974. Transoceanic diffusion and Nuclear America. In *Prehispanic America,* edited by S. Gorenstein, pp. 124–44. Thames and Hudson, London (commented bibliography).

———. 1978. Western Mesoamerica before A.D. 900. In *Chronologies in New World archaeology,* edited by R. E. Taylor, and C. W. Meighan, pp. 241–84. Academic Press, New York.

Tolstoy, P., S. K. Fish, M. W. Boksenbaum, K. B. Vaughn, and C. E. Smith. 1977. Early sedentary communities of the Basin of Mexico. *Journal of Field Archaeology* 4:91–106.

Topic, J. R. 1982. Lower-class social and economic organization at Chan Chan. In *Chan Chan: Andean desert city,* edited by M. E. Moseley, and K. C. Day, pp. 145–75. University of New Mexico Press, Albuquerque.

Torquemada, J. de. 1975–83. *Monarquía indiana,* edited by M. León Portilla, 7 vols. Universidad Nacional Autónoma de México, Instituto de Investigaciones Históricas, México.

Tourtellot, G., and J. A. Sabloff. 1972. Exchange systems among the ancient Maya. *American Antiquity* 37:126–35.

Tovar, J. de. 1972. *Manuscrit Tovar, origines et croyances des indiens du Mexique, relación del origen de los yndios . . . ,* edited by J. Lafaye. Akademische Druck- und Verlagsanstalt, Graz.

Townsend, R. F. 1979. *State and cosmos in the art of Tenochtitlan.* Dumbarton Oaks, Washington.

———. 1992. *The Aztecs.* Thames and Hudson, London.

Tozzer, A. M. 1957. *Chichén Itzá and its Cenote of Sacrifice: A comparative study of contemporaneous Maya and Toltecs.* Memoirs of the Peabody Museum of American Archaeology and Ethnology, vol. 11, 12, Harvard University, Cambridge.

Tozzer, A. M., transl. 1941. *Landa's Relación de las cosas de Yucatán.* Papers of the Peabody Museum of Archaeology and Ethnology, vol. 18. Harvard University, Cambridge.

Trautmann, W. 1968. *Untersuchungen zur indianischen Siedlungs- und Territorialgeschichte im Becken von Mexico bis zur frühen Kolonialzeit.* Hamburgisches Museum für Völkerkunde und Vorgeschichte, Hamburg.

Treiber, H. 1987. *Studien zur Katunserie der Pariser Handschrift.* Acta Mesoamericana 3. Verlag von Flemming, Berlin.

Trigger, B. G. 1970. Aims in prehistoric archaeology. *Antiquity* 44:26–37.

———. 1971. The archaeology of government. *World Archaeology* 2:321–36.

———. 1978. The archaeology of government. In *Time and traditions; essays in archaeological interpretation,* edited by B. G. Trigger, pp. 153–66. Edinburgh University Press, Edinburgh.

Trimborn, H. 1923–24. Der Kollektivismus der Inkas in Peru. *Anthropos* 18-19:978–1001.

———. 1925. Der Kollektivismus der Inkas in Peru. *Anthropos* 20:579–606.

———. 1927. Die Gliederung der Stände im Inka-Reich. *Journal de la Société des Américanistes de Paris, N.S.* 19:303–44.

Trimborn, H., and A. Kelm. 1967. *Francisco de Avila.* Gebrüder Mann Verlag, Berlin.

Troll, C. 1943. Die Stellung der Indianer-Hochkulturen im Landschaftsaufbau der tropischen Anden. *Zeitschrift der Gesellschaft für Erdkunde zu Berlin,* Heft 3, 4:93–128.

Trombold, C. D. 1990. A reconsideration of chronology for the La Quemada portion of the Northern Mesoamerican Frontier. *American Antiquity* 55:308–24.

Tschohl, P. 1964. *Kritische Untersuchungen zur spätindianischen Geschichte Südost-Mexikos, Teil I: Die aztekische Ausdehnung nach den aztekischen Quellen und die Probleme ihrer Bearbeitung.* Dissertation, Hamburg University.

———. 1987. Tlacaelel als aztekischer Übergangskönig bei J. Rounds: über das falsche und richtige Anwenden von Theorien. In *Mit Theorien arbeiten: Untersuchen in der Kulturanthropologie,* edited by S. Küsting, A. Bruck, and P. Tschohl, pp. 205–20. Lit, Münster.

Tudela de la Orden, J., ed. 1980. *Códice Tudela.* 2 vols. Ediciones Cultura Hispánica, Madrid.

Tudela, J., ed. 1977. *Relación de las ceremonias y ritos y población de los indios de la provincia de Michoacán.* Balsal Editores, Morelia/México.

Turner, B. L. 1979. Prehispanic terracing in the central Maya lowlands: Problems of agricultural intensification. In *Maya archaeology and ethnohistory,* edited by N. Hammond and G. R. Willey, pp. 103–15. University of Texas Press, Austin.

Uchmany, E. A. 1978. Huitzilopochtli, dios de la historia de los azteca-mexitin. *Estudios de Cultura Nahuatl* 13:211–37.

Urioste, G. L., ed. 1983. *Hijos de Pariya Qaqa: La tradición oral de Waru Chiri, mitología, ritual y costumbres.* Maxwell School of Citizenship and Public Affairs, Syracuse.

Urteaga, H. H. 1931. *El imperio incaico.* Librería e imprenta Gil, Lima.

Urteaga, H. H., ed. 1920. *Discurso sobre la descendencia y gobierno de los Incas.* Sanmartí y ca., Lima.

Valcárcel, L. E. 1925. *Del ayllu al imperio.* Editorial Garcilaso, Lima.

———. 1946. The Andean calendar. In *Handbook of South American Indians,* edited by J. Steward, vol. 3: 471–76. Smithsonian Institution, Bureau of American Ethnology, Bulletin 143, Washington.

———. 1966. El imperio de los incas: Una nueva visión. In *Actas y Memorias del XXXVI Congreso Internacional de Americanistas,* vol. 2:15–22. Sevilla.

Vázquez Chamorro, G. 1981a. La mujer Azteca. *Historia* "16" 58:105–15.

———. 1981b. Las reformas socio-económicas de Motecuhzoma II. *Revista Española de Antropología Americana* 11:207–17.

———. 1986. Karl Marx, la teoría de la sociedad oriental y el México precortesiano: Una observación al artículo de E. Corona, "Sobre el nivel de desarollo de las fuerzas productivas para la caracterización del Estado en Mesoamérica." *Revista Española de Antropología Americana* 16:43–62.

Vázquez de Tapia, Bernardino. 1972. *Relación de méritos y servicios del conquistador,* edited by J. Gurría Lacroix. Universidad Nacional Autónoma de México, México.

Vega, El Inca Garcilaso de la. 1960. *Primera parte de los comentarios reales.* Atlas, Madrid.

Wachtel, N. 1971. *La vision des vainçus: Les indiens du Pérou devant la conquête espagnole (1529–1570).* Gallimard, Paris.

———. 1973a. Rebeliones y milenarismo. In *Ideología mesiánica del mundo andino,* edited by J. M. Ossio A., pp. 105–42. I. Prado Pastor, Lima.

———. 1973b. La reciprocidad y el estado Inca: De Karl Polanyi a John V. Murra. In *Sociedad e ideología: Ensayos de historia y antropología andinas,* edited by N. Wachtel, pp. 59–78. Instituto de Estudios Peruanos, Lima.

———. 1976. *Los vencidos: Los indios del Perú frente a la conquista española.* Alianza, Madrid.

———. 1977. *The Vision of the Vanquished: The Spanish Conquest in Peru through Indian Eyes,* transl. by B. and S. Reynolds. Barnes and Noble, New York.

———. 1978. Hommes d'eau: Le problème Uru (XVIe-XVIIe siècle). *Annales—Economies, Sociétés, Civilisations* 33:1127–59.

———. 1981a. Reciprocity and the Inca state: From Karl Polanyi to John V. Murra. In *Research in economic anthropology,* edited by G. Dalton, vol. 4:38–50. JAI Press, Greenwich.

———. 1981b. Les mitimas de la valle de Cochabamba: La politique de colonisa-

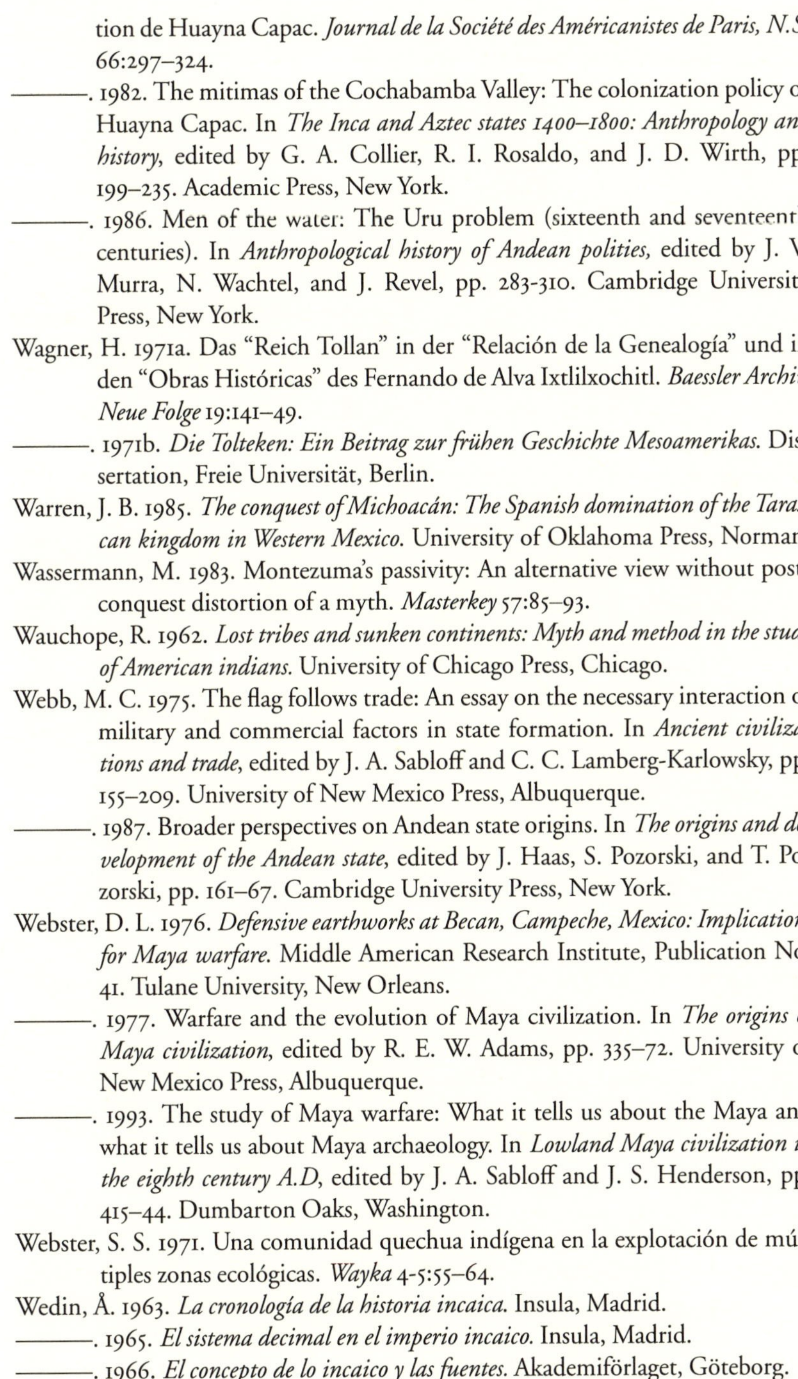

tion de Huayna Capac. *Journal de la Société des Américanistes de Paris, N.S.* 66:297–324.

———. 1982. The mitimas of the Cochabamba Valley: The colonization policy of Huayna Capac. In *The Inca and Aztec states 1400–1800: Anthropology and history,* edited by G. A. Collier, R. I. Rosaldo, and J. D. Wirth, pp. 199–235. Academic Press, New York.

———. 1986. Men of the water: The Uru problem (sixteenth and seventeenth centuries). In *Anthropological history of Andean polities,* edited by J. V. Murra, N. Wachtel, and J. Revel, pp. 283-310. Cambridge University Press, New York.

Wagner, H. 1971a. Das "Reich Tollan" in der "Relación de la Genealogía" und in den "Obras Históricas" des Fernando de Alva Ixtlilxochitl. *Baessler Archiv, Neue Folge* 19:141–49.

———. 1971b. *Die Tolteken: Ein Beitrag zur frühen Geschichte Mesoamerikas.* Dissertation, Freie Universität, Berlin.

Warren, J. B. 1985. *The conquest of Michoacán: The Spanish domination of the Tarascan kingdom in Western Mexico.* University of Oklahoma Press, Norman.

Wassermann, M. 1983. Montezuma's passivity: An alternative view without post-conquest distortion of a myth. *Masterkey* 57:85–93.

Wauchope, R. 1962. *Lost tribes and sunken continents: Myth and method in the study of American indians.* University of Chicago Press, Chicago.

Webb, M. C. 1975. The flag follows trade: An essay on the necessary interaction of military and commercial factors in state formation. In *Ancient civilizations and trade,* edited by J. A. Sabloff and C. C. Lamberg-Karlowsky, pp. 155–209. University of New Mexico Press, Albuquerque.

———. 1987. Broader perspectives on Andean state origins. In *The origins and development of the Andean state,* edited by J. Haas, S. Pozorski, and T. Pozorski, pp. 161–67. Cambridge University Press, New York.

Webster, D. L. 1976. *Defensive earthworks at Becan, Campeche, Mexico: Implications for Maya warfare.* Middle American Research Institute, Publication No. 41. Tulane University, New Orleans.

———. 1977. Warfare and the evolution of Maya civilization. In *The origins of Maya civilization,* edited by R. E. W. Adams, pp. 335–72. University of New Mexico Press, Albuquerque.

———. 1993. The study of Maya warfare: What it tells us about the Maya and what it tells us about Maya archaeology. In *Lowland Maya civilization in the eighth century A.D,* edited by J. A. Sabloff and J. S. Henderson, pp. 415–44. Dumbarton Oaks, Washington.

Webster, S. S. 1971. Una comunidad quechua indígena en la explotación de múltiples zonas ecológicas. *Wayka* 4-5:55–64.

Wedin, Å. 1963. *La cronología de la historia incaica.* Insula, Madrid.

———. 1965. *El sistema decimal en el imperio incaico.* Insula, Madrid.

———. 1966. *El concepto de lo incaico y las fuentes.* Akademiförlaget, Göteborg.

Weigand, P. C., G. Harbottle, and E. V. Sayre. 1977. Turquoise sources and source analysis: Mesoamerica and the southwestern U.S.A. In *Exchange systems in prehistory*, edited by T. K. Earle and J. E. Ericson, pp. 15–34. Academic Press, New York.

Whitecotton, J. W. 1977. *The Zapotecs: Princes, priests and peasants.* University of Oklahoma Press, Norman.

Whittaker, G. 1982. The tablets of Mound J at Monte Albán. In *Los indígenas de México en la época prehispánica y en la actualidad*, edited by M. Jansen and T. J. J. Leyenaar, pp. 50–86. Rutgers, Leyden.

———. 1992. The Zapotec writing system. In *Epigraphy*, edited by V. R. Bricker. Handbook of Middle American Indians Supplement, vol. 5:5–19. V. R. Bricker, general editor. University of Texas Press, Austin.

Wilk, R. R. 1985. The ancient Maya and the political present. *Journal of Anthropological Research* 41:307–26.

Wilkerson, S. J. K. 1974. The ethnographic work of Andrés de Olmos, precursor and contemporary of Sahagún. In *Sixteenth-century Mexico; the work of Sahagún*, edited by M. S. Edmonson, pp. 27–77. University of New Mexico Press, Albuquerque.

Willey, G. R. 1953. *Prehistoric settlement patterns in the Virú valley.* Bureau of American Ethnology, Washington.

———. 1974a. Das alte Amerika. In *Propyläen Kunstgeschichte* 18, Ullstein und Propyläen Verlag, Berlin.

———. 1974b. The classic Maya hiatus: A rehearsal for the collapse? In *Mesoamerican archaeology: New approaches*, edited by N. Hammond, pp. 417–30. University of Texas Press, Austin.

———. 1977. The rise of Maya civilization: A summary view. In *The origins of Maya civilization*, edited by R. E. W. Adams, pp. 383–423. University of New Mexico Press, Albuquerque.

———. 1991. Horizontal integration and regional diversity: An alternating process in the rise of civilizations. *American Antiquity* 56:197–215.

Willey, G. R., G. F. Ekholm, and R. F. Millon. 1964. The pattern of farming life and civilization. In *Natural Environment and Early Cultures*, edited by R. C. West, pp. 446–98. Handbook of Middle American Indians, vol. 1. R. Wauchope, general editor, University of Texas Press, Austin.

Willey, G. R., and D. B. Shimkin. 1971. The collapse of classic Maya civilization in the southern lowlands. *Southwestern Journal of Anthropology* 27:1–18.

———. 1973. The Maya collapse: A summary view. In *The classic Maya collapse*, edited by T. P. Culbert, pp. 457–501. University of New Mexico Press, Albuquerque.

———. 1974. The collapse of classic Maya civilization in the southern lowlands. In *The rise and fall of civilizations*, edited by J. A. Sabloff and C. C Lamberg-Karlovsky, pp. 104–18. Cummings Publishing Co., Menlo Park.

Williams, B. J. 1989. Contact period rural overpopulation in the Basin of Mexico, carrying capacity models tested with documentary data. *American Antiquity* 54:715–32.

Wilson, D. J. 1983. The origins and development of complex prehispanic society in the lower Santa valley, Peru: Its implications for theories of state origins. *Journal of Anthropological Archaeology* 2:209–76.

Winfield Capitaine, F. 1988. La estela 1 de La Mojarra, Veracruz, México. *Research Reports on Ancient Maya Writing* 16, Center for Maya Research, Washington.

Winning, H. von. 1987. *La iconografía de Teotihuacán: Los dioses y los signos.* 2 vols. Universidad Nacional Autónoma de México, Instituto de Investigaciones Estéticas, México.

Wintzer, H. 1930. Das Recht Altmexikos. *Zeitschrift für vergleichende Rechtswissenschaft* 45:323–480.

Wittfogel, K. A. 1972. The hydraulic approach to pre-Spanish Mesoamerica. In *Chronology and Irrigation* (The Prehistory of the Tehuacan Valley, vol. 4), edited by F. Johnson, pp. 59–80. University of Texas Press, Austin.

Woodbury, R. B., and J. A. Neely. 1972. Water control systems of the Tehuacan Valley. In *Chronology and Irrigation* (The Prehistory of the Tehuacan Valley, vol. 4), edited by F. Johnson, pp. 81–153. University of Texas Press, Austin.

Wright. H. T. 1977. Recent research on the origin of state. *Annual Review of Anthropology* 6:379–97.

———. 1986. The evolution of civilization. In *American archaeology, past and future,* edited by D. J. Meltzer, D. D. Fowler, and J. A. Sabloff, pp. 323–65. Society for American Archaeology, Smithsonian Institution Press, Washington.

Yadeùn Angulo, J. 1975. *El estado y la ciudad: El caso de Tula, Hgo.* Instituto Nacional de Antropología e Historia, México

Yeakel, J. A. 1983. The accounting-historian of the Incas. *The Accounting Historian Journal* 10:39–51.

Zambardino, R. A. 1980. Mexico's population in the sixteenth century: Demographic anomaly or mathematical illusion. *Journal of Interdisciplinary History* 11:1–27.

Zantwijk, Rudolf van. 1962. La paz azteca: La ordenación del mundo por los Mexica. *Estudios de Cultura Nahuatl* 3:101–35.

———. 1963. Principios organizadores de los mexicas: Una introducción al estudio del sistema interno del régimen aztec. *Estudios de Cultura Nahuatl* 4:187–222.

———. 1965. Introducción al estudio de la division en quince partes en la sociedad azteca y su significación en la estructura interna. *Journal de la Société des Américanistes de Paris, N.S.* 54:211–22.

———. 1967a. La organización de once guarniciones aztecas: Una nueva interpretación de los folios 17v y 18r del Códice Mendocino. *Journal de la Société des Américanistes de Paris, N.S.* 56:149–60.

———. 1967b. *Servants of the saints: The social and cultural identity of a Tarascan community in Mexico.* Van Gorcum & Co., Assen.

———. 1969. La estructura gubernamental del estado de Tlacupan (1430–1520). *Estudios de Cultura Nahuatl* 8:123–55.

———. 1970. Las organizaciones social, económica y religiosa de los mercaderes gremiales aztecas. *Boletín de Estudios Latinoamericanos* 10:1–20.

———. 1973. Politics and ethnicity in a prehispanic Mexican state between the 13th and 15th centuries. *Plural Societies* 4:23–52.

———. 1978. Iquehuacatzin, un drama real azteca. *Estudios de Cultura Nahuatl* 13:89–96.

———. 1980. El carácter de la autoridad en el imperio azteca y su expresión en la retórica oficial. *Indiana* 6:71–87.

———. 1981. The Great Temple of Tenochtitlán: Model of Aztec cosmovision. In *Mesoamerican sites and worldviews,* edited by E. P. Benson, pp. 71–86. Dumbarton Oaks, Washington.

———. 1982. La entronización de Acamapichtli de Tenochtitlán y las características de su gobierno. *Estudios de Cultura Nahuatl* 15:17–26.

———. 1985. *The Aztec arrangement.* University of Oklahoma Press, Norman.

———. 1986a. La historicidad de Tlacaelel, el cihuacoatl del imperio azteca (1430–1477). *Xochipilli* 1:5–18.

———. 1986b. Quetzalcoatl y Huemac, mito y realidad azteca. In *Myth and the imaginary of the New World,* edited by Edmundo Magaña and Peter Mason, pp. 321–58. Foris, Amsterdam.

———. 1992. *'Met mij is de zon opgegaan'.* Prometheus, Amsterdam.

Zantwijk, R. A. M. van (commentary). 1979. *Anales de Tula.* Akademische Druck- und Verlagsanstalt, Graz.

Zevallos Quiñones, J. 1975. La visita del pueblo de Ferreñafe (Lambayeque) en 1568. *Historia y Cultura (Lima)* 9:155–78.

Zimmermann, G. 1963. *Die Relationen Chimalpahin's zur Geschichte Mexico's.* Teil 1, Die Zeit bis zur Conquista. Cram, Hamburg.

Zorita, Alonso de. 1891. Breve y sumaria relación de los señores y maneras y diferencias que había de ellos en la Nueva España. In *Nueva Colección de documentos para la historia de México,* edited by J. García Icazbalceta, vol. 3:71–227. Andrade y Morales, México (2nd ed., 1941, vol. 3:67–205. Editorial Salvador Chávez Hayhoe, México).

Zuidema, R. T. 1964. *The ceque system of Cuzco: The social organization of the capital of the Inca.* E. J. Brill, Leiden.

———. 1966. El calendario Inca. In *Actas y Memorias del XXXVI Congreso Internacional de Americanistas,* vol. 2:25–30. Sevilla.

———. 1977a. The Inca kinship system: A new theoretical view. In *Andean kinship and marriage,* edited by E. Mayer and E. Bolton, pp. 240–81. American Anthropological Association, Washington.

———. 1977b. The Inca calendar. In *Native American astronomy,* edited by A. F. Aveni, pp. 219–59. University of Texas Press, Austin.

———. 1980a. El calendario Inca. In *Astronomía en la América antigua,* edited by A. F. Aveni, pp. 263–311. México.

———. 1980b. Parentesco inca. In *Parentesco y matrimonio en los Andes,* edited by E. Mayer and E. Bolton, pp. 55–114. Pontificia Universidad Católica del Perú, Fondo Editorial, Lima.

———. 1986. *La civilisation inca au Cuzco.* Presses Universitaires de France, Paris.

———. 1987. Calendars: South American Calendars. In *Encyclopedia of Religion,* edited by M. Eliade and C. J. Adams, vol. 3:16–21. Macmillan, New York.

———. 1990. *Inca civilization in Cuzco.* University of Texas Press, Austin.

Zuidema, R. T., and D. Poole. 1981. Los límites de los cuatro suyus incaicos en el Cuzco. *Bulletin de l'Institut Française d'Etudes Andines* 9:83–89.

Chronologies

PRECOLUMBIAN CULTURES OF MESOAMERICA
ACCORDING TO ARCHAEOLOGICAL SOURCES

Preclassic 1500 B.C.–A.D. 300
- Early Preclassic 1500–700 B.C.
  - Olmecs
- Middle Preclassic 700–300 B.C.
  - Monte Albán
- Late Preclassic 300 B.C.–A.D. 250
  - Monte Albán
  - Cuicuilco
  - Teotihuacán

Classic: A.D. 250–900
- Early Classic A.D. 300–500
  - Monte Albán
  - Teotihuacán
  - Cholula
  - Maya of the Lowlands
  - Izapa culture
- Classic: A.D. 500–700
  - Monte Albán
  - Teotihuacán
  - Maya of the Lowlands
- Late Classic: A.D. 700–900
  - Xochicalco
  - Cacaxtla
  - Veracruz culture (El Tajín)
  - Maya of the Lowlands

Postclassic: A.D. 900–1520/1540
- Early Postclassic: A.D. 900–1200
  - Tula (to A.D. 1000)
  - Maya of northern Yucatán (to ca. 1000, often called Terminal Classic)
- Late Postclassic: A.D. 1200–1520/1540 (Historical Epoch)
  - Chichimec immigration
  - Tepanec Empire (until 1430)
  - Aztec expansion (from 1430)
  - Maya states in northern Yucatán and highlands of Guatemala

PRECOLUMBIAN CULTURES (CERAMIC STYLES) OF THE CENTRAL ANDES ACCORDING TO ARCHAEOLOGICAL SOURCES

Formative: Initial Period: 2100–1400 B.C.
- Haldas
- Kotosh

Formative: Early Horizon: 1400–400 B.C.
- Cupisnique
- Chavín
- Ocucaje
- Wichqana
- Chanapata
- Paracas
- Qaluyu
- Chiripa

Early Intermediate Period: 400 B.C.–A.D. 550
- Vicús
- Moche
- Salinar
- Gallinazo
- Lima
- Nasca
- Recuay
- Huarpa
- Pukara
- Tiahuanaco

Middle Horizon: A.D. 550–900
- Moche V
- "Huari-Norteño"
- Nievería
- Tiahuanaco
- Huari

Late Intermediate Period: A.D. 900–1476
- Chimú
- Chancay
- Ica
- Chanka
- Killke
- Chincha

Late Horizon: A.D. 1476–1534
- Altiplano states
- Chincha
- Inca expansion

IMPORTANT EVENTS IN PRECOLUMBIAN HISTORY OF CENTRAL MEXICO ACCORDING TO SOURCES OF THE INDIGENOUS TRADITIONS

before 1100	Decline of Tollan
1125?	Dynasty of Colhuacan
ca. 1250	Arrival of the Mexica in the Valley of Mexico
1298?	Tetzcoco: Quinatzin accession
1325?	Founding of Tenochtitlán
ca. 1350	Decline of Colhuacan
1371	Tenochtitlan: Acamapichtli accession
1372	Tlatelolco: Cuacuapitzahuac Epcoatl accession
1377	Tetzcoco: Techotlalatl accession
1391	Tenochtitlán: Huitzilihuitl accession
1409	Tetzcoco: Ixtlilxochitl accession
1409	Tlatelolco: Tlacateotl accession
1414	Start of war Tetzcoco-Azcapotzalco
1415	Tenochtitlán: Chimalpopoca accession
1418	Tetzcoco: Ixtlilxochitl killed, Nezahualcoyotl into exile
1426	Azcapotzalco: Tezozomoc dead, succession problems
1427	Tlatelolco: Cuauhtlatoa accession
1427	Azcapotzalco: Maxtla accession
1427	Tenochtitlán: Itzcoatl accession
1428	Conquest of Azcapotzalco by Tenochtitlán and allies Formation of Triple Alliance: Tenochtitlán, Tetzcoco, Tlacopan
1430	Tenochtitlán: Cihuacoatl Tlacaelel accession
1431?	Death of Maxtla
1433	Tetzcoco: Nezahualcoyotl accession
1440	Tenochtitlán: Moteuczoma I Ilhuicamina accession
1449–54	Flood and famine in the Basin of Mexico
1465	Conquest of Chalco
1467	Tlatelolco: Moquihuix accession
1471	Tenochtitlán: Axayacatl accession
1472	Tetzcoco: Nezahualpilli accession
1473	Tlatelolco conquered by Tenochtitlán, death of Moquihuix
1478	Defeat at Taximaroa against the Tarascans
1482	Tenochtitlán: Tizoc accession
1486	Tenochtitlán: Ahuitzotl accession
1498	Tenochtitlán: Flood from Acuecuexatl wells
1499	Defeat of Tenochtitlán in Atlixco
1502	Tenochtitlán: Moteuczoma II Xocoyotzin accession
1516	Tetzcoco: Cacama accession
1519, 11/8	Tenochtitlán: Spaniards arrive

1520, 6/30	Tenochtitlán: Flight of the Spaniards in Noche Triste
1520	Tenochtitlán: Cuitlahuac accession
1521	Tenochtitlán: Cuauhtemoc accession
1521, 8/13	Tenochtitlán conquered by Spaniards, Cuauhtemoc prisoner

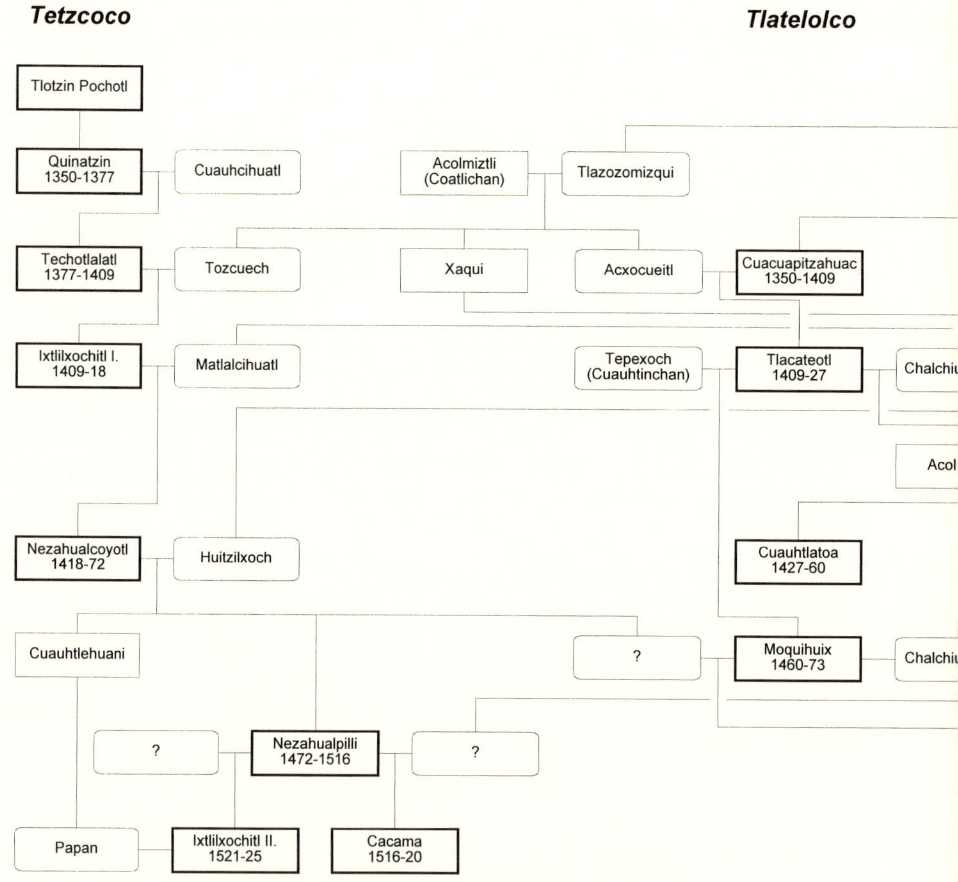

DYNASTIES IN THE VALLEY OF MEXICO

Rectangular: male person; heavy frame: ruler (period of rulership); double line at side: Cihuacoatl of Tenochtitlán; rectangular with round corners: female person

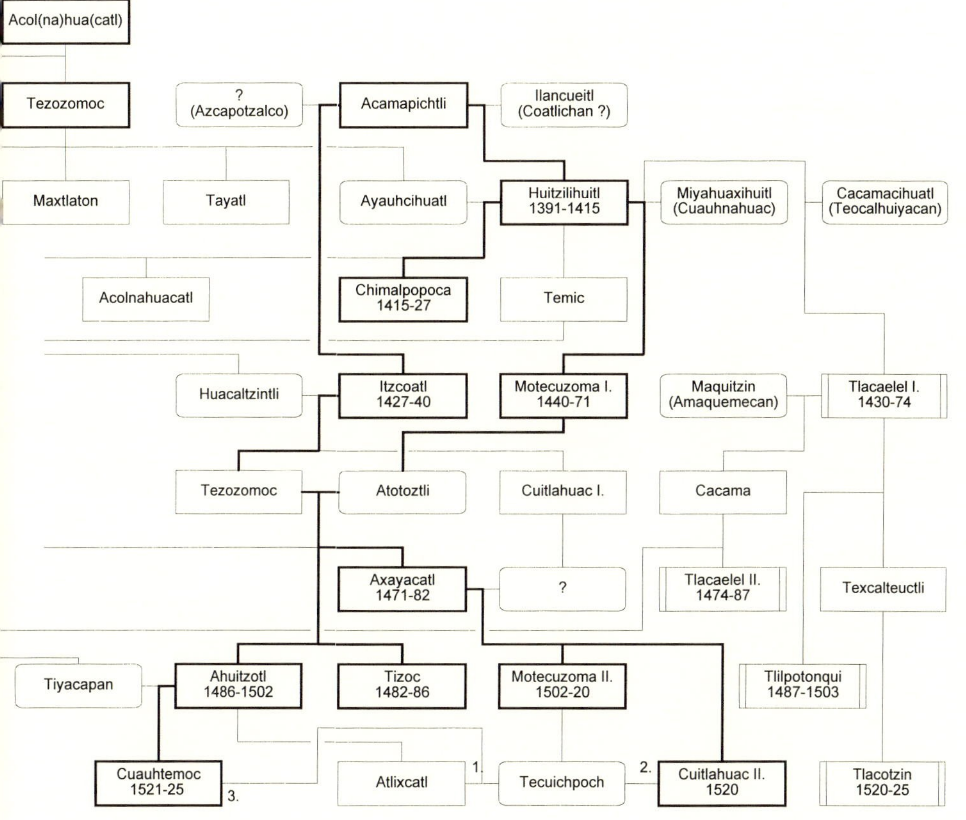

Azcapotzalco
Tenochtitlan
Acol(na)hua(catl)
Tezozomoc
? (Azcapotzalco)
Acamapichtli
Ilancueitl (Coatlichan ?)
Maxtlaton
Tayatl
Ayauhcihuatl
Huitzilihuitl 1391-1415
Miyahuaxihuitl (Cuauhnahuac)
Cacamacihuatl (Teocalhuiyacan)
Acolnahuacatl
Chimalpopoca 1415-27
Temic
Huacaltzintli
Itzcoatl 1427-40
Motecuzoma I. 1440-71
Maquitzin (Amaquemecan)
Tlacaelel I. 1430-74
Tezozomoc
Atotoztli
Cuitlahuac I.
Cacama
Axayacatl 1471-82
?
Tlacaelel II. 1474-87
Texcalteuctli
Tiyacapan
Ahuitzotl 1486-1502
Tizoc 1482-86
Motecuzoma II. 1502-20
Tlilpotonqui 1487-1503
Cuauhtemoc 1521-25
3.
Atlixcatl
1.
Tecuichpoch
2.
Cuitlahuac II. 1520
Tlacotzin 1520-25

HJP '95

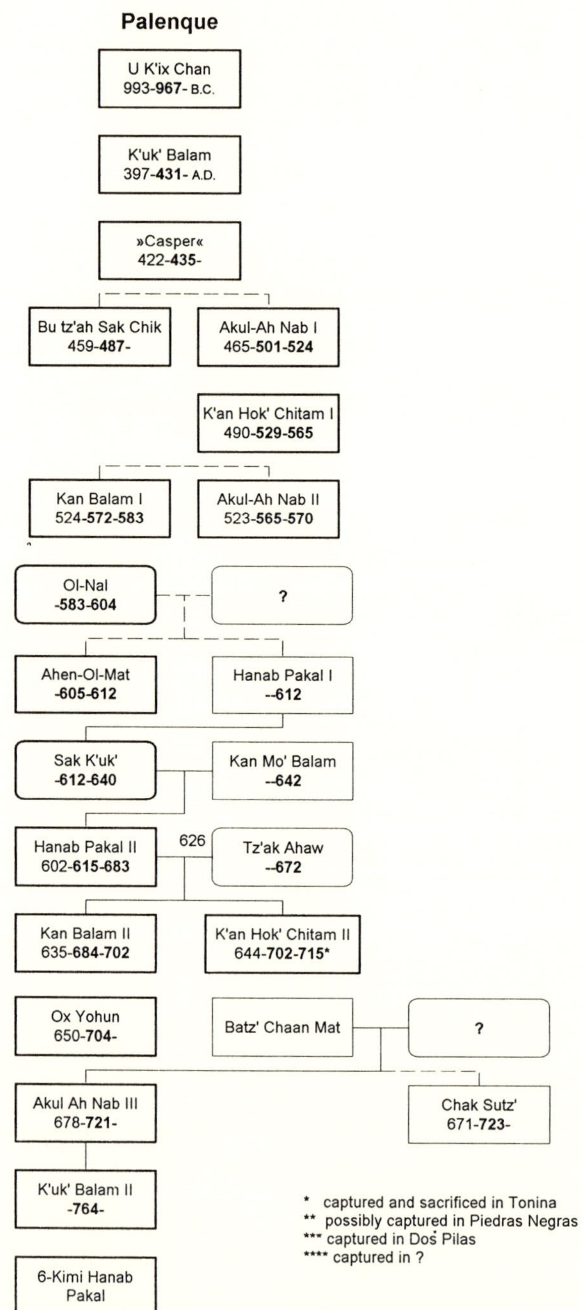

DYNASTIES OF PALENQUE AND YAXCHILAN

Rectangular: male person; heavy frame: ruler (birth, accession, death); rectangular with round corners: female person. Names in "…" are paraphrases of glyphs.

Yaxchilan

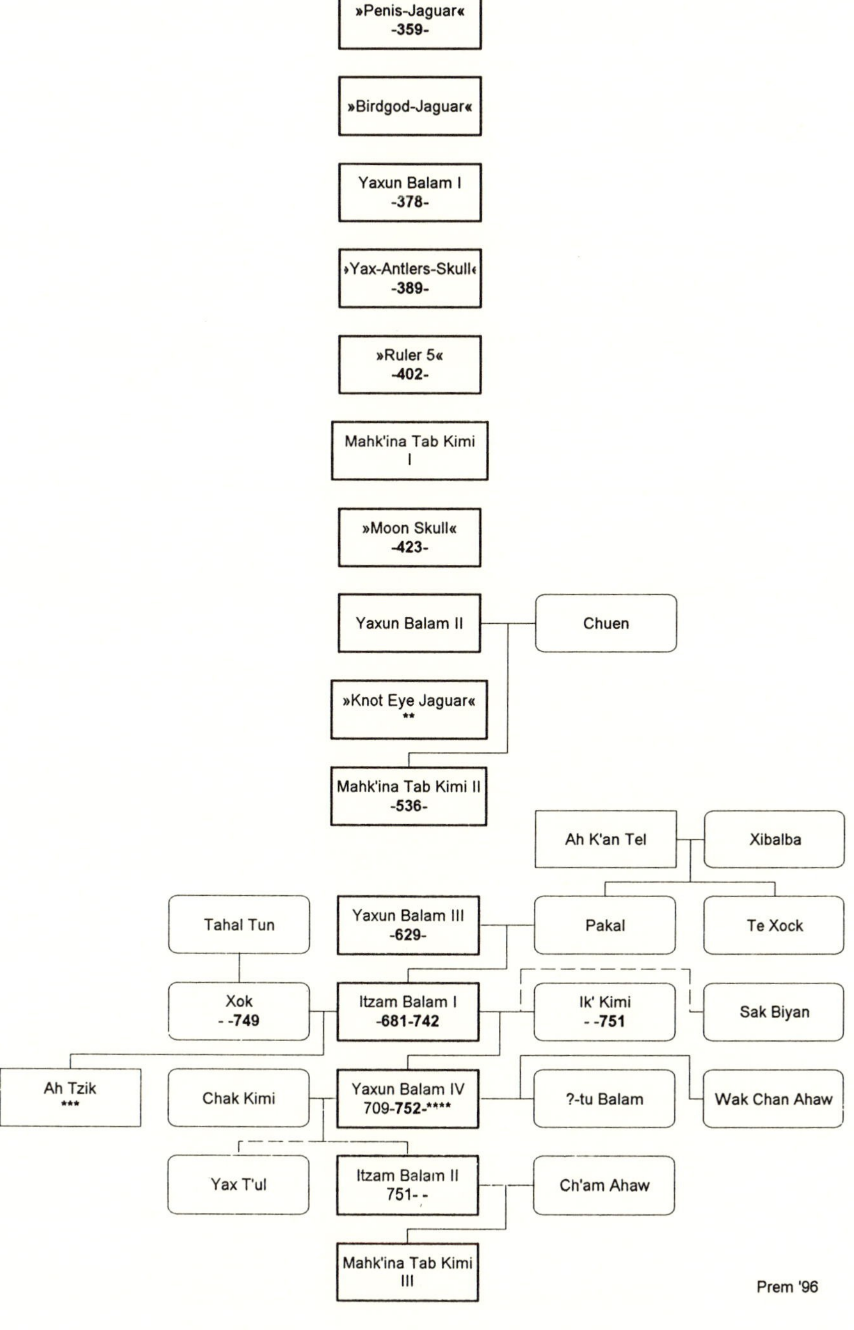

Prem '96

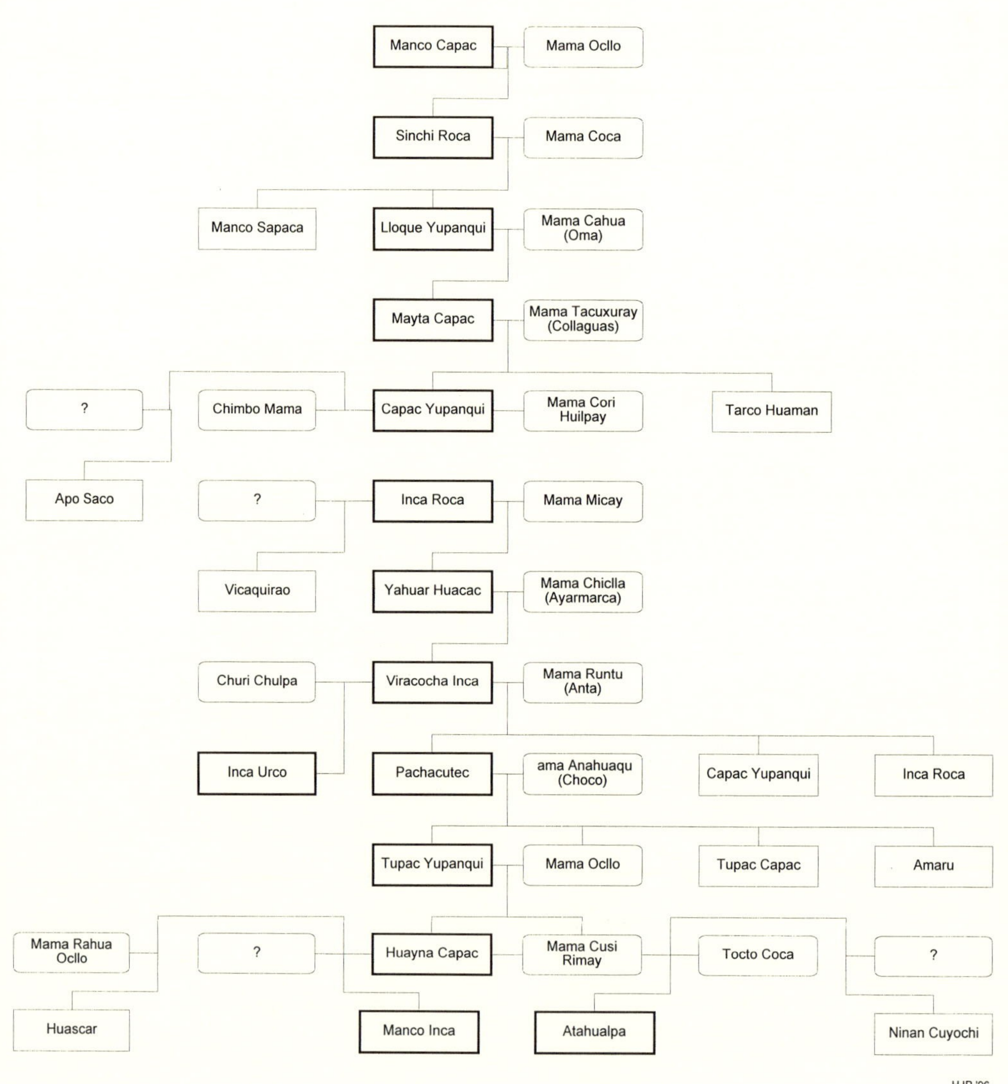

DYNASTIES OF THE INCA

Rectangular: male person; heavy frame: ruler; rectangular with round corners: female person

EASTERN MESOAMERICA

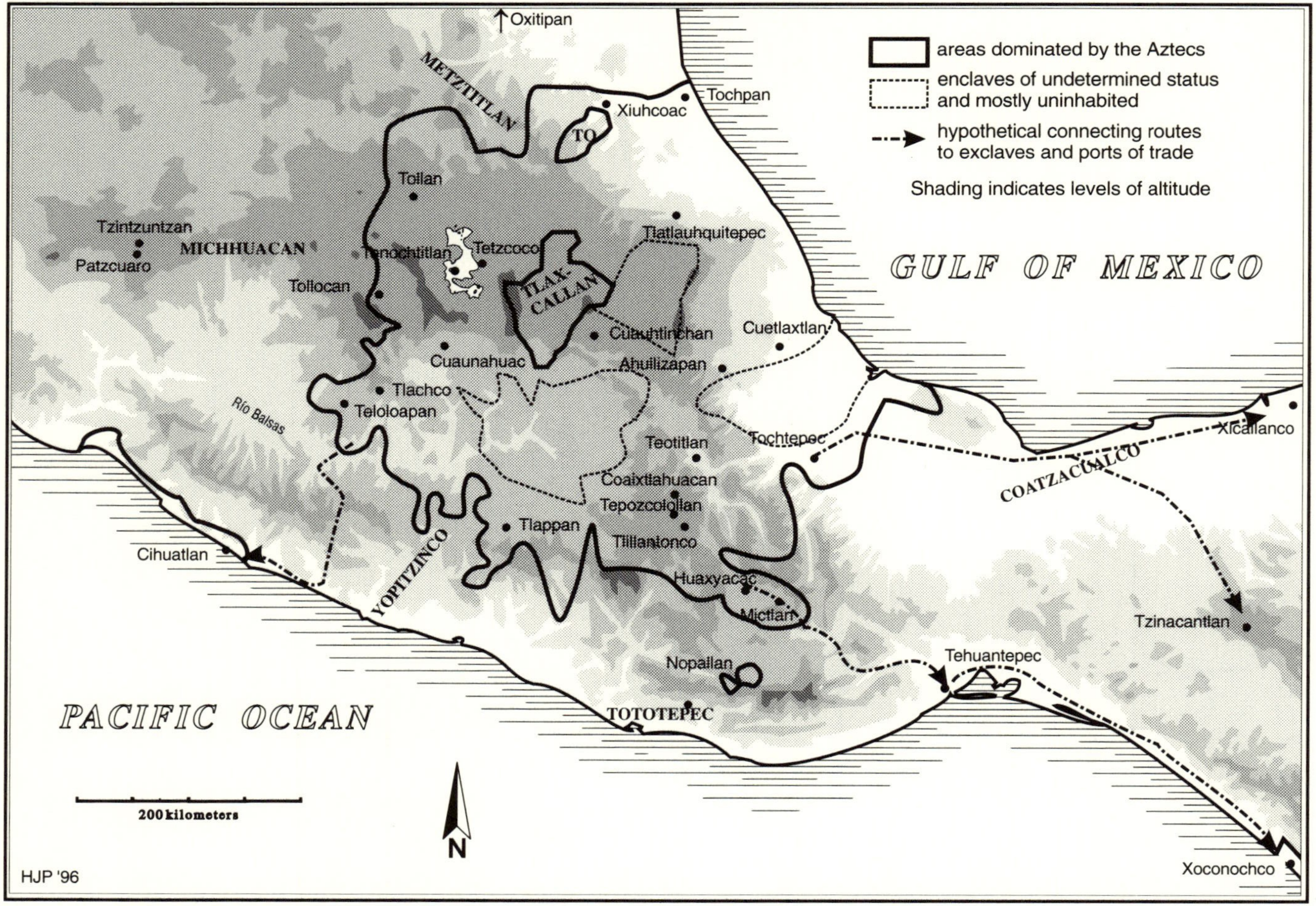

areas dominated by the Aztecs
enclaves of undetermined status and mostly uninhabited
hypothetical connecting routes to exclaves and ports of trade
Shading indicates levels of altitude

Oxitipan
METZTITLAN
Tochpan
Xiuhcoac
TO
Tollan
Tzintzuntzan
Patzcuaro
MICHHUACAN
Tenochtitlan
Tetzcoco
TLAX-CALLAN
Tlatlauhquitepec
GULF OF MEXICO
Tollocan
Cuauhtinchan
Cuetlaxtlan
Cuaunahuac
Ahuilizapan
Tlachco
Teloloapan
Río Balsas
Teotitlan
Tochtepec
Xicallanco
COATZACUALCO
Coaixtlahuacan
Tepozcolollan
Tlappan
Tlillantonco
Cihuatlan
YOPITZINCO
Huaxyacac
Mictlan
Tzinacantlan
Tehuantepec
Nopallan
TOTOTEPEC
PACIFIC OCEAN
200 kilometers
N
HJP '96
Xoconochco

WESTERN MESOAMERICA

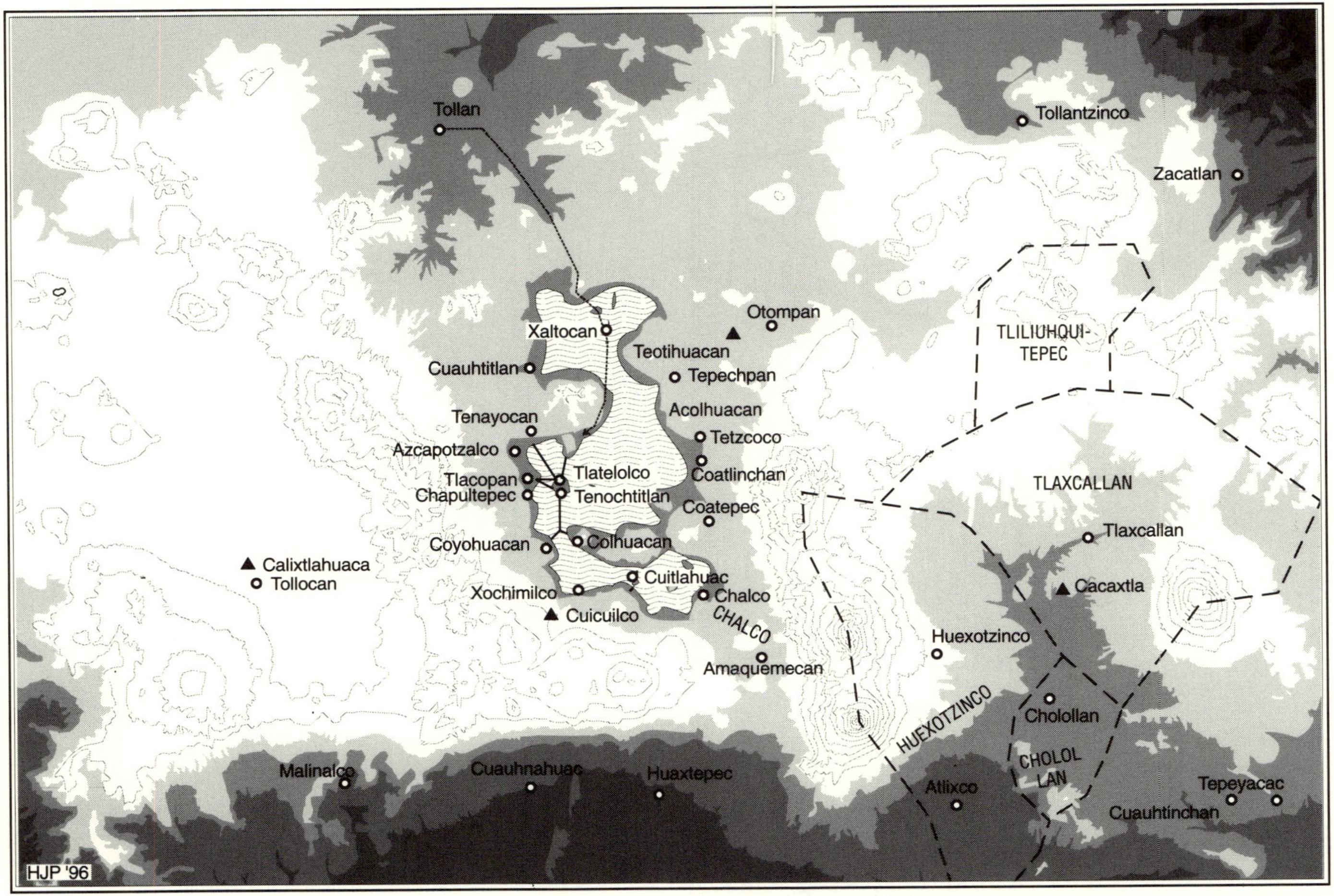

CENTRAL MEXICAN VALLEY ZONE

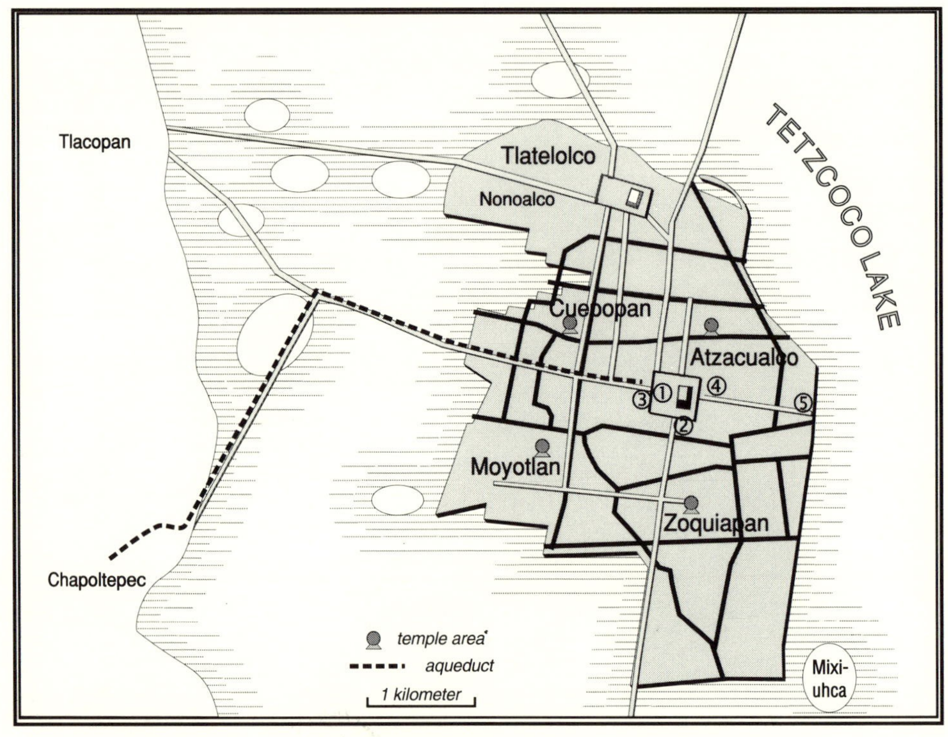

TENOCHTITLÁN

(1) Main temple, (2) Palace of Moteuczoma II., (3) Palace of Axayacatl, (4) Palace of Moteuczoma I., (5) Harbor.

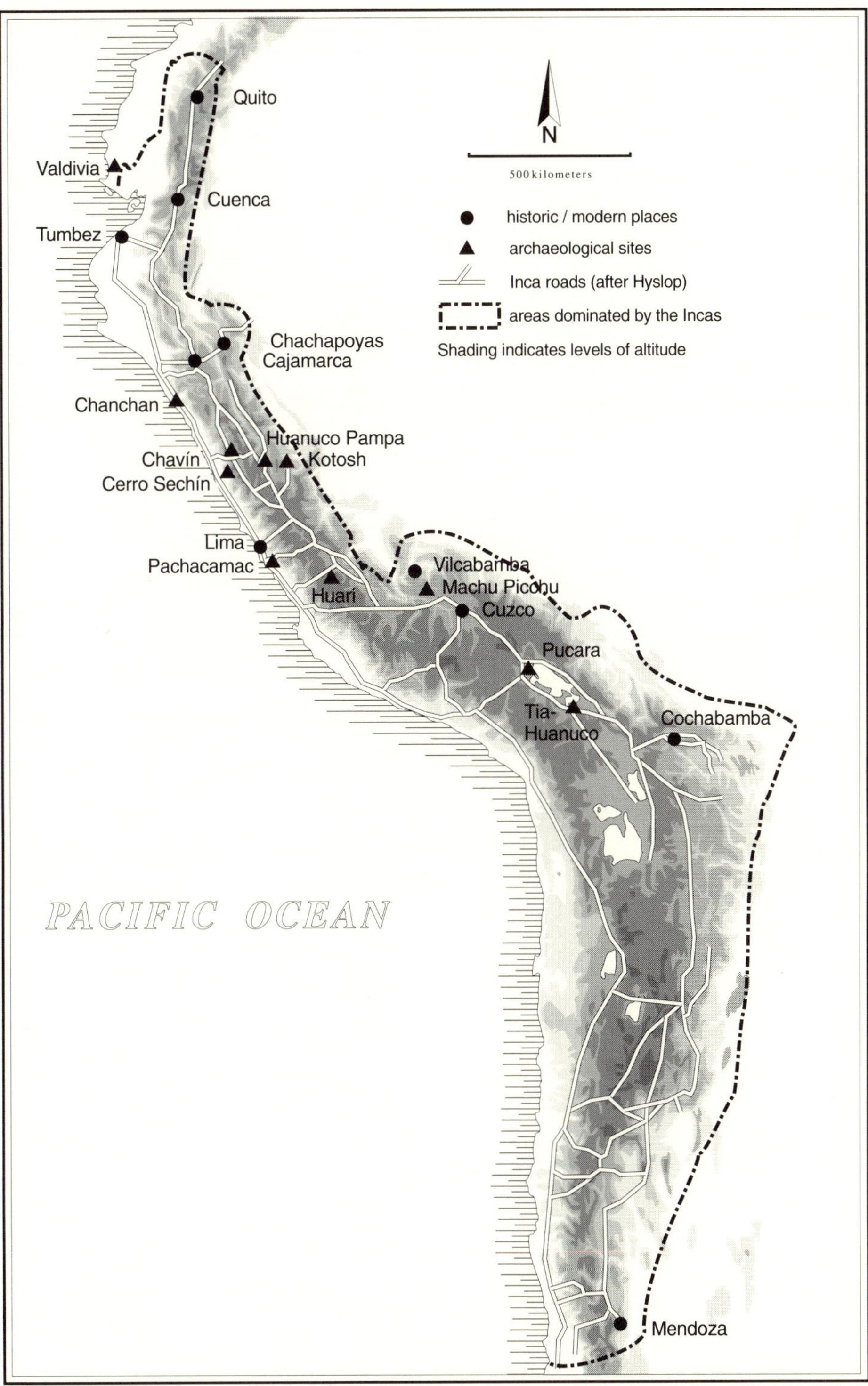

ANDEAN REGION

Index

About the Author and Translator

HANNS J. PREM is professor of American anthropology at the University of Bonn. He has conducted several years of field- and archival work in Mexico and is currently directing an archaeological project in Yucatán. Among his publications are monographs on precolonial and early colonial history of Mexico and edited volumes on Maya archaeology.

KORNELIA KURBJUHN holds a Ph.D. in ethnology from the University of Tübingen. She has held lectureships in Germany and the United States and has published numerous articles on the Maya. She lives and works in New York City.